Designing Economic Mechanisms

LEONID HURWICZ

University of Minnesota

STANLEY REITER

Northwestern University

CAMBRIDGE
UNIVERSITY PRESS

CAMBRIDGE UNIVERSITY PRESS
Cambridge, New York, Melbourne, Madrid, Cape Town, Singapore,
São Paulo, Delhi, Dubai, Tokyo, Mexico City

Cambridge University Press
The Edinburgh Building, Cambridge CB2 8RU, UK

Published in the United States of America by Cambridge University Press, New York

www.cambridge.org
Information on this title: www.cambridge.org/9780521724104

First published 2006
Reprinted 2007 (twice), 2008
First paperback edition 2008

A catalogue record for this publication is available from the British Library

Library of Congress Cataloguing in Publication Data
Hurwicz, Leonid.
Designing economic mechanisms / Leonid Hurwicz, Stanley Reiter.
p. cm.
Includes bibliographical references and index.
ISBN 0-521-83641-7 (hardback)
1. Economics, Mathematical. 2. Economics – Mathematical models.
3. Mathematical optimization. 4. Game theory. I. Reiter, Stanley. II. Title.
HB135.H87 2006
330.01′5195 – dc22 2005034796

ISBN 978-0-521-83641-8 Hardback
ISBN 978-0-521-72410-4 Paperback

Designing Economic Mechanisms

A mechanism is a mathematical structure that models institutions through which economic activity is guided and coordinated. There are many such institutions; markets are the most familiar ones. Lawmakers, administrators, and officers of private companies create institutions in order to achieve desired goals. They seek to do so in ways that economize on the resources needed to operate the institutions and that provide incentives to induce the required behavior. This book presents systematic procedures for designing mechanisms that achieve specified performance and economize on the resources required to operate the mechanism, i.e., informationally efficient mechanisms. Our systematic design procedures can be viewed as algorithms for designing informationally efficient mechanisms. Most of the book deals with these procedures of design. Beyond this, given a mechanism that implements a goal function in Nash equilibrium, our algorithm constructs a decentralized, informationally efficient mechanism that implements that goal function in correlated equilibrium.

Leonid Hurwicz is Regents' Professor of Economics Emeritus at the University of Minnesota. Internationally renowned for his pioneering research on economic theory, particularly in the areas of mechanism and institutional design and mathematical economics, he received the national Medal of Science in 1990. A member of the National Academy of Sciences and the American Academy of Arts and Sciences, Professor Hurwicz is a former President and Fellow of the Econometric Society. The recipient of six honorary doctorates, he serves on the editorial board of several journals and coedited and contributed to two collections for Cambridge University Press, *Studies in Resource Allocation Processes* (1978, with Kenneth Arrow) and *Social Goals and Social Organization* (1987, with David Schmeidler and Hugo Sonnenschein). His recent publications include papers in *Economic Theory* (2003, with Thomas Marschak), *Review of Economic Design* (2001, with Stanley Reiter), and *Advances in Mathematical Economics* (2003, with Marcel K. Richter).

Stanley Reiter is Morrison Professor of Economics and Mathematics in the Weinburg College of Arts and Sciences and Morrison Professor of Managerial Economics and Decision Sciences in the Kellogg School of Management, Northwestern University, where he directs the Center for Mathematical Studies in Economics and Management Science. He previously served as Krannert Professor of Economics and Mathematics at Purdue University. A Fellow of the American Academy for the Advancement of Science, the American Academy of Arts and Sciences, the Guggenheim Foundation, and the Econometric Society, Professor Reiter is coauthor (with Kenneth R. Mount) of *Computation and Complexity in Economic Behavior and Organization* (Cambridge University Press, 2002). He also edited *Studies in Mathematical Economics* (1987), coedited *Information, Incentives, and Economic Mechanisms* (1987), and serves as Associate Editor of the journals *Economic Design* and *Complex Systems*.

Contents

Acknowledgements

We thank Leonard Shapiro, Portland State University, for helpful discussions at an early stage of the research reported in this book. We are indebted to Thomas Marschak, U.C. Berkeley, for many helpful discussions, useful references, and other contributions. Don Saari and Steven Williams participated in our early exploration of the ideas underlying decentralized mechanism design in the setting of calculus on manifolds. We have benefited from many discussions with Steve Williams in the course of our research.

We thank Mary Wilcox, Economics Department, University of Minnesota, for typing portions of our manuscript, and Frances M. Walker, Center for Mathematical Studies in Economics and Management Sciences, Northwestern University, for word-processing the manuscript for publication.

Introduction

This book presents an approach to the design of decentralized, informationally efficient economic mechanisms. We provide a systematic process by which a designer of mechanisms, who is presented with a class of possible situations by a client (perhaps a private agent, or a government) and with the client's aims and objectives, can produce informationally efficient decentralized mechanisms that achieve the client's aims in that class of situations.

HISTORY

Formal treatment of economic mechanisms and mechanism design began with Hurwicz's paper (1960). The background against which that paper was set included a debate on the comparative merits of alternative economic systems. The main participants in that debate included Lange (1938) and Lerner (1937, 1944) on one side, and von Mises (1920, 1935) and Hayek (1935, 1945) on the other. Hurwicz's paper provided for the first time a formal framework in which significant issues in that debate could be addressed. In a subsequent paper, Hurwicz (1972) treated the formal theory of mechanisms again. The problem is to select a mechanism from a set of alternative possible mechanisms. A mechanism is viewed as a value of a variable whose domain of variation is a set of possible mechanisms. Informational tasks entailed by the mechanism imply costs in real resources used to operate the mechanism (as distinct from the resources used in economic production and other real economic activities). Desiderata by which the performance of a mechanism is evaluated also come into play. Hurwicz recognized the fact, emphasized in the earlier debate, that information about the economic environment, the facts that enable or constrain economic possibilities, such as resource endowments and stocks of goods inherited from the past, and individuals' preferences for goods, is distributed among economic agents.

It is obvious, but nevertheless worth saying, that those who do not directly observe some aspect of the prevailing environment do not have that information to guide their actions unless it is communicated to them by someone who does directly observe it.

Hurwicz introduced a formal model of a process of communication that incorporated this constraint – a dynamic message exchange process modeled after the Walrasian tatonnement. He used the term *privacy* (suggested by the inability of one to observe the private information of another) to refer to this restriction. His 1960 model includes as a formal element a language used for communication. The elements (words) used in that language are resource flow matrices which model production and exchange of commodities among the agents. He imposed restrictions on the language and on the functions used to model the communication process in order to generalize properties of the competitive mechanism that are deemed desirable.[1]

Hurwicz (1972) also recognized that dispersion of private information among economic agents can create incentive problems. He formalized this class of problems by introducing *game forms as mechanisms,* and also the concept and analysis of *incentive compatibility of mechanisms.*

Although the original formulation includes a tatonnement-like exchange of messages, attention soon focused on statics, that is, on the task of recognizing the equilibria of message exchange processes, rather than on the task of *finding* equilibria. In this literature, the *verification scenario* isolates the problem of recognizing equilibrium, or solution, from the process of finding equilibrium. In a verification scenario each agent reacts to an announced message by saying yes or no. The responses verify a proposed equilibrium when all agents say yes. (In the language of computer science a verification scenario is a nondeterministic algorithm.)

Mount and Reiter (1974) considered mechanisms that *realize* a given goal function. (*Realize* is the term used to refer to a situation in which the outcomes of the mechanism are precisely those specified by the goal function when agents do not attempt to use their private information strategically. The term *implement* is used when agents behave strategically.) Defining informational decentralization in terms of the structure of the language, and of related restrictions on permissible messages, as is done in Hurwicz (1960) creates two classes of mechanism: decentralized and not decentralized. Instead, Mount and Reiter provided a mathematical characterization

---

[1] Marschak and Radner (1971) and Radner (1972a, 1972b, 1972c) took a different approach to mechanism design, called theory of teams. This approach incorporates uncertainty about environments, and about an agent's knowledge about the knowledge of other agents.

of privacy-preserving message correspondences, and a concept of the *informational size* of a space. This formalization requires all mechanisms to be privacy preserving. It allows privacy-preserving mechanisms to be compared according to the informational sizes of their message spaces, and thereby creates an ordering of mechanisms by the informational size of their message spaces.[2]

The Mount–Reiter concept of the informational size of spaces (and other related concepts) applies to finite spaces, and to continua, including Euclidean spaces and more general topological spaces. They applied it in the 1974 paper to the competitive market mechanism in a class of pure exchange environments, a class in which the message space is Euclidean. Thus, an agent in a message exchange process could send signals based on his private information to another agent, at a cost that is increasing in the size of the messages. In some cases, that communication might require unfeasibly large messages. (This observation also applies to verification scenarios, with suitable adjustments.) This formulation produces an ordering of mechanisms, instead of classifying them as decentralized and not decentralized. Since then, the term informationally decentralized has come to be used for mechanisms whose communications respect privacy, and the size of the message space is used to indicate the real costs of communication. Mount and Reiter assumed, as in Hurwicz, that the initial distribution of information about the prevailing environment is given, and, as in Hurwicz, required that privacy be respected.

The mathematical characterization of privacy-preserving mechanisms (now called decentralized mechanisms) defines a structure of product sets in the space of environments (the parameter space). The relationship between product structures in the parameter space and privacy-preserving (henceforth decentralized) mechanisms is central to the design of mechanisms.

As already noted, the set of mechanisms from which a mechanism can be chosen is a formal element in the Hurwicz approach. One way to think of the problem is to construe the choice of economic organization as a problem of constrained optimization. In this view, there is a set of alternative mechanisms, each required to satisfy certain structural constraints (for instance, privacy preservation), a set of environments, an objective function (the goal function), and, for each candidate mechanism, the real costs (in resources) of operating that mechanism. The problem is to find one or more mechanisms in the set of available mechanisms whose outcomes

---

[2] For finite spaces, Euclidean spaces and topological spaces that have dimension this ordering is complete.

in each environment match those specified by the goal function for that environment, and also minimize, in a vectorial sense, the real costs of operating the mechanism. But generally the set of mechanisms is not known. Some elements in this set might be known mechanisms, for instance, the competitive market mechanism, or one or another version of central planning mechanisms; but this short list surely does not exhaust the universe of conceivable mechanisms. Therefore we must seek a method, or methods, of discovering, or constructing, the elements of that set that are capable of realizing the given goal function.

This task requires that, among other things, we identify the determinants of the real costs of operating each mechanism. Resource costs have been identified as generated by:

- The need for agents to observe the part of the environment to which they have direct access. The precision with which agents must perform this observation determines part of the real cost of operating the mechanism.
- The amount of communication required by the mechanism. The informational size of the message space required has been taken as an indicator of this cost.
- The information processing, including computation, required for each agent to decide whether to say yes or no to an announced message. This dimension of cost is studied in Mount and Reiter (2002) and is not treated formally in this book, although it is commented on in places.
- The losses that arise because of deviation from full realization of the specified goals when agents behave strategically.
- Enforcement of rules of the game, when agents behave in ways that violate those rules.

A second formal element is the set of environments under consideration, and the goal function defined on that set of environments. More generally, goals can be formalized by a correspondence. Analysis in which goals are represented by a correspondence usually reduces to analysis of selections (functions) from that correspondence. In this book we restrict attention to goal functions. Goals can arise in a wide variety of contexts. Some familiar ones arise in the context of neoclassical economic theory. Some arise in the context of organizations that are themselves part of a larger economic system, for example, firms, government agencies, nonprofit entities, and other institutions. Legislation can define socio-economic or political-economic goals. These considerations give emphasis to the need for systematic methods of discovering or designing new mechanisms, in a variety of formal (mathematical) settings.

Reiter realized in 1977 that the mathematical condition (given in Mount and Reiter 1974) that characterizes privacy-preserving message correspondences can be used to design decentralized mechanisms. He showed the relationship between a *product structure*, or an *indexed production structure*, and decentralized mechanisms in examples with two different goal functions. This discovery has led to an approach to systematic design of decentralized mechanisms, specifically, to the discovery of an algorithm (with variants) that accepts a finite set of agents, a factored environment space, and a goal function, and puts out one or more informationally decentralized mechanisms that realize the goal function. That is, the algorithm's output is a mechanism whose output in each environment recognizes the outcome specified by the goal function for that environment.

A decentralized mechanism that realizes a given goal function (it is implicit that the set of agents and the factorization of the space of environment are given) is itself an algorithm. It can be visualized as a machine that accepts as input an environment, and a possible value of the goal function at that environment, and produces as its output either yes or no. Yes, if the candidate value of the goal function is the one prescribed by the goal function, and no otherwise. This machine is presented graphically in Figure 1.

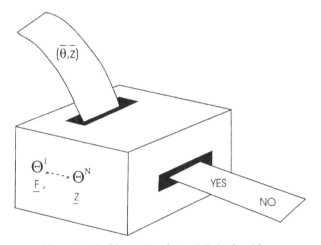

Figure 1. Machine 1: Nondeterministic algorithm.

An algorithm for *designing such mechanisms* can also be represented graphically as a machine that accepts as input a set of agents, a (factored) set of environments, and a goal function and produces as output a machine of the kind shown in Figure 1– a decentralized mechanism that realizes the given goal function. This second machine is shown in Figure 2.

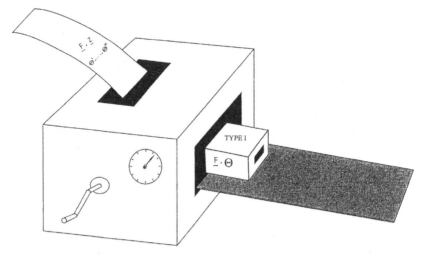

Figure 2.[3] Machine II: Algorithm for producing type I Mechanisms.

Reiter presented these ideas to Don Saari, who then suggested using methods of calculus on manifolds, including methods from differential geometry, and the theory of foliations, specifically the Frobenius theorem on integrable distributions (see Warner 1971), to develop an approach to mechanism theory based on parameter-indexed product structures. Reiter also discussed these ideas with K. Mount, who helped him clarify certain mathematical elements. The research program opened by these ideas led first to joint work by Hurwicz, Reiter and Saari (1980). Steven Williams, at that time a student of Saari, provided a proof of a conjectured extension of the Frobenius theorem to products of distributions and the corresponding product integrable distributions. Subsequently, Saari (1984) published a paper using a somewhat different mathematical apparatus. These approaches to mechanism design in one way or another entail solving systems of partial differential equations. Steven Williams followed the calculus on manifolds approach. His work is presented in a forthcoming book (*Communication in Mechanism Design: A Differential Approach*. Cambridge University Press) that extends and applies that approach.

We (Hurwicz and Reiter) undertook to develop systematic methods of designing decentralized mechanisms that do not rely on the heavy machinery of calculus on manifolds, or the theory of foliations, and that do not

---

[3] Machine II is shown with a dial indicating that there are several settings of the machine. It is shown in Chapters 2 and 3 that the order in which we carry out certain steps of the algorithm for designing mechanisms can result in different machines of Type I.

require solving partial differential equations. The results of that program are reported in this book. This book presents two basic algorithms called rectangles method and condensation method, respectively. This book presents several versions of the rectangles method algorithm in different mathematical settings. The methods presented here use more elementary mathematics to construct indexed product structures and from them construct informationally efficient decentralized mechanisms. Here informational efficiency includes *observational efficiency* and *communication efficiency*, with limited attention to a form of *computational complexity* called *equation efficiency* when environmental parameters are real numbers, and relations are given by equations.

Going beyond this, we consider mechanisms that are incentive compatible, specifically mechanisms that *implement* a given goal function in dominant strategies, and also mechanisms that *implement* a goal function in Nash equilibrium. We apply our algorithms to modify a given mechanism that implements a given goal function (in dominant strategies or in Nash equilibrium) so that the modified mechanism is both informationally efficient and implements that goal function.

We present, for the case of finite environment spaces, an algorithm that modifies Nash-implementing mechanisms to make them informationally efficient, while preserving their incentive properties. It seems clear that the methods used in the finite case generalize to the case of Euclidean environment spaces; we present an example, but we have not carried out a general analysis.

A GUIDE TO THE CHAPTERS

Chapter 1 introduces the basic ideas of our process for constructing a decentralized, informationally efficient mechanism whose outcomes match those specified by a given goal function defined on a specified class of factored environments. In this chapter these ideas are presented mainly with the help of two examples. In the first, we use a pure exchange environment – two goods, two agents with quasi-linear utility functions – to present the ideas of our approach in a familiar and concrete setting in which relations are modeled by equations. The discussion is relatively informal. It demonstrates how a known mechanism, the competitive market mechanism, can be obtained as the output of our design procedure, and also shows how that procedure can be used to construct other mechanisms, not the customary one. The analysis of this example is developed in Chapter 2. The second example is one in which logging in a National Forest is under the control of an agency of the government and so is subject to political pressures. This situation is modeled set-theoretically. This example introduces the analysis in Chapter 3.

Chapter 1 contains an informal discussion of ideas about resource costs of operating a mechanism that arise from information processing requirements associated with that mechanism. This chapter also contains a brief discussion of game forms and strategic behavior.

In Chapter 2, the primary focus is on the case in which economic environments and goal functions are modeled by systems of equations. The goal function is typically assumed to be smooth, and to have a nonzero Jacobian. The Walrasian goal function is used several times in simple examples to illustrate the ideas and methods presented in this book, and to provide a continuing connection with received economic theory. Finite examples are also used to illustrate some ideas. The methods of analysis and the constructions presented in this chapter use mathematics that should be familiar to an economics graduate student. Our aim here is to make the ideas and the analyses accessible to a broad range of economists, including those who work in applied fields, and to do this without oversimplifying the ideas or the processes of construction. The pace and formality of our presentation reflect these objectives. Examples are used freely to illustrate our techniques. For most of this chapter the examples discussed stay close to familiar economic models, and to mathematical techniques familiar to economists. However, toward the end of the chapter, where the condensation method is presented, the exposition unavoidably becomes somewhat more technical.

The condensation method is based on a mathematical structure presented in Chapter 4, specifically on Theorem 4.4.6, which is stated and proved in that chapter. The mathematics there is a bit more complex, although the methods are still those of multivariable calculus, and so are not very different from the mathematics used elsewhere in Chapter 2.

We include the entire paper (Mount and Reiter 1996) in Chapter 4 rather than just Theorem 4.4.6, because that paper addresses subjects fundamental to mechanism design and informational efficiency that arise in the mathematical setting of Chapter 2, but are not treated in full formality elsewhere in this book. In Chapter 2 an agent evaluates a function that depends on the goal function to be realized. The arguments of the goal function are parameters that specify the environment. An agent's function has as its arguments some environmental parameters and some additional message variables. The function to be evaluated may be given by one equation, or several. The more the variables that appear in ask agent's equation system, the more difficult is his task. The number of environmental parameters in ask agent's equation system depends on the number of environmental parameters related to that agent that are arguments of the goal function. But reality does not present us with a set of environmental parameters, and a goal function the way a rose bush presents us with a rose. The parameter space and goal function are the result of modeling choices. Two different modelers might produce two different mathematical expressions that model the same situation, but do not necessarily do so equally efficiently from the standpoint of the costs implied by the modeling choice. The number of variables that are arguments of the functions that form the model determine with other elements the resource costs required to operate the mechanism.

The introduction to Chapter 4 contains a simple example in which one modeling choice results in a function of two variables whose partial derivatives with respect to those variables in not zero, but in which there is another way to set up the space and function so that the same relation between the dependent and independent elements, the same abstract function, can be written as a function of one variable. The number of variables in the model affects the observation of the environment that is required, the amount of communication that is required, the number of equations that must be dealt with, and more generally the complexity of the computations that are entailed; it is desirable to know how many variables, and which ones, the underlying abstract function really depends on, as distinct from the number it appears to depend on.

There is a body of literature in computer science that analyzes the question "How many variables does a function written as a function of N Boolean variables really depend on?" That is: "Can a function of N Boolean variables be written as a function of fewer than N such variables?" (References are cited in Chapter 4.) This literature presents a procedure that yields the fewest variables possible for a given function to be evaluated. Reducing the number of variables reduces the computational complexity of evaluating that function. It also has an effect on other dimensions of informational efficiency, for instance, the number of equations that are required to represent the function.

To answer the same question is a much more subtle and complex task in the case of smooth functions defined on Euclidean spaces, and the methods that work in the discrete case do not work in the continuous case, the case dealt with in Chapter 2. Mount and Reiter (1996) reprinted here as Chapter 4 presents new and different methods to answer the question: "How many variables does a smooth function of N variables *really* depend on?" The results and methods presented in Chapter 4 are basic to the analysis of several kinds of complexity. This topic is discussed further in the section of this introduction that deals with Chapter 4.

In Chapter 3 our basic approach to mechanism design is developed using the language of sets and functions, that is, without requiring that sets and functions be represented by equations in real variables, and without regularity conditions such as continuity or differentiability. Consequently, this development is in a sense more general than that in Chapter 2. It covers cases in which the set of environments is finite, or infinite but discrete, as well as cases in which sets are continua. This added generality brings with it a significant benefit. A problem of mechanism design can present itself in a setting where it is difficult to model environments and goals using equations that are sufficiently regular to permit the methods presented in Chapter 2 or 4 to be used. For instance, in some situations the relevant environments and goals are designated in legislation written in legal language. In such a case, set-theoretic language might be a better tool for modeling the situation, whereas it might be quite difficult to capture its essential elements in a formalization of the kind needed to apply the methods presented in Chapter 2 or 4. Furthermore, an analysis using set-theoretic language sometimes leads to a clearer view of the essentials.

With these considerations in mind, Chapter 3 begins with a brief discussion of two examples intended to illustrate the range of possible situations that might be presented for analysis. These examples are drawn from American economic history. After presenting the set-theoretic methods of mechanism design in Sections 3.1 through 3.7, Section 3.8 returns to the National Forest example presented in Chapter 1, Section 1.8. This example is used first to illustrate the informational aspects of our approach to mechanism design, and then in Section 3.9.1; to exemplify the conversion of a decentralized informationally efficient mechanism into one that implements the goal function in dominant strategies, and is decentralized and informationally efficient.

In Section 3.9.2 we consider strategic behavior modeled by game forms that implement a given goal function F in Nash equilibrium. For a given a goal function F that satisfies "Maskin monotonicity" and "no veto power," we present a two-stage procedure – an algorithm – for constructing a game form that Nash implements F and whose equilibrium message correspondence generates an informationally efficient covering of the underlying space of environments – the parameter space. That is, we construct an informationally efficient decentralized mechanism that in a coordinated ex post equilibrium implements the goal function.

Section 3.9.2 is written by Reiter and Adam Galambos.

The mathematics used in Chapter 3 is not esoteric. The theory of informational efficiency is presented more formally than in earlier chapters, and the theorems that relate message space size and coarseness of the covering of the parameter space are presented in detail. The methods and techniques presented in Chapter 3 will, we hope, provide guidance to modeling in applications that, on their face, seem not to lend themselves to formalization.

Chapters 2 and 3 can be read in either order.

Chapter 4 is a slightly reedited version of Mount and Reiter (1996). We reprint it here for two reasons. First, it contains the theorem, and the mathematical structure needed to state and prove it, that is the basis for the condensation method of constructing decentralized mechanisms that is presented in Chapter 2.

Second, it sheds light on an aspect of the theory of decentralized mechanisms that is interesting in itself. It has been intuitively clear that the communication complexity and the computational complexity of a function each depend in different ways on the number of variables on which that function depends. The number of variables on which a function depends is an elusive concept, as the beginning sections of Chapter 4 make clear. Arbib and Spira have given a lower bound on the complexity of a function when the domain of that function is a finite set (Arbib 1960, Spira 1969, Spira and Arbib 1967.) The concept of complexity they use is the one commonly used for computations performed by a finite state automaton. In obtaining their lower bound they use a concept that corresponds to the number of Boolean variables on which the function being computed *actually* depends, as distinct from the variables that appear in the mathematical expression used to define the function – the variables on which it might appear to depend. In the finite case the number of variables is easily counted. But their methods do not extend to functions between infinite sets, or continua. In our cases, where a goal function can have a more general space as its domain or range, the counting procedure is replaced by construction of a *universal object in a category*. The category is the *category of encoded revelation mechanisms* that realize the function whose complexity is being analyzed. The universal object is a minimal encoded revelation mechanism called an *essential revelation mechanism*. The dimension (when it exists) of the message space of the universal object is the number of variables on which the function being analyzed *really* depends. The concepts mentioned in this paragraph are all defined and discussed in Chapter 4.

The analysis in Chapter 4 makes extensive use of the concept of a product structure. As noted above, a product structure, for a given set of economic environments and a goal function, captures formally the concept of informational decentralization, or privacy preservation. The universal element in the category of encoded revelation mechanism extends a familiar property of functions that do not satisfy privacy preservation to the case where privacy preservation is required. Briefly, this is as follows. Consider a space Ψ of functions from some space, U, to the space of contour maps of the functions in Ψ. For instance, F and G are elements of Ψ, where $F : X \to Y$ and $G : W \to Z$. Let the mapping Φ associate to each element of Ψ its contour map; thus, for any element F in Ψ, $\Phi(F) = X/F$. The assertion is that the mapping Φ determines a diagram for each function F in Ψ, in which

- $F : X \to Y$ is represented by a horizontal line at the top of the diagram,
- there is a function $g : X \to \Phi(F) = X/F$, and
- there is a function $\rho_F : \Phi(F) \to Y$, such that $F(x) = \rho_F \circ g(x)$.

Economists are familiar with this structure; when F is a utility function then $\Phi(F) = X/F$ is its indifference map. Furthermore, a function can be defined that attaches to each level set in the indifference map, X/F, the utility that F assigns to that level set. That is, each utility function F can be expressed as the composition of the map Φ with a map ρ_F that depends on the function F – the map Φ is *universal* in the sense that it is defined for all functions in Ψ, and does not depend functionally on F.

In the case of interest in this book, decentralization or privacy preservation is involved. In that case the domain X is a Cartesian product of sets, and, in that case, the decomposition of F sketched above does not respect privacy. To obtain an analogous decomposition of F, that does respect privacy one must use a *product structure* in the domain of F.

There are in general many product structures for a given function F. In this more complicated case, the mathematical entity that corresponds to the universal mapping φ is, as explained in Chapter 4, a *universal element in the category of essential revelation mechanisms that realize F*.[4] The result obtained from this analysis is that the set of decentralized mechanisms that are in principle available for a given goal function is essentially determined by the set of possible product structures on the domain of that goal function.

---

[4] A universal element (or object) is an object in a category that represents a functor from that category to the category of sets. A functor that has such a representing object is a representable functor. The essential revelation mechanism is such a universal object. For the complete definition of the concept of representable functor and several other examples of representable functors and representing objects; see MacLane (1971, p. 55–62).

The analysis in Chapter 4 uses several bordered Hessian matrices associated with a twice continuously differentiable (goal) function to characterize the variables on which that function actually depends. Theorem 4.4.6 that establishes this result is used in Chapter 2 as the basis for an algorithm, the condensation method, for constructing decentralized mechanisms that realize a goal function that satisfies the differentiability and rank hypotheses of that theorem.

Mechanisms and Mechanism Design

1.0 Introduction

Our aim in this book is to present systematic methods for designing decentralized economic mechanisms whose performance attains specified goals. We begin with an informal discussion of the general problem, and of our approach to it. A (decentralized) mechanism is a formal entity intended to represent a system for organizing and coordinating economic activity. The need for such mechanisms can arise at different levels of economic entities, ranging from households, or firms, to government agencies, to entire economies. We discuss examples at several levels.

Economic activity has been classified as production, consumption, and exchange. These activities are constrained by restrictions on resource availabilities, and on knowledge of technological possibilities. Resource availabilities and technological possibilities form part of the *economic environment*, that is, at any one time they are exogenously given, either from nature, or inherited from the past. Knowledge of resource constraints and of technological possibilities is generally distributed among economic agents. Consequently no economic agent, or other entity, can know the totality of what is *feasible* and what is not. The preferences of economic agents are also distributed among agents; they are typically interpreted as private information and are usually taken as exogenously given. They play a dual role: they underlie the motivations of agents, and in that role form part of the economic environment, and they also play a role in determining the criteria of economic efficiency and hence in defining the goals of economic activity. In neoclassical economic theory, notably general equilibrium theory the concept of economic efficiency is usually taken to be Pareto optimality. But Pareto optimality is a relatively weak requirement, and in many situations the goals of economic activity embody stronger, or at least different, requirements.

Economic activity takes place in a setting of institutions and arrangements, a framework of laws, customs, formal organizations, and less formal structures. These range from relatively simple, informal, often subtle, arrangements, to highly complex and formalized structures. We refer to structures of this kind formally as *mechanisms*. In a modern developed economy, such as the one we see in the United States, economic activity encompasses activities that are neither production, consumption nor exchange. Instead, a very substantial amount of what is generally recognized as economic activity, for instance, activities from which people earn incomes, includes involvement in *creating* or *operating* a mechanism. These activities include acquiring information, processing information, and communicating information to or from others. Resources used in these activities are not available for use in production or consumption. Thus, the evaluation of mechanisms should not avoid considering the real costs of creating, operating, and maintaining the institutions required for the existence and functioning of those mechanisms.

New goals, and mechanisms intended to achieve them, are created from time to time, in the United States often by acts of Congress or other legislative bodies. Often, perhaps even typically, they arise because of some unsatisfactory aspect of the performance of an existing economic system or institution, or from the efforts of agents to establish systems that they expect to give them advantage. For instance, the milk supply to a city typically comes from a number of individual farmers who together made up what is called the milk-shed of the city. In the case of Chicago, the milk-shed is made up mainly of dairy farms in Illinois, Iowa, and Wisconsin. In an earlier time milk delivered to the city was likely to be infected with tuberculosis. There was a public–policy conflict that went on for many years over whether to require farmers to test their herds for tuberculosis, and to cull infected cows. Requiring pasteurization was also a policy issue. There were modern clean dairies that produced unadulterated milk, but they co-existed with a large number of small milk producers who sold filthy adulterated milk and were not driven to clean up their product until forced by law and inspection to do so. Elimination of tubercular cows would, and eventually did, improve the health and well-being of those who drank milk, but testing cows and culling herds lowers the wealth of some farmers. Testing and culling could not be justified on grounds of Pareto optimality, nor could pasteurization.[1]

---

[1] See Pegram, T. R. (1991) Public health and progressive dairying in Illinois. Agricultural History, 65, 36–50, for an account of the attempt to regulate the quality of the milk supplied to Chicago in the late 19th and early 20th century.

In more recent times issues of public health and quality of life have led Congress to create new official goals, such as "clean air" and "clean water," and to create agencies intended to attain them. But the legislation that establishes an agency is typically stated in general terms that may restrict, but not completely specify, the means by which the agency is to attain its assigned objectives.

Knowledge of economic theory and experience with economic analysis are useful to anyone faced with a problem of this kind, but until quite recently economic theory did not offer much specific guidance for the design of mechanisms in this sort of situation. In the past few decades economic theory has addressed the implications of the fact that information about the environment is distributed. Relevant information that is known to one person, but not observable by anyone else, creates incentives to use that information for private advantage.

There is now a considerable body of theory that focuses on strategic issues arising from distributed information (asymmetric information). In this theory a mechanism is modeled as a *game form*. The desired outcomes are given by a *goal function* (sometimes called a social choice function in this literature), a function that specifies the outcome desired in each possible environment. A game form that has the property that its equilibria (Nash or otherwise) coincide (on a given class of environments) with the outcomes specified by a given goal function is said to *implement* that goal function in the type of game theoretic solution specified. Thus, an agency entrusted with the task of administering a goal function specified by a Congressional act faces the task of designing a game form that implements the goal function. But agreement between equilibriums and the outcome specified by the goal function is alone not sufficient. The game form must be feasible, in the sense that the informational tasks required by the mechanism can actually be carried out by all of the agents involved, including those who make up the agency. For instance, if the operation of the mechanism were to require infinite amounts of information to be observed, or communicated or otherwise processed by agents, or by the agency, then the mechanism would clearly be infeasible. Indeed, if the costs of operating a particular mechanism were to exceed the available budget, the mechanism would be infeasible. To put this slightly differently, if the budget provided for the mechanism were too small, it would make it impossible for the prescribed goal function to be implemented.[2]

---

[2] The Renegotiation Act in World War II provides an interesting example. The situation called for rapid conversion of production from civilian products to military products. The

The implementation literature contains many examples of mechanisms in which astronomical amounts of information must be transmitted, and astronomically complicated strategies are used. The relevance of results of that kind to the design of mechanisms that are intended to guide actual application is, to say the least, unclear.[3] Without knowledge of the informational requirements of game forms that implement a given goal function, the applicability of implementation theory in that instance is in question.

It is intuitive, and has been demonstrated formally, that for a given goal function the informational costs associated with a mechanism when information about the environment is distributed, but when the agents do not attempt to take strategic advantage of their private information, provide a lower bound on the informational requirements of implementing that goal function. The extent of the additional costs required for implementation would be a measure of the informational cost of attaining incentive compatibility. There may well be cases in which it is in some sense better to use a mechanism that is not fully incentive compatible, but is informationally feasible. In such cases we are weighing information costs against incentive costs – a kind of calculation not unknown to economics.

government sought to induce rapid conversion by offering cost-plus contracts to producers. But, with the experience of wartime government contracting in earlier periods still fresh in mind, the administration wanted to prevent "profiteering" and the appearance of profiteering, in order to create the public perception of equal sacrifices for the war effort. To this end the Renegotiation Act provided that "excess profits" on government contracts could be recovered later, after examination of each contracting firm's experience. Evidently with the intent to avoid creating perverse incentives, the law provided that, for example, profits that resulted from superior efficiency, or especially valuable qualities of the items produced, would justify retention of more of the profit. There were five such factors provided in the Renegotiation Act, known as the *statutory factors*. But the agency created to administer the Act, was quite small. To the eye of an outside observer, the resources provided were not sufficient to allow the statutory factors to be taken into account effectively. It must perforce be administered by rules-of-thumb. There are indications that this was in fact the case. It is also likely that the lawmakers were aware of this, and preferred this performance to the one in which there were intrusive investigations into the internal workings of the private contractors. Because the contracting firms were allowed to keep their total profits for years before being renegotiated by the agency, thereby getting the use of the money without interest, the recovery of so-called excess profits by gross rules-of-thumb appeared to be acceptable. Indeed, the Act applied to defense contracts for decades after the end of World War II.

Recovery of excess profits by renegotiation was first authorized in the Sixth Supplemental National Defense Appropriation Act of 1942 (PL 77-528). It was elaborated in the Renegotiation Act of 1944, and extended through 1945, when it was allowed to expire. It was revived in 1948 (PL80-547) and extended in a sequence of Acts through 1968. See *Congress and the Nation*, vol. 1 for the period 1945–64, and vol. 2 for 1965–68.

[3] On the other hand, theorems that tell us that the information required to implement a goal function is astronomical are impossibility theorems and so are useful.

Going beyond these considerations, the process of inventing mechanisms to accomplish a given purpose has been somewhat ad hoc. It seems desirable to have systematic procedures for designing decentralized mechanisms that implement a given goal function. In keeping with the spirit of the preceding paragraph, a systematic process for designing decentralized mechanisms on the assumption that agents do not act strategically is a good place to start. If under this assumption it were shown that any mechanism that could achieve the goal would require infinite resources, then it would be known decisively that the specified objective could not be met when agents behave strategically. As we said to begin with, our aim is to provide systematic procedures for designing mechanisms whose outcomes agree with those specified by a given goal function, when information about the environment is distributed among the agents. In addition we require that the mechanisms be *informationally efficient*. To put it a bit differently, we present an "algorithmic process" or "machine" that accepts as inputs a set of agents, a set of possible environments, a distribution of information about the environments among the agents, and a goal function that expresses the desired outcomes of action. The output of this machine is an informationally efficient decentralized mechanism whose result for any environment in the given class is the one specified by the goal function for that environment. In this chapter we seek to motivate and explain the steps of the design procedure and the concepts used in an informal and intuitive way. Therefore, to the extent possible, we carry on the discussion in this chapter in simple settings, and with a minimum of technical apparatus. We begin in the setting of classical welfare economics, and in Section 1.8 take up an example of the kind mentioned in the discussion of mechanism design problems that arise in political–economic settings. The example is one of government regulation of a National Forest. Analysis in that example is set theoretic. It uses the methods developed in Chapter 3. The discussion of that example in this introductory chapter is informal and intuitive; in Chapter 3 it is revisited in Section 3.8 to show the formal analysis.

1.1 Mechanisms and Design

The question "How should economic activity be organized?" arises at different levels, from organizing an entire economy to organizing a small sector of economic activity, including even a single firm or household. Whatever the scope or domain of economic activity, as long as more than one agent is involved, the fact that essential information about the environment is distributed among the agents is at the root of the problem of designing economic mechanisms.

If there is only one way of organizing, then there is nothing to choose. But we see that institutions, laws, and less formal arrangements that govern and mediate economic activity vary across space, time, and types of economic activity. This makes it plausible that there is more than one possibility in the set of systems that could conceivably organize economic activity. To choose rationally from this variety of possible arrangements requires an analytic structure that permits us to describe the performance and operating characteristics of different systems. It also requires that there be criteria for comparing different systems.

The system, or mechanism, we are most familiar with is the market mechanism. For markets, the prototype of an explicit description of an adjustment process is the Walrasian tatonnement. It has served as a basic expository device for explaining how prices tend to reach their equilibrium levels under perfect competition.[4] Its stability properties have been studied extensively. But even in the neoclassical framework there are many reasons economics cannot confine itself to the tatonnement model. To begin with, there are questions about its behavioral justification. Second, there is a large class of economic environments in which competitive equilibria exist, but price adjustment processes along the lines of the Walrasian tatonnement do not converge to an equilibrium, even locally. Third, there are environments in which competitive equilibrium may not exist (as when there are significant indivisibilities) or cannot exist (as when there are increasing returns). There are environments in which competitive equilibria can be inefficient (as in the presence of indivisibilities, externalities, or public goods). The Walrasian tatonnement is not satisfactory in these cases. Finally, even if the tatonnement process does converge to an efficient competitive ("Walrasian") equilibrium, the resulting resource allocation may fail to satisfy other desiderata, such as fairness or providing a minimum standard of living for a significant segment of the population.

The inadequacies of the Walrasian mechanism have long been recognized. Almost universally, there are "remedies" in the form of policies, such as social insurance or transfer payments supported by taxation. Remedies for failures of the competitive mechanism in nonclassical environments have

---

[4] The textbook story of excess demand dynamics adjustment does not extend to the full class of general equilibrium models with three or more commodities and three or more agents. So far, there is no theorem that guarantees convergence of general markets to equilibrium.

also been proposed. These include marginal cost pricing under increasing returns, Lindahl pricing in economies with public goods, and a variety of schemes, including Pigouvian taxes and marketable pollution rights for harmful externalities. And models have been formulated whose stability properties are superior to those of tatonnement.

In many cases proposed solutions to the design problem were found to have serious deficiencies or disadvantages. This fact often leads in practice to a process of modifications intended to improve performance, though often those modifications result in increasing bureaucratization and to centralization of decision making. Institutions based on such proposed solutions often turn out to entail heavy costs for information processing and enforcement of rules. Experience of this kind suggests that we should distinguish two kinds of desiderata:

- those that apply to the (intended) outcomes of the mechanism (as we shall see, these are expressed by a goal function), and
- those that are associated with the operation of a mechanism, for example, the costs of information processing and communication (these are not expressed by a goal function; the same outcome can in general be attained in different ways, with different costs).

Another significant matter arises from the problem of incentive compatibility and the cost of enforcing behavior rules, as well as the costs of enforcing the rules of the game.

Certain game-theoretic models designed to "implement" given social objectives sometimes use – in existence proofs at least – very large strategy spaces. These imply high communication costs. When, as is often the case, the strategy spaces are infinite-dimensional, the required calculations cannot be carried out in finite time. Going further, in some cases proposed solutions, not necessarily game theoretic, postulate individual behavior patterns that are inconsistent with what is believed about natural incentives. Those disadvantages may sometimes be unavoidable, but in other cases superior alternatives may exist. Thus we are led to ask two questions: how can we determine which deficiencies are unavoidable (as has been shown, for instance, for economies with increasing returns), and how can we go about discovering superior alternatives if they are not known?

With brilliant inspiration or luck, the second question can be answered by the ad hoc invention of a superior alternative. But even then, we might not know whether one could do still better, either in terms of social desiderata or costs. To know whether one can do better than the existing solutions, or whether acceptable solutions are possible, even in principle, several things are needed. One must be able to consider a complete class of processes or mechanisms that satisfy the given desiderata, and be able to determine whether these desiderata are at all achievable. That is, we must be able to determine whether that class of mechanisms is nonempty, and, if it is not empty, to be able to compare its various members in terms of criteria such as efficiency and cost requirements. A first prerequisite for this analysis is to have a well-defined concept of a mechanism or an adjustment process. Once the concept of mechanism is defined, one can formalize a concept of decentralization, in particular, of informational decentralization. Being decentralized may be viewed as a requirement of feasibility that applies to a mechanism when information (about preferences, resources, or technologies) is initially dispersed among the individual agents, as is typically the case in most economies. Decentralization may also be considered to have a social value in itself. In any case, the focus of our investigation in this book is on adjustment processes and mechanisms that are informationally decentralized. Hence, for analytical purposes, it is essential to have a clearly defined concept of informational decentralization. There is, of course, some freedom in choosing such a definition. The one we use in this book, called the "privacy preserving" property, is in a sense minimal. It requires that no agent can condition his or her messages on environmental parameters that he does not observe directly. This requirement is less demanding than, for instance, that used by Hurwicz (1960). The concept of an adjustment process corresponds to the one used there as well as to the one used in Mount and Reiter (1987). In this book we study the equilibria of mechanisms, whether in the form of adjustment processes or in their equilibrium forms.

Our basic point of view is to treat the mechanism as the value of a variable, to be solved for as the "unknown" of a problem. The problem we address is not just to analyze how a given mechanism works, but rather to find decentralized mechanisms that have performance properties specified by goal functions in a given class of environments and that also have minimal information processing costs.

In much standard microeconomic analysis, the criterion of social desirability is taken to be the Pareto optimality of outcomes (although, more recently, equity or fairness considerations have also entered the picture), but our model is intended for a broader class of performance criteria. The search for, and comparison of, alternative mechanisms that satisfy a specified performance criterion also takes place in settings much smaller than the economic organization of a national economy, for example, in the internal organization of a firm, or in the context of regulation of a branch of industry, or of some area of economic activity. The example in Section 1.8

of this chapter is of this kind. Criteria other than Pareto optimality may well come into play in those cases. Even if Pareto optimality remains the criterion, the agents whose preferences count might be a relatively limited group. As for information processing costs, many come under the headings of observation, communication, or complexity. In this book we concentrate mainly on the costs of observation and communication. We take the cost of observation to be an increasing function of the precision with which the environment must be observed, and we take the cost of communication to be an increasing function of the size of messages that must be processed by the participants. Cost of observation and communication is interpreted here in several related ways; these are discussed in this chapter under the rubric of informational efficiency. In particular, when the messages transmitted among agents consist of sets of numbers, one meaning of informational efficiency is that the mechanism uses messages that consist of as few numbers as possible, that is, the message space of the mechanism is Euclidean and that it has as small a dimension as possible.

It is known from previous research that, for any given criterion of desirability, there is a (tight) lower bound on the dimension of the message space of a mechanism whose outcomes satisfy that criterion.[5] It has been shown that in classical (convex) economies, when the criterion is Pareto optimality, the lower bound is the size of the message space used by the Walrasian tatonnement. Significantly, the bound depends only on the number of agents and commodities – and not on such factors as the number of parameters in the utility or production functions. On the other hand, in nonconvex economies the message space is usually larger. In environments with increasing returns to scale, there is usually no finite lower bound; that is, an infinite-dimensional message space (entailing infinite costs) might be required. Informational costs, including communication costs, seem to be particularly important in the organization of firms. The recent wave of corporate downsizing suggests that the use of computers, computer networks, the world-wide-web, and related communication devices has led to a radical reorganization of firms; layers of middle management, formerly occupied mainly with information processing and communication functions, were eliminated.

---

[5] Although it is important to attain the lower bound, we recognize that there may be a tradeoff between the dimension of the message space and the complexity of the mechanism. Thus, one might choose a mechanism whose message space dimension is above the minimum in order to lower the level of complexity. It would generally be necessary to make this tradeoff in order to minimize information processing costs. This tradeoff in a Walrasian example is analyzed in Mount and Reiter (2002).

Lower bounds on the sizes of message spaces are relevant to evaluating the merits of game-theoretic models that use infinite-dimensional strategy spaces to prove that a wide class of criteria of desirability can be implemented in wide classes of environments. Where, as in nonconvex environments, infinite-dimensional strategy spaces must be used to achieve exact implementation, we may have to be satisfied with approximate or second-best solutions. It is important to have a theory that tells us where such situations arise. Furthermore, one cannot be satisfied with mechanisms that use an infinite-dimensional space where a finite-dimensional one would work. Hence, again, we need a theory that tells us when a finite-dimensional space would be adequate, and how low a dimension it could possibly have.[6]

As is well known, much contemporary economic analysis, including that using game-theoretic models, has the limitation of being focused on equilibrium, that is, statics. The analysis in this book shares this limitation. It is important to understand the operational meaning of the distinction between statics and dynamics in the context of mechanism design. To design a *dynamic* mechanism for a given criterion of desirability means to define a decentralized iterative procedure whose successive steps converge to a desirable outcome, and which stops, or otherwise signals, when a desirable outcome is attained. (Here we do not intend to exclude processes that operate in continuous time.) On the other hand, a *static* mechanism design is not required to converge, only to recognize equilibrium. More precisely, it can be viewed as a "verification scenario," in which a *given* proposed outcome is tested for desirability. This involves asking each participant whether the proposed outcome is acceptable to her.[7] The proposed outcome is judged acceptable if and only if all the participants' responses are affirmative. We do not undertake the dynamic design task in this book. Our aim here is to develop the techniques of static design, that is, to formulate systematic procedures for designing a verification scenario, given only the class of environments over which the scenario is to be effective (including the initial distribution of information among the participants and the criterion of desirability).[8] The aim of this chapter is to present a minimally technical

---

[6] Here, too, the possibility of a tradeoff with other determinants of information processing costs, including complexity, should be taken into account.

[7] In the light of private information available to that participant.

[8] There do exist results in the literature (Jordan 1987, Mount and Reiter 1987, Reiter 1979, and Saari and Simon 1978) showing how message space size requirements increase when dynamic stability requirements are imposed. We hope that further research on design of stable mechanisms will build on this work. But it seems that a necessary first step in the development of systematic design procedures is the static aspect and the present work does not go beyond this.

introduction to the concepts used in the design process. These include:

- the concept of an adjustment process (specifically, a message exchange process),
- the concept of informational decentralization (in particular, privacy preserving), and
- what it means when we say that a given process "realizes" a given desirability criterion.

The process of design includes two steps. The first is called the rectangles method (abreviated RM). This is followed by a second step, which can be one of the two possibilities, called respectively, the transversals method (abbreviated TM) and the condensation method (CM).

To make the concepts easier to absorb, we initially illustrate them with two examples. The first example, the class of environments, consists of two-person pure exchange (Edgeworth box) environments. In this example the criterion of desirability requires a Walrasian outcome. This may seem somewhat paradoxical, considering that our basic objective is to go beyond Walrasian theory, but it is helpful as an expository device. The example is presented in Section 1.6. Our second example in this chapter has a more political flavor. It is representative of a class of situations in which there is an authority, perhaps an agency of a government, that regulates the actions of agents, in our example, whose interests conflict. It is presented in Section 1.8. This example illustrates many of the ideas that underly our approach to mechanism design. In addition, there are also nonWalrasian illustrations[9] in other chapters. These two examples are presented here in some detail. However, the analyses presented in subsequent chapters do not rely on the details of these examples.

The reader should also be aware of two limitations on the class of problems that we analyze in this book. First, in Chapter 2, an environment is specified by a finite number of real parameters. This specification is typical of models used in applications, but not of those in economic theory. Second, the criteria of desirability that we use are (single-valued) functions. We have used correspondences (for example, the Pareto correspondence) in a more general theory presented elsewhere. Furthermore, in our Walrasian examples we limit ourselves to cases in which there is a unique Walrasian equilibrium.

The rest of this chapter following the examples consists of two parts: the exposition of basic concepts, primarily illustrated by the two examples, and

---

[9] In particular, the inner product goal criterion.

a sample of first step design procedures using the rectangles method. The exposition begins with a review of some basic concepts of mechanism theory. Environments, outcomes, and goal functions are introduced; the initial dispersion of information is discussed; and the elements of message exchange processes and game forms are reviewed briefly and with little formality. The concepts of realizing a goal function by a decentralized mechanism, and of implementing a goal function by a game form, are reviewed. Following that, ideas underlying the rectangles method are presented in the context of examples.

1.2 Environments and Goal Functions

The performance of a mechanism, and therefore the choice of mechanism to realize a given goal function, depends on elements that constrain the situation, such as technological possibilities, or that define preferences, but are not subject to the control or influence of the designer of the economic organization – that is, on the relevant "givens" of the problem. The totality of such elements is called the set of (economic) environments or the *environment space*. In economic theory the environment space is usually taken to be infinite dimensional; for example, all convex preference relations may be admitted. Here in Chapters 2 and 4 we assume that the agents are characterized by a finite number of parameters, and that an environment is represented by the parameters characterizing the agents. This is the usual assumption in models used in empirical applications.

It is typically the case that no one, including the mechanism designer, knows the prevailing environment. We usually assume that an agent knows only her own parameters, but not those of other agents, and that the designer knows only the environment space, Θ, and the goal function, F, that is, the class of environments for which a mechanism is to be designed and the criterion of desirability.[10]

We suppose that mechanisms are designed for a client, who may be "society," a firm, or a political authority. The goal function, F, reflects the client's criteria for evaluating outcomes (often resource allocations). The client's concerns can be with efficiency, fairness, or other attributes of the outcome. The goal function has the environment as its argument, because the desirability of an allocation depends on the prevailing point

---

[10] Other assumptions can be made about the initial distribution of information among the agents, perhaps limiting what an agent knows to what can be unambiguously inferred from signals that the agent can observe. Generally, this would mean that an agent would know less about the prevailing environment than knowing his own parameters.

θ in the environment space Θ. The goal function does not capture or reflect the things that might vary when different mechanisms are used to realize that goal function. Factors that determine informational costs generally are not related to outcomes alone, but depend on the means of arriving at outcomes. Because the goal function represents criteria for judging the outcomes, but not the means of achieving them, it is important to distinguish the goal function from the mechanism, which is a means of achieving the goal. In formal notation we write $F : \Theta \rightarrow Z$, where Z is the outcome space. In many economic models, the outcome space is a vector space, for instance, the space of allocations. But frequently, especially in examples, we take the space of outcomes to be the real numbers, that is, $Z = R$.

In a more general treatment of mechanism design, the goal F is a correspondence rather than a function. In that case, the correspondence F goes from the joint parameter space to the outcome space, and the value $F(\theta)$ then describes the set of outcomes that are desirable, or at least acceptable, according to the criterion embodied in F when the prevailing environment is θ. The Pareto correspondence, say P, is an example. In that case $P(\theta)$ is the set of outcomes that are Pareto optimal when the prevailing environment is θ.

1.3 Mechanisms: Message Exchange Processes and Game Forms

A message exchange process, or mechanism, in equilibrium form consists of three elements, a message space, denoted M, a (group) equilibrium message correspondence, denoted μ, where $\mu : \Theta \Rightarrow M$, and an outcome function, denoted h, $h : M \rightarrow Z$. Let $\pi = (M, \mu, h)$. Such a mechanism is perhaps most naturally understood as representing the stationary or equilibrium states of a dynamic message exchange process. The message space M consists of the messages available for communication. Here we take it to be a (finite-dimensional) Euclidean space.

Messages may include, for instance, formal written communications within a firm, such as sales, production, or accounting reports. These typically have conventional formats. They usually consist of an array of blank spaces in which numerical (sometimes alphanumeric) entries are made according to given instructions. Therefore, such a report is an ordered array of variables, whose possible values form a (vector) space.

Less formal communications, such as business letters or memos, can be represented in the same way, if we abstract from personal chit-chat. It does not require a great stretch of imagination to see how the relevant substance of conversations might be treated in the same way.

The group equilibrium message correspondence μ associates with each environment, θ, the set of messages, $\mu(\theta)$, that are equilibrium or stationary messages for all the agents. We interpret these as messages that each agent individually finds acceptable. If the messages were proposed actions, then those in $\mu(\theta)$ would consist of all the proposals to which each agent would agree when the environment is θ.

The outcome function h translates messages into outcomes.

Thus, the mechanism $\pi = (M, \mu, h)$ when operated in an environment θ leads to the outcomes $h(\mu(\theta))$ in Z.

If it is the case that for all environments in the given space, Θ, the mechanism π leads to an outcome desired by the client in that environment, then we say that π *realizes*[11] F on Θ, or, that π *realizes* F.

Briefly, π realizes F if for all θ in Θ, $h(\mu(\theta)) = F(\theta)$.

This concept can be represented in a commuting diagram, shown in Figure 1.3.1.

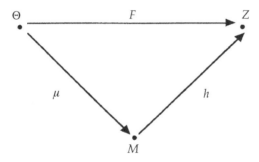

Figure 1.3.1

The equilibrium message correspondence μ represents the behavior of the agents. We consider two different cases. First, ignoring incentives, we may suppose that the behavior of the agents is known or prescribed; this is customarily assumed in the case of the competitive mechanism, for instance, in general equilibrium theory.[12] Second, we may suppose that the behavior of the agents is chosen by them strategically in a game.

A game is defined by the individual strategy domains, $S^1, \ldots, S^N$ of the players and their payoff functions $\Psi^1, \ldots, \Psi^N$. The N-tuples $S^1, \ldots, S^N$ of individual strategies constitute the joint strategy space S.[13] The ith

---

[11] The term "realizes" is used to distinguish this concept from implementation by a game form.

[12] There it is assumed that agents' actions maximize utility taking prices as given.

[13] Thus, S is the Cartesian product of the individual strategy domains: $S = S^1 \times \cdots \times S^N$.

player's payoff function represents his/her utility when the joint strategy $s = (s^1, \ldots, s^N)$ is used by the players. On the other hand, the value, $h(s)$, of the outcome function h of a game represents the (physical) outcome prescribed by the rules of the game when the joint strategy, s, is used. The value of the ith player's payoff function when s is used is the value of the composition $\psi^i(s) = \varphi^i(h(s))$, where $\varphi^i(s)$ represents his utility as a function of the (physical) outcomes.

The game form, $G = G(S, h)$, consists of the joint strategy space S and the outcome function h; it determines a game as follows. When the environment is θ, each agent's preferences (represented by a utility function) allow him to evaluate the payoff resulting from any joint strategy, when the outcome function is h.

In a one-shot game with a specified message space (the actions available to the players), the move of a player is to select a message. A solution concept such as Nash equilibrium determines a set of messages, to be called solution messages.

In a multimove game with a specified message space, at each opportunity to move, each player selects a message depending on his information at that point in the game. A strategy is a function whose arguments are the player's type,[14] and his information at each point of the game at which he has the move. A solution concept, such as Nash equilibrium, determines a set of N-tuples of such functions. With finitely many stages, each equilibrium N-tuple determines the final message array. The set of all Nash equilibria of the game therefore determines a set of Nash equilibrium final message arrays, called solution messages.

Whether one-shot or multimove, the game form with a specified message space, and a solution concept, induces both individual and privacy preserving[15] group correspondences from the set of types (to be identified with the parameter space) into the message space. These correspondences can be identified with the correspondences μ^i and μ in Figure 1.3.1. Therefore, the game form generates a privacy-preserving mechanism in which the individual message correspondences specify the behavior determined by a game solution concept, rather than prescribed directly by a designer. The strategic behavior of each player is represented by a correspondence μ^i from the information that agent i has about θ (which we assume is θ^i) to the message space M. Thus, a game is defined, with N-tuples $(\mu^1, \ldots, \mu^N)$ as elements of the joint strategy space of the N players.

---

[14] A player's type is characterized by his private information.
[15] They are privacy preserving because the behavior of an individual player cannot depend directly on the type of another player.

If such an N-tuple $(\mu^1, \ldots, \mu^N)$ is an equilibrium (Nash or other) of the game, then the resulting messages in each environment θ define a correspondence from Θ to M, which we denote by μ. It is the equilibrium message correspondence seen above. To distinguish it from the individual correspondence μ^i we shall sometimes refer to the correspondence μ as the group correspondence.

If the equilibrium correspondence μ determined by a game form makes the diagram in Figure 1.3.1 commute, that is, if, roughly speaking, the outcomes determined by equilibria of the game form G agree with those specified by the goal function F for every environment in Θ, then the game form G is said to *implement* the goal function F (in whatever type of equilibrium is used as the game theoretic solution concept).

It is immediately clear that if a game form G implements a goal function F, then there is a corresponding mechanism π that realizes F. This mechanism is the one defined by taking the message correspondence determined by the equilibrium of the game to be the group message correspondence of the mechanism, and the outcome function of G to be the outcome function of the mechanism. Therefore, the informational requirements of realizing a given goal function provide a lower bound for the informational requirements of implementing that goal function; see Reichelstein and Reiter (1988).

1.4 Initial Dispersion of Information and Privacy Preservation

As we have said, we assume that each agent knows only his own characteristic. When the environment is θ, agent i knows only θ^i. (In the game theoretic setting this is agent i's private information, and his type.) Agent i's behavior, whether strategic or not, can depend only on the information he has. That is, agent i's behavior can depend on the environment θ only through θ^i.[16] The effect of this requirement is that once the mechanism is specified, there must exist individual equilibrium message correspondences for each agent, denoted μ^i, where $\mu^i \colon \Theta^i \to M$ such that $\mu(\theta) = \bigcap_{i=1}^N \mu^i(\theta^i)$.

Suppose, as is often the case in applications, that each of these correspondences, μ^i, is defined by an equilibrium equation of the form

---

[16] For future reference, we note that an agent is not assumed to know the set of possible environments, including in particular the set of other agents, and the possible environments of other agents. Nor do we assume that any agent knows the goal function, and the rule that governs his behavior in the mechanism in which he participates. The rule is either in the form of the individual message correspondence, μ^i, or the equilibrium equation, g^i.

$g^i(m, \theta^i) = 0.$[17] Then the value of the group message correspondence μ is given by

$$\mu^i(\theta^i) = \{m \in M : g^i(m, \theta^i) = 0\}, \qquad i = 1, \ldots, N.$$

We see that the group equilibrium message set $\mu(\theta)$ contains only messages that can be individually verified by each agent, that is, messages that satisfy that agent's individual equilibrium equation(s), and furthermore, that the equations of agent i have only the component θ^i of θ as an argument. The group message correspondence μ is given by the system of equations

$$g(m, \theta) = 0,$$

which is shorthand for the equation system

$$g^i(m, \theta^i) = 0, \qquad \text{for } i = 1, \ldots, N.$$

Because the verification carried out by an agent only requires the knowledge of his own characteristic θ^i, the mechanism π is said to *preserve privacy*; as we have seen, a corresponding property holds in the game theoretic formulation, where strategies of an agent can depend only on that agent's private information.

Note that the mechanism π can be written either as (M, μ, h) or in equation form as (M, g, h).[18]

1.5 Mechanism Design

The problem of mechanism design is: given a class Θ of environments, an outcome space Z, and a goal function F, find a privacy preserving mechanism (or a class of mechanisms) $\pi = (M, \mu, h)$ (in equation form, $\pi = (M, g, h)$) that realizes F on Θ.

We want to find mechanisms that realize the goal function, and do it with as low a burden of processing information as possible. (We might also want to take account of other costly aspects, such as the burden of policing the behavior of agents.)

Thus, in a design problem, the goal function is the main "given," while the mechanism is the unknown. Therefore, the design problem is the "inverse" of traditional economic theory, which is typically devoted to the analysis of the performance of a given mechanism.

---

[17] g^i might consist of several equations.

[18] As we have indicated, the equilibrium form of a mechanism can be derived from a more intuitive dynamic message exchange process. This is done explicitly in Hurwicz (1960)

The chief emphasis of this book is, as we have said, on developing systematic methods of solving the design problem using only the information about the function F (including its domain Θ) and without prior preconceptions as to the precise nature of the mechanism that might realize it.[19] By following this approach, we have sometimes discovered mechanisms that realize a given function that were previously unknown, and sometimes discovered them in cases where it was not known whether a mechanism with the required properties was possible. On the other hand, it is also interesting that our procedures have constructed mechanisms that were already known, such as the competitive mechanism, or parameter transfer processes.

1.6 Mechanism Design Illustrated in a Walrasian Example

1.6.1 An Edgeworth Box Economy

Consider a two-agent two-commodity economy in which each agent has a quasi-linear quadratic utility function characterized by two parameters, denoted (α_i, β_i) for agent i. In what follows X_i denotes the total holdings of (or consumption by) agent i of the first commodity, Y_i denotes i's holdings of the second commodity, and w_i and v_i are respectively i's initial endowments of the two commodities. The parameter vector $(\alpha_i, \beta_i, w_i, v_i)$ is the *characteristic* of agent i.[20] The characteristics of both agents together determine both the set of feasible allocations – the Edgeworth box – the set of feasible trades, and the set of Pareto-optimal trades as well.

In terms of the total consumption vector (X_i, Y_i) the utility function U^i of agent i is

$$U^i(X_i, Y_i) = \alpha_i X_i + (1/2)\beta_i X_i^2 + Y_i, \qquad i = 1, 2.$$

We assume that both β_i are negative (hence U^i is strictly concave on X_i), and both $\alpha_i > 0$. We also assume that the whole Edgeworth box is in the range where U^i increases with X_i.

The ith agent's net trades are

$$x_i = X_i - w_i$$

---

[19] Although the search might be limited to a class of mechanisms that is of particular interest, especially because of informational efficiency considerations.

[20] More generally, the agent's characteristic would include the functional form of the utility function, here specified as quadratic (or other attributes of his/her preferences) as well as the admissible consumption set.

and

$$y_i = Y_i - v_i.$$

The no-disposal feasibility (balance) conditions then imply

$$x_1 + x_2 = 0,$$

and

$$y_1 + y_2 = 0.$$

Substituting $x_i + w_i = X_i$ and $y_i + v_i = Y_i$ into U^i gives the utility function u_i of agent i for net trades. That utility function is

$$u_i(x_i, y_i) = \alpha_i(x_i + w_i) + (1/2)\beta_i(x_i + w_i)^2 + y_i + v_i \qquad i = 1, 2.$$

1.6.2 The Walrasian Goal Function

In this example we assume that the goal is to achieve the (unique) Walrasian trade in each environment specified by the parameter vectors.

To simplify the exposition, we suppose that the initial endowments are constant, and transform the notation somewhat. Each agent i has two variable parameters, α_i and β_i. To make the algebra simpler we use $\gamma_i = \alpha_i + \beta_i w_i$ in place of α_i for each agent i. We introduce the following notation, which is also used subsequently. We denote the parameters of agent 1 by a's, and the parameters of agent 2 by b's. Let θ^i be the parameter vector characterizing agent i.

Thus, $\theta^1 = (a_1, a_2)$ stands for (β_1, γ_1), and $\theta^2 = (b_1, b_2)$ stands for (β_2, γ_2). The parameter point characterizing the environment is $\theta = (\theta^1, \theta^2)$. The corresponding parameter spaces are denoted by capital letters, so that θ is in $\Theta = \Theta^1 \times \Theta^2$.

We take outcomes to be *net trades*, and so focus our attention on the net trade x_1.[21] Then we can take the outcome space Z to be the real number space R.

The function F_W associates to each environment θ its unique Walrasian trade x_1. The subscript W stands for "Walrasian." Thus, we are assuming that the goal function is

$$F_W : \Theta^1 \times \Theta^2 \to Z.$$

---

[21] Knowing x_1 is sufficient to determine the complete resource allocation: $x_2 = -x_1$ and $y_i = -px_i$, $i = 1, 2$. (The value of p, the price of good X, can be determined from the equilibrium messages of the mechanism to be used below.)

In the notation just introduced, its value is

$$F_W(\theta) = \frac{(b_2 - a_2)}{(b_1 + a_1)}. \qquad (+)$$

This goal function is derived as follows:

$$U^i(X_i, Y_i) = \alpha_i X_i - (1/2)\beta_i X_i^2 + Y_i, \qquad \alpha_i > 0, \beta_i > 0,$$

where X_i and Y_i denote the respective total consumptions of the two goods by trader i. However, we deal with *net trades in good X* denoted by x_i.

Let ω denote the initial endowment of good X held by trader i; use the relation $X_i = \omega_i + x_i$, and drop the constant terms. Then the utility function of the ith trader can be written as

$$u^i(x_i, Y_i) = (\alpha_i - \beta_i\omega_i)x_i - (1/2)\beta_i x_i^2 + Y_i.$$

Define a_1, a_2, b_1 and b_2 by

$$\alpha_1 - \beta_1\omega_1 = a_2, \qquad \beta_1 = a_1$$
$$\alpha_2 - \beta_2\omega_2 = b_2, \qquad \beta_2 = b_1.$$

Then we get

$$u^1(x_1, Y_1) = a_2 x_i - (1/2)a_1 x_i^2 + Y_1$$

and

$$u^2(x_2, Y_2) = b_2 x_2 - (1/2)b_1 x_2^2 + Y_2.$$

Since $\beta_i < 0$, for $i = 1, 2$, it follows that a_1 and b_1 are both strictly positive. Furthermore, in order to guarantee that the equilibrium solutions will stay on the increasing side of the (vertex upward) parabolas, we also assume that a_2 and b_2 are positive. (This amounts to assuming that, for each i, the endowment is small enough to satisfy the inequality $\omega_i < \alpha_i/\beta_i$.)

Next, we consider the Walrasian equilibrium conditions for interior solutions for the net trades in good X. Because of quasi-linearity for each $i = 1$, 2, this implies equating the marginal utility of X with the relative price p of X in terms of Y. The resulting equations are

$$-a_1 x_1 + a_2 = p$$
$$-b_1 x_2 + b_2 = p.$$

Furthermore, we have the market clearing condition

$$x_1 + x_2 = 0.$$

Hence the equilibrium conditions can be rewritten in terms of $x = x_2$ as

$$a_1 x + a_2 - p = 0$$
$$-b_1 x + b_2 - p = 0.$$

Because a_1 and b_1 are positive by hypothesis, the system is uniquely solvable, and the equilibrium values of x and p are

$$x = (b_2 - a_2)/(b_1 + a_1)$$
$$p = (a_1 b_2 + a_2 b_1)/(b_1 + a_1).$$

Note that the price p is always positive, because we assumed that the four parameters (a's and b's) are positive.

We define the goal function $F(\theta)$ at θ to be the quantity of the second trader's net trade $x_2 = x$; i.e.,

$$F_W(\theta) = (b_2 - a_2)/(b_1 + a_1), \tag{2}$$

where

$$\theta = (a, b), \qquad a = (a_1, a_2), \qquad b = (b_1, b_2).$$

In deriving the Walrasian goal function F_W we began with a two-person, two-good pure exchange environment in which the utility functions of the agents and their initial endowments are given. The natural parameters that specify the environment are the parameters of the two utility functions of the agents, and their initial endowments. The efficient (Pareto optimal) trades are naturally described in terms of those parameters. In doing so, the expressions that characterize efficient or desired trades involve both parameters of the utility functions and endowments, and variables that specify quantities of the traded commodities. But instead of using those parameters, we have carried out certain transformations of them, being careful to preserve the identification of parameters of individual agents, with the result that efficient, or desired, trades are characterized by the goal function, F_W, in terms of the new transformed parameters alone. It is these parameters that we take as specifying an environment. In this example they are the parameters denoted (a_i, b_i), $i = 1, 2$. In our approach to mechanism design theory, we generally assume that an environment is characterized by a vector of parameters, and that a goal function has those parameters as its arguments. As the Walrasian example (Example 1.2) illustrates, to arrive at those parameters may involve some analysis. It is important to keep in mind that choosing the Walrasian function F_W as our *goal* function does not commit us to using the Walrasian (that is, the competitive) *mechanism* to realize it! In fact, we consider a variety of mechanisms, some of them not at all in the spirit of Walras, that realize this function. The only requirement at this point is that each such mechanism should yield the net trade in good X for agent 1 that is equal to the value specified by the Walrasian goal function, formula (+), as its equilibrium outcome in any admissible environment. The mechanism used to attain this outcome need not (but can) be the competitive mechanism. We consider several mechanisms that give the outcome specified by formula (+) as their equilibrium outcomes in Section 1.6.8 in this chapter, and also in Chapter 2. However, we start here by considering the customary competitive mechanism well known from standard textbooks.

1.6.3 Mechanisms: The Competitive Mechanism

Although our aim is to show a systematic process for solving the design problem, we begin by going in the other direction. Starting from a mechanism, we show that it determines the instruments that will be used to solve the design problem more generally. Because the competitive mechanism is familiar to economists, and realizes the goal function F_W, we use the competitive mechanism to illustrate two important concepts. The first is the representation of the goal function by a rectangular covering of the parameter space Θ (a partition in this example) and the second is the labeling of the sets of that covering in a useful way.

1.6.4 Competitive Equilibrium Conditions

We apply the interior first-order conditions for utility maximization subject to the budget constraint, and from them we derive the competitive equilibrium conditions in terms of net trades. These are

$$\alpha_i + \beta_i(w_i + x_i) = p, \qquad i = 1, 2,$$

where p is the price of X in terms of Y.

Using the fact that

$$x_2 = -x_1$$

and the variables γ_1 and γ_2, as defined above, the equilibrium conditions become

$$\gamma_1 - b_1 x = p$$
$$\gamma_2 - b_2 x = p.$$

Hence, $x = \frac{\gamma_2 - \gamma_1}{b_1 + b_2}$.

In the notation we have defined, the equilibrium conditions become

$$a_2 + a_1 x = p$$
$$b_2 - b_1 x = p, \tag{*}$$

which yield

$$x = \frac{b_2 - a_2}{b_1 + a_1}. \tag{**}$$

The denominator in (**) does not vanish because of the assumption that the β_i's are both negative.[22]

The equations (*) are the equilibrium equations of the competitive mechanism. The resulting equilibrium is, of course, the Walrasian equilibrium, and the allocation it produces is the Walrasian allocation. For that reason we have chosen its outcome for x, as given in (**), as the Walrasian goal function $F_W(\theta)$, making the right-hand sides of (+) and (**) identical.

Our derivation of (*) shows that the competitive equilibrium realizes the Walrasian goal function F_W. But it remains to be shown that the competitive process qualifies as a mechanism in the sense of our definition.

1.6.5 The Competitive Mechanism Is a Mechanism

In the formalism of mechanisms, a message of the competitive mechanism has the form

$$m = (m_1, m_2) = (x, p).$$

Here X is the quantity, p is the price, and therefore m is in the competitive message space $M_c = \mathbf{R}^2$. (The subscript c stands for "competitive.")

The individual message correspondences of the competitive mechanism, obtained from (*) above, are

$$\mu_c^1(a_1, a_2) = \{(m_1, m_2) \in M_c \mid a_2 + a_1 m_1 - m_2 = 0\}$$
$$\mu_c^2(b_1, b_2) = \{(m_1, m_2) \in M_c \mid b_2 - b_1 m_1 - m_2 = 0\}. \tag{$\wedge$}$$

The (group[23]) equilibrium message correspondence μ_c then turns out to be singleton-valued, because we are assuming that $a_1 + b_1 < 0$, and hence the two equations (*) that define the individual message correspondences have a unique solution for $m = (m_1, m_2)$ in terms of the a's and b's.

---

[22] The case $b_2 - a_2 = 0$ characterizes allocations on the contract curve.
[23] As distinct from the individual.

The (group) equilibrium message correspondence is

$$\mu_c(a_1, a_2, b_1, b_2) = \{(m_1, m_2) \in M_c \mid m_1 = (b_2 - a_2)/(b_1 + a_1),$$
$$\text{and} \quad m_2 = (a_1 b_2 + a_2 b_1)/(b_1 + a_1)\},$$

and the outcome function is the projection of the vector (m_1, m_2) onto its first component. Thus,

$$h_c(m_1, m_2) = m_1 = (b_2 - a_2)/(b_1 + a_1).$$

Thus the competitive mechanism $\pi_c = (M_c, \mu_c, h_c)$ does qualify formally as a mechanism in our sense. We see that the competitive mechanism does realize F_W on Θ in the sense of our definition, because the formula for m_1 is the same as that for F_W.

Next, we make use of this formulation to illustrate concepts basic to mechanism design.

1.6.6 The Competitive Mechanism Illustrates Some Concepts Used in Mechanism Design

The commuting diagram in Figure 1.3.1 shows that, when the mechanism (M, μ, h) realizes the goal function F, the composition of μ and h is the same function as F. To help interpret this representation, we decompose the message correspondence μ into the composition of two functions, the first from the parameter space Θ into the set of subsets of that space Θ the second is a function that labels those sets by elements of M. The logic of this decomposition of μ can be illustrated by an analogy with the theory of consumer choice. If Θ were a commodity space, and F the utility function of an agent, we would be looking at the familiar decomposition of the utility function into its indifference map (that is, a function from Θ to the indifference classes of F in Θ) and then a labeling of those indifference sets (that is, a function from the indifference classes to the values of F, making M equal to the range of F). The first function (to the set of level sets of F) is uniquely determined by F. Having decomposed μ this way, the outcome function needed in order to make the diagram in Figure 1.3.1 commute is the identity function on the range of F, now the same as M. (In this decomposition of μ we might have labeled the level curves of F in some other way. In that case, to make the diagram commute, the outcome function h would be the one-to-one function that converts the label of each level set into the value of F on that set.)

1.6.7 Privacy Preservation in the Competitive Mechanism

If there were only one agent, then the requirement that μ preserve privacy would, of course, be satisfied automatically. In that case we could choose μ to be the composition of the function that maps each point of Θ to the level set of F that contains it, and label those level sets with the appropriate F values.

However, when there are two or more agents the privacy requirement excludes the possibility that μ maps Θ to the labels of level sets of F, except for a few very special functions F. (The reason for this is made clear in Chapters 2 and 3.)

We use the example with the Walrasian goal function F_W and the competitive mechanism π_c to see what happens in the presence of the privacy requirement when there are two agents.

Consider some trade, specified by a value of x in our example, say, $x = c$. The level set $F_W^{-1}(c)$ is given by

$$F_W^{-1}(c) = \left\{ (\theta^1, \theta^2) \in \Theta^1 \times \Theta^2 : c = \frac{b_2 - a_2}{b_1 + a_1} \right\}.$$

The equation defining the level set can be written as

$$b_2 - cb_1 = a_2 + ca_1, \qquad (\#)$$

thus separating the parameters of agent 1 from those of agent 2. To take advantage of this separation, we introduce the auxiliary variable d, and express the equation $(\#)$ in the equivalent form

$$\begin{aligned} a_2 + ca_1 &= d \\ b_2 - cb_1 &= d. \end{aligned} \qquad (\#\#)$$

Notice that these are the equations $(*)$, that is, the individual equilibrium equations of π_c, with c in place of x and d in place of p.

There are two things to be noted about the subset of the parameter space Θ defined by the equations $(\#\#)$ in a_1, a_2, b_1, b_2, when c and d are fixed. First, because c is fixed, the set given by the preceding two equations is a subset of the level set of the goal function F determined by c; we say that the subset is *F-contour contained*, abbreviated F-cc. Second, using our jargon, it is a *rectangle*.[24]

---

[24] In this and other chapters, by a *rectangle* we mean a Cartesian product of *any* two sets one of which lies in the parameter space of agent 1 and the other in the parameter space of agent 2. In this case, the *rectangle* is a product of slanted straight lines, but the product would qualify as a *rectangle* even if its components had been curved.

Furthermore, any point in this level set belongs to some rectangle obtained by choosing a suitable value of d, keeping c fixed.

Thus, for fixed c, the *level set $F_W^{-1}(c)$ is expressed as a union of rectangles,* one side of which is in the parameter space of agent 1 and the other in the parameter space of agent 2, each rectangle labeled by the value of d. Formally, the level set defined by c can therefore be written as

$$F_W^{-1}(c) = \bigcup_{d \in R} \{(a_1, a_2, b_1, b_2) \in \Theta \mid a_2 + ca_1 = d \quad \text{and} \quad b_2 - cb_1 = d\}$$

$$= \bigcup_{d \in R} \{\{(a_1, a_2) \in \Theta_1 : a_2 + ca_1 - d = 0\}$$

$$\cap \{(b_1, b_2) \in \Theta_2 \mid b_2 - cb_1 - d = 0\}\}.$$

This decomposition of the level sets of F_W into rectangles is fully determined by the equilibrium equations (*) of the mechanism. A similar, not necessarily identical, covering of the level sets of F_W by rectangles is determined by the equilibrium equations of *any* (privacy-preserving) mechanism that realizes F_W.

It follows that the message correspondence μ_c is the composition of a function that maps the parameter space into *rectangles in Θ that fit inside of level sets* of the goal function F_W (for this reason we call this an F_W-*contour contained (abbreviated F_W-cc) covering*) and a function that labels each rectangle with the two numbers, c and d. These are values of two real variables. Because these numbers are sufficient to identify the rectangle, we can use them as the means by which the agents communicate, that is, as messages.

Thus,

$$m_1 = x = c$$
$$m_2 = p = d.$$

In the static case, an agent *verifies* a given joint message if given her parameters the message satisfies her equilibrium equations.

As we have seen, these rectangles cover all of Θ. It is worth noting that this covering is in fact a partition of Θ. Furthermore, this labeled, F-cc covering has the following *informational properties*:

(i) Each agent can verify the joint message $(m_1, m_2) = (x, p) = (c, d)$ knowing only his own parameters, that is, without knowing the other agent's parameters; that is, agent i looks only at the component m_i and accepts or agrees to the entire message if and only if m_i is acceptable given his parameters. (This is the privacy-preserving property of the covering, and of the mechanism.)

(ii) Given their parameters (a_1, a_2) and (b_1, b_2) respectively, both agents independently and simultaneously verify a particular message $(m_1, m_2) = (x, p) = (c, d)$ if and only if $m_1 = x = c = F(a_1, a_2, b_1, b_2)$, and $m_2 = p = d$.

(iii) The messages consist of two real numbers (two is the dimension of the message space), although the number of parameters of agents is four.

Further, it is the case that messages and equations like (*) that have the properties (i) and (ii) do not exist for messages consisting of fewer than two real numbers. (To see this, note that if there were a mechanism that realizes F_W and uses only a one-dimensional message, that mechanism would have to distinguish different values of F_W. Therefore the one-dimensional message would have to label the level sets of F_W in Θ. But the level sets of F_W are not rectangles. Therefore there do not exist functions $F_W^i : \Theta^i \to M$ such that

$$F_W(\theta) = F_W^1(\theta^1) \cap \cdots \cap F_W^N(\theta^N).$$

Further, for the same number of agents and goods, even if the agents' utilities depended on more than two parameters each, say fifty each, the same two-dimensional messages would have the properties, (i), (ii), and (iii).

What we have noticed so far is that if we know the mechanism, that is, the equilibrium equations, we can construct an F-cc covering (in this case a partition) of the level sets of F_W by rectangles. But, it is also the case that if we somehow managed to find an F_W-cc covering of the level sets of F_W by rectangles, and a way to label the rectangles by variables, $m_1, \ldots, m_r$, then we could obtain a system of equilibrium message equations of a mechanism with properties (i) and (ii) from that covering. (The messages would, of course, be r-dimensional instead of two-dimensional.)

1.6.8 Deriving a Mechanism (Not the Competitive Mechanism) from a Covering for the Walrasian Goal Function

Suppose we are given the F_W-cc covering that consists of the rectangles $A(d_1, d_2) \times B(c)$, where

$$A(d_1, d_2) = \{(a_1, a_2) \in R^2 \mid a_1 = d_1, a_2 = d_2\} = \{d_1, d_2\},$$

which is a singleton in Θ^1, and

$$B(c) = \left\{ (b_1, b_2) \in R^2 \left| \frac{(b_2 - d_2)}{(b_1 - d_1)} = c \right. \right\},$$

which is a straight line in Θ^2. Given two different vectors (d_1, d_2, c) and (d_1', d_2', c'), the rectangles determined by them are disjoint. That is, this covering is a partition of Θ.

Then, for each value of the real variable c, the corresponding contour set is

$$F_W^{-1}(c) = \bigcup_{d_1, d_2} \left\{ (a_1, a_2) \in R^2 \mid a_1 = d_1, a_2 = d_2 \right\}$$

$$\times \left\{ (b_1, b_2) \in R^2 \left| \frac{(b_2 - d_2)}{(b_1 + d_1)} = c \right. \right\}.$$

In this partition of the level sets of F_W, each rectangle is labeled by its values of d_1, d_2, and c. In a way analogous to what was done with the competitive mechanism, these labels can be used as messages by a mechanism whose message space is R^3. That mechanism realizes F_W, but it is not the competitive mechanism. This is done as follows. Let

$$m_1^1 = d_1, \qquad m_2^1 = d_2, \qquad m^2 = c.$$

And, let the individual equilibrium equations of the mechanism be

$$g_1^1(m, a) = m_1^1 - a_1 = 0,$$

$$g_1^1(m, a) = m_2^1 - a_2 = 0,$$

for agent 1, and

$$g^2(m, a) = \left(\frac{(b_2 - m_2^1)}{(b_1 + m_1^1)} \right) - m^2 = 0,$$

for agent 2.

Let the outcome function be

$$h^*(m_1^1, m_2^1, m^2) = m^2.$$

We see that the mechanism $\pi^* = (R^3, g_1^1, g_2^1, g^2, h^*)$ (in equation form) realizes F_W. That is, for all admissible parameter values (a_1, a_2, b_1, b_2) the solution of the equilibrium equations gives a value of m_2 such that

$$F_W(a_1, a_2, b_1, b_2) = m_2$$

(We call this a *parameter transfer mechanism from 1 to 2*, abbreviated $PT_{1 \to 2}$ or $PT_{a \to b}$, because agent 1 tells agent 2 the value of his parameters (that is, he "transfers" his parameters, a, to agent 2), and agent 2 uses that information to calculate the value of F_W.)[25]

By constructing a parameter transfer mechanism, we have exhibited a privacy preserving mechanism that realizes the Walrasian goal function (that is, results in the same resource allocation as the Walrasian mechanism), but that is quite different from the "customary" competitive mechanism.

We see in these examples that the message space in each case *labels*, or *indexes a rectangular covering* of the joint parameter space Θ, with the property that each level set of the goal function can be represented as a union of some of those rectangles. In both cases the covering turns out to be a partition. Observe, however, that each *partition* of the full parameter space Θ defines a *covering*, not necessarily a partition, of the *individual* parameter spaces Θ^i of the agents.[26]

Each of these two privacy-preserving mechanisms (competitive and parameter transfer) constitutes a solution of the design problem for F_W. However, they have different informational properties.

1.6.9 Informational Properties of the Two Mechanisms

First, the competitive mechanism uses two-dimensional messages, whereas the parameter transfer mechanism uses three-dimensional messages.

---

[25] The general form of $PT_{a \to b}$ for a given F and $\Theta = \Theta^1 \times \Theta^2$, with $\theta^1 = a$ and $\theta^2 = b$, is

$$g^1(m, a) = m^1 - a = 0, \qquad g^2(m^2, b) = m^2 - F(m^1, b) = 0$$

dim m^1 = dim Θ^1, dim $m^2 = 1$; dim $M = 1 +$ dim Θ^1. Parameter transfer mechanisms, as well as other mechanisms that realize F_W are discussed in the context of the Walrasian example and in more general settings in Chapter 2.

[26] The covering of Θ^i defined by the partition of Θ is obtained by projection. A set A belongs to the covering of Θ^i if and only if there is a rectangle R in the partition of Θ that has A as its Θ^i-side.

Rectangular coverings are discussed more formally in Chapters 2 and 3. A labeled (or indexed) rectangular F-contour contained covering is called a *product structure* for F. The label or index of each rectangle in a covering can be a point of the rectangle. In that case, the product structure is called a parameter indexed product structure (PPS). It can alternatively be indexed in some other way, i.e., by a message. In that case the product structure is called a message indexed product structure (MPS). These concepts are defined more precisely in Chapters 2 and 3.

The interpretation of a partition of the parameter space in terms of information is that less information about the parameter value is conveyed by identifying the set (not a singleton) it belongs to than would be conveyed by identifying the point itself. When the collection of sets forms a covering rather than a partition, it is still the case that identifying a set that contains the parameter point conveys less information than identifying the point, but, because there may be several sets that contain a given parameter point, a covering opens the possibility of choosing a particular set to represent the parameter point conditional on the set (i.e., the message) transmitted by the other agent. This possibility is sometimes useful.

Second, we have already pointed out that the size of messages of the competitive mechanism is the same no matter how many parameters characterize the agents, whereas the dimension of the messages used by the parameter transfer mechanism π^* depends on the number of parameters that characterize agent 1.

Third, the rectangular F_W-cc covering of Θ induced by the competitive mechanism consists of two-dimensional rectangles in R^4; the rectangles induced by the parameter transfer mechanism are one-dimensional rectangles in R^4. This corresponds to the fact that the competitive mechanism uses two-dimensional message and the parameter transfer uses three-dimensional ones; in these cases $2 + 2 = 4 = 3 + 1$, the dimension of R^4. Neither partition is a refinement of the other, so it cannot be claimed that one is more (or less) informative than the other. However, in the parameter transfer π^*, agent 1 must identify his parameters exactly, whereas this is not the case for agent 1 in the competitive mechanism.

Fourth, in the competitive mechanism each agent must verify one equation; in the parameter transfer agent 1 verifies two equations, whereas agent 2 verifies one equation.

From the standpoint of computational complexity, in the case of the competitive mechanism both agents have equally complex equations to verify, whereas in the parameter transfer agent 2 has a more complex equation to verify and agent 1 has two trivial ones. In the case of the competitive mechanism, the parameter point θ^i of agent i is contained in several (in this case infinitely many) sets of the covering. But the sets labeled by a particular message consists of many parameter points. This means that the agents can coordinate by each transmitting a message that signals a set of parameter values rather than having to signal the precise parameter values.

Comparisons of the informational properties illustrated in this example are important elements of the design problem. The method we propose for designing privacy-preserving mechanisms that realize a given goal function produces mechanisms that have properties of informational efficiency in one or another of the senses illustrated in the Walrasian example.[27]

As we have said, the preceding examples illustrate the connection between mechanisms that realize a given goal function, on the one hand, and rectangular coverings of the level sets of the goal function, on the other. They suggest a general way of solving a problem of mechanism design posed in a goal function, including its domain. That is, given only the goal function

---

[27] Several concepts of informational efficiency are introduced in Section 1.7 of this chapter, in section 2.6 of Chapter 2, and are also discussed more formally in Chapter 3, Section 3.7.

(including its domain, and its range) and the initial dispersion of information among the agents, expressed in terms of parameters that characterize the agents, first construct a rectangular covering of the level sets of the goal function, and then a labeling of the rectangles in that covering, thus producing a *product structure* for the goal function. Next, use the labeled rectangular covering to construct the message space and the equilibrium equations, or message correspondences, of the agents, and the outcome function; these together define the mechanism.

It would be desirable to carry out these steps by a routine or algorithmic procedure, rather than to have to rely on inspiration or brilliant insights. We present next an outline of such a procedure. The procedure has two main steps. The first, called the rectangles method (RM), constructs a rectangular, F-cc, covering of the level sets of F. The second step can be one of three alternatives, called the flagpole method, the transversals method, and the condensation method, respectively. Each second step method labels the rectangles, constructs a message space, the equilibrium equations, or the message correspondence and the outcome function of a mechanism. A mechanism so constructed realizes the goal function, and is informationally efficient.

A more complete and formal treatment is given in subsequent chapters. Here we continue in the setting of the Walrasian example.

1.6.10 The Rectangles Method Applied to the Walrasian Goal Function – Informal

We are given a goal function

$$F : \Theta^1 \times \Theta^2 \to Z.$$

In our Walrasian example,

$$F(\theta^1, \theta^2) = F_W(a_1, a_2, b_1, b_2) = (b_2 - a_2)/(b_1 + a_1),$$

whose level sets, $F_W^{-1}(c)$, are given by the equation

$$(b_2 - a_2)/(b_1 + a_1) = c.$$

To construct a rectangular covering of a given level set, we must construct a collection of rectangles each of which is completely contained in that level set, and whose union is the level set. A rectangle is the product of two sets, one of which is in the parameter space of the first agent and the other in the parameter space of the second agent. We refer to these as *sides* of the rectangle. Our procedure is to construct these sides. We outline the principles underlying the *rectangles method* in the case of two agents.

In general, when there are two agents, the method of rectangles involves constructing a "generic" rectangle by following these three steps:

1. select a *base point*, $\bar{\theta}$ in the parameter space;
2. select a *starting agent*,[28] say agent 1 and correspondingly select a θ^1 side for the rectangle, to be denoted by $A(\bar{\theta})$, in such a way that the rectangle $A(\bar{\theta}) \times \{\bar{\theta}\}$ does not go outside the level set $F^{-1}(\bar{\theta})$; and
3. construct the θ^2 side of the rectangle, denoted by $B^*(A(\bar{\theta}), \bar{\theta})$, so that the set $B^*(A(\bar{\theta}), \bar{\theta})$ is the largest possible without making the rectangle $A(\bar{\theta}) \times B^*(A(\bar{\theta}), \bar{\theta})$ go outside the level set of $\bar{\theta}$.

It is intuitively clear that several properties of a rectangular covering of the level sets of F is related to, and perhaps determines, informational costs. For instance, the coarser the covering, the less precisely the agents have to observe their parameters. Furthermore, when the level sets of the goal function are finite, the coarser the covering, the "smaller" is the set needed to index its sets, and hence, the "smaller" the messages that must be communicated in order to transmit the information needed to realize the goal function. However, in general, the coarseness of the covering and the size of the message space are different (not equivalent) concepts. Informational properties of rectangular coverings, and of message spaces, are discussed subsequently in this chapter, and more formally in Chapters 2 and 3. Here we content ourselves with only a hint of their existence.

Having constructed a rectangular covering, the next step is to construct a labeling, or indexing, of its sets. Finding a good way of indexing a covering of the parameter space is a major part of the problem. One approach that is helpful is by the construction of a *transversal*. The basic idea of indexing a family of sets by a transversal can be illustrated easily by using the level sets of the function F, a case that corresponds to the one agent situation. A systematic discussion of the theory of transversals is given in Chapters 2 and 3 and illustrated there.

Suppose, for example, that $F : R^k \to R$ is a smooth function. We assume that the level sets of F are $(k-1)$-dimensional, as they would be when the Jacobian of F has rank $(k-1)$. Viewed geometrically, the level sets can be identified by taking a curve Γ (one-dimensional) transversal to the level sets,

---

[28] The procedure starting with making 2 the starting agent is analogous. We speak of *left rectangles method* when 1 is the starting agent, and *right rectangles method* when 2 is the starting agent.

that is, a curve Γ such that each level set intersects Γ exactly in one point. We arbitrarily chose a point A on the curve, and for each level set $a = F^{-1}(c)$, measure the arc length from A to the (unique) point B_a at which the level set a intersects the curve (see Figure 1.6.1.). This construction amounts to indexing the level sets of F, using the measured arc length as the index. (An alternative indexing using the same curve Γ is given by the point B_a itself. We will sometimes use the latter indexing in what follows.) An indexing system that does not distinguish the level sets of F cannot serve as a message system of a mechanism that realizes F; that is, no message correspondence that induces a partitioning or covering of Θ coarser than the contour map of F can realize F.

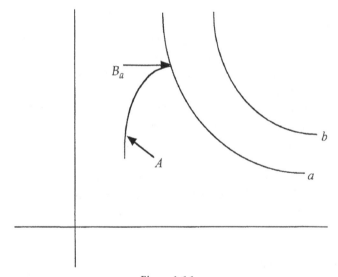

Figure 1.6.1

1.7 Introductory Discussion of Informational Efficiency Concepts

If no informational efficiency requirements are imposed, the task of designing a privacy-preserving mechanism that realizes a given goal function is trivial, because it can easily be accomplished by direct revelation or parameter transfer. But a direct revelation mechanism uses a message space whose dimension is equal to the number of parameters of all participants. A parameter transfer process uses a smaller message space; when there are two agents, we can get by with a message space of dimension equal to one plus the smaller of the two numbers of parameters characterizing the agents. Because, other things being equal, information processing costs rise with the size of messages agents must handle, it is desirable to lessen this burden.

Our earlier examples show that this may be possible. In Section 1.8 (logging in a National Forest) there are privacy preserving mechanisms with four-, three-, or two-dimensional message spaces that realize the goal function. Similarly, we have shown that to realize the Walrasian goal function F_W, direct revelation uses four messages (i.e., a four-dimensional message space), parameter transfer uses three, but the competitive process uses only two. If one goes beyond our highly simplified Walrasian example, the contrast is even greater: in an economy with two goods and two agents, if the two agents had utility functions in the form of polynomials of degree p, direct revelation would require $2p$ messages, and parameter transfer $p + 1$; hence the number of messages required could become arbitrarily high. But the competitive mechanism needs only two messages, regardless of the degree of the polynomials!

But the situation is not always so pleasant. There are goal functions that cannot be realized by any mechanism with fewer messages than are used by the parameter transfer process. One example of such a goal function is the inner product,[29] defined by

$$F(a, b) = \sum_{r=1}^{p} a_r b_r,$$

with p an arbitrary positive integer. It is known (see, e.g., Hurwicz (1986)) that this goal function cannot be realized with a message space of dimension less than $p + 1$, the same as that for the parameter transfer process.

These considerations lead to one kind of informational efficiency concept for mechanisms; the dimension of the message space, abbreviated as *m-efficiency*. But there are others. For instance, whereas parameter transfer is more m-efficient than direct revelation, it places the burden of calculating the value of the goal function on one of the agents. Thus, in the case of two agents, if the transfer is from 1 to 2, the equilibrium equation to be verified by agent 2 is

$$m_2 - F(m_1, b) = 0, \tag{1}$$

where m_2 is a real number but the dimension of m_1 is equal to that of agent 1's parameter vector.[30] On the other hand, in the direct revelation mechanism,

---

[29] The inner product is the prototype of goal functions that express strong complementarities between the parameters of the two agents. There are many such functions. See Williams (1984) for the genericity of such functions in the smooth case.

[30] Since agent 1's equation is $m^1 - a = 0$, the outcome function for $PT_{1\to2}$ is $h(m) = m^2$. Hence no additional calculation is required. On the other hand, for direct revelation the outcome function is $h(m) = F(m^1, m^2)$, and does require additional calculation by the coordinating computer.

agent 2's equilibrium equation is

$$\tilde{m}_2 - b = 0. \tag{2}$$

The task of agent 1 is the same in both cases: to verify the equilibrium equation

$$m_1 - a = 0. \tag{3}$$

We see that whereas the parameter transfer process is more m-efficient than direct revelation, it might raise the cost of computations, because agent 2's computation might be more complex. Whether the tradeoff between lowering the number of messages and raising the complexity is advantageous depends on the technologies of information processing and their relative prices.[31]

Another aspect of the informational efficiency issue is brought out by comparing the two parameter transfers: from agent 1 to agent 2, and vice versa. Suppose at first that the individual parameter vectors a and b have the same dimension. Then either parameter transfer uses the same number of messages, namely, one plus the dimension of the parameter vector a (or b). Hence the two transfers have the same m-efficiency. However, the person bearing the burden of more complex computations might be different in the two cases. Because their skills or costs may differ, we cannot claim that it does not matter who does the computations. Thus, the complexity of computations, roughly indicated by the number of equations to be verified by each agent, constitutes another aspect of informational efficiency.

In cases that satisfy certain mathematical regularity conditions, namely, smoothness of the functions and the nonsingularity of the system's Jacobian matrix, the total number of equations to be solved by the two agents in the two parameter transfers will be the same – equal to the dimension of the message spaces, i.e., one plus the number of components in the vector a (or b). But because which agent bears the burden makes a difference, we can use as an efficiency measure the vector $q = (q_1, q_2)$ where q_i is the number of equations to be solved by agent i. The vector q is called the *equation efficiency vector* (sometimes abbreviated as *eq-vector*) For *parameter* transfer from 1 to 2, these numbers are ($q_1 = \dim a$, $q_2 = 1$), so the eq-vector is $(\dim(a), 1)$. For transfer from 2 to 1, the eq-vector is $(1, \dim(a))$. (If the dimensions of a and b are different, the eq-vector for transfer from 2 to 1 is $(1, \dim(b))$.) Other things being equal, the lower these numbers are, the

---

[31] From here on, we shall with a few exceptions ignore complexity issues. Complexity in economic settings is treated extensively in Mount and Reiter (2002).

better. We therefore refer to this (vectorial) measure as *equation efficiency*, abbreviated as *eq-efficiency*. Thus a privacy-preserving mechanism whose eq-vector is $q = (q_1, q_2)$ is said to be eq-efficient for F if it realizes F, and if there does not exist another privacy-preserving mechanism, say p', that also realizes F, whose eq-vector (q_1', q_2') is vectorially lower, that is, is such that $q_i' \leq q_i$ for $i = 1, 2$, and at least one inequality is strict.

It is important to note that the eq-efficiency measure generates a partial ordering, not a complete one.

It is not difficult to see that, in regular cases, m-efficiency implies eq-efficiency. But the reverse is not true; there are examples of mechanisms that are eq-efficient but not m-efficient.

We have already noted briefly that the coverings induced by equilibrium message correspondences can differ in their coarseness, and suggested that it seems plausible to suppose that the finer a covering, the more effort is required to determine the set of the covering that one is in. Hence, a less coarse covering would entail higher information processing costs. Thus, other things being equal, the coarser the better. This leads us to a third informational efficiency concept called *covering efficiency*. A privacy-preserving mechanism that realizes a goal function F is called *covering-efficient* (or maximally coarse, or minimally fine) if there does not exist another mechanism that realizes F whose covering is coarser. It is shown in later chapters that the rectangles method (RM) has the attractive property of being covering-efficient. However, it is shown by examples that it is not always eq-efficient, hence not always m-efficient.[32]

We turn next to Section 1.8.

Section 1.8 is representative of a class of situations in which there is an authority, usually an agency of a government, that is created to regulate actions of economic agents in situations in which markets do not assure satisfactory outcomes. Sometimes agencies are created to intervene when the balance of economic power of private agents becomes systematically one-sided, and there is sufficient political pressure for intervention. The Interstate Commerce Commission of the Federal Government is a classic example; there are many others. The law(s) that establish an agency of this kind usually specify a mission or objective, but rarely specify the means by which the agency is to achieve that objective. Therefore, the agency has

---

[32] In terms of the concepts of informational size referred to in footnote 32, chapter 2 and coarseness of the associated covering, it is shown in Chapter 3 that minimal informational size of the message of a mechanism implies maximal coarseness of the covering, but, as the example of the parameter transfer mechanism shows, maximum coarseness of the covering does not imply minimal informational size of the message space.

a design problem, sometimes in a setting that is not among the familiar formulations of economic theory. The following example is a highly stylized formulation intended to capture certain key features of the situations just alluded to, and to show how they relate to the formal model of mechanisms and mechanism design presented in this book. Our example is not offered as a realistic representation of a real case. We present it to begin with in the form of a narrative, in which named agents interact in a situation that can be seen as a stylized account of a real situation. But real situations are usually much richer, much more complicated, and more nuanced than is our stylized story. We do not intend that our story should be read as an account of any real case.

1.8 A National Forest

In our example there is a National Forest. The forest can produce two products, forest products, briefly "wood", and the experience of a natural environment, briefly "nature." Forest products are produced by logging. But logging changes the natural environment. Thus, wood and nature are joint products of logging in this forest. The commodity space is R_+^2, the nonnegative quadrant of the two-dimensional Euclidean space. The intensity, or amount, of logging in this forest determines the amount of wood produced, and also the degree of degradation of the original natural environment, measured as the amount of unspoiled nature that remains.

The National Forest is run by a Federal agency, which is responsible for deciding how much logging can be done there. Therefore we want a representation of the technology of logging in terms of the variable controlled by the regulating agency. Let that variable be $\lambda \in [0, 1]$. This is the amount of logging, normalized for this particular forest so that $\lambda = 0$ represents no logging, and $\lambda = 1$ represents cutting the entire forest. The following diagram represents the technology.

The piecewise linear curve shown in Figure 1.8.1 is the production set. It is not necessarily the efficient frontier of a larger set, as it would appear to be in a conventional representation of production, although the example could be reformulated to fit that interpretation. Note that the point in the commodity space that represents the result of no logging in this forest is the point $(0, N)$, where N denotes the amount of nature provided by the uncut forest. The curve shown in Figure 1.8.1 is the image of the unit interval by the function $\phi : [0, 1] \to R_+^2$, where $\phi(\lambda) = (\phi_1(\lambda), \phi_2(\lambda))$. Here $\phi_1(\lambda)$ is the amount of wood produced when the intensity (amount) of logging is λ, and $\phi_2(\lambda)$ is the amount of nature so produced.

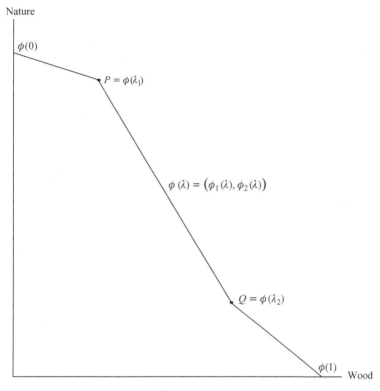

Figure 1.8.1

We assume that the curve $\phi([0, 1])$ is piecewise linear in order to simplify the example without making it trivial.[33]

The points P and Q in Figure 1.8.1 are points of (jump) discontinuity of the derivative of the curve $\phi([0, 1])$. These points occur at the values corresponding to $\lambda = \lambda_1$ and $\lambda = \lambda_2$.

The community of those who benefit from logging includes sellers of forest products, producers for whom forest products are inputs, and consumers of goods made from forest products. These people prefer to have more logging.

On the other hand, those who use the forest for recreation, and those who value it as their descendents' heritage prefer less logging, even though they may also be consumers of some forest products. We suppose that the preferences of people in the two different groups are diametrically opposed.

---

[33] This assumption is modified in Section 3.8, where this example is revisited.

For simplicity we assume that there are two lobbyists – political–economic agents – agent 1 and agent 2. Agent 1 represents the group of loggers; agent 2 represents the preservationists. Agent 1 knows that the loggers are willing to support political action that advocates more logging. Agent 1 also knows that the amount of support forthcoming from the logging community depends on the amount of logging that would be allowed, that is, on the value of λ. If $\lambda = 0$ is the proposed or prevailing amount of logging, then loggers are willing to support more intense, or extensive political action than they would if $\lambda = 1$, in which case they might be unwilling to pay much. Thus, agent 1 knows the function $P_1 : [0, 1] \rightarrow R$ whose value, $p_1 = P_1(\lambda)$, is the intensity of political pressure that agent 1 expects to be generated from the support of the community of loggers when the amount of logging allowed is λ.

Similarly, agent 2 knows the function $P_2 : [0, 1] \rightarrow R$, whose value is the amount of political pressure agent 2 generates at the logging amount λ. We call the functions P_i *political action functions*, or *p-functions*, for short. For simplicity, we treat the p-functions as primitives.[34] We make two assumptions directly about them. First, we assume that the function P_i takes values in the interval $[\tau^i_{min}, \tau^i_{max}]$, $i = 1, 2$. The end points of the interval are the minimum and maximum levels of political pressure Agent i can bring to bear. We assume that the function P_1 takes its maximum at 0, and is *strictly decreasing* on the interval $[0, 1]$, and that P_2 takes its minimum at 0, and is *strictly increasing* on $[0, 1]$. Furthermore, we assume that each p-function is piecewise linear; it consists of three line segments corresponding to the three line segments in the graph of φ. It follows that a possible p-function P_1 for agent 1 is completely specified by its value at each of four points,

$$\lambda = 0, \qquad \lambda = \lambda_1, \qquad \lambda = \lambda_2, \qquad \lambda = 1.$$

Let

$$\tau^1_{max} = P_1(0), \quad a_1 = P_1(\lambda_1), \quad a_2 = P_1(\lambda_2), \quad \text{and} \quad \tau^1_{min} = P_1(1).$$

Similarly for P_2, we write

$$\tau^2_{min} = P_2(0), \quad b_1 = P_2(\lambda_1), \quad b_2 = P_2(\lambda_2), \quad \text{and} \quad \tau^2_{max} = P_2(1).$$

In this notation, the graph of P_1 consists of three line segments, one with the endpoints $((0, \tau^1_{max}), (\lambda_1, a_1))$, the second with the endpoints

---

[34] In a more detailed model, the group political actions would be derived from the underlying technology and utility or profit functions.

(λ_1, a_1), (λ_2, a_2), and the third with endpoints (λ_2, a_2), $(1, \tau^1_{min})$. The assumption that P_1 takes its maximum at 0 and its minimum at 1, and is strictly monotone is expressed by the requirement that $\tau^1_{max} > a_1 > a_2 > \tau^1_{min}$. The two endpoints of the middle segment correspond to the points at which the graph of φ has kinks. Similarly, P_2 consists of three line segments with endpoints $(0, \tau^2_{min})$, (λ_1, b_1), (λ_1, b_1), (λ_2, b_2), and (λ_2, b_2), $(1, \tau^2_{max})$, respectively, where $\tau^2_{min} < b_1 < b_2 < \tau^2_{max}$. These graphs are shown in Figure 1.8.2.

We are assuming that the function φ is fixed, and known to everyone. Hence, the values λ_1 and λ_2 are constants known to everyone. To simplify matters further, we assume that the minimum and maximum values are the same for all functions P_1 under consideration, and the same for all functions P_2. That is, τ^1_{max}, τ^2_{max}, τ^1_{min}, τ^2_{min} are constants that are known to everyone. Therefore, a p-function P_1 is uniquely specified by two numbers, a_1, a_2.

Similarly, P_2 is characterized by two numbers, b_1 and b_2. Thus, an environment consists of a possible pair of functions (P_1, P_2). It is specified by four numbers, $\theta = (a_1, a_2, b_1, b_2)$.[35] The set, $\Theta = \Theta^1 \times \Theta^2$ of environments is the set of all $\theta = (\theta^1, \theta^2)$ that satisfy the conditions

$$\tau^1_{max} > a_1 > a_2 > \tau^1_{min},$$

and

$$\tau^2_{min} < b_1 < b_2 < \tau^2_{max}.$$

Thus,

$$\Theta^1 = \left\{ (a_1, a_2) : \tau^1_{max} > a_1 > a_2 > \tau^1_{min} \right\},$$

and

$$\Theta^2 = \left\{ (b_1, b_2) : \tau^2_{min} < b_1 < b_2 < \tau^2_{max} \right\}.$$

We let $a = (a_1, a_2)$ and $b = (b_1, b_2)$, and, where needed, we identify the p-function corresponding to the parameters a and b as $P_1(\bullet, a)$, and $P_2(\bullet, b)$.

The government agency that controls the National Forest assigns responsibility for that forest to a bureaucrat, who is represented here by an agent, called the *Forester*. The role of the Forester is to decide how much logging to permit, that is, to choose the value of λ. The Forester knows the function ϕ,

---

[35] It is not an essential feature of our general framework that an environment be represented by finitely many parameters. As can be seen subsequently, indivisibilities and nonlinearity do not present special difficulties.

but does *not* know the functions P_i, $i = 1, 2$; that is, the Forester does not know the prevailing environment, namely,

$$\theta = (a_1, a_2, b_1, b_2) = (a, b).$$

The Forester is supervised by superiors, by one or more Congressional committees, and ultimately by the President. Therefore, the Forester must be able to justify his decision on the basis of some coherent principle. Such a principle, or set of principles, can be represented formally by a goal function that associates the desired level of logging, $\lambda = F(\theta)$, with each possible environment θ.

What might the goal function express in this problem? The Forester can be motivated by several factors. First, he is responsible for the state of the forest. Second, he is a bureaucrat in an administration that might have political obligations to one or the other of the parties, and thus wish to favor one of the parties. Third, he may want to minimize, or limit the intensity of political conflict. The Forester might decide how much logging to permit without considering the political pressure that might be brought to bear by the agents. But suppose the Forester wants to, or must, allow political pressures to bear on the decision, then the goal function should reflect this factor. Although the set of possible goal functions is fairly large, to keep the example simple we assume here that the objective of the Forester is to balance the political pressures.[36] Specifically, we assume that the Forester would like to choose that logging level at which the political pressure brought to bear by agent 1 equals that of agent 2. This situation is illustrated in Figure 1.8.2, where the point (λ^*, τ^*) is the one at which political pressures are equal in the environment represented there.

To put this into practice, the Forester must, in one way or another, get information about the environment, and be able to explain or rationalize his decision. Someone, perhaps the Forester, or his superiors, or a Congressional committee, must design a systematic process – a mechanism – that will allow him to take the desired decisions in each possible environment. We express this by saying that the mechanism must "realize the goal function."[37]

A natural way of thinking about a mechanism is to think of the private agents, agents 1 and 2, sending information – messages – to the Forester,

---

[36] This example is revisited in Section 3.8 where it is used to illustrate graphically the formal methods if constructing mechanisms that are presented in Sections 3.2 to 3.5. Other goal functions are also considered there.

[37] This corresponds to "implementing a social choice or goal function" in the game-theoretic approach. We consider incentives in Section 3.9. The term "mechanism" has a slightly different meaning there.

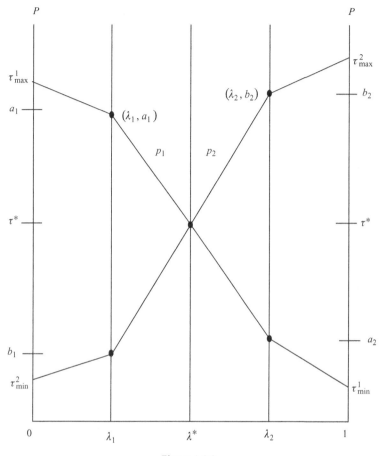

Figure 1.8.2

perhaps in an ongoing dialogue. This suggests some sort of dynamic process, for instance, a discrete time message exchange or adjustment process as follows.

At time t the Forester announces a provisional logging rate $\lambda(t) \in [0, 1]$. Agent i responds with the message $p_i(t) = P_i(\lambda(t), \theta^i)$, $i = 1, 2$. At time $t + 1$ the Forester calculates

$$\Delta(\lambda(t)) = P_1(\lambda(t), a) - P_2(\lambda(t), b)$$

and adjusts the value of $\lambda(t)$ according to the rule

$$\lambda(t + 1) = \lambda(t) + \eta(\Delta(\lambda(t))),$$

where η is a sign preserving function of Δ such that $\eta(0) = 0$. Thus, according to this process the Forester proposes a logging rate, each agent responds with a message that informs the Forester of the amount of political pressure that the agent can bring to bear. If the pressure from the loggers exceeds the pressure from the preservationists, the Forester proposes a higher logging rate, if the pressure from the loggers is smaller than that from the preservationists, the Forester proposes a lower logging rate. If the pressures are equal, the Forester announces that rate as his decision.

The assumptions we have made about the functions P_i, $i = 1, 2$, ensure that there is a unique logging rate λ^* at which $\Delta(\lambda^*) = 0$, and that the adjutment process we have defined converges to it. However, there are other environments, in which the functions P_i, $i = 1, 2$, do not satisfy all our assumptions, in which the Forester's response to political pressure could lead to more complex adjustments and different outcomes.[38]

Now we restrict attention to equilibrium. Then we can use the *verification scenario*, to achieve the same result as we would get by looking only at the stationary points – the equilibria – of the dynamic process. According to rules of a verification scenario, the Forester "posts" a message (sends it to each agent); both agents 1 and 2 see the message, and each responds either "yes" or "no." Here we are assuming that both agents answer truthfully. (We drop this assumption subsequently.) If both agents answer "yes," then the Forester translates the posted message into a logging rate according to a fixed rule called the *outcome function* – a function known by all three agents. What messages can the Forester post? In a more realistic case, it seems clear that communication between the Federal agency, the industry and the environmentalists is likely to be complicated and voluminous. This leads to the idea that it is desirable to have a mechanism that realizes the goal function while using messages that are as "small" as possible. We consider the mechanisms that are available in our example.

A revelation mechanism is an obvious possibility. If the Forester posts a four-dimensional vector (a_1, a_2, b_1, b_2), and both agents 1 and 2 respond "yes," then as far as equilibrium is concerned, it is just as if each agent told the Forester their parameters. Thus, the message is $m = (a_1, a_2, b_1, b_2; x)$, where $x \in \{yes, no\} \times \{yes, no\}$ is the reply of the two agents.

Note that the set of possible replies of the agents is the same in the verification scenario no matter what the nature of the message the Forester posts. Therefore, when trying to minimize message size, we can ignore the reply part of the message – the x – and concentrate attention on the message

---

[38] We consider one such example in Section 3.8.

that the Forester posts. When the Forester sees that all replies are "yes," he can then calculate the value of the outcome function at the agreed upon message, and choose that value to be the logging rate. If the designer chose the (obviously) correct outcome function, the mechanism would realize the goal function. The obviously correct outcome function is

$$h(m) = h(a_1, a_2, b_1, b_2) = F(a_1, a_2, b_1, b_2).$$

The mechanism just described is *privacy preserving*, because each agent can decide whether or not to say "yes," knowing only her own parameters, but not those of the other agent, and the Forester can translate the responses into an outcome, because he knows the message he posted, and he knows the goal function. The message space of this mechanism is four dimensional, and the mechanism realizes the goal function. This mechanism is, of course, the *complete revelation mechanism*.

Is it possible in this example to do better than complete revelation? Note that the goal function is initially known by the Forester, and by the designer of the mechanism, and may or may not be known by the private agents. We assume here that it is announced by the Forester, perhaps published in the Federal Register.

Assuming that either agent 1 or agent 2 knows the goal function, there is a privacy-preserving mechanism that realizes the goal function and whose message space is three dimensional, namely, a *parameter transfer mechanism*. Suppose agent 1 knows the goal function.

The Forester posts a message that consists of three numbers, (u, v, w). In the environment (a_1, a_2, b_1, b_2) agent 2 says "yes" to this message if and only if $v = b_1$, $w = b_2$, and agent 1 says "yes" if and only if $u = F(a_1, a_2, v, w)$. Let the outcome function be

$$h(m) = h(u, v, w) = u.$$

It is clear that this mechanism is privacy preserving, and does realize the goal function. It has a message space smaller than that of the complete revelation mechanism. If neither agent 1 nor agent 2 knows the goal function, then this mechanism is not available.

Is there a privacy-preserving mechanism that realizes the goal function F and does so with a one-dimensional message space? The answer is "no." The obvious candidate for a mechanism with a one-dimensional message space is one in which the Forester posts a proposed amount of logging, say, λ^*. Agent 1 replies "yes" if and only if there is a real number τ such that the point (λ^*, τ) lies in the graph of his p-function. But this is evidently the case for any value of τ in $[\tau^1_{max}, \tau^1_{min}]$. Therefore agent 1 always answers "yes," if τ is in $[\tau^1_{max}, \tau^1_{min}]$, or always answers "no," if not. Similarly for agent 2. No matter what parameter point is the true one, the Forester cannot identify it by this mechanism, except by chance. A more complete mathematical analysis shows that no alternative one-dimensional message would work either.[39]

A message space whose dimension is two is the only remaining possibility. We next describe a privacy-preserving mechanism that uses two-dimensional messages, and that realizes the goal function.

The Forester posts a two-dimensional message (λ, τ), where the logging rate, λ, is in $[0, 1]$, and τ is a real number. Agent 1 says "yes" if and only if (λ, τ) is a point in the graph of P_1; agent 2 says "yes" if and only if (λ, τ) is a point in the graph of P_2. When both the logger and the nature lover each say "yes," the point (λ, τ) is a point of intersection of the graphs of their p-functions. Thus, when both agents say "yes," to the announced point (λ, τ), that point uniquely satisfies the equation

$$P_1((\lambda, \tau); a) - P_2((\lambda, \tau); b) = 0.$$

In that case the political pressures are equal – exactly balanced.

Let the outcome function be the projection onto $[0, 1]$. It follows that the logging rate λ is the value of the goal function at that environment. This mechanism realizes the goal function, and as we have seen, has a message space whose dimension is two.

The increase in informational efficiency, as measured by the difference in dimensions of the message spaces, can be illustrated by comparing the revelation mechanism, whose message space is four dimensional, with the mechanism whose message space is two dimensional. This comparison can be made in an intuitive way by comparing Figure 1.8.2 with Figures 1.8.3a and 1.8.3b. In Figure 1.8.2 we see that a message identifies exactly one parameter vector, which identifies exactly one pair of p-functions, that is, one environment. Figure 1.8.2 shows a case in which the Forester has posted (λ^*, τ^*), where $\lambda_1 \leq \lambda^* \leq \lambda_2$, and $P_1(\lambda^*; a) = P_2(\lambda^*; b)$.

The Forester can then solve the corresponding system of two linear equations for the value of λ, which we see is the one specified by the goal function. But Figures 1.8.3a and 1.8.3b make it clear that there are many pairs of p-functions that intersect at a given point (λ, τ). Thus, the mechanism, and the Forester, can verify the logging rate specified by the goal function without identifying the particular environment that prevails. Figures 1.8.3a and

---

[39] That analysis originates in Mount and Reiter (1974) and Hurwicz (1986).

1.8.3b together exhibit that class of environments for a particular value of (λ, τ).

More formally, let $gr(f)$ denote the graph of the function, (or correspondence) f. Sometimes we abuse the notation and write f for $gr(f)$, when the intention is clear from the context. It is evident that for any parameter point $(a, b) = (a_1, a_2, b_1, b_2)$, $gr(P_1 (\bullet; a))$ and $gr(P_2 (\bullet; b))$ intersect at exactly one point. Figure 1.8.2 shows the graphs of two p-functions such that the point of intersection of their graphs lies between λ_1 and λ_2. The situation is essentially the same, but simpler, when the point of intersection lies in one of the other two possible intervals. Therefore, we focus on the case shown in Figure 1.8.2.

Given a point (λ, τ) in $P_1 (\bullet; a)$, where $\lambda_1 \leq \lambda \leq \lambda_2$, and the value of agent 1's first parameter a_1, we can uniquely identify the function $P_1 (\bullet; a)$ by the pair $(a_1; (\lambda, \tau))$. To see this notice that (λ, τ) is a convex combination of (λ_1, a_1) and (λ_2, a_2). Thus

$$(\lambda, \tau) = \mu\left(\lambda_1, a_2^1\right) + (1 - \mu)\left(\lambda_2, a_2^2\right),$$

where $\mu \in [0, 1]$.

It follows that

$$a_2 = \frac{\tau - \mu a_1}{1 - \mu}, \qquad \text{where } \mu = \frac{\lambda - \lambda_1}{\lambda_1 - \lambda_2}. \tag{+}$$

We write

$$a_2 = \xi_1(a_1, (\lambda, \tau)),$$

where the function ξ_1 is defined for $a_1 > \tau^*$, and also satisfies the condition that $\xi_1(a_1, (\lambda, \tau)) \geq \bar{\tau}_2$.

Similarly for agent 2, if we are given $b = (b_1, b_2)$ and a point (λ, τ) in the $gr(P(\bullet; b))$, with $\lambda_1 \leq \lambda \leq \lambda_2$, we can write

$$b_2 = \xi_2(b_1, (\lambda, \tau)),$$

where $\bar{\tau}_2 < b_2$ and satisfies $\xi_2(b_1, (\lambda, \tau)) < \hat{\tau}_2$.

Suppose we begin with the environment (a, b) shown in Figure 1.8.2, and suppose we hold the parameters b of agent 2 fixed. Then the function $P_2 (\bullet; b)$ is determined, and hence its graph is fixed. For which parameter points, a of agent 1 does $P_1 (\bullet; a)$ contain the point (λ^*, τ^*)?

Let $D_1(\lambda^*, \tau^*)$ denote the domain of the function $\xi_1(\bullet, (\lambda^*, \tau^*))$. In Figure 1.8.3a it is the open interval (τ^*, τ_1'), where τ_1' is the largest value of a_1 such that $\xi_1(a_1, (\lambda^*, \tau^*)) > \tau_{min}^1.$[40]

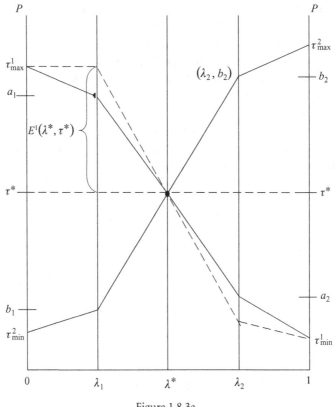

Figure 1.8.3a

Thus, for any environment a of agent 1 such that $a_1 \in (\tau^*, \tau_1')$ the pair $(a_1, \xi_1(a_1, (\lambda^*, \tau^*)))$ is a point in Θ^1 such that the p-function of agent 1 contains the point (λ^*, τ^*). This means that the information about the environment of agent 1 conveyed when agent 1 says "yes" to the Forester's posted message (λ^*, τ^*) is that agent 1's p-function is in the set

$$E^1(\lambda^*, \tau^*) = \{a \in \Theta^1 \mid a = (a_1, a_2) = (a_1, \xi_1(a_1, (\lambda^*, \tau^*)),$$
$$a_1 \in D_1(\lambda^*, \tau^*)\}$$

---

[40] Here we really mean the supremum of the set of values of a_1 such that the corresponding value of a_2 is not less than τ_{min}^1.

Similarly, the domain $D_2(\lambda^*, \tau^*)$ of $\xi_2(\bullet, (\lambda^*, \tau^*))$ is the open interval (τ_2', τ^*). Thus, the set

$$E^2(\lambda^*, \tau^*) = \{b \in \Theta^2 \mid b = (b_1, b_2) = (b_1, \xi_2(b_1, (\lambda^*, \tau^*))),$$
$$b_1 \in D_2(\lambda^*, \tau^*)\}.$$

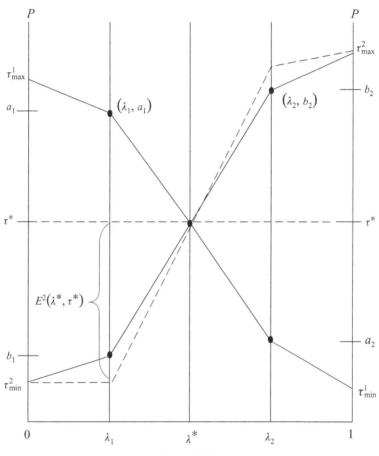

Figure 1.8.3b

Notice that the product $E^1(\lambda^*, \tau^*) \times E^2(\lambda^*, \tau^*) \subseteq \Theta$

1. is a rectangular subset of the parameter space,
2. is contained in the contour set $F^{-1}(\lambda^*)$, and
3. there is no subset of Θ that has the properties 1 and 2, and also includes $E^1(\lambda^*, \tau^*) \times E^2(\lambda^*, \tau^*)$ as a proper subset.

Property 3 indicates a kind of informational efficiency. This claim is justified, because we have shown that when the message is one dimensional the Forester cannot be sure of taking the desired decision.

Furthermore, as τ varies, the sets $E^1(\lambda^*, \tau) \times E^2(\lambda^*, \tau)$ make up a covering of $F^{-1}(\lambda^*)$. Denote this covering by $C(F^{-1}(\lambda^*))$, or $C(\lambda^*)$. Note that the covering $C(\lambda^*)$ is a partition. This is evident from the fact that if $a' \in E^1(\lambda, \tau)$ and $b' \in E^2(\lambda, \tau)$, then $gr(P_1(a')) \cap gr(P_2(b')) = (\lambda, \tau)$. But the intersection $gr(P_1(a')) \cap gr(P_2(b'))$ consists of a unique point. It follows that the parameter point (a', b') cannot belong to any other set in $C(\lambda^*)$, nor can it belong to any other set in the covering $C = \bigcup_{\lambda \in [0,1]} C(\lambda)$.

The covering C is _indexed_ by the messages posted by the Forester, namely, by (λ, τ). This kind of structure is called a "message indexed product structure."

The designer of a mechanism for this example would have to do his job knowing only the set of possible parameter points (environments) and the goal function. In this chapter and also in Chapters 2 and 4 we present different systematic procedures that enable a designer who knows only the set of possible environments and the goal function to construct a mechanism that:

(i) does not require that any agent take actions that depend on information the agent would not know given the initial distribution of information about the environment and

(ii) does not require the designer to know the prevailing environment or the message space before he constructs the mechanism.

So far we have assumed that the agents do not take strategic advantage of their private information. This is because our objective is present an algorithm (algorithms) for designing informationally efficient decentralized mechanisms. However, in Chapter 3, Section 3.9, we study combining our algorithms with methods of designing _incentive compatible_ mechanisms to produce decentralized mechanisms that are both incentive compatible and informationally efficient.

TWO

From Goals to Means: Constructing Mechanisms

Introduction

Our objective in this chapter is to provide a somewhat informal[1] description of systematic procedures for constructing informationally efficient decentralized mechanisms that realize a given goal function.

A *goal function* represents outcomes or actions deemed desirable in each possible environment under consideration. An *environment* is specified by the values of finitely many parameters that together form the parameter space. Their values define feasibility of allocations and preferences of the agents. A goal function has as its domain a *factored*[2] parameter space (in this chapter usually Euclidean or finite), and a Euclidean or finite *outcome space*[3] as its range.

A *mechanism* is a triple consisting of (i) a *message space*, (ii) a system of decentralized *equilibrium relations* (correspondences, equations), and (iii) the *outcome function* that translates equilibrium messages into outcome choices. A mechanism models communication through messages, their verification by agents, and the outcomes associated with equilibrium messages.

DEFINITION. We say that a mechanism *realizes*[4] the goal function if

(i) (*existence*) for every parameter point θ, there exists a corresponding equilibrium point m in the message space.

---

[1] A more formal exposition is found in Chapter 3.

[2] The factorization of the parameter space represents the initial dispersion of information among agents, i.e., it specifies which parameters are known to which agents.

[3] We often use the real numbers as the outcome space, but an extension of results to multi-dimensional Euclidean spaces is straightforward.

[4] Using this term (as distinct from "implements") reminds us that there is no claim of incentive-compatibility.

(ii) (*optimality*) if m is an equilibrium message for θ, then the outcome z specified for m by the outcome function is desirable according to the goal function – *F-optimal*.

Our procedures for designing mechanisms that realize a given goal function are intended to be *systematic* (or "*algorithmic*") in the sense that, given the initial data (the goal function and the factorized parameter space), a decentralized informationally efficient mechanism that realizes the given goal function is obtained as the end stage of a well defined sequence of prescribed steps[5,6] when the parameter space is Euclidean or finite. In the Euclidean case the goal function is required to satisfy regularity conditions, and so is the mechanism. In this chapter we focus on two methods of mechanism design. In one of them – the method of rectangles – one of the steps is to construct a transversal. In some cases this step uses the axiom of choice.

The mechanisms obtained are *(informationally) decentralized* in the following sense. In the communication stage (often called the *verification scenario*) an individual agent, say agent i, is asked only to verify whether a message m is compatible at equilibrium with that agent's characteristic – the vector θ^i of parameters known to agent i. Equilibrium prevails if and only if each agent replies in the affirmative. *Informational decentralization*[7] means that no agent needs to know other agents' parameters. The mechanisms we construct are *informationally efficient*.[8] Informational efficiency includes two components: the coarseness of coverings of the parameter spaces and the informational size of the message space.

The coarseness property of informational efficiency is meaningful for finite as well as Euclidean spaces, and it has some intuitive appeal. However, maximal coarseness does not necessarily yield minimal size or dimension of the message space, though it sometimes does. The theorem in Section 2.6.5.2 states that among the maximally coarse mechanisms for a given goal function there is at least one whose message space has minimum informational size.

The rectangles method of mechanism design consists of *two phases*. In *phase one* we construct a correspondence $V(\cdot)$, with the parameter space Θ

---

[5] Since more than one informationally efficient decentralized mechanism is usually available, some steps may give the designer choice among a number of alternatives.

[6] A step may involve the solution of a finite system of nonlinear equations.

[7] Also called the *privacy-preserving* property.

[8] For finite spaces, size is measured by cardinality; for Euclidean spaces, by vectorial dimension.

as its domain, and whose range consists of Cartesian *products*[9] (inaccurately called *"rectangles"*) in the parameter space. The correspondence is *self-belonging* – for each θ in Θ, θ belongs to $V(\Theta)$. The products (rectangles) represent decentralization in that they correspond to a given factorization of the parameter space, which reflects the initial dispersion of information among the agents. Also, the "rectangles" are compatible with the goal function F in that all elements of a "rectangle" are in the same F-contour set. *This property is called F-contour compatibility (abbreviated F-cc).* Finally, in virtue of the self-belonging property of the correspondence, each point of the parameter space belongs to at least one of the rectangles – the correspondence *generates* a *covering* of the parameter space. This correspondence is sometimes referred to as a *parameter-indexed product structure* (PPS).

In order to achieve the maximal coarseness component of informational efficiency, we construct the correspondence V by means of a procedure called the *method of rectangles*, abbreviated RM, but more specifically *reflexive* RM (rRM). To produce reflexivity requires a (finite) number of iterative steps.[10] These concepts are defined formally later in this chapter.

Phase one constructs an rRM maximally coarse covering of the domain Θ of the parameter-indexed correspondence $V(\cdot)$. The sets that compose the covering can be labeled – *indexed*. The set of indexing elements can be viewed as a first approximation to a message space. But that set is, in general, excessively large. We therefore need a procedure (*phase two*) for "shrinking" the indexing set. To state it more precisely, we want to find a correspondence, say $W(\cdot)$, whose domain is a set M, as "small" in cardinality or dimension as we can make it, that identifies the same sets that V does – satisfying the condition $W(M) = V(\Theta)$. Thus, the set of rectangles generated by W is exactly the same as the set of rectangles generated by V, but the indexing set – the message space to be used in the mechanism we are designing – is "smaller." A factored correspondence indexed by the message space is, naturally, referred to as the *message-indexed product structure* (MPS).

When the parameter space is Euclidean, and the V-generated coverings are partitions, and if certain regularity (rank, smoothness) conditions are satisfied, we have two special procedures, respectively called the *condensation* and *flagpole* methods, for shrinking the space of rectangles, and thus gaining the informational advantage afforded by a smaller message space.

---

[9] Corresponding to the factoring of the parameter space. The term "rectangle" refers to the geometric appearance when there are just two agents, each with one-dimensional parameter space Θ^i.

[10] As many steps as there are agents.

In more general situations[11] the construction of the message space involves a theorem that guarantees the existence of a transversal for coverings generated by self-belonging correspondences. This more general approach is called the method of transversals (TM). As noted above, when the parameter space is Euclidean our general existence results involve the use of the axiom of choice. The condensation and flagpole methods, although of more limited applicability, do not use the axiom of choice, and hence are more "constructive."

Note again that we are dealing with two distinct components of informational efficiency: maximal coarseness of the covering and minimal size of the message space. We have examples of maximal coarseness without minimal message space size, but for a given goal function there always exists a mechanism that is both maximally coarse and has a message space of minimal size.

Organization of Chapter 2

To a considerable extent Chapter 2 is a simplified exposition of results and proofs reported in Chapter 3, but it contains a number of illustrative examples worked out in some detail: the "L-dot" example, a finite example, and Euclidean examples – the augmented two-dimensional inner product, and the Walrasian example. In these examples, elements of the mechanisms are given by equations. Consequently, an additional component of informational efficiency applies. The sections that deal with informational efficiency comparisons contain results not present in other chapters.

All of Section 2.1 deals with phase one, that is, with procedures involved in constructing product structures that define decentralized coverings of the parameter space by rectangles $V(\bar{\theta})$ indexed by $\bar{\theta}$, and represented by equations written as $G(\bar{\theta}, \theta) = 0$. The main such procedure is called the method of rectangles (RM) described in Section 2.1.3, and more specifically the reflexive RM, abbreviated as rRM. Illustrative examples follow in Sections 2.1.3.1 to 2.1.3.3 (L-dot, augmented inner product, Walrasian) and 2.1.3.4 (the "hyperbolic" example).

Sections 2.2–2.6 deal mainly with phase two, the transition from parameter indexed equation system $G(\bar{\theta}, \theta) = 0$ to message-indexed equation systems $g(m, \theta) = 0$ using the transversals method (TM). Two specialized techniques are introduced for coverings free of intersections – partitions: "flagpoles" (Section 2.3) and "condensation" (Section 2.4). Coverings with

---

[11] See Chapter 3.

overlaps are discussed in Section 2.1.3 (the "hyperbolic" example) and 2.5. Section 2.6 is devoted to informational efficiency, a particular result is that rRM does not always lead to a message space of minimal dimension (2.6.7), but that a minimal dimension message space mechanism can always be achieved with rRM (2.6.5).

Basic Concepts and Notation

We begin with the goal. This is formalized as follows. We first introduce the outcome space Z. For example, the elements of Z might be resource allocations.[12] The elements of Z are divided into those that are and those that are not "optimal". Whether an element of Z is or is not optimal depends on two factors. First, it depends on the criterion ("goal") in terms of which the optimality judgment is made, such as, for instance, Pareto optimality or the maximization of a social welfare function. Second, it depends on the prevailing characteristics of the agents, such as (in economic environments) their preferences, endowments, or production capabilities. In the jargon of microeconomics the totality of such characteristics is often called *the economy*; in the mechanism design literature it is called *the (economic) environment*, not to be confused with the natural environment, although the natural environment is a component of the economic environment.

DEFINITION. Let there be N agents, and denote by e^i – the ith agent's individual characteristic; for instance, e^i might describe this agent's preferences, endowment, or production possibility set. In turn the environment (the economy) is defined as the N-tuple $e =: (e^1, \ldots, e^N)$ describing the totality of all the agents' characteristics.[13]

The range of admissible variation of the ith agent's individual characteristic – the ith characteristic space, is denoted by E^i, so that e^i is an element of E^i.

The range of admissible variation of the environment – of the N-tuples e – is denoted by E and is called the environment space. Throughout, we make the important assumption of independence of the admissible range of variation of the individual characteristics: an environment

---

[12] Although our illustrations are mostly taken from economics, the framework we use has a broader domain of applicability.

[13] This formulation does not imply absence of externalities. For instance, if agent 1 is a firm whose productivity depends on the output of agent 2, e^1 defines 1's production possibility as a correspondence with 2's output as the domain and the space of 1's input–output vectors as the range. (See Camacho (1982).)

$e = (e^1, \ldots, e^N)$ is admissible, $e \in E$, if and only if all its components are individually admissible – if and only if $e^i \in E^i$ for $i = 1, \ldots, N$. Formally, $E = E^1 \times \cdots \times E^N$.[14]

Returning to the concept of optimality, we introduce the second factor on which the optimality of a given outcome depends: the prevailing environment. This dependence is in part due to the fact that any reasonable optimality criterion presupposes feasibility, and feasibility in turn is determined by (or constitutes part of the specification of) the prevailing environment (e.g., endowments or production capabilities). But the optimality of a feasible outcome also depends on the agents' preferences, and these, too, are determined by and constitute a part of the specification of the prevailing environment. Thus, in a typical microeconomic pure exchange model, the ith agent's characteristic is specified as $e^i = (\omega^i, C^i, R^i)$ where ω^i is the ith agent's endowment, C^i the ith agent's admissible consumption set, and R^i the ith agent's preference relation (possibly represented by a utility function $u^i(\cdot)$). When the optimality criterion is Pareto-optimality, the optimality of an allocation depends on all the components of the characteristic, including the preference component R^i (or $u^i(\cdot)$). If the symbol F represents the optimality criterion (e.g., Pareto-optimality), we denote by $F(e)$ the set of outcomes that are *optimal with respect to the criterion F when the prevailing environment is e*. Thus, $F(e)$ is a subset of the outcome space Z. It is natural to use the symbol F also to represent the correspondence from E onto Z; we write $F : e \Rightarrow F(e)$,

$$F(e) \subseteq Z,$$

or

$$F : E \Rightarrow Z.$$

We call F the *goal correspondence*,[15] although "optimality correspondence" or "evaluation correspondence" might have been better terms.

Thus, for z in Z and e in E, the outcome is F-optimal[16] at e if and only if

$$z = F(e).[17]$$

---

[14] Note that this notation does not rule out the presence of externalities. (See footnote 13.)

[15] Maskin (1977, 1999) and others call it the social choice rule (SCR) or social choice correspondence (SCC). Reiter (1974) has called it the performance standard.

[16] When F is set-valued, "F-acceptable" might be more appropriate.

[17] We now write $z = F(\theta)$ rather than $z \in F(\theta)$ because $F(\theta)$ is a singleton for every θ in Θ and $F(\cdot)$, a (single-valued) function.

In this book we simplify the model by specializing the goal correspondence in two respects. First, we make $F(\cdot)$ a function – by definition single-valued – rather than a correspondence. So, for instance, rather than dealing with a set-valued criterion such as Pareto optimality, we choose a specific function that associates a particular (possibly Pareto-optimal) outcome. F is then called a *goal function*.

Second, we *parametrize* the domain of F – the spaces of characteristics and environments. For instance, instead of dealing with the class of convex preferences, we assume that an agent's preferences are represented by a utility function of a given form with a finite number of parameters, such as a polynomial of a specified (finite) degree. *When components of the characteristic other than the parameter of the utility function remain constant, the ith agent's characteristic can then be represented by a point in the finite-*dimensional (parameter) space Θ^i of the coefficients of the polynomial.

When the environment is parametrized, we consider the ith agent's characteristic space E^i to be represented by Θ^i; in turn, the environment space E is represented by the factored parameter space $\Theta = \Theta^1 \times \cdots \times \Theta^N$. (The Cartesian product form is due to the independence assumption, $E = E^1 \times \cdots \times E^N$, mentioned above.)

Thus when the outcome z is F-optimal at a given parametrized environment θ, where $\theta = (\theta_1, \ldots, \theta_N)$, we write

$$z = F(\theta);$$

here θ is a point in the parameter space Θ and z is, as before, an element of the outcome space Z.

The goal correspondences or functions tell us the outcomes that are desired (*F-optimal*) in a given environment. Processes or mechanisms are the instruments used to achieve these goals. More specifically, the parametrized *optimization problem* is to determine the outcome that is optimal in a given environment. If all the relevant information resided in one center, it would be just a matter of using this centralized information to determine the prevailing parameter value θ, and then to calculate (at the center) the corresponding outcome $z = F(\theta)$. But our interest is focused on situations where *information* about the prevailing parameters is initially *dispersed*. For example, say agent 1 knows θ^1, agent 2 knows θ^2, etc., but no agent knows the parameters of other agents. Hence the collective parameter point (N-tuple) $\theta = (\theta^1, \ldots, \theta^N)$ is not known to any single agent, nor is there any center, or coordinator, who knows θ.

Obviously, some exchange of information is necessary to determine the outcome to be associated with N-tuple θ. For instance, the Walrasian tâtonnement process may be viewed as such an exchange; under favorable conditions tâtonnement would asymptotically yield the optimal values.

In this book we do not attempt to design dynamic (iterative) *processes* that would lead to optimal answers. Instead, we undertake a more modest task, that of *verifying* whether a proposed outcome, however generated, is optimal. We refer to this procedure as a *verification scenario*.[18] And, as we shall see, this procedure is somewhat roundabout.

The reason for roundaboutness is that the seemingly obvious approach, that in which every agent i communicates her parameter value θ^i to some central coordinator, or computer (the *direct revelation* process) might be very costly (hence informationally inefficient) as compared with alternatives, for example, with the following alternative procedure.

First, each agent i is provided with what we call the ith *individual equilibrium function* g^i. Second, a fixed set (*message space*) M of symbols denoted by m, and called *messages*, is chosen.

The ith equilibrium function g^i is a function of two (vectorial) variables, m and θ^i, taking values in a Euclidean vector space.[19]

The ith agent is in equilibrium if and only if

$$g^i(m, \theta^i) = 0,$$

where 0 denotes the null vector of the range of g^i.

Now suppose a message m is announced simultaneously to all agents. Since agent i is assumed to know his own parameter θ^i and his equilibrium function $g^i(\cdot, \cdot)$, and to have received the message m, the agent can now (correctly) calculate the value $g^i(m, \theta^i)$, and determine whether $g^i(m, \theta^i) = 0$.

If all agents are in equilibrium – if $g^i(m, \theta^i) = 0$, $i = 1, \ldots, N$, abbreviated as $g(m, \theta) = 0$ – we say that m is an *equilibrium message* for θ.[20] (Here N denotes the number of agents.)

Then the equilibrium message m is communicated to, say, an external computer which in turn uses an *outcome function* $h : M \to Z$ to obtain the desirable outcome as

$$z = h(m).$$

---

[18] This scenario is an operational interpretation of (general equilibrium) *statics*.

[19] Suppose $g^i : M \times \Theta^i \to \mathbb{R}^q_i$. Then g^i is a q_i-tuple of *real-valued* functions. Hence, $g^i(m, \theta^i) = 0$, where $0 = (0, \ldots, 0)$ with q_i components, is equivalent to q_i equations $g^i_1(m, \theta^i) = 0, \ldots, g^i q_i(m, \theta^i) = 0$, where the RHS symbol 0 is the real number zero.

[20] If even one agent, j, is not in equilibrium at θ, i.e., if there is a $j \in \{1, \ldots, N\}$ such that $g^j(m, \theta^j) \neq 0$, then some other message m' where $m' \neq m$, must be tried in order to attain equilibrium.

This external computer needs to know the outcome function and the equilibrium message, but not the individual parameter values. The tools used to carry out this verification procedure constitute what we call a *mechanism*, denoted by π.

DEFINITION. The mechanism π in equation form consists of (is defined by) the message space M, the individual equilibrium functions $g^1, \ldots, g^N$, and the outcome function h, where $h : M \to Z$, and $g^i : M \times \Theta^i \to \mathbb{R}^q_i$, $i = 1, \ldots, N$. We write this as

$$\pi = (M; g^1, \ldots, g^N; h) \qquad \text{or} \qquad \pi = (M, g, h),$$

where it is understood that

$$g(m, \theta) = (g^1(m, \theta^1), \ldots, g^N(m, \theta^N)), \theta = (\theta^1, \ldots, \theta^N);$$

i.e., the ith component g^i of $g(m, \theta)$ depends only on θ^i, and not on any component Θ^j, $j \neq i$.

Because the ith equilibrium function does not contain any θ^j, $j \neq i$, as an argument, the mechanism is said to be *informationally decentralized* or *privacy preserving*.[21]

The idea of informational efficiency behind this procedure is that, in certain situations at least, one can use a message space that is in some sense "smaller" than the parameter space.[22] When that is the case the (roundabout) verification scenario may be less costly than direct revelation.[23] In the verification scenario described above, only the message m is transmitted from the center to the agents. Their characteristic parameters are not known to the center; they are "plugged into" the equilibrium functions by the agents themselves.[24] So if the message space is smaller than the parameter space, there may be a saving in transmission costs.

How should the verification scenario work?

---

[21] It is worth noting that a mechanism that produced a Nash equilibrium outcome qualifies as an example of a decentralized mechanism. Hence some results for decentralized mechanisms apply to Nash implementation procedures; this is especially the case for certain impossibility theorems.

[22] For instance, if M and Θ are vector spaces, their dimensionalities may be taken as measures of "size." When Θ and M are finite, cardinality is a natural measure of size.

[23] Direct revelation is a verification scenario in which the message space is a "copy" of the parameter space, so that the two are of equal size.

[24] This process of verification may be interpreted either as behavioral or computational, or a combination of both. In a microeconomics framework, it corresponds to statics (as opposed to dynamics).

To begin with, for every parameter point θ in Θ there should be at least one equilibrium message m in M.

First,

(*i*) for every θ in Θ,

there exists m in M such that

$$g^1(m, \theta^1) = 0, \ldots, g^N(m, \theta^N)) = 0, \qquad \text{i.e.,} \qquad g(m, \theta) = 0.$$

Because (*i*) requires that there be an equilibrium message for every parameter point in the parameter space, we say that a mechanism satisfying (*i*) *covers* the parameter space Θ.[25]

Secondly, we do not want the mechanism to yield non-optimal equilibrium values. That is,[26]

$$(ii) \left\{ \begin{array}{c} \text{if } m \text{ is an equilibrium message for } \theta \\ \text{and } h(m) = z, \text{ then } z = F(\theta), \text{ so that} \\ h(m) = F(\theta). \end{array} \right\}$$

Thus the process, as defined, results in an *F-optimal* outcome.[27]

DEFINITION. A *mechanism* $\pi = (M; g^1, \ldots, g^N; h)$ is said to *realize the goal function F* over the parameter space Θ iff:

(*i*) (*Existence*) $\forall \theta \in \Theta, \exists m \in M$ such that
$$g^i(m, \theta^i) = 0, \quad i = 1, \ldots, N,$$

and

(*ii*) (*F-optimality*) $\forall \theta \in \Theta$ and $m \in M$,
$$\text{if } g^i(m, \theta^i) = 0, \quad i = 1, \ldots, N,$$
$$\text{then } h(m) = F(\theta).$$

[*Here* $\theta = (\theta^1, \ldots, \theta^1) \in \Theta = \Theta^1 \times \cdots \times \Theta^N$, $F : \Theta \to Z$, $h : M \to Z$, $g^i : M \times \Theta^i \to \mathbb{R}^q_i, i = 1, \ldots, N.$]

The preceding section introduced the concept of a mechanism in *equation form*, so called because the verification scenario involves checking whether the *equations* $g^i(m, \theta^i) = 0$ are satisfied. But an alternative, set-theoretic,

---

[25] This covering property corresponds to the class of economies in general equilibrium analysis for which constructive equilibria exist, i.e., it is an existence requirement.

[26] Recall that m is an equilibrium message $\theta = (\Theta^1, \ldots, \Theta^N)$ if and only if $g^i(m, \theta^i) = 0, \ i = 1, \ldots, N.$

[27] Note that (ii) is an analog of the conclusion of the first fundamental theorem of welfare economics, while (i) is reminiscent of the conclusion of an existence theorem for competitive equilibrium. In (ii), the goal function (or, more generally, correspondence) F is the counterpart of the Pareto criterion. Hence we refer to (ii) as the *F-optimality* requirement.

way of defining mechanisms is important for later analysis that is explored in Chapter 3. To begin with, for any parameter point θ in Θ, we consider the set of messages

$$\mu(\theta) = \{m \in M : g(m, \theta) = 0\},$$

where $g(m, \theta) = 0$ is short for $g^i(m, \theta^i) = 0$, $i = 1, \ldots, N$, and $\theta = (\theta^1, \ldots, \theta^N) \in \Theta^1 \times \cdots \times \Theta^N$. Because the equation system $g(m, \theta) = 0$ may have more than one solution for m given θ, the set $\mu(\theta)$ need not be a singleton.

DEFINITION

1. Let $\mu : \Theta \Rightarrow M$ be a correspondence from the parameter space onto the message space, that associates with each point θ of the parameter space all those messages that are equilibrium messages for that point θ. $\mu(\cdot)$ is called the *(collective or group) equilibrium correspondence*.
2. Define an analogous correspondence $\mu^i : \Theta^i \Rightarrow M$ for each agent i by defining the set of messages $\mu^i(\theta^i) = \{m \in M : g^i(m, \theta^i) = 0\}$, for each value of that agent's parameter point θ^i. $\mu^i(\cdot)$ is the ith individual equilibrium correspondence.

Since $g(m, \theta) = 0$ in the definition of $\mu(\theta)$ is equivalent to $g^i(m, \theta^i) = 0$ for all i, and hence to $m \in \mu^i(\theta^i)$ for all i, it follows that, for all

$$\theta = (\theta^1, \ldots, \theta^N) \in \Theta^1 \times \cdots \times \Theta^N = \Theta,$$

we have

$$\mu(\theta) = \mu^1(\theta^1) \cap \cdots \cap \mu^N(\theta^N). \tag{$*$}$$

This relation expresses the informational decentralization – privacy-preserving property – of the mechanism in terms of the equilibrium correspondences

$$\mu, \mu^1, \ldots, \mu^N,$$

rather than in terms of properties of the equilibrium functions. The intersection operation in equation $(*)$ formalizes the requirement that m is an equilibrium message if and only if every agent i approves m as an equilibrium message given his individual parameter vector θ^i.

We often find it convenient to think of the mechanism as defined in terms of these correspondences, thus writing

$$\pi =: (M; \mu^1, \ldots, \mu^N; h) \qquad \text{or} \qquad \pi = (M, \mu, h),$$

where it is understood that the domains of the correspondences are Θ for μ and Θ^i for the μ^i respectively, and that the intersection equality (*) above holds between μ and the μ^i's.[28]

2.1 Phase One: Mechanism Construction

The question is: How to design a decentralized mechanism that realizes a given (factored) goal function F, with a factorization that is known to the designer?

2.1.1 Two Examples

The task of design could be accomplished very easily if we were willing to ignore requirements of informational efficiency. The simplest and well-known way is by using *the direct revelation mechanism* which we describe next. To simplify exposition we consider the case in which there are only two agents ($N = 2$).

2.1.1.1 Direct Revelation

To specify the direct revelation mechanism for two agents we first choose a message space M that is a copy of the parameter space – $M = M^1 \times M^2$, with $M^1 = \Theta^1$, $M^2 = \Theta^2$, so that $M = \Theta$.

As before, the individual equilibrium functions are defined by

$$g^i(m, \theta^i) \equiv m^i - \theta^i, \qquad i = 1, 2$$

and the outcome function by

$$h(m) \equiv F(m).$$

At equilibrium $g^i(m, \theta^i) = 0$, i.e., $m^i = \theta^i$, $i = 1, 2$. So equilibrium requires that each agent's message vector be equal to that agent's parameter vector – hence the name "direct revelation." In turn, the outcome function (perhaps operated by a computer or an administrative center) plugs the message vector into the outcome function. Since at equilibrium $m = \theta$, it follows that $h(m) = F(m) = F(\theta)$, hence the specified optimal outcome is

---

[28] In the preceding presentation the correspondences μ and μ^i were defined in terms of the equilibrium function g^i. But it is possible to proceed in reverse order, considering the correspondences as primitives and defining the ith equilibrium function g^i by $g^i(m, \theta^i) = 0$ if $m \in \mu(\theta)$, and $g^i(m, \theta^i) = s^i$ where s^i is any non-zero point in $\mathbb{R}^q_i$, if $m \notin \mu(\theta)$.

obtained. Thus the direct revelation mechanism is informationally decentralized, and does realize the given goal function F.

However, this mechanism might be very costly to operate if the parameter space Θ is "large," – if it is a vector space of high dimension. In that case the number of equations to be verified is large and the message space is also "large." Specifically, suppose that the individual parameter spaces respectively have dimensions and that

$$\dim \Theta^i = k_i, \quad i = 1, 2, \quad \dim \Theta = k, \quad k = k_1 + k_2,$$

then the vector equation $g^i(m, \theta^i) \equiv m^i - \theta^i = 0$ consists of k_i scalar (real-valued) equations and the message space has dimension k, $\dim M = k$, which might be a large number.

2.1.1.2 Parameter Transfer

One alternative to the direct revelation mechanism is the *parameter transfer mechanism*. Here each agent but one reveals his parameter values as in direct revelation. But the remaining agent's role, instead of revealing her parameter value, is to calculate the F-optimal value of the outcome using the messages of the other agents. To minimize the dimension of the message space, and to lower communication costs, the nonrevealing agent must be the one with the smallest parameter space. If $k_1 \leq k_j$ for $j \in \{2, \ldots, N\}$ we use *parameter transfer from agent j to agent 1*. To simplify exposition suppose $N = 2$.

Thus, suppose $\dim \Theta^1 = k_1 \leq k_2 = \dim \Theta^2$. Then we choose $\tilde{M} = \tilde{M}^1 \times \tilde{M}^2$ where $\tilde{M}^1 = \Theta^1$, while $\tilde{M}^2$ is a copy of the outcome space (i.e., $\tilde{M}^2 = Z$).[29] We write $\tilde{m}^1 \in \tilde{M}^1$, $\tilde{m}^2 \in \tilde{M}^2$, and $\tilde{m} \in \tilde{M}$. Then

$$g^1(\tilde{m}, \theta^2) \equiv \tilde{m} - \theta^1,$$

as in direct revelation, but the second equilibrium function is different:

$$g^2(\tilde{m}, \theta^2) \equiv \tilde{m}^2 - F(\tilde{m}^1, \theta^2).[30]$$

(So agent 1 may be viewed as transmitting his parameter, to agent 2.) Thus, at equilibrium, $\tilde{m}^1 = \theta^1$, and

$$\tilde{m}^2 = F(\tilde{m}^1, \theta^2) = F(\theta^1, \theta^2) = F(\theta),$$

---

[29] To achieve gain in informational efficiency or compared with direct revelation, it must be the case that $\dim Z < \dim \Theta^2$.

[30] We assume here that agent 2 is informed about the goal function F. This does not violate the privacy-preserving requirement.

which is the F-optimal outcome. So for the outcome function we take

$$h(\tilde{m}) = h(\tilde{m}^1, \tilde{m}^2) \equiv \tilde{m}^2.$$

Consequently, if $\tilde{m}$ is an equilibrium message when θ prevails, we have $h(\tilde{m}) = F(\theta)$, as required by F-optimality. Requirement (i) – existence – is also satisfied, since the two equilibrium equations can be solved for $\tilde{m}^1$ and $\tilde{m}^2$ given any θ^1 and θ^2. Hence the parameter transfer mechanism does realize the given goal function.

Here agent 1 checks k_1 equations and dim $\tilde{M}^1 = k_1$, while agent 2 verifies equations whose number equals the dimension of the outcome space Z (i.e., dim $\tilde{M}^2 = $ dim Z), and so dim $\tilde{M} = k_1 + $ dim Z. This is lower than dim M of the direct revelation mechanism whenever dim $Z < k_2 = $ dim Θ^2.

It should be noted that, while parameter transfer from agent 1 to agent 2 lowers the dimension of the message space (when dim $Z < k_2$), at the same time it imposes a more complex computational task on agent 2 – that of calculating the value of the outcome $z = F(\tilde{m}^1, \theta^2)$, even though it involves fewer equations whenever $k_1 < k_2$.

By contrast, in the direct revelation mechanism, agent 2 needs only to verify that $m^2 = \theta^2$, which requires no calculation. (The calculation $z = F(m^1, m^2)$, here with $m^2 = \theta^2$, must still be carried out in the direct revelation mechanism, but that can be done by an external computer or a coordinator rather than by one of the agents.)

The tradeoff between the size of the message space and the number of equations to be verified by the agents, as well as the complexity of the computational task imposed on the agents, is important but it is not examined further in this chapter. Certain aspects of it are analyzed in Chapter 4 of this volume and more completely in Mount and Reiter (2002). Instead we concentrate on the problem of *minimizing the size of the message space and the number of equations* ($q = q_1 + q_2$) *to be verified by the agents, and on maximizing the coarseness of the relevant covering.*

2.1.1.3 Mechanisms and Indexed Product Structures

THE SEARCH FOR SMALLER MESSAGE SPACES. We approach this task in a somewhat indirect manner, namely, by studying *coverings* of the parameter space that are induced by the mechanisms designed to realize the goal function. It turns out that, with the help of such coverings, one can construct mechanisms with certain features of informational efficiency. Since we also have a technique for constructing the coverings from a given goal function, the combination of the two procedures (the construction of a covering and the construction of the mechanism from the covering) may be viewed as an algorithm for constructing decentralized mechanisms that realize the goal functions and have desirable informational efficiency properties, when the goal function is given.

In this chapter our approach is partly set-theoretic and mostly algebraic.

We call our procedure for constructing the coverings *the method of rectangles* (abbreviated RM), and a general procedure for making the transition from coverings to mechanisms the *method of transversals* (abbreviated TM).[31] There are also two specialized procedures for constructing transversals called *flagpoles* and *condensation*.

As a point of departure we observe that a mechanism (in equation form) $\pi =: (M, g, h)$ that realize the goal function F induces a covering of the parameter spaces Θ called a *message-indexed product structure* (MPS).

Since π realizes F, there exists for any θ in Θ an equilibrium message m in M, such that $g(m, \theta) = 0$. In general, there may be more than one point m of M that satisfy the equation $g(m, \theta) = 0$. The set of equilibrium messages m for a given parameter point θ, namely $\{m \in M : g(m, \theta) = 0\}$, introduced above, is denoted by $\mu(\theta)$, where $\mu(\cdot)$ is a correspondence from the parameter space Θ into the message space M. Formally, $\mu : \Theta \Rightarrow M$. μ is called the (collective or group) *equilibrium correspondence*.

It may happen that for certain messages m in M, the message m is not an equilibrium for any parameter point – $g(m, \theta) \neq 0$ for all θ in Θ. Denote by M' a subset of M that consists of those points that are equilibrium for some θ in Θ. So M' is the *image* of Θ by μ, written as $M' = \mu(\Theta)$, or $M' =$ image μ.

For $m \in M'$ we denote by $U(m)$, or sometimes U_m, the set of all such parameter points θ such that $U_m =: \{\theta \in \Theta : g(m, \theta) = 0\}$ or, equivalently,

$$U_m =: \{\theta \in \Theta : m \in \mu(\theta)\}.$$

This set has two important properties. First, *it is contained in one of the contour (level) sets of the goal function F* – if $F(\theta') = z$ and $\theta' \in U_m$, then for any other element θ of U_m, we have $F(\theta) = z$.

More concisely, this can be expressed by saying that for every m in M' there is a z in the image of Θ by F – a point z in $F(\Theta)$, such that

$$U_m \subseteq F^{-1}(z). \tag{$*$}$$

---

[31] An early insight leading to TM owes much to Professor Leonard Shapiro, Portland State University, and his notion of "flagpoles."

Here is the reason. For $\theta' \in U_m$, we have $g(m, \theta') = 0$. Hence m is an equilibrium message for θ'. The outcome function yields the outcome $h(m) = z$. Since π realizes F, it follows that $z = F(\theta')$. Now if also $\theta'' \in U_m$, we have $g(m, \theta'') = 0$ with the *same equilibrium message m*; hence for θ'' the outcome is again $h(m) = z$, and because π realizes F, it follows that $h(m) = z = F(\theta'')$, thus $z = F(\theta')$ and $z = F(\theta'')$, hence $F(\theta') = F(\theta'')$. Hence all points of U_m have the same value of the goal function, and that is equivalent to the inclusion in formula (*) above.

DEFINITION 2.1.1.3. We say that, for every m in M', U_m is F-cc.

A second important property of the set U_m is related to informational decentralization – the privacy-preserving property of the mechanism π.

Suppose that two points θ' and θ'' of the parameter space belong to the *same set* $U_m - \theta' = (\theta'_1, \theta'_2)$ and $\theta'' = (\theta''_1, \theta''_2)$, $\theta'_i, \theta''_i \in \Theta^i$, $i = 1, 2$, and also $\theta' \in U_m$ and $\theta'' \in U_m$.

Since the mechanism is decentralized, this means that[32]

$$\begin{cases} g^1(m, \theta'_1) = 0 \\ g^2(m, \theta'_2) = 0 \end{cases}$$

and

$$\begin{cases} g^1(m, \theta''_1) = 0 \\ g^2(m, \theta''_2) = 0 \end{cases}.$$

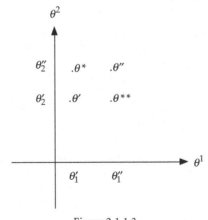

Figure 2.1.1.3

---

[32] On the right-hand sides of equations below, the symbol 0 is a vector with q_1 or q_2 components (each component being the real number 0).

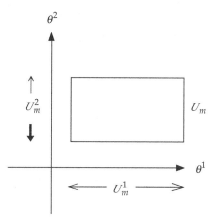

Figure 2.1.1.4

But then it follows that the point $\theta^* =: (\theta_1', \theta_2'')$ also belongs to U_m because the first and last of the above equations hold respectively for θ_1' and θ_2''. Similarly $\theta^{**} =: (\theta_1'', \theta_2')$ belongs to U_m.

Thus, U_m is the Cartesian product of two sets $U_m^1 \subseteq \Theta^1$ and $U_m^2 \subseteq \Theta^2$ where U_m^i is the projection of U_m into Θ^i, written $U_m^i = pr_i U_m$, $i = 1, 2$.

Formally, for all $m \in M$,

$$U_m = U_m^1 \times U_m^2, \ \ U_m^i \subseteq \Theta^i, \ i = 1, 2, \tag{+}$$

where

$$U_m^i = pr_i U_m, \ i = 1, 2, \tag{++}$$

In simple cases dim $\Theta^i = 1$, $i = 1, 2$ the picture looks like Figure 2.1.1.4. For this reason, we refer to sets such as the U_m in this figure as rectangles or *rectangular*. But this terminology is somewhat misleading, because if Θ^1 is, say, two-dimensional, the set U_m^1 can have any shape whatsoever. The term "rectangle" is used as a synonym for the Cartesian product relations[33] expressed by $(+)$ and $(++)$ above. Thus *every set U_m is F-cc and rectangular.*

Since a set U_m is defined for every message in M', this defines a correspondence denoted by U(or $U_{(.)}$ or $U(\cdot)$) such that $U : m \Rightarrow U_m$, so that $U : M' \Rightarrow \Theta$, where $M' = \mu(\Theta)$, and $\mu(\Theta) = \text{IM}\mu$.

(Recall that μ is a correspondence from Θ onto M, such that $m \in \mu(\theta)$ is, by definition, equivalent to $g(m, \theta) = 0$.) In what follows we continue

---

[33] Corresponding to the factoring of the parameter space, $\Theta = \Theta^1 \times \cdots \times \Theta^N$.

to write U_m rather than $U(m)$, and often represent the correspondence as an indexed family of sets, written as $\{U_m : m \in M'\}$.

Consider the image of this correspondence – the collection C of sets $K \subseteq \Theta$ such that

$$K = U_m$$

for some m in M. The collection C is a collection of subsets of the parameter space Θ that constitute the image of $U(\cdot)$ denoted by IM $U(\cdot)$.

Formally, we define

$$C = IM\ U(\cdot) = \{K : K \subseteq \Theta, K = U_m \text{ for some } m \in U_m\}.$$

It is important to distinguish between the correspondence $U(\cdot)$ and its image C; if it happens that two distinct messages, say m' and m'', produce the same rectangle $K = U'_m = U''_m$, the set C contains K only once!

Assuming that the given mechanism $\pi = (M, g, h)$ realizes F, its covering property (i) above guarantees that, for every θ in Θ, there is $m \in M$ such that $g(m, \theta) = 0$ – such that $\theta \in U_m$. By definition this means that C is a *covering* of the parameter space Θ, because it is a collection of subsets of Θ such that each point θ of Θ belongs to at least one of those sets; more succinctly, the union of the sets belonging to the collection equals the space Θ. An important subclass of coverings consists of *partitions* – these are coverings whose constituent sets are disjoint. Formally a covering, B of Θ is a partition if for any two constituent sets $\beta' \in B$, $\beta'' \in B$, $\beta' \cap \beta'' = \varnothing$ (the two sets are disjoint), or $\beta' = \beta''$ (they are identical).

These observations are summarized as Theorem 2.1.1. A more formal statement and proof is found in the Appendix to this chapter.

THEOREM 2.1.1. *If* $\pi = (M, \mu, h)$ *is an informationally decentralized mechanism that realizes* F *over* Θ, *then it defines a correspondence* $U(\cdot) : M' \Rightarrow \Theta$ *that is* F-cc *and rectangular, with the domain* $M' = \mu(\Theta)$.

It is then natural to ask the "converse" question: suppose we have an arbitrary set A and a correspondence $\sigma : A \Rightarrow \Theta$ from A into the parameter space. When does such a correspondence define an informationally decentralized mechanism realizing F? An answer is provided by Theorem 2.1.2.

THEOREM 2.1.2 *(for proof, see the Appendix)*. Suppose that $\Theta = \Theta^1 \times \Theta^2$ is the (factored) parameter space, S an arbitrary set (the "index set"), and D is a correspondence from S into Θ such that, for every s in S, the set $D(s)$ is F-cc and rectangular, and such that the image $D(S)$ is a covering of Θ – D: $S \Rightarrow \Theta$ is "onto."

Then there exist correspondences $\sigma^i : \Theta^i \Rightarrow S$, $i = 1, 2$, and a function $h : S \to Z$ such that the mechanism in correspondence form, defined by

$$\pi = (S, \sigma, h), \qquad \text{where } \sigma(\theta^1, \theta^2) = \sigma^1(\theta^1) \cap \sigma^2(\theta^2),$$

is privacy-preserving, and realizes F.

Furthermore, a corresponding mechanism in equation form is constructed by defining, for each $i = 1, 2$, the ith individual equilibrium function by the requirement

$$g^i(s, \theta^i) = 0 \quad \text{if and only if } s \in \sigma^i(\theta^i).$$

REMARK. For instance, one may set

$$g^i(s, \theta^i) = 0 \quad \text{if } s \in \sigma(\theta^i)$$

and

$$g^i(s, \theta^i) = 1 \quad \text{if } s \notin \sigma^i(\theta^i).$$

Thus Theorem 2.1.2 provides a recipe for designing a decentralized mechanism that realizes the given goal function F: namely, construct a correspondence, such as D in the theorem, that generates a rectangular F-cc covering of Θ.

If no informational efficiency desiderata are required of the mechanism, we already know two mechanisms that would accomplish this: direct revelation and parameter transfer.

In *direct revelation* the conditions of Theorem 2.1.2 are satisfied when we set $S = \Theta$, $S = S^1 \times S^2$, $S^i = \Theta^i$, $i = 1, 2$, and $D(s) = D(\theta) = \{\theta\}$. Here the covering C of Θ generated by the correspondence D is *the finest possible partition* of Θ, with the partition sets being singletons consisting of the individual points of Θ. Hence, in equation form we obtain the decentralized mechanism with $S = \Theta$ as the message space and $g^i(s, \theta^i) \equiv s^i - \theta^i$, $i = 1, 2$, where $s = (s_1, s_2) \in S^1 \times S^2 = S$, and the outcome function defined by $h(s) \equiv F(s)$.

In *parameter transfer*, say, from agent 1 to agent 2, again we have $S = S^1 \times S^2$, $S^1 = \Theta^1$, $S^2 = F(\Theta)$ and, for each s in S, the set $D(s)$ is a rectangle, $D(s) = A(s) \times B(s)$, with, for $s = (s_1, s_2)$,

$$A(s) = \{\theta^1\} \qquad \text{where } \theta^1 = s^1,$$
$$B(s) = \{\theta^2 \in \Theta^2 : s^2 = F(s^1, \theta^2)\}.$$

Here the decentralized mechanism in equation form, again with S as the message space, is $S = S^1 \times S^2$, $S^1 = \Theta^1$, $S^2 = F(\Theta)$; the individual equilibrium functions are

$$g^1(s, \theta^1) \equiv s^1 - \theta^1$$
$$g^2(s, \theta^2) \equiv s^2 - F(s^1, \theta^2),$$

and the outcome function is defined by

$$h(s) \equiv s^2,$$

where

$$s = (s^1, s^2).$$

If informational efficiency is measured by dim M, there are cases in which one cannot do better than to use direct revelation:

EXAMPLE: $\Theta = \mathbb{R}^2_{++} = \Theta^1 \times \Theta^2 \equiv \mathbb{R}_{++} \times \mathbb{R}_{++}$, $F(\theta^1, \theta^2) = \theta^1 \theta^2$ (a "Cobb–Douglas" goal function). Direct revelation is the only possible mechanism, since only a point qualifies as an F-cc rectangle.

There are also situations where one can do better than direct revelation but, subject to certain regularity conditions on the mechanism, no better than parameter transfer (Hurwicz 1986).

EXAMPLE (inner product of dimension $P \geq 2$):

$$\Theta = \Theta^1 \times \Theta^2, \qquad \Theta^i = \mathbb{R}^P_{++}, \qquad P \geq 2,$$

$$F(\theta) = \theta^1 \times \theta^2 = \sum_{j=1}^{P} \theta^1_j \theta^2_j.$$

Additionally, there are other cases where one can do better than parameter transfer. An important example is the Walrasian goal function F in an Edgeworth box environment (two agents, two goods) discussed in Chapter 1. There dim $\Theta^i = 2$, $i = 1, 2$, hence dim $\Theta = 4$, but a decentralized mechanism that realizes F (corresponding to the price mechanism) uses a message space M whose dimension is only 2. By contrast, parameter transfer requires dim $M = 3$, while direct revelation requires dim $M = 4$.

2.1.2 Constructing a "Universal" Method of Designing Informationally Efficient Mechanisms Realizing a Given Goal Function

2.1.2.0

The facts set out in the preceding section lead to a search for a general systematic procedure that would, for any given goal function, design an informationally efficient mechanism that realizes that goal function.

2.1.2.1 Informational Efficiency

In much of the existing literature informational efficiency is identified with minimum size[34] of the message space. Our analysis of the problem has led to additional informational concepts; one of them is called *F-maximal coarseness* of the covering generated by the mechanism.[35, 36] These two concepts – informational size of the message space and *F*-maximal coarseness – capture different, but related aspects of informational efficiency. To make the concept of *F*-maximal coarseness precise, we introduce some terminology.

By definition, the *covering C_π induced (or generated) by a mechanism* $\pi = (M, g, h)$ is the collection of subsets of the parameter space

$$\{U_m \subseteq \Theta : g(m, \theta) = 0, \, m \in M\}.$$

DEFINITION 2.1.2.2. A covering C' of a space is said to be a *coarsening* of the covering C of that space if every set of C is contained in some set of C'. It is a *proper coarsening* if it is a coarsening and one of the inclusions is strict.

A covering C' of a space is an *F-maximal covering* of that space if it is *F*-cc, rectangular, and there is no *F*-cc, rectangular covering of that space that is a proper coarsening of C'.

With these concepts we can state our informational efficiency objectives. First, we want the mechanism $\pi = (M, g, h)$ we are designing to generate a collection of sets C_π that is an F-maximal covering. Second, given such a

---

[34] For example, the dimension of the message space when the parameter space is Euclidean (implicit in the preceding examples), and a message space of minimum cardinality when the parameter space is finite.

[35] A related notion was proposed in Hurwicz (1960), Section 9, pp. 44–6.

[36] The intuition behind the use of coarseness as an indicator of informational efficiency is discussed in Section 3.7.

covering, we want to choose a message space M (i.e., the domain of $U(.)$) of the minimal size compatible with that covering.[37]

We could define a mechanism $\Pi = (\Theta, G, H)$ that uses the space of environments, Θ, as its message space, and whose outcome function H is chosen so that Π realizes F. But a mechanism with Θ as the message space would in general not minimize the size – dimension or cardinality – of the message space, and hence would have no regard for informational efficiency. Thus, in phase 1 of the design process we use the method of rectangles – rRM – to construct a covering correspondence $V : \Theta \rightarrow \Theta$ that generates an F-cc, rectangular covering

$$C_V = \{K \subseteq \Theta : K = V(\theta), \theta \in \Theta\}$$

that is maximally coarse. The equation form of $V(\cdot)$ is defined by

$$V(\bar{\theta}) = \{\theta \in \Theta : G(\bar{\theta}, \theta) = 0\}.$$

In phase 2 we use the method of transversals – TM – to construct a message space and an outcome function.

We accomplish the goal of maximal coarseness of covering by the rRM procedure. The rRM procedure is followed by constructing a *transversal*. This involves finding a *system of distinct representatives* (SDR) – a point from each rectangle in the covering C_V that identifies that rectangle uniquely. When Θ is infinite and no regularity conditions are imposed on F, the proof of existence of an SDR uses the axiom of choice. However, under conditions of smoothness and solvability of the equation system $G(\bar{\theta}, \theta) = 0$ for θ, and when with the covering C_V is a partition, and the relevant Jacobians are non-singular, we have two special constructive methods (*flagpole, condensation*) for finding transversals, and hence constructing the appropriate message spaces M, the equilibrium functions $g(m, \theta)$, and the outcome functions h. In many Euclidean examples, the functions $G(\bar{\theta}, \theta)$ are linear[38] in θ, but there are cases in which we must solve non-linear systems.

Examples show that F maximality does not imply minimal size of the message space (see example Z below, and in Chapter 3, Section 3.7.4). In

---

[37] The desired size-minimality can only be required relative to the covering because – as seen in various examples – there may exist different F-maximal mechanisms that realize a given goal function F, with different minimum-size message spaces. However, it is shown in Chapter 3, Section 3.7.4, Theorem 3.7.4.1, that a decentralized mechanism that realizes F and has a message space of minimal information size, also has a maximal covering of the parameter space, if the covering induced by the mechanism is an rRM covering. The converse is not true.

[38] Sometimes after algebraic simplifications that do not change the covering.

fact, in example Z, an rRM covering can exhibit *redundancy*. This is discussed below. Nevertheless, there is some consolation in the following result (see Section 2.5): among decentralized mechanisms that realize F and have a message space of minimal size, one is guaranteed to be obtainable by the rRM recipe. An efficient method of constructing a minimal covering when Θ is finite is presented in Section 3.4.1 of Chapter 3.

REMARK 1. Since rRM coverings have the maximum coarseness property, it is useful to know a simple way of deriving an rRM correspondence V. It involves using in the initial step the *maximal correspondence* $A(\bar{\theta}) : \Theta \Rightarrow \Theta^1$ (resp. $B(\bar{\theta}) : \Theta \Rightarrow \Theta^2$), followed by the L-RM (resp. R-RM procedure). In equation form, the equilibrium relation $G^1(\bar{\theta}, a) = 0$ is defined by the equation

$$F(a, \bar{b}) - F(\bar{a}, \bar{b}) = 0; \tag{*}$$

alternatively, $G^2(\bar{\theta}, b) = 0$ is defined by the equation

$$F(\bar{a}, b) - F(\bar{a}, \bar{b}) = 0. \tag{**}$$

If (*) is chosen, the B-side of the L-RM rectangle is, as usual, $B^*(A(\bar{\theta}), \bar{\theta})$. But then $A^*(B^*(A(\bar{\theta}), \bar{\theta})) = A(\bar{\theta})$, because expanding the A-side any further would make the rectangle extend into a different F-contour set. Thus, we achieve reflexivity. If (**) is initially chosen, the situation is analogous.

This simple method of guaranteeing reflexivity is used in many examples.

REMARK 2. In order to use the special techniques – flagpole or condensation – for constructing a transversal, the covering C_V must be a partition. To make sure that this is the case when $V(\cdot)$ is specified by the equation system $G(\bar{\theta}, \theta) = 0$, and $V(\cdot)$ is an rRM correspondence, we use a result – Theorem 3.6.1 – proved in Chapter 3: when $V(\cdot)$ is rRM, C_V is a partition if and only if $V(\cdot)$ is *symmetric*, that is, if for all $\theta, \theta' \in \Theta$, $\theta \in V(\theta')$ if and only if $\theta' \in V(\theta)$. In equation form, the symmetry condition is that $G(\bar{\theta}, \theta) = 0$ is equivalent to $G(\theta, \bar{\theta}) = 0$ for all θ and $\bar{\theta}$ in Θ. Thus we need only to check whether the equation remains valid when the arguments are interchanged. We illustrate this verification process in Section 2.1.3.2 for the augmented inner product example – $F(a, b) \equiv a_1 b_1 + a_2 b_2 + b_3$ – after first deriving the parameter-indexed system $G(\bar{\theta}, \theta) = 0$. We use L-RM, with maximal $A(\bar{\theta})$ to guarantee reflexivity, thus obtaining an rRM system $G(\bar{\theta}, \theta) = 0$.

In the following section we present the method of rectangles (RM and especially rRM) which carries out phase one – constructing a self-belonging rectangular correspondence $V : \Theta \Rightarrow \Theta$ that yields F-coarseness maximal coverings. This is followed by phase two where, taking as given a self-belonging correspondence $V : \Theta \Rightarrow \Theta$ that generates an F-maximal covering, we construct a corresponding decentralized mechanism that realizes F with a message space whose size is in general smaller than that of the parameter space, and in special cases whose size is minimal for the covering generated by V.

In phase two we also present the (general) method of transversals (TM) of constructing mechanisms as well as the special cases of TM – of condensation and flagpoles for regular smooth partitions generated by the correspondence V.

2.1.3 The Method of Rectangles (RM)

The method of rectangles (RM) is a way of creating a particular kind of covering correspondence that satisfies the assumptions made in Theorem 2.1.2, and possesses an important informational efficiency property – "maximal coarseness" – defined formally below. In describing it, we again specialize to $N = 2$.

DEFINITION 2.1.3.1. The domain ("index set") of the correspondence $V : \Theta \Rightarrow \Theta$ is the parameter space Θ itself – $\Theta = \Theta^1 \times \Theta^2$. We sometimes refer to this correspondence as a *parameter-indexed product structure* (abbreviated PPS).

DEFINITION 2.1.3.2. The correspondence $V : \Theta \Rightarrow \Theta$ has the property that for every $\theta \in \Theta$, the set $V(\theta)$ contains θ as one of its elements, i.e.,

$$\forall \theta \in \Theta, \ \theta \in V(\theta).$$

We say that V is *a self-belonging correspondence*.

This property has an important consequence: since the domain of the correspondence $V(\cdot)$ is the parameter space Θ, it follows that, for every $\theta \in \Theta$, there is a θ' such that $\theta \in V(\theta')$ – we can take $\theta' = \theta$. Hence the image of the correspondence $V(\cdot)$, denoted by $C_V = V(\Theta)$, is a *covering* of Θ. It remains to define the "rectangular" sets

$$V(\theta) = V^1(\theta) \times V^2(\theta), \qquad V^i(\theta) \subseteq \Theta^i, \qquad i = 1, 2$$

so that they are F-cc "rectangles" and the covering is maximally coarse. This can be accomplished as follows.

The Rectangles Method

First, for each $\bar{\theta}$ in Θ, $\bar{\theta} = (\bar{\theta}^1, \bar{\theta}^2)$, $\theta^i \in \Theta^i$, $i = 1, 2$, let A be an arbitrarily chosen correspondence[39] $A : \Theta \Rightarrow \Theta^1$ that satisfies the conditions:
(1) for every θ in Θ,

$$A(\bar{\theta}) \times \{\bar{\theta}^2\} \subseteq F^{-1}(F(\bar{\theta})).$$

We form a "rectangle" by choosing a set $B \subseteq \Theta^2$ so that, for $\bar{\theta} = (\bar{\theta}^1, \bar{\theta}^2)$,
(2) $\bar{\theta}^2 \in B$
and
(3) $A(\bar{\theta}) \times B \subseteq F^{-1}(F(\bar{\theta}))$.
Clearly, any set $K = A(\bar{\theta}) \times B$ where A and B satisfy conditions (1)–(3) is an F-cc rectangle.

For the sake of informational efficiency, we add one more condition – we make B as "tall" as possible without going outside the contour set $F^{-1}(F(\bar{\theta}))$. This maximal set B is written as $B^*(A(\bar{\theta}), \bar{\theta})$.

Formally, for any θ and $A(\theta)$, we define
(4) $B^*(A(\bar{\theta}), \bar{\theta}) =: \cup\{B \subseteq \Theta^2 : \bar{\theta}^2 \in B \text{ and } A(\bar{\theta}) \times B \subseteq F^{-1}(F(\bar{\theta}))\}$.

In a two-dimensional diagram the rectangle $A(\bar{\theta}) \times B^*(A(\bar{\theta}), \bar{\theta})$ is maximally tall among F-cc rectangles with $A(\bar{\theta})$ as base. The correspondence $L : \Theta \Rightarrow \Theta$ so obtained, written as $L(\theta) =: A(\theta) \times B^*(A(\theta), \theta)$, is called *the left-RM correspondence*. It is self-belonging, F-cc, and rectangular. ("Self-belonging" means that for every θ in Θ, θ is in $L(\theta)$.)

Alternatively, we can start by first defining an arbitrarily chosen[40] correspondence $B : \Theta \Rightarrow \Theta^2$ such that, for $\bar{\theta} = (\bar{\theta}^1, \bar{\theta}^2)$, (1') $\bar{\theta}^2 \in B(\theta)$, and (2'){$\bar{\theta}^1$} $\times B(\bar{\theta}) \subseteq F^{-1}(F(\bar{\theta}))$.
In turn, define $A^*(B(\bar{\theta}), \bar{\theta})$ by

$$A^*(B(\bar{\theta}), \bar{\theta}) =: \cup\{A \subseteq \Theta^1 : \bar{\theta}^1 \in A \text{ and } A \times B(\bar{\theta}) \subseteq F^{-1}(\bar{\theta})\},\ ^{41}$$

and write $R(\theta) =: A^*(B(\theta), \theta) \times B(\theta)$. This defines a correspondence $R : \Theta \Rightarrow \Theta$, again self-belonging, F-cc, and rectangular. It is called the *right-RM correspondence*.

---

[39] In terms of a two-dimensional diagram of the parameter space dim Z < dim Θ^2, the set Θ^1 is on the horizontal axis, and the set Θ^2 on the vertical. Hence the set $A(\bar{\theta})$ is a subset on the horizontal axis. It is not necessarily an interval.
[40] $B(\bar{\theta})$ is a subset of the vertical axis in a two-dimensional diagram.
[41] Thus making the rectangle $A^*(B(\bar{\theta}), \bar{\theta})$ maximally wide among F-cc rectangles with $B(\bar{\theta})$ as base.

In general, the two RM correspondences can be different. But maximal coarseness is achieved precisely when, for a given F, the left and right RM's yield the same V-generated covering C_V when

$$A^*(B^*(A(\bar{\theta}), \bar{\theta}) = A(\bar{\theta}) \qquad \text{for all } \bar{\theta} \in \Theta.$$

Fortunately, it is shown in Chapter 3 that there is a simple *iteration procedure* that requires N steps when there are N agents, therefore only two steps when there are two agents, that constructs a covering that qualifies as both left- and right-RMs – is *reflexive*. The first step is to form for each $\bar{\theta}$ a left-RM correspondence that consists of rectangles $A(\bar{\theta}) \times B^*(A(\bar{\theta}), \bar{\theta})$. In the second step, using the correspondence $\bar{B}(\bar{\theta}) =: B^*(A(\bar{\theta}), \bar{\theta})$ as a point of departure for each point $\bar{\theta}$, we form the right-RM correspondence by constructing, for each $\bar{B}(\bar{\theta})$, the "maximally wide" set

$$A^*(\bar{B}(\bar{\theta}), \bar{\theta})$$

while staying within the contour set $F^{-1}(F(\bar{\theta}))$. Rather remarkably, it turns out that the set $A^*(\bar{B}(\bar{\theta}), \bar{\theta})$ created at the end of the second step equals the set $A(\bar{\theta})$ used at the beginning of the first step.

In this way we obtain a correspondence that is not only right-RM, but also left-RM (since $A(\bar{\theta}) =: A^*(\bar{B}(\bar{\theta}), \bar{\theta})$). Thus, we obtain a rectangular F-cc correspondence, say $V(\bar{\theta}) = \tilde{A}(\bar{\theta}) \times \tilde{B}(\bar{\theta})$ such that

$$\tilde{B}(\bar{\theta}) = B^*(\tilde{A}(\bar{\theta}), \bar{\theta})$$

and, at the same time,

$$\tilde{A}(\theta) = A^*(\tilde{B}(\theta), \theta).$$

We call such a correspondence *reflexive*-RM (written as rRM). Reflexive-RM coverings have important informational efficiency features that are discussed below.

A reflexive RM correspondence $V(\cdot)$ need not generate a partition. The following example shows that a covering C defined by an rRM, V.

2.1.3.1 Example 1 (L-dot)

Let

$$\Theta = \{\alpha, \beta, \gamma, \delta\},$$
$$F(\alpha) = F(\beta) = F(\gamma) \neq F(\delta)$$

As seen in the graph in Figure 2.1.3.1,

$$\alpha = (a_1, b_2), \qquad \beta = (a_1, b_1), \qquad \gamma = (a_2, b_1), \qquad \delta = (a_2, b_2).$$

To obtain a *reflexive* correspondence $V(\cdot)$, we apply the left-RM procedure using the maximal $A(\cdot)$ correspondence. Thus

$$A(\beta) = (a_1, a_2), \qquad A(\gamma) = (a_1, a_2),$$
$$A(\alpha) = a_1, \qquad A(\delta) = a_2.$$

Then

$$B^*(A(\beta), \beta) = (b_1, b_2)$$

is a column vector,

$$B^*(A(\gamma), \gamma) = b_1, \qquad B^*(A(\gamma), \gamma) = (b_1, b_2)$$

is a column vector, and

$$B^*(A(\delta), \delta) = b_2.$$

This yields the *reflexive* correspondence $V(\cdot)$, where

$$V(\alpha) = V(\beta) = \{\alpha, \beta\}$$

is a column vector, and

$$V(\gamma) = \{\beta, \gamma\}, \qquad V(\delta) = \delta.$$

Analogous procedure with the maximal $B(\cdot)$ set as the first step followed by right-RM procedure yields the correspondence $\tilde{V}(\cdot)$. The correspondence differs from $V(\cdot)$ only in that $\tilde{V}(\beta) = \{\beta, \gamma\}$. The two correspondences yield the same unique reflexive covering C:

$$\tilde{V}(\alpha) = \{\alpha, \beta\}, \qquad \tilde{V}(\beta) = \{\beta, \gamma\}, \qquad \tilde{V}(\gamma) = \{\beta, \gamma\}, \qquad \tilde{V}(\delta) = \{\delta\}.$$

The covering C consists of rectangles K', K'', and K''', where $K' = \boxed{\begin{matrix}\alpha\\\beta\end{matrix}}$, $K'' = \boxed{\beta\ \gamma}$, and $K''' = \boxed{\delta}$ is the unique F-maximal covering, and it is obtained from the rRM correspondence $V(\cdot)$ defined by

$$V(\alpha) = V(\beta) = \{\alpha, \beta\}, \qquad V(\gamma) = \{\beta, \gamma\}, \qquad V(\delta) = \{\delta\},$$

and from $\tilde{V}(\cdot)$ defined above.

In what follows we choose the reflexive correspondence $V(\cdot)$:

$$V(\alpha) = \{\alpha, \beta\}, \qquad V(B) = \{\beta, \gamma\}, \qquad V(\gamma) = \{\beta, \gamma\}, \qquad V(\delta) = \{\delta\}.$$

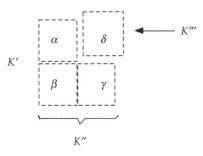

Figure 2.1.3.1

That it must be obtainable via rRM follows, by Theorem 2.1.2 ("necessity"), from the fact that it is F-maximal, maximally coarse. Conversely, Theorem 2.1 ("sufficiency") implies that any rRM leads to an F-maximal covering. In particular, since $V(\cdot)$ is rRM, it constructs a covering that is F-maximal.

2.1.3.2 Example 2: The Augmented Two-Dimensional Inner Product

We now proceed with the phase one analytics of another instructive example, that of the *augmented inner product* on the restricted domain

$$F : \mathbb{R}^5 \backslash \{(a, b) : b_1 \neq 0\},$$

where

$$F = a_1 b_1 + a_2 b_2 + b_3.$$

First, we choose the $A(\cdot)$ correspondence defined by

$$a_1 \bar{b}_1 + a_2 \bar{b}_2 + \bar{b}_3 = F(\bar{\theta}) = \bar{a}_1 \bar{b}_1 + \bar{a}_2 \bar{b}_2 + \bar{b}_3.$$

Since this A is maximal, a reflexive L-RM will result.

Thus $G^1(\bar{\theta}, a) \equiv a_1 \bar{b}_1 + a_2 \bar{b}_2 + \bar{b}_3 + \bar{b}_3 - \bar{F}$, where $\bar{F} = \bar{a}_1 \bar{b}_1 + \bar{a}_2 \bar{b}_2 + \bar{b}_3$.

After cancellation of $\bar{b}_3$ terms and division by $\bar{b}_1 \neq 0$, we obtain

$$a_1 + a_2 \frac{\bar{b}_2}{\bar{b}_1} = \bar{a}_1 + \bar{a}_2 \frac{\bar{b}_2}{\bar{b}_1}. \tag{1}$$

Solving equation (1) for a_1, we get

$$a_1 = \left(\bar{a}_1 + \bar{a}_2 \frac{\bar{b}_2}{\bar{b}_1} \right) - \left(a_2 \frac{\bar{b}_2}{\bar{b}_1} \right).$$

Substituting this value of a_1 into $F(a, b) = \bar{F}$, we obtain

$$b_1 \left[\left(\bar{a}_1 + \bar{a}_2 \frac{\bar{b}_2}{\bar{b}_1} \right) - \left(a_2 \frac{\bar{b}_2}{\bar{b}_1} \right) \right] + a_2 b_2 + b_3 = \bar{F}, \quad \forall a_2,$$

which must be an identity in a_2.

Thus the coefficient of a_2 yields

$$-b_1 \frac{\bar{b}_2}{\bar{b}_1} + b_2 = 0,$$

while the constant term yields

$$b_1 \left(\bar{a}_1 + \bar{a}_2 \frac{\bar{b}_2}{\bar{b}_1} \right) + b_3 = \bar{F}.$$

These two equations define the set $B(\bar{\theta})$.

Thus the G-functions for agent 2 are

$$G^{21}(\bar{\theta}, b) \equiv -b_1 \frac{\bar{b}_2}{\bar{b}_1} + b_2,$$

and

$$G^{22}(\bar{\theta}, b) \equiv b_1 \left(\bar{a}_1 + \bar{a}_2 \frac{\bar{b}_2}{\bar{b}_1} \right) + b_3 - \bar{F}.$$

The equation system

$$G^1(\bar{\theta}, a) = 0, \qquad G^2(\bar{\theta}, b) - G(\bar{\theta}, \theta) = 0$$

is equivalent to the relation $\theta \in V(\bar{\theta})$, $\theta = (a, b)$.

This completes phase one for the augmented inner product example. Phase two is analyzed in Section 2.1.3.3.

Next, preparatory to phase two, we show that the covering C_V is a partition. Using the symmetry theorem, Chapter 3, Theorem 3.6.1, this is accomplished by proving that $G(\bar{\theta}, \theta)$ is symmetric, that is

$$G(\bar{\theta}, \theta) = 0 \Leftrightarrow G(\theta, \bar{\theta}) = 0 \qquad \text{for all } \theta, \bar{\theta} \text{ in } \theta, \tag{+}$$

which amounts to showing that after interchanging $\bar{\theta}$ and θ, the (+) equations are still satisfied.

Proof: The interchanged equations are

$$\bar{a}_1 b_1 + \bar{a}_2 b_2 + b_3 = a_1 b_1 + a_2 b_2 + b_3 \tag{1'}$$

$$-\bar{b}_1 \frac{b_2}{b_1} + \bar{b}_2 = 0 \tag{2.1'}$$

$$-\bar{b}_1\left(a_1 + a_2\frac{b_2}{b_1}\right) + \bar{b}_3 = a_1 b_1 + a_2 b_2 + b_3. \tag{2.2'}$$

Note first that (2.1′) is identical with (2.2′). Hence we have proved that (2.1′) holds.

Rewrite (1) as

$$a_1 + a_2\frac{\bar{b}_2}{\bar{b}_1} = \bar{a}_1 + \bar{a}_2\frac{\bar{b}_2}{\bar{b}_1}. \tag{$\bar{1}$}$$

Consider the equivalent of (1′), viz ($\tilde{1}'$) : $\bar{a}_1 + \bar{a}_2\frac{b_2}{b_1} = a_1 + a_2\frac{b_2}{b_1}$.

In virtue of (2.1) or (2.1′) we may replace b_2/b_1 by b_2/b_1. Then ($\tilde{1}'$) becomes

$$a_1 + a_2\frac{\bar{b}_2}{\bar{b}_1} = a_1 + a_2\frac{\bar{b}_2}{\bar{b}_1}\left(= a_1 + a_2\frac{b_2}{b_1}\right) \tag{$\tilde{1}'$}$$

which is the same as ($\bar{1}$), hence equivalent to (1).

It remains to prove (2.2′). In virtue of ($\tilde{1}'$) and (2.1), Equation (2.2′) can be replaced by

$$b_1\left(\bar{a}_1 + \bar{a}_2\frac{\bar{b}_2}{\bar{b}_1}\right) + \bar{b}_3 = a_1 b_1 + a_2 b_2 + b_3,$$

that is,

$$\bar{b}_1\bar{a}_1 + \bar{a}_2\bar{b}_2 + \bar{b}_3 = a_1 b + a_2 b_2 + b_3,$$

that is,

$$\bar{a}_1\bar{b}_1 + \bar{a}_2\bar{b}_2 + \bar{b}_3 = F.$$

or

$$b_1\left(a_1 + a_2\frac{b_2}{b_1}\right) + b_3 = \bar{F}$$

that is,

$$b_1\left(a_1 + a_2\frac{\bar{b}_2}{\bar{b}_1}\right) + b_3 = \bar{F}.$$

But, by ($\bar{1}$), this is equivalent to

$$b_1\left(\bar{a}_1 + \bar{a}_2\frac{\bar{b}_2}{\bar{b}_1}\right) + b_3 = F,$$

which is (2.2). So $G(\bar{\theta}, \theta) = 0$ implies $G(\theta, \bar{\theta}) = 0$, as was to be shown.

Thus the rRM covering for $F = a_1 b_1 + a_2 b_2 + b_3$, $\Theta = \{\theta \in \mathbb{R}^{5,b}$, $b_1 \neq 0\}$, generated by the ("maximal") specification of the A-set by $A(\bar{\theta}) = \{(a, b) \in \mathbb{R}^5 : \bar{b}_1 \neq 0, a_1 \bar{b}_1 + a_2 \bar{b}_2 + \bar{b}_3 = F(\bar{a}, \bar{b})\}$, is symmetric. Hence the rRM correspondence $V(\bar{\theta})$, represented by $G^1(\bar{\theta}, a) = 0$, $G^2(\bar{\theta}, b) = 0$ is symmetric. Hence, the rRM covering C_V is a partition.

2.1.3.3 The Walrasian Example

The next illustrative example is labeled *Walrasian*. Recall that the goal function in the Walrasian example in Chapter 1 is

$$F(a, b) = \frac{(b_2 - a_2)}{(b_1 + a_1)}.$$

In Chapter 1 we promised to derive the Walrasian goal function from utility functions and endowments for a two agent economy. This derivation is meant to justify calling this goal function Walrasian – it is not a part of the mechanism design procedure. A designer would be given F and Θ and need not know anything about where they come from.

Recall from Chapter 1, Section 1.6.2 that we are dealing with a two-good two-trader pure exchange economy (the Edgeworth box) with no free disposal. The goods are X and Y, and preferences are represented by quasilinear (additively separable and linear in Y) utility functions, quadratic in X. The ith trader's utility function is

$$u^i = \alpha_i X_i - \frac{1}{2}\beta_i(X_i)^2 + Y_i, \quad \text{with } \beta_i > 0.$$

Capitalized X_i, Y_i are the respective *totals* consumed. *Net trades* are denoted by lower case letters, and initial endowments of good X held by agent i by ω_i, so that $X_i = x_i + \omega_i$. In terms of net trades, interior first-order conditions for utility maximization are

$$(\alpha_i - \beta_i \omega_i) - \beta_i x_i = p, \quad i = 1, 2, \quad X_i > 0, Y_i > 0, \quad i = 1, 2,$$

where p is the price of good X in terms of the numéraire Y. (We are assuming an interior equilibrium, $X_i > 0$, $Y_i > 0$, $i = 1, 2$, with all marginal utilities positive.)

At competitive equilibrium, $x_1 + x_2 = 0$. Using this equality and defining

$$\gamma_i = \alpha_i - \beta_i \omega_i$$
$$x = x_1,$$

we obtain equilibrium conditions in the form

$$\gamma_1 - \beta_1 x = p$$
$$\gamma_2 + \beta_2 x = p.$$

Solving these equations leads to

$$x = (\gamma_2 - \gamma_1)/(\beta_1 + \beta_2)$$
$$p = (\gamma_1 \beta_2 + \gamma_2 \beta_1)/(\beta_1 + \beta_2).$$

Our goal function $F(\theta)$ will be the value x of the net trade of trader 2 in terms of the four parameters. (Of course, this also yields the net trade x_1 of trader 1, since $x_1 = -x$.)

In this section we confine ourselves to phase one of the Walrasian example. Phase two is dealt with in a later section. Since the approach is analytic, we derive the functions $G(\bar{\theta}, \theta)$ that define the covering correspondence $V : \Theta \Rightarrow \Theta$. The functions constituting the mapping $G : \Theta \times \Theta \to \mathbb{R}^d$ is, in decentralized form, $G^i : \Theta \times \Theta^i \to \mathbb{R}^{d_i}, i = 1, 2$.

Before proceeding further, for the sake of uniformity with other sections, we change the notation so that 1's parameters are denoted by a's, and 2's by b's. Thus we write

$$a_1 = \beta_1, \qquad a_2 = \gamma_1, \qquad b_1 = \beta_2, \qquad b_2 = \gamma_2,$$

and hence, the goal function given to the designer is

$$F(\theta) = F(a, b) = \frac{b_2 - a_2}{b_1 + a_1}, \qquad \text{with } b_1 > 0, \quad a_1 > 0,$$

where

$$\theta = (a, b), \qquad a = (a_1, a_2), \qquad b = (b_1, b_2).$$

This completes the derivation of the goal function F for the Walrasian example.

The designer is given this function, but not the derivation. What follows is the start of phase one for the Walrasian example. Phase two follows in Section 2.2.

Next, we obtain the G-equations for L-RM[42] representing a V-correspondence.

---

[42] The same equations would be obtained if the b-equations obtained from L-RM were used as the starting point – the system is reflexive (rRM) since $A(\cdot)$ is maximal.

The A-equation is defined by[43]

$$F(a, \bar{b}) = F(\bar{a}, \bar{b}), \tag{1}$$

therefore

$$\frac{\bar{b}_2 - a_2}{\bar{b}_1 + a_1} = \frac{\bar{b}_2 - \bar{a}_2}{\bar{b}_1 + \bar{a}_1} \tag{1'}$$

This is equivalent to

$$a_1 \frac{\bar{b}_2 - \bar{a}_2}{\bar{b}_1 + \bar{a}_1} + a_2 = \frac{\bar{a}_1 \bar{b}_2 + \bar{a}_2 \bar{b}_1}{\bar{b}_1 + \bar{a}_1}, \tag{2}$$

which is

$$G^1(\bar{\theta}, a) = 0, \tag{2'}$$

where

$$G^1(\bar{\theta}, a) \equiv a_1 \bar{F} + a_2 - \bar{p}, \tag{2''}$$

using the abbreviations

$$\bar{F} = \frac{\bar{b}_2 - \bar{a}_2}{\bar{b}_1 + \bar{a}_1} \quad \text{and} \quad \bar{p} = \frac{\bar{a}_1 \bar{b}_2 + \bar{a}_2 \bar{b}_1}{\bar{b}_1 + \bar{a}_1}.$$

Solving Equation (2) for a_2 and substituting this solution into

$$F(a, b) = F(\bar{a}, \bar{b}),$$

we obtain the equation

$$b_2 + \left(a_1 \frac{\bar{b}_2 - \bar{a}_2}{\bar{b}_1 + \bar{a}_1} - \frac{\bar{a}_1 \bar{b}_2 + \bar{a}_2 \bar{b}_1}{\bar{b}_1 + \bar{a}_1} \right) = (b_1 + a_1) \frac{\bar{b}_2 - \bar{a}_2}{\bar{b}_1 + \bar{a}_1}, \tag{3}$$

which must be an identity in a_1. The a_1-terms cancel out, and we are left with the b-equation guaranteeing that Equation (3) is an identity in a_1 for all $\bar{\theta}$, namely

$$b_1 \frac{\bar{b}_2 - \bar{a}_2}{\bar{b}_1 + \bar{a}_1} - b_2 = -\frac{\bar{a}_1 \bar{b}_2 + \bar{a}_2 \bar{b}_1}{\bar{b}_1 + \bar{a}_1}. \tag{4}$$

Equation (4) can be written as

$$G^2(\bar{\theta}, b) = 0, \tag{4'}$$

---

[43] The A-set thus chosen is *maximal*: any proper superset would violate the F-cc property of the resulting covering.

where

$$G^2(\bar{\theta}, b) \equiv b_1 \bar{F} - b_2 + \bar{p}. \tag{4''}$$

Thus the equation form of the covering correspondence for the Walrasian example consists of Equations (2′) and (4′), with their left-hand sides defined by (2″) and (4″), respectively.

Step 2. In order to apply the flagpole technique, it is essential to know that the covering C_V generated by the correspondence V is a *partition* of the parameter space – that its rectangles do not overlap.

To prove this we use Theorem 3.6. It states that an rRM covering is a partition if and only if it is symmetric.[44] Because our correspondence is rRM, it is sufficient to show that $G(\bar{\theta}, \theta) = 0$ if and only if $G(\theta, \bar{\theta}) = 0$.

We show that if Equations (3) hold, then Equations (4) below are satisfied if the overbars are switched from $\bar{F}$ where the variables are $\bar{a}, \bar{b}$ to the coefficients a and b. The equations that result are

$$\begin{aligned} G^1(\theta, \bar{a}) &\equiv \bar{a}_1 F + \bar{a}_2 - p = 0 \\ G^2(\theta, \bar{b}) &\equiv -\bar{b}_1 F + \bar{b}_2 - p = 0 \end{aligned} \tag{4.1}$$

$(F = g^2(m, b) - g^1(m, a)$ and $p = (a_1 b_2 + a_2 b_1)/(b_1 + a_1).)$

We first establish that

$$\bar{F} = F \tag{5.1}$$

and

$$\bar{p} = p. \tag{5.2}$$

Subtracting (3.1) from (3.2), we obtain

$$-(b_1 + a_1)\bar{F} + (b_2 - a_2) = 0,$$

which is equivalent to (5.1).

Thus we are entitled to replace $\bar{F}$ by F in (3.1), which yields

$$\bar{p} = a_1 F + a_2 = a_1[(b_2 - a_2)/(b_1 + a_1)] + a_2 = p.$$

This proves (5.2).

Next, we establish the identity

$$\bar{a}_1 \bar{F} + \bar{a}_2 = \bar{p}. \tag{6.1}$$

[44] The covering CV is said to be *symmetric* if $\theta \in V(\bar{\theta})$ if and only if $\bar{\theta} \in V(\theta)$ for all $\bar{\theta}, \theta$. In equation form this is equivalent to the condition $G = (\bar{\theta}, \theta) = 0$ if and only if $G = (\theta, \bar{\theta}) = 0$.

After substituting for $\bar{F}$ and $\bar{p}$ their values in terms of the four parameters with overbars, we obtain an identity in these parameters. Hence (6.1) follows. In turn, relations (5.1), (5.2), and (6.1) yield (4.1).

Next, analogously to (6.1), we prove the identity

$$-\bar{b}_1 \bar{F} + \bar{b}_2 = \bar{p}, \tag{6.2}$$

and use it with (5.1) and (5.2) to prove (4.2).

The reverse argument – showing that Equations (4) imply Equations (3) – is carried out in an analogous fashion. Hence C_V is a partition.[45]

2.1.3.4 Phase 1. Coverings with Overlaps in the Euclidean Continuum: The Hyperbolic Example

An instructive and extremely simple example of a goal function defined over the two-dimensional factored parameter space $\Theta = \mathbb{R} \times \mathbb{R}$ is

$$F(a, b) = a b, \qquad (a, b) \in \mathbb{R}^2,$$

with both a and b ranging over all reals.

A contour set defined by the equation $a b = \gamma$, with the constant $\gamma \neq 0$, is a rectangular hyperbola, located in the first or third quadrants when $\gamma > 0$ and in the other two quadrants when $\gamma < 0$. But when $\gamma = 0$, the contour set defined by $a b = 0$ is the union of the two numerical axes.

Consider a rectangular F-cc covering for the contour map of this function. To fill a hyperbolic contour set, say $a b = 1$ in the first quadrant, the only "rectangles" we can use are singletons, one-point sets each consisting of an ordered pair $(a, b) >> 0$, with $b = 1/a$. Every point in the interior of the first quadrant is such a "rectangle" for some $\gamma > 0$. The situation is analogous in the interiors of the other three quadrants, with $\gamma > 0$ or $\gamma < 0$. But things change when $\gamma = 0$. In fact, the contour set defined by $a b = 0$ consists of the union of the two numerical axes (it has the shape of a plus sign), and cannot be covered by a single "rectangle," but it can be filled by two "rectangles," each consisting of one of the axes. Of course, each axis can be split into rectangular F-cc subsets, but only the two axes provide an rRM, hence "informationally efficient" (in the sense of maximally coarse[46]) covering. It then turns out that this covering is not a partition since the

---

[45] For an alternative approach to proving that C_V is a partition, see the remark in Section 2.3.4.

[46] In another context we define "informationally efficient" mechanism to include the requirement that its message space has minimal informational size.

origin belongs to both axes. The two "rectangles," consisting of the two axes, constitute the *unique maximally coarse covering;* it has an overlap at the origin.[47] Note that the "rectangles" covering the $\gamma = 0$ contour set have a different dimension from those covering the contour sets with $\gamma \neq 0$.

We now proceed to apply the analytical RM techniques (as opposed to geometric) to finding an rRM covering for the goal function $F(a, b) = ab$, $a \in \mathbb{R}$, $b \in \mathbb{R}$. It is natural to divide the problem into two parts, depending on whether (i) we are dealing with the hyperbolic contour sets for $\gamma \neq 0$, or (ii) when $\gamma = 0$, where the only contour set is the union of the two axes,

$$\{(a, b) \in \mathbb{R}^2 : ab = 0, a \in \mathbb{R}, b \in \mathbb{R}\}.$$

(i) The case $\bar{a} \neq 0$, $\bar{b} \neq 0$. Without loss of generality we start with L-RM and use the maximal A-correspondence, defined by the equation

$$F(a, \bar{b}) = F(\bar{a}, \bar{b}).$$

Here the equation becomes

$$a\,\bar{b} = \bar{a}\,\bar{b},$$

with $\bar{a} \neq 0$, $\bar{b} \neq 0$. Since $\bar{b} \neq 0$ permits cancellation, we are left with

$$a = \bar{a},$$

and the $A(\cdot)$ correspondence is defined by

$$A(\bar{\theta}) \equiv \{a \in \mathbb{R}; a = \bar{a}, a \neq 0\} = \{\bar{a}\}.[48]$$

Following the L-RM recipe we now seek the B-set corresponding to this $A(\bar{\theta})$ set, the set written formally as $B^*(A(\bar{\theta}), \bar{\theta})$. This set is defined by the requirement that it consist of those elements $b \in \Theta^2$, $\Theta^2 = \mathbb{R}$, that satisfy the equation

$$F(a, b) = F(\bar{\theta}) \tag{+}$$

for all a in $A(\bar{\theta})$ and all $\bar{\theta} \in \Theta$. In this case (i), with $F(\bar{\theta}) = \bar{a}\,\bar{b} \neq 0$, and $a \in A(\bar{\theta})$ equivalent to $a = \bar{a}$, equation (+) becomes

$$\bar{a}\,b = \bar{a}\,\bar{b}, \tag{++}$$

---

[47] The origin of $\mathbb{R}^2$ is in this example the only overlap point. The situation is analogous to the (finite Θ) L-dot example where the unique maximally coarse covering has an overlap at the "elbow" point we usually label β.

[48] Thus, in this case, the maximal A-set is a singleton, hence, somewhat paradoxically, also minimal.

or, after cancellation of $\bar{a} \neq 0$,

$$b = \bar{b}. \qquad\qquad (+++)$$

Thus $B^*(A(\bar{\theta}), \bar{\theta}) = \{\bar{b}\}$. Therefore, the generic "rectangle" $V(\bar{\theta})$ of the rRM covering is of the form $\{\bar{a}\} \times \{\bar{b}\}$, $\bar{a}\,\bar{b} \neq 0$, hence a singleton $V(\bar{\theta}) \equiv \{(\bar{a}, \bar{b})\}$, in agreement with the geometric insight.[49] In equation form, the covering correspondence $V(\cdot)$ for the region of case (i) is written as

$$G^1(\bar{\theta}, a) \equiv a - \bar{a} = 0, \qquad G^2(\bar{\theta}, b) \equiv b - \bar{b} = 0.$$

We now proceed to Case (ii), $\bar{a}\,\bar{b} = 0$.

This case will be divided into three sub-cases: first with $\bar{a} = 0$, $\bar{b} \neq 0$, second with $\bar{a} \neq 0$, $\bar{b} = 0$, and the third with $\bar{a} = 0$, $\bar{b} = 0$, i.e., $\bar{\theta} =$ the origin.

In the first sub-case if

(ii.1), $\bar{a} = 0$, $\bar{b} \neq 0$, the maximal A-set again satisfies the equation

$$a\,\bar{b} = 0, \qquad \bar{b} \neq 0, \qquad\qquad (°)$$

hence $\bar{b}$ can be canceled, and so

$$a = 0 = \bar{a}.$$

Therefore,

$$A(\bar{\theta}) = \{0\} = \{\bar{a}\}. \qquad\qquad (°°)$$

In turn we seek the B-set. As always in L-RM, this set is defined by the equation

$$F(a, b) = F(\bar{\theta}) \qquad \text{for all} \quad a \in A(\bar{\theta}) \qquad \text{and} \quad \text{all } \bar{\theta} \in \Theta,$$

which translates into

$$\bar{a}\, b = 0 \qquad \text{for} \quad \bar{a} = 0, \quad \text{or} \quad 0 \cdot b = 0.$$

Thus, the B-set consists of all $b \in \mathbb{R}$ that satisfies the requirement $0 \cdot b = 0$ which does not exclude any real value b. Thus in this sub-case the B-set is the whole b-(vertical) axis, or formally,

$$B^*(A(\bar{\theta}), \bar{\theta}) = \mathbb{R} \qquad \text{for all} \quad \bar{\theta} = (\bar{a}, \bar{b}), \quad \bar{a} = 0, \quad \bar{b} \neq 0.$$

The resulting "rectangle" of the covering correspondence $V(\cdot)$ is of the form $V(\theta) = \{0\} \times \mathbb{R}$, again in accord with the geometric insight.

---

[49] That this covering will turn out to be rRM is clear. Its reflexivity can be verified directly by using rRM starting with the B-set using $B(\bar{\theta}) = \{\bar{b}\}$ as the initial correspondence.

In equation form, when $\bar{a} = 0$, $\bar{b} \neq 0$, with L-RM and maximal A-set, we can write

$$G^1(\bar{\theta}, a) \equiv a \equiv 0$$
$$G^2(\bar{\theta}, b) \equiv 0 \cdot b \equiv 0.$$

Note that this yields

$$F(a, b) = 0.$$

(ii.2) We now take up the second sub-case of case (ii), where $\bar{a} \neq 0$, $\bar{b} = 0$. Here the equation $F(a, \bar{b}) = F(\bar{a}, \bar{b})$ defining the maximal A-set becomes

$$a \cdot 0 = 0,$$

so that

$$A(\bar{\theta}) = \mathbb{R} \qquad \text{(all of the reals)}.$$

Hence the B-defining equation $F(a, b) = F(\bar{a}, \bar{b})$ for all a in $A(\bar{\theta})$ and all $\bar{\theta}$ in Θ translates into

$$a b = 0 \qquad \text{for all } a \text{ in } \mathbb{R}.$$

Clearly, the only value of b that satisfies this requirement is $b = 0$, so that

$$B^*(A(\bar{\theta}), \bar{\theta}) = \{0\} = \{\bar{b}\}.$$

The resulting "rectangle" is $V(\bar{\theta}) = \mathbb{R} \times \{0\}$, i.e., the whole a-axis, again in agreement with the geometry.

In equation form, when $\bar{\theta} \neq 0$, $\bar{b} = 0$, we have for L-RM with maximal $A(\bar{\theta})$, we have

$$G^1(\bar{\theta}, a) \equiv 0 \cdot a \equiv 0,$$
$$G^2(\bar{\theta}, b) \equiv b \equiv 0,$$

and again, $F(\theta) = 0$.

(ii.3) There remains the third sub-case of (ii) where $\bar{\theta} = (\bar{a}, \bar{b}) = (0, 0)$. Here again $A(\bar{\theta})$ is defined by

$$a \cdot 0 = 0.$$

Hence, when $\bar{\theta} = (0, 0)$, we *can* use as the corresponding B-"rectangle" the set $\mathbb{R} \times \{0\}$, i.e., the a-axis. But, unlike in the previous two sub-cases, we have an alternative: we can choose to use R-RM. This would lead to $\tilde{V}((0, 0)) = \{0\} \times \mathbb{R}$, i.e., the b-axis. Of course, we must choose between the two possibilities, since – by the RM rules – one, but only one, rectangle is associated with each point $\theta \in \Theta$. In equation form,[50] for L-RM with $\bar{\theta} = (0, 0)$, we have $G^1(\bar{\theta}, a) = a \cdot 0 = 0$, $G^2(\bar{\theta}, b) = b = 0$, and again, $F(\theta) = 0$.

Perhaps it is not quite obvious that such alternatives do not exist in the previous two sub-cases of case (ii). Here are the reasons.

Consider, for example, the sub-case $\bar{a} = 0$, $\bar{b} \neq 0$. Suppose there were an alternative to $V(\bar{\theta}) = \{0\} \times \mathbb{R}$, to the b-axis. Such an alternative cannot be a proper subset of $\{0\} \times \mathbb{R}$ because then the resulting covering would fail to be maximally coarse, hence would not qualify as rRM. So an alternative would have to contain a point (a, b) with $a \neq 0$. If also $b \neq 0$, then $F(a, b) \neq 0$, hence the alternative rectangle fails to be F-contour contained and so does not qualify as RM.

So suppose the alternative contains a point $\theta' = (a', b')$ with $a' \neq 0$, $b' = 0$, a point on the a-axis other than the origin. Since RM produces a self-belonging correspondence, the resulting rectangle must also contain the point $\bar{\theta}$. But since the covering correspondence is rectangular, the rectangle containing both $\theta' = (a', b')$ and $\bar{\theta} = (\bar{a}, \bar{b})$ must also contain the point $\theta'' = (a'', b'') = (a', \bar{b})$, with both components nonzero. However, since (a'', b'') has both components nonzero, we find that the "rectangle" in question contains both $\bar{\theta}$ with $F(\bar{\theta}) = 0$ and θ'' with $F(\theta'') \neq 0$, hence it violates the F-cc requirement for an RM "rectangle." Hence, in the first subcase of case (ii) there is no alternative to $V(\bar{\theta}) = \{0\} \times \mathbb{R}$. The argument for the second subcase is analogous.

2.2 Phase 2: Constructing Decentralized Mechanisms, from Parameter Indexed Product Structures: Transition to Message-Indexed Product Structures

2.2.0 Introduction

The transition from parameter-indexed structures to message-indexed structures is motivated by our desire for increased informational efficiency. Gain in informational efficiency is exemplified by the price mechanism, with prices and quantities as component messages, as compared with the direct revelation mechanism with parameters as messages.

In the direct revelation scenario, the coordinator tries out points in what may be a huge parameter space (e.g., when preferences are represented by polynomials of high degree). By contrast, in the price mechanism, the coordinator, the Walrasian auctioneer, asks each agent i whether a point in the

---

[50] When the choice $V((0, 0, 0)) = \mathbb{R} \times \{0\}$ is made.

(p, q^i) – price-quantity space – is acceptable, a space whose dimensionality depends only on the number of goods and persons in the economy, and does not increase with the complexity of individual preferences.

This section is devoted to phase two of the procedure for constructing a mechanism that realizes a given goal function F. This phase takes as given a parameter-indexed product structure (correspondence) that is F-cc, and shows how to construct a message-indexed product structure (correspondence) that can be informationally more in a sense[51] maximally efficient.

2.2.1 Basic Concepts

Suppose that for a specified goal function $F : \Theta \to Z$ a parameter-indexed product structure is given. By this we mean a correspondence $V : \Theta \Rightarrow \Theta$, where $\Theta = \Theta^1 \times \cdots \times \Theta^N$. We assume that V is defined on all of Θ, V is F-cc self-belonging, and "rectangular". (To simplify exposition we usually take $N = 2$.)

Thus with each point $\bar{\theta}$ in the parameter space Θ, the (covering) correspondence $V(\cdot)$ associates a subset $V(\bar{\theta})$ of the parameter space that has these properties:

(i) *F-cc*: given any two points θ', θ'' in $V(\bar{\theta})$, the values of the goal function are the same – $F(\theta') = F(\theta'')$;

(ii) *self-belonging*: the set $V(\bar{\theta})$ contains its "generator" $\bar{\theta}$ – for any $\bar{\theta} \in \Theta$, we have $\bar{\theta} \in V(\bar{\theta})$;

(iii) *rectangularity*:[52] given any $\bar{\theta} = (\bar{\theta}_1, \bar{\theta}_2) \in \Theta^1 \times \Theta^2$,
(stated for $N = 2$)
$V(\bar{\theta}) = V^1(\bar{\theta}) \times V^2(\bar{\theta})$ where $V^i(\bar{\theta}) \subseteq \Theta^i$, $i = 1, 2$.

We sometimes impose additional requirements, such as that V be rRM (reflexive method of rectangles).

It typically happens that a set K in Θ is "generated" by different points – there may be two distinct points $\bar{\theta}'$, $\bar{\theta}'' \in \Theta$, $\bar{\theta}' \neq \bar{\theta}''$ such that

$$V(\bar{\theta}') = V(\bar{\theta}'') = K.$$

The correspondence V generates a *covering* C_V of Θ, where

$$C_V = \{K \subseteq \Theta : K \subseteq \Theta, K = V(\bar{\theta}) \text{ for some } \bar{\theta} \in \Theta\}.$$

(We sometimes omit the subscript V.)

---

[51] Minimal fineness – maximal coarseness of the covering.

[52] Rectangularity corresponds to privacy-preserving and informational decentralization.

It turns out that a covering generated by self-belonging correspondences has a property that is crucial for our procedure. It is shown in Chapter 3, Section 3.5, Theorems 3.5.1 and 3.5.2, that when V is self-belonging, it is possible to choose in each set K of the covering C an element, say θ_K, called its *representative*, so that (i) each representative belongs to the set it represents; and (ii) distinct sets have *distinct representatives*; formally

(i) $\theta_K \in K$
(ii) $K' \neq K'' \Rightarrow \theta'_K \neq \theta''_K$.

Conversely, if a covering C admits a system of distinct representatives, then there exists a self-belonging correspondence $V : \Theta \Rightarrow \Theta$ that generates C. To see this, suppose the covering C has an SDR. Then for every $k \in C$, there is $\theta_k \in K$, where θ_k is the representative of the set K. Define $V\theta_k$ to be K. Then $\theta_k \in K = V(\theta_k) - V$ is self-belonging.

The system of distinct representatives (SDR) is a (single-valued) function $\Lambda : C \to \Theta$. So $\Lambda(K)$ corresponds to what we denoted above by θ_K.

To see that an SDR is always possible for a self-belonging correspondence, consider the following construction.[53]

Given a set K of a covering C_V generated by the self-belonging correspondence $V : \Theta \Rightarrow \Theta$, let Θ_K denote a generator of $K - V(\theta_K) = K$, and let Θ_K be the set of all "generators" of K. Thus, $\Theta_K = \{\bar{\theta} \in \Theta : V(\bar{\theta}) = K\}$.

Choose[54] an arbitrary element, say θ', of the set Θ_K and declare θ' to be the representative of the set K, i.e., $\theta' = \theta_K$, or

$$\theta' = \Lambda(K).$$

Since θ' was chosen from Θ_K, it follows that

$$V(\theta') = K.$$

But V is self-belonging, so $\theta' \in V(\theta')$. Hence SDR (i) is satisfied. Note also that Θ'_K is disjoint from Θ''_K if $K' \neq K''$. If it were not so, there would exist some $\bar{\theta}$ such that $K' = V(\bar{\theta})$ and $K'' = V(\bar{\theta})$, which is impossible since $\bar{\theta}$ uniquely defines the set $V(\bar{\theta})$.

It follows that, when $K' \neq K''$, their representatives θ'_K and θ'_K, respectively, chosen from distinct sets, must be different. That is,

$$K' \neq K'' \Rightarrow \Lambda(K') \neq \Lambda(K''),$$

and so SDR (ii) is also satisfied.

---

[53] Not the only possible one!
[54] Justified by the axiom of choice.

So the existence of the system of distinct representatives is implied by the self-belonging property of the correspondence V.

The theorem that guarantees the existence of an SDR applies not only to correspondences that generate partitions of the parameter space, but also to those that produce coverings with overlapping K-sets.

As we shall see below, these coverings are much simpler to deal with; since any element of a set K can serve as its representative θ_K. (When C_V is a partition, $K = \Theta_K$ for all K.)

Clearly, such a choice satisfies SDR(i). SDR(ii) is also satisfied because if θ' represents K', θ' was chosen from K', and $K' \cap K'' = \varnothing$, then θ' cannot be chosen from K''.

2.2.2 The L-dot Example

The overlap situations are less obvious. It is helpful to look again at the L-dot example.

EXAMPLE 1.

Figure 2.2.2.1

There are two F-contour sets: $\{\alpha, \beta, \gamma\}$ and $\{\delta\}$. Clearly, $V(\delta) = \{\delta\}$. It can be shown that the only rRM covering consists of the three sets $K' = \boxed{\begin{array}{c}\alpha\\\beta\end{array}}$, $K'' = \boxed{\beta\ \gamma}$, and $\boxed{\delta}$. Hence there is an overlap at β. There are two possible rRM correspondences generating the above rRM coverings.

We must have $V(\alpha) = \{\alpha, \beta\}$, $V(\gamma) = \{\beta, \gamma\}$. The two alternatives are $V(\beta) = \{\alpha, \beta\}$, or $V(\beta) = \{\beta, \gamma\}$.

The analysis is the same for the two specifications of V. The choices available for the SDR are

$$\Lambda(K') = \alpha, \Lambda(K'') = \gamma,$$
$$\Lambda(K') = \alpha, \Lambda(K'') = \beta,$$

or

$$\Lambda(K') = \beta, \Lambda(K'') = \gamma.$$

Since Θ is finite, there is no need to appeal to the axiom of choice. But there are interesting examples with overlaps where Θ is infinite (e.g., a

Euclidean space), and yet an SDR is easy to construct, even with an overlapping parameter-indexed rRM covering.

2.2.3 More Examples

EXAMPLE 2: AUGMENTED TWO-DIMENSIONAL INNER PRODUCT. When

$$F = a_1 b_1 + a_2 b_2 + b_3, \qquad F : \mathbb{R}^5 \to \mathbb{R},$$

with the domain unrestricted, then there are overlaps.

But if we restrict the domain so that, $b_1 \neq 0$, $F : \mathbb{R}^5 \backslash \{\theta \in \mathbb{R}^5 : b_1 \neq 0\} \to \mathbb{R}$, then there are no overlaps.

EXAMPLE 3: THE "HYPERBOLIC" GOAL FUNCTION

$$F = ab \qquad (a \in \mathbb{R}, b \in \mathbb{R})$$

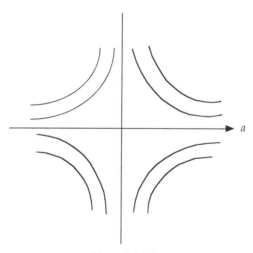

Figure 2.2.3.1

Here, if $\theta = (a, b)$, the rRM yields $V(\theta) = \{\theta\}$ whenever $a \neq 0$, $b \neq 0$. If $a = 0$, $b \neq 0$, we find $V((a, b)) = \{(a, b) \in \mathbb{R}^2 : a = 0\}$ = the b-axis =: $\mathbb{R}_b$.

Similarly, if $a \neq 0$, $b = 0$, we have $V((a, b)) = \{(a, b) \in \mathbb{R}^2 : b = 0\}$, = the a-axis =: $\mathbb{R}_a$. Only for $(a, b) = (0, 0)$ do we have a choice of two rectangles: $V((0, 0)) = \mathbb{R}_a$ or $V((0, 0)) = \mathbb{R}_b$. (Not both!) In either case, the resulting rRM covering C_V consists of all singletons $\{(a, b)\}$ with $a \neq 0$, $b \neq 0$, and the two axes $\mathbb{R}_a$ and $\mathbb{R}_b$.

What about an SDR? Clearly, if $a \neq 0$, $b \neq 0$, $K = \{(a, b)\}$, then $(a, b) = \Lambda(K)$ – the single element must be its own representative. But for $K = \mathbb{R}_a$ we have an infinity of choices: any point on the a-axis can serve as the representative of $\mathbb{R}_a$.

If the chosen representative of $\mathbb{R}_a$ is any non-zero point, then any point of $\mathbb{R}_b$ (including the origin) can be chosen as representative of $\mathbb{R}_b$. But, of course, if $0 = \Lambda(\mathbb{R}_a)$, then $\Lambda(\mathbb{R}_b)$ must be chosen from among points on $\mathbb{R}_b$ that are not the origin.

EXAMPLE 4. Another interesting Euclidean case with overlap is that of a "Leontief" goal function $F = \min(a, b)$, $a \in \mathbb{R}_+$, $b \in \mathbb{R}_+ (\Theta = \mathbb{R}_+^2)$, $\mathbb{R}_+ =$ nonnegative real numbers, $\mathbb{R}_+^2 = \mathbb{R}_+ \times \mathbb{R}_+.$)

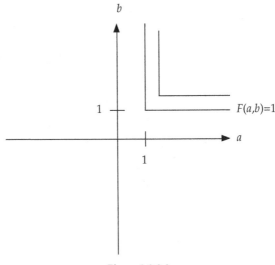

Figure 2.2.3.2

Here the rRM covering of a "typical" contour set, say $F(a, b) = 1$, consists of two (closed) half-lines that overlap at the "elbow" where $a = b = 1$. So:

$$\text{For } \theta = (a, 1), \quad \text{with } a \geq 1,$$
$$V(\theta) = \{(a, b) \in \mathbb{R}_+^2 : 1 \leq a, \ b = 1\}$$
$$\text{For } \theta = (1, b), \quad \text{with } b > 1,$$
$$V(\theta) = \{(a, b) \in \mathbb{R}_+^2 : a = 1, \ b \geq 1\}$$

and the (overlapping) rRM rectangles of the covering for the contour set $F(a, b) = 1$ are the two rectangles

$$K' = \{(a, b) : 1 \leqq a, b = 1\}$$

and

$$K'' = \{(a, b) : a = 1, b \geqq 1\}.$$

For an SDR, we can choose any point of K' and any point of K'', provided we do not choose the same "elbow point" for both.

EXAMPLE 5: "A PARABOLIC" GOAL FUNCTION

$$F = (a - b)^2 - (a + b), \qquad (a, b) \in \mathbb{R}_+^2$$

The interesting phenomenon is that every rRM rectangle consists of *two isolated points* even though F is "smooth." For instance, the contour set $F(a, b) = 0$ contains the rRM rectangles $\underbrace{\{(1, 0), (1, 3)\}}_{K'}$ and $\underbrace{\{(0, 1), (3, 1)\}}_{K''}$.

There are overlaps; for instance, the two rectangles $\{(0, 0), (1, 0)\}$ and $\{(0, 0), (0, 1)\}$ both in the contour set $F(a, b) = 0$ have in common the point $(0, 0)$. Moreover, the graph of $F(a, b)$ contains an L-dot configuration, consisting of the three points $\{(0, 1), (0, 0), (1, 0)\}$ in the set $F(a, b) = 0$, together with the point $(1, 1)$ belonging to the contour $F(a, b) = -2 \neq 0$.

2.2.3.1 Transversals and Other Message Spaces

The message space M can be taken to be the image of the covering C_V by the SDR function Λ, the set $\Lambda(C_V)$ of distinct representatives, known as the *transversal* (T)[55] of the covering.

In the L-dot example (Example 1), with the choice

$$\Lambda(K') = \alpha, \qquad \Lambda(K'') = \gamma,$$

we have

$$T = \{\alpha, \gamma, \delta\}.$$

With the two alternative choices of SDR the transversal is $\{\alpha, \beta, \delta\}$ or $\{\beta, \gamma, \delta\}$.

---

[55] We use the term "transversal," because when the space is Euclidean, and F is smooth, the set defined by Λ is typically a geometric transversal.

Here the reduction in size from Θ to $M' = T$ is not very impressive four points in Θ down to three in T.

In the Leontief example (Example 3) the reduction from Θ to T is more significant: each half-line is replaced by a single point.

The objective of reducing the size of the message space is sometimes accomplished by choosing as the message space M (a superset of M') that is not T, but some set that has a subset that is in 1-1 correspondence with T. This is illustrated in the Leontief example – Example 3.

The rectangles of the covering are written as $K'_{b'} = \{(a, b) \in \mathbb{R}^2_+ : a \geqq b',$ $b = b' \geqq 0\}$, a horizontal closed half line starting at (and including) the point $(a, b) = (a', b')$, and $K''_{a'} = \{(a, b) \in \mathbb{R}^2_+ : a = a', b \geqq a' \geqq 0\}$, a vertical closed half-line starting at (and including) the point $(a, b) = (a', b')$. The values of a' and b' are fixed for each rectangle, but range over all nonnegative values for the covering correspondence V. Each contour set is L-shaped and equals the union $K'_{b'} \cup K''_{a'}$, with $a' = b'$.

Define the SDR function $\Lambda : C_V \to \Theta$ as follows: $\Lambda(K'_{b'}) = (2b', b')$ for all $b' \geqq 0$, $\Lambda(K''_{a'}) = (a', 2a')$ for all $a' > 0$;[56] but for the vertical half-line starting at the origin, K''_0, we must avoid the origin. So we must choose some point $(0, c) \in K''_0$, $c > 0$, say $\Lambda(K''_0) = (0, 1)$. We obtain the transversal $T = T_1 \cup T_2 \cup \{(0, 1)\}$, with $T_1 = \{(a, b) \in \mathbb{R}^2_+ : a = 2b, b \geqq 0\}$, $T_1 = \{(a, b) \in \mathbb{R}^2_+ : b = 2a, a > 0\}$. Clearly, T is a two-dimensional set. However, we can project it into a negative $45°$ straight line such as $M = \{(a, b) \in \mathbb{R}^2 : b = -a\}$ so that $M = v(T)$, so that $v(a, b) \in \{(\bar{a}, \bar{b}) : \bar{b} = -\bar{a}, |\bar{a}| < a\}$ for $(a, b) \in T_1 \cup T_2$, while $v(0, 1) = (-1, +1)$. Clearly, M is of dimension 1, but the choice $\Lambda(K''_0) = (0, 1)$ results in a discontinuity, apparently due to the overlap at the origin.

However, it is clear that the equilibrium message set M' is one-dimensional whereas $\Theta = \mathbb{R}^2_+$ is two-dimensional. So there is a significant informational benefit.

2.2.3.2 Example 6: A Goal Function That Depends On One Agent's Parameter Only

Suppose $\Theta = \mathbb{R}^2$, $F(\theta) = b$, $(\theta = a, b)$.

Here each contour set is a horizontal line and each such line is covered by a single rRM rectangle.

$$V(a, b') = \{(a, b) \in \mathbb{R}^2 : b = b'\}.$$

---

[56] But not for $a' = 0$ since this would result in two different rectangles (those starting at the origin) having the same representative.

A transversal T is obtained, e.g., as

$$T = \{(a, b) \in \mathbb{R}^2 : a = a^*\}$$

with $\Lambda(K) = a^*$, b_k for $K = \{(a, b) \in \mathbb{R}^2 : b = b_K\}$.

We can use the projection v into the b-axis, so that $v = T \to b$-axis, $v(a^*, b) = (0, b)$, $b \in \mathbb{R}$. Here again $\Theta = \mathbb{R}^2$ while T, M, and $M'(= M)$ are equivalent to $\mathbb{R}$. Both $\Lambda(\cdot)$ and $v(\cdot)$ are smooth.

2.2.4 General Issues in Mechanism Construction

As these examples indicate, it is sometimes easy to find an SDR function Λ and the corresponding transversal; indeed there may be many possibilities. But two questions arise. First, what about more complex examples where the choice of SDR function Λ for the given V is not self-evident? And, secondly, supposing we have found an SDR function Λ for the given V, how do we go about constructing a mechanism that realizes the given goal function F?

Consider the second question first. So suppose we have a self-belonging F-cc rectangular correspondence V that generates a covering C_V of the parameter space Θ, and we also have an SDR function Λ, hence also its transversal T. How do we construct a mechanism?

To simplify matters, suppose we use the transversal T as the message space M, so that $M = M' = T$. (In the examples above, this corresponds to using the identity transformation on T as v.)

A mechanism (in set-theoretic form) is defined as a triple (M, μ, h) where M is the message space, $\mu : \Theta \Rightarrow M$ is the equilibrium message correspondence, and $h : M \to Z$ is the outcome function.

We want such a mechanism to *realize* the goal function $F : \Theta \to Z$ on the parameter space Θ, to satisfy the two requirements: existence and F-optimality:

(i) *existence* $\forall\, \theta \in \Theta$, there is $m \in M$ such that

$$m \in \mu(\theta);$$

(ii) *F-optimality* $\forall\, (\theta, m) \in \Theta \times M$, if $m \in \mu(\theta)$, then $h(m) = F(\theta)$.

By the simplifying assumptions made above we have $M = M' = T$, but we must still construct the equilibrium correspondence μ, and the outcome function h.

In the simplified case, the outcome function (in general defined on M) has $T \subseteq \Theta$ as its domain. Hence it is legitimate to use $m \in M$ as an argument for $h(\cdot)$ and to define $h(\cdot)$ on M by

$$h(m) = F(\theta)|_{\theta=m}$$

i.e.,

$$h(m) = F(m).$$

This will be our construction of $h(\cdot)$.[57]

It remains to construct the equilibrium correspondence μ, and that turns out to be more complicated, primarily because we want our mechanism to be informationally decentralized – privacy-preserving.

To make the strategy of our construction more transparent, we first show how the construction works when the requirements of decentralization are ignored – how one verifies that the mechanism does realize the goal function. If the requirements of decentralization are ignored, it is as if the two agents were able to pool their information instead of acting only on the basis of their own characteristics (parameter vectors).

Given this framework we define the equilibrium message correspondence as follows.

We say that $m \in M$ is *an equilibrium message for* the parameter point $\theta \in \Theta$ if and only if $m = \Lambda(K)$ for some set K of the covering C of Θ such that θ is a point of K.

Hence the equilibrium message $\mu(\theta) = \{m \in M : m = \Lambda(K)$ for some $K \in C$ such that $\theta \in K\}$.

Equivalently, $m \in \mu(\theta)$ if and only if $m = \Lambda(K)$ for some $K \in C$ and $\theta \in K$. (Here $C = C_V$).

To see that the mechanism (M, μ, h) we have constructed does realize the goal function F, note first that the existence requirement (i) is satisfied – $\mu(\theta)$ is nonempty for every $\theta \in \Theta$. This is so since C is a covering of Θ such that $\theta \in K$, and so its representative $\Lambda(K)$ is an element of $\mu(\theta)$.

It remains to prove F-optimality of the mechanism – that if $m \in \mu(\theta)$ then $h(m) = F(\theta)$. By property SDR (i), $\Lambda(K)$ is in the set K, and, by the definition of $\mu(\theta)$, θ is also in the set K. But, by the F-cc property of the covering C, all points in K are in the same F–contour set. Hence

$$F(\Lambda(K)) = F(\theta).$$

Since $\Lambda(K) = m$, this becomes

$$F(m) = F(\theta). \qquad (+)$$

---

[57] Note that this construction of the outcome function remains valid and unchanged when informational decentralization is introduced into our procedure.

turn, by the definition of the outcome function h,

$$h(m) = F(m). \qquad (++)$$

Equations $(+)$ and $(++)$ yield

$$h(m) = F(\theta),$$

and F-optimality follows.

We drop the assumption $M = M' = T$.

As noted in connection with the examples, it is often desirable to choose as message space a set M different from the transversal T, but "rich" enough so that it contains a subset M' that is in 1–1 correspondence with T. When M is such a set, there exists a (single-valued) function $v : T \to M$, and a subset $M' \subseteq M$, such that $M' = v(T)$, and v is 1–1 between T and M' v is a *bijection* from T into M'. Hence v has a single-valued inverse v^{-1} from M' onto T. Thus, if $m = v(t)$, $m \in M'$, $t \in T$, $t' \in T$, $t' \neq t$, then $v(t') \neq m$.

Note that the simplified case where $M = M' = T$ is a special case, in which v is the identity mapping between T and M.

In the more general situation where v might, but need not be, the identity, we generalize the construction of the outcome function in a natural way. That is we define the outcome function $h : M \to Z$

$$h(m) = F(v^{-1}(m)) \qquad \text{for all } m \in M.$$

We now say that $m \in M$ is an *equilibrium message* at $\theta \in \Theta$ if and only if

$$m = v(\Lambda(k))$$

for some set K of the covering C_V of Θ such that θ is a point of K. Hence the equilibrium correspondence μ is defined by

$$\mu(\theta) = \{m \in M : m = v(\Lambda(K)) \text{ for some } K \in C_V \text{ such that } \theta \in K\}.$$

The proof that this more general mechanism[58] (M, μ, h) realizes F follows the previous pattern. Existence follows from the fact that C_V covers Θ. As for F-optimality, if $m \in \mu(\theta)$, then

$$m = v(\Lambda(K)) \text{ for some } K \text{ satisfying } \theta \in K. \qquad (0)$$

By the F-cc property of C, again

$$F(\Lambda(K)) = F(\theta), \qquad (\dagger)$$

---

[58] More explicitly, one might have written the mechanism as $(M, \mu, h; \Lambda, v)$.

since both $\Lambda(K)$ and θ are in K. Now $h(m) = F(v^{-1}(m))$ by the definition of

$$h = F(v^{-1}(v(\Lambda(K)))) - \text{by } (0)$$
$$= F(\Lambda(K)) - \text{by } v^{-1} \circ v = \text{ identity}$$
$$= F(\theta) - \text{by } (\dagger),$$

as was to be shown.

The preceding exercise, ignoring as it did the problem of *informational decentralization,* is useful in displaying the strategies we use both in defining the elements used in the construction of the mechanism, and also in proving the crucial property of the mechanism – that it realizes the goal function.

But now we must come to grips with the issue of informational decentralization.

Assuming, for the sake of simplicity, that there are only two agents ($N = 2$), we now deal with a *factored parameter space* $\Theta = \Theta^1 \times \Theta^2$, so that if $\theta \in \Theta$, then $\theta = (\theta^1, \theta^2)$, with $\theta^1 \in \Theta^1$ and $\theta^2 \in \Theta^2$.

Requiring decentralization does not affect the construction of an SDR function Λ or of the outcome function; we still define $h(m) = F(v^{-1}(m))$ and $M \supseteq M' = v(\Lambda(C_V))$. It is the construction of the equilibrium function μ that becomes more complicated.

As before, we start by considering the *special case* where the transversal is the message space – $M = M' = T = \Lambda(C_V)$. The (collective) equilibrium correspondence $\mu : \Theta \Rightarrow M$ is by definition the intersection of two *individual* equilibrium correspondences μ^1, μ^2, where each $\mu^i : \Theta^i \Rightarrow M$, $i = 1, 2$, and, for $\theta = (\theta^1, \theta^2)$,

$$\mu(\theta) = \mu(\theta^1, \theta^2) = \mu^1(\theta^1) \cap \mu^2(\theta^2).$$

In particular, the individual correspondence μ^1 is so constructed that agent 1 is able to determine whether $m \in \mu^1(\theta^1)$ without knowing θ^2, and vice versa for agent 2.

To help our intuition, let us think in terms of the *verification scenario.* First, assume that the covering C_V, the spaces Θ^1, Θ^2, and the SDR function Λ are public knowledge – known to both agents.

The coordinator displays to both agents an element m of the message space M; m is a candidate for an equilibrium message for the parameter point $\theta = (\theta^1, \theta^2)$, whose components are respectively known to agent 1 and agent 2.

The important new aspect of the situation, ignored in the preceding exposition, is the assumption of "rectangularity" of the covering C_V – the fact that each set K in C_V is a Cartesian product, a "rectangle" $K = K_1 \times K_2$, where $K_1 \subseteq \Theta^1$ and $K_2 \subseteq \Theta^2$. "Rectangularity" formalizes the idea that each agent be able to make a decision based only on her own private information – her parameters – and thus enable the mechanism to be informationally decentralized.

The question asked of agent 1 with parameter θ^1 is: given the information available to you, does there exist a "rectangle" $K^* \in C$ such that, for some $\tilde{\theta}^2 \in \Theta^2$, the parameter point $(\theta^1, \tilde{\theta}^2) \in K^*$ and $m = \Lambda(K^*)$, i.e., that $\theta^1 \in pr_{\Theta^1} K^*$ and $\tilde{\theta}^2 \in pr_{\Theta^2} K^*$ and $m = \Lambda(K^*)$? We say that $m \in \mu^1(\theta)$ if and only if the answer is "yes."

Formally, the first agent's individual equilibrium message correspondence is defined by

$$\mu^1(\theta^1) = \left\{ \begin{array}{l} m \in M : m = \Lambda(K^*) \text{ for some } K^* = K_1^* \times K_2^* \in C, \\ K_i^* \in \Theta^i, i = 1, 2 \text{ such that } \theta^1 \in K_1^* \end{array} \right\}$$

analogously,

$$\mu^2(\theta^2) = \left\{ \begin{array}{l} m \in M : m = \Lambda(K^{**}) \text{ for some } K^* \in C, \\ K^{**} = K_1^{**} \times K_2^{**}, K_i^{**} \in \Theta^i, i = 1, 2, \text{ and } \theta^2 \in K_2^{**} \end{array} \right\}.$$

Clearly, each agent i is able to answer her question without knowledge of the other agent's parameter θ^j, $j \neq i$.

Now for $\theta = (\theta^1, \theta^2)$, let $m \in \mu(\theta)$ where $\mu(\theta) = \mu^1(\theta^1) \cap \mu^2(\theta^2)$ by definition.

This means by definition of $\mu^i(\cdot)$ that

$$m = \Lambda(K^*), \qquad K^* \in C_V, \qquad \theta^1 \in K_1^*,$$

and

$$m = \Lambda(K^{**}), \qquad K^{**} \in C, \qquad \theta^2 \in K_2^{**}$$

hence

$$\Lambda(K^*) = \Lambda(K^{**}).$$

But by SDR (ii) it follows that $K^* = K^{**}$. Thus $m \in \mu(\theta)$ means that there exists $\bar{K}$ such that

$$m = \Lambda(\bar{K}), \qquad \bar{K} \in C, \qquad \bar{K} = \bar{K}_1 \times \bar{K}_2, \qquad \theta^1 \in \bar{K}_1, \qquad \theta^2 \in \bar{K}_2,$$

hence (by the rectangularity of C_V) $\theta = (\theta^1, \theta^2) \in \bar{K}$. That is,

$$\mu(\theta) = \left\{ \begin{array}{c} m \in M : m \in \Lambda(\bar{K}) \text{ for some } \bar{K} \in C_V \\ \text{such that } \theta \in \bar{K} \end{array} \right\}.$$

The mechanism (M, μ, h) thus constructed is informationally decentralized because $\mu((\theta^1, \theta^2)) = \mu^1(\theta^1) \cap \mu^2(\theta^2)$, and each $\mu^i(\theta^i)$, $i = 1, 2$, is privacy preserving, i.e., each agent can answer her verification question without knowing the other agent's parameter value.

2.2.5 Mechanism Construction for L-dot

Before generalizing, we first illustrate the preceding "recipes" for mechanism construction by a simple, though nontrivial example, that of the L-Dot configuration (Example 1 above). The goal function is

$$F(\alpha) = F(\beta) = F(\gamma) = p, \qquad F(\delta) = q \neq p.$$

As seen above, there is only one rRM covering; it consists of three rectangles: the column vector $K' = \{\alpha, \beta\}$, the row vector $K'' = \{\beta, \gamma\}$, and $K''' = \{\delta\}$. However, there are three different correspondences that generate that covering.

We must use $V(\alpha) = K'$, $V(\gamma) = K''$, and $V(\delta) = K'''$. Where we have alternatives, we choose $V(\beta) = K'$.

The individual parameter spaces are

$$\Theta^1 = \{a_1, a_2\}, \qquad \Theta^2 = \{b_1, b_2\}, \qquad a_1 < a_2, \qquad b_1 < b_2,$$

with

$$\alpha = (a_1, b_2), \qquad \beta = (a_1, b_1), \qquad \gamma = (a_2, b_1), \qquad \delta = (a_2, b_2).$$
$$(a_1, a_2, b_1, b_2 \text{ are real numbers }).$$

We make the following choices for the SDR function:

$$\Lambda(K') = \alpha, \qquad \Lambda(K'') = \gamma, \qquad \Lambda(K''') = \delta.$$

Hence our transversal is

$$T = \{\alpha, \gamma, \delta\}.$$

Since we are still in the simplified case where $M = M' = T$, the message space consists of α, γ, and δ. However, when we treat these elements as messages, we denote them respectively as $m' = \alpha$, $m'' = \gamma$, $m''' = \delta$.

To construct a mechanism, we must define the equilibrium correspondences and the outcome function.

The outcome function construction is simple. The recipe prescribes

$$h(m) = F(\theta)|_{\theta=m}.$$

Thus,

$$h(m') = F(\alpha) = p, \qquad h(m'') = F(\delta) = p, \qquad h(m''') = q \qquad (q \neq p).$$

The construction of the two equilibrium correspondences μ^1 and μ^2 is more complicated. To find correspondence μ^1, we must find two sets: $\mu^1(a_1) \subseteq M$ and $\mu^1(a_2) \subseteq M$. We start with $\mu^1(a_1)$. Since $M = \{m', m'', m'''\}$ is finite, we can find $\mu^1(a_1)$ by answering three questions: Does m' belong to $\mu^1(a_1)$? Does m'' belong to $\mu^1(a_1)$? Does m''' belong to $\mu^1(a_1)$?

Is $m' \in \mu^1(a_1)$ true? By definition of $\mu'(\theta)$, the question means: Is there a rectangle K in the covering C_V such that $m' = \Lambda(K)$ and $a_1 \in K_1$? (Here $\mathbb{R} = \mathbb{R}_1 \times \mathbb{R}_2$, $K_1 \subseteq \Theta^1$, $K_2 \subseteq \Theta^2$.)

Now $m' = \alpha$, so $m' = \Lambda(K)$ only if $K = K'$, $K' = \{\alpha\}$, so $K' = \{a_1\} \times \{b_1, b_2\}^+ \cdot K'_1 = \{a_1\}$. Since $a_1 \in \{a_1\}$, it follows that $m' \in \mu^1(a_1)$.

To complete the construction of $\mu^1(a_1)$, we must still find out whether $m'' \in \mu^1(a_1)$, and whether $m''' \in \mu^1(a_1)$. Consider the first question.

The question whether $m'' \in \mu^1(a_1)$ means: Is there a rectangle $K \in C_V$ such that $m'' \equiv \gamma = \Lambda(K)$ and $a_1 \in K_1$? The only rectangle satisfying the first requirement is K'', and so $K''_1 = \{a_1, a_2\}$, so $a_1 \in K''_1$, and hence $m'' \in \mu^1(a_1)$.

In turn, whether $m''' \in \mu^1(a_1)$ means: Is there a rectangle K such that $K \in C_V$, $M''' = \delta = \Lambda(K)$, and $a_1 \in K_1$. The only qualifying rectangle is K'', since only K''' is represented by δ. Now $K''' = \{(a_2, b_2)\}$ so $K'''_1 = \{a_2\}$. But $a_1 \notin \{a_2\}$. Therefore $m''' \notin \mu^1(a_1)$. It follows that $\mu^1(a_1) = \{m', m''\} = \{\alpha, \gamma\}$.

To find $\mu^1(a_2)$, we have to answer the corresponding three questions: whether m', m'', m''' belong to $\mu^1(a_2)$. To know the correspondence μ^1 : $\Theta^1 \Rightarrow M$ means in this case knowing the sets $\mu^1(a_1)$ and $\mu^1(a_2)$.

The correspondence $\mu^2 : \Theta^2 \Rightarrow M$ of the second agent is found by the analogous procedure.

Finally, to obtain the full ("collective") equilibrium correspondence $\Theta^1 \times \Theta^2 \Rightarrow M$, we calculate μ^1, μ^2, and then their intersection – for every $\theta = (\theta^1, \theta^2)$, $\theta^i \in \Theta^i$, $i = 1, 2$, we find the subset $\mu(\theta)$ of M the equation

$$\mu(\theta) = \mu(\theta^1, \theta^2) = \mu^1(\theta^1) \cap \mu^2(\theta^2).$$

The three components of the decentralized mechanism still satisfy the definitions:

$$M = \Lambda(C),$$

$$h(m) = F(m),$$

and

$$\mu(\theta) = \left\{ \begin{array}{c} m \in M : m = \Lambda(K) \text{ for some } K \in C \\ \text{such that } \theta \in K \end{array} \right\}.$$

But these were the only properties used in the proof that the mechanism (M, μ, h) realizes F on Θ. Hence that earlier proof remains valid, line by line!

Moreover, the same is true if we generalize by using a set M other than $\Lambda(C_V)$, *provided this M has a subset rich enough to be in one-to-one correspondence with the transversal $T = \Lambda(C_V)$.* We have thus constructed a mechanism that is informationally decentralized, and realizes the given goal function on the parameter space, from a given F-cc, rectangular covering of the parameter space that has an SDR.

In fact, we have constructed a whole family of such mechanisms, because there is leeway in choosing the SDR function Λ, and in choosing the message space M, as well as the mapping function $v : T \to M'$ where $M' = v(\Lambda(C))$. Since the set $\Lambda(C)$ is the transversal of the covering, we speak of the "method of transversals" abbreviated *TM*.

The mechanisms so constructed take as given a covering C_V of the parameter space that is F-cc, rectangular, and has an SDR. The latter property is (by Theorem 3.A.1) equivalent to the covering being generated by a self-belonging correspondence, say $V : \Theta \Rightarrow \Theta$. The reflexive *RM* correspondence is self-belonging, as well as F-cc and rectangular. Hence our result (the construction of an informationally decentralized mechanism that realizes F) applies in particular to coverings generated by rRM (reflexive method of rectangles) correspondences. But its scope is broader, since rRM has an additional property, viz., that of maximal coarseness, a type of informational efficiency.

As we have seen, coverings generated by rRM can have overlaps, or they can be partitions of the parameter space. The mechanism construction procedure we have just defined is applicable in either case, but is much easier for partitions.

2.3 Smooth Transversal Construction for Partitions by the "Flagpole" Method[59]

2.3.1 Flagpoles: General Principles

This section describes a method of constructing a transversal (by the "flagpole approach") for a mechanism that realizes a given goal function $F : \Theta \to Z$, when the covering correspondence $V : \Theta \Rightarrow \Theta$ for F is known and is represented by an equation system. This approach makes possible the discovery of mechanisms that realize a given goal function without requiring any prior knowledge or conjecture about the form of the mechanism. (Such a procedure is illustrated by the example below.)

The system representing V is written in vector form as $G(\bar{\theta}, \theta) = 0$, $G : \Theta \times \Theta \to R^d$, where d is a positive integer. (The parameter space Θ is a subset of the Euclidean space of dimension $k \geq d > 1$). That $G = 0$ represents V means that

$$G(\bar{\theta}, \theta) = 0 \quad \text{if and only if} \quad \theta \in V(\bar{\theta}), \tag{1}$$

As in most of our work, the correspondence V is assumed to be *self-belonging* and F-cc, that is $G(\bar{\theta}, \bar{\theta}) = 0$ for all $\bar{\theta}$ in Θ, and if $G(\bar{\theta}, \theta) = 0$, then $F(\theta) = F(\bar{\theta})$.

When the parameter space Θ factors into two individual spaces (of dimensions k_1 and k_2, with $k_1 + k_2 = k = \dim \Theta$), $\Theta = \Theta^1 \times \Theta^2$, the correspondence V is rectangular: if $\theta = (a, b) \in \Theta^1 \times \Theta^2$, then $V(\theta) = V^1(\theta) \times V^2(\theta) \subseteq \Theta^1 \times \Theta^2$. In equation form this means that the system $G(\bar{\theta}, \theta) = 0$ of d equations is equivalent to two subsystems of equations, written as $G^1(\bar{\theta}, a) = 0$, $G^2(\bar{\theta}, b) = 0$ where again $\theta = (a, b) \in \Theta^1 \times \Theta^2$, $G^i : \Theta \times \Theta^i \to R^{di}$ and $d_1 + d_2 = d$. (It is assumed that $d_i \leq k_i$, $i = 1, 2; d \leq k$.)

The preceding assumptions are standard in much of this chapter. We make additional specializing assumptions that enable us to carry through the flagpole approach, although at the cost of limiting its applicability.

The chief such assumption is that the covering C_V of Θ generated by V, is assumed to be a partition. Hence, by the *symmetry* property of coverings that are partitions,

$$G(\bar{\theta}, \theta) = 0 \Leftrightarrow G(\theta, \bar{\theta}) = 0.$$

See Theorem 3.6.1.

---

[59] The "flagpole" approach, due to Professor Leonard Shapiro, Portland State University, was the earliest technique of constructing a mechanism given the equation system $G(\bar{\theta}, \theta) = 0$.

The flagpole approach also relies on differentiability of the function G, and on properties of its derivatives that justify the use of the implicit function (or, with additional conditions, univalence) theorems. Therefore, we assume that G is continuously differentiable, with the parameter space Θ an open Euclidean set.

Furthermore, we assume that the $d \times k$ Jacobian matrix of $G(\bar{\theta}, \theta)$ denoted $\partial G/\partial\theta$ with respect to its second argument, $\theta = (a, b)$, is of rank d, with the following structure. Let $a = (a^*, a^{**}) \in \Theta^1$, $\dim(a^*) = d_1$, and similarly $b = (b^*, b^{**}) \in \Theta^2$, $\dim(b^*) = d_2$. Where convenient, we refer to the sub-vectors a^{**}, and b^{**} as the residual sub-vectors. We assume that the two Jacobians $J^1 = \partial G^1/\partial a^*$ and $J^2 = \partial G^2/\partial b^*$ are nonsingular. (Except in trivial cases, at least one of the two sub-vectors a^{**}, b^{**} will be nonempty. In most of our examples both are nonempty.)

Let G be defined and smooth – C^1 – in a neighborhood of a parameter point θ°. A "*flagpole*" is a subset P of the parameter space Θ, defined by specifying fixed values, say α^{**} and β^{**} respectively, for the two residual subvectors a^{**} and b^{**}. Write $H(a, b) = 0$, to stand for the equation system $a^{**} = \alpha^{**}$ and $b^{**} = \beta^{**}$ ($H^1 = 0$ and $H^2 = 0$). Then $P = \{\theta \in \Theta : H(\theta) = 0\}$.[60] We sometimes write $\theta = (\theta^*, \theta^{**})$, where $\theta^* = (a^*, b^*)$, $\theta^{**} = (a^{**}, b^{**})$.

Consider the k by k system consisting of $G^1(\bar{\theta}, a)) = 0$, $G^2(\bar{\theta}, b) = 0$, $H(a, b) = 0$. By hypothesis, there is a point θ° in the neighborhood where these equations are all satisfied, and all functions are continuously differentiable. Furthermore, the Jacobian J of this system is nonsingular, since it can be written as the following triangular block matrix:

$$
J = \begin{array}{c} \\ \partial G^1/ \\ \partial G^2/ \\ \partial H^1/ \\ \partial H^2/ \end{array}
\begin{array}{cccc} /\partial a^* & /\partial b^* & /\partial a^{**} & /\partial b^{**} \\ \left(\begin{array}{cccc} J^1 & 0 & 0 & x \\ 0 & J^2 & 0 & x \\ 0 & 0 & I_{a^{**}} & 0 \\ 0 & 0 & 0 & I_{b^{**}} \end{array} \right) \end{array}, \tag{2}
$$

where $I_{a^{**}}$ and $I_{b^{**}}$ are identity matrices, respectively, with the dimensions of a^{**} and b^{**}, and the submatrices J^1 and J^2 are assumed nonsingular. (As usual, 0's stand for null matrices and the x's for matrices whose values do not affect the argument.)

[60] Typically, there are alternative choices of vector partitions resulting in the selection of a flagpole. However, some choices are unacceptable because they would lead to failure of "coverage," others because the resulting J matrix would be singular. In any case, the number of candidates for such choice within the present framework is finite, hence this phase of mechanism construction does not negate its "algorithmic" nature.

The equation $G(\bar{\theta}, \theta) = 0$ represents a point θ in the rectangle $K = V(\bar{\theta})$ of the covering C_V associated with the "source" $\bar{\theta}$ (in K), and $H(\theta) = 0$ locates this point on the flagpole P. Hence the solution of the system (whose local existence and uniqueness is guaranteed by the implicit function (or univalence) theorems[61]), written as $\hat{\theta} = \tau(\bar{\theta})$. $\hat{\theta}$ is the point on the flagpole $P = \{\theta : H(\theta) = 0\}$ "representing" the "source" $\bar{\theta}$ in the rectangle $G(\bar{\theta}, \theta) = 0$. Hence, indirectly it represents the rectangle K. (Because C_V is a partition, different "source" points in the same rectangle would yield the same $\hat{\theta}$.) In fact, because C_V is a partition, $\hat{\theta}$ is a representative of the rectangle K in the sense of an SDR, i.e., $\hat{\theta} = \tau(\bar{\theta}) = \Lambda(K)$ in our usual notation for an SDR. It follows that $\tau(\Theta)$ is a *transversal* for C_v.[62] Hence the flagpole P contains (or is) the transversal T. From here on we construct the functions that define equililibrium, and the outcome functions.

To clarify the mechanism construction procedure used in the example below, and to make this subsection more nearly self-contained, we outline the construction used.

Write $M' = \tau(\Theta)$, and choose a set containing M' to be the *message space* M. Next define the equilibrium function $g : M \times \Theta \to R^d$ for any m in M and θ in Θ by

$$g(m, \theta) = \left\{ \begin{array}{ll} G((m, \alpha^{**}, \beta^{**}), \theta) & \text{if } m \in M' \\ 3 & \text{otherwise} \end{array} \right\}.$$

[61] Additional assumptions (à la Gale/Nikaido) would be required to apply the univalence theorems. The simplest case of global validity is that in which $G(\bar{\theta}, \theta)$ is affine in its second argument, θ, i.e., when the system is of the form $A(\bar{\theta})\theta - B(\bar{\theta}) = 0$, and all entries in both matrices, $A(\bar{\theta})$ and $B(\bar{\theta})$, are continuously differentiable with respect to $\bar{\theta}$ at all points $\bar{\theta} \in \Theta$, and where the matrix $A(\bar{\theta})$ is nonsingular at all points $\bar{\theta} \in \Theta$. (That is the situation in the example below, as well as in many of our other examples, including the Walrasian.)

[62] To justify the equality $\hat{\theta} = \tau(\bar{\theta}) = \Lambda(K)$, where $K = V(\bar{\theta})$, we first show that $\hat{\theta} = \tau(\theta)$ for every $\theta \in K$ and (ii) for no $\theta \notin K$.

To prove (i), let $\theta' \in K$, i.e., $\theta' \in V(\bar{\theta})$ and let $\theta\# = \tau(\theta')$. Now by the definition of $\tau(.)$, $\theta\# \in V(\theta')$. But $V(\theta') = V(\bar{\theta})$. (If not, $V(\Theta)$ would not be a partition, because θ' would belong to two distinct sets; θ' belongs to $V(\theta')$ by self-belonging, and also belongs to $V(\bar{\theta})$ by hypothesis.) But then $G(\bar{\theta}, \theta\#) = 0$ and also $G(\bar{\theta}, \hat{\theta}) = 0$. But the system $G(\bar{\theta}, \theta) = 0$, $H(\theta) = 0$ has a unique solution for θ (at least locally by the IFT, or, with additional assumptions, globally). Hence $\theta\# = \hat{\theta}$. This completes the proof of (i).

As for (ii), it follows from the fact that if $\hat{\theta} = \tau(\theta)$ for some $\theta \in V(\theta)$, $\theta \notin K$, then θ would belong to two distinct rectangles, thus violating the assumption that C_V is a partition.

Given (i) and (ii), if we define Λ by $\Lambda(K) = \tau(\theta)$ for some θ such that $K = V(\theta)$, the two properties defining an SDR are satisfied, and we see that $\tau(\Theta) = \Lambda(\Theta)$, hence $\tau(\Theta)$ qualifies as a transversal in the SDR sense.

Finally, we define the outcome function $h()$ at m in M' by

$$h(m) = F((m, \alpha^{**} \beta^{**})).$$

Then the mechanism (M, g, h) is decentralized (privacy preserving), and realizes F.

That it realizes F is seen as follows.

(*Existence:* for every θ in Θ, there exists m in M such that $g(m, \theta) = 0$). Given θ, let $m = \tau^*(\theta)$ where $\tau^*(\theta)$ is defined by

$$\tau(\theta) = (\tau^*(\theta), (\alpha^{**}, \beta^{**})).$$

Then, by definition,

$$g(m, \theta) = G((\tau^*(\theta), (\alpha^{**}, \beta^{**})), \theta) = G(\tau(\theta), \theta).$$

Now $G(\theta, \tau(\theta)) = 0$ by the definition of $\tau(\theta)$. Hence $G(\tau(\theta), \theta) = 0$ by the assumed symmetry of G (because V generates a partition). Hence $g(m, \theta) = 0$.

(*F-optimality:* if $g(m, \theta) = 0$, then $h(m) = F(\theta)$.)

By construction, if $g(m, \theta) = 0$ then $(m, \alpha^{**} \beta^{**}) = \tau(\theta)$. Hence, by definition, $h(m) = F(\tau(\theta))$. But, by the F-cc property of V (and hence of G), it follows that $F(\tau(\theta)) = F(\theta)$ because $G(\theta, \tau(\theta)) = 0$ and hence $\tau(\theta) \in V(\theta)$. Thus $h(m) = F(\theta)$ and so the mechanism realizes F.

That $g(m, \theta)$ is decentralized follows from the definition of g. This is so because according to this definition, each equation of $g = 0$ is inherited from the corresponding equation of G. Therefore, because G is decentralized, so is g.

Admittedly, the flagpole approach requires specializing assumptions. It has, however, two advantages: it is in a sense, algorithmic, and the solutions it produces have desirable smoothness properties.

We provide two illustrations: Example 2 (augmented two-dimensional inner product) and the Walrasian example.

2.3.2 Flagpoles: Example 2 (Augmented Inner Product)

Our example is the two-dimensional augmented inner product where the goal function is $F \equiv a_1 b_1 + a_2 b_2 + b_3$ and every one of the five parameters ranges over all real values, except that zero is not a possible value of b_1; thus,

$$\Theta = \{\theta \in \mathbb{R}^5 : b_1 \neq 0\}.$$

We first construct an rRM correspondence V for F by constructing its $G = 0$ equation system. The A-set for any $\bar{\theta} = (\bar{a}, \bar{b})$ in Θ, defined by the equation $G^1(\bar{\theta}, a) = 0$, is chosen so as to be *maximal* in Θ. It follows that the resulting left-RM covering is guaranteed to be reflexive. Thus, in the present example, this A-set is defined by

$$G^1(\bar{\theta}, a) \equiv \bar{b}_1 a_1 + \bar{b}_2 a_2 + \bar{b}_3 - (\bar{b}_1 \bar{a}_1 + \bar{b}_2 \bar{a}_2 + \bar{b}_3) = 0 \qquad (1\#)$$

or, equivalently,[2]

$$G^1(\bar{\theta}, a) \equiv a_1 + (\bar{b}_2/\bar{b}_1)a_2 - (\bar{a}_1 + (\bar{b}_2/\bar{b}_1)\bar{a}_2) = 0. \qquad (i)$$

To obtain equations of the B-set, we solve (1) for a_1 as a function of a_2 and substitute this expression into the equation $F(a, b) - F(\bar{a}, \bar{b}) = 0$, thus obtaining an equation in a_2 and b. According to the L-RM construction rules, the latter equation must be an identity in a_2, hence the coefficients of a_2 must vanish. This yields the two equations in b and $\bar{\theta}$ that define the B-set. They are

$$G^{21}(\bar{\theta}, b) \equiv -(\bar{b}_2/\bar{b}_1)b_1 + b_2 = 0, \qquad (2.1)$$

and

$$G^{22}(\bar{\theta}, b) \equiv [\bar{a}_1 + (\bar{b}_2/\bar{b}_1)\bar{a}_2]b_1 + b_3 - F(\bar{\theta}) = 0. \qquad (2.2)$$

Next, we show that the system $G = 0$, consisting of equations (1), (2.1), and (2.2), has the property of *symmetry*, so that the covering is a partition. This is accomplished by interchanging parameters with overbars with those without, and verifying that the system so obtained, $G(\theta, \bar{\theta}) = 0$, is equivalent to $G(\bar{\theta}, \theta) = 0$.

First, the equation obtained by interchange in (2.1), viz.

$$-(b_2/b_1)\bar{b}_1 + \bar{b}_2 = 0, \qquad (2.1')$$

is identical, except in appearance, to (2.1). In turn, performing the interchange in (1) we get

$$\bar{a}_1 + (b_2/b_1)\bar{a}_2 - (a_1 + (b_2/b_1)a_2) = 0. \qquad (1')$$

By (2.1'), Equation (1') is equivalent to

$$\bar{a}_1 + (\bar{b}_2/\bar{b}_1)\bar{a}_2 - (a_1 + (\bar{b}_2/\bar{b}_1)a_2) = 0, \qquad (1'')(1')$$

which is the same as (1).

Finally, the result of interchange in (2.2) is

$$[a_1 + (b_2/b_1)a_2]\bar{b}_1 + \bar{b}_3 - F(\theta) = 0. \qquad (2.2')$$

By (2.1′) and (1″) this is equivalent to

$$F(\bar{\theta}) - F(\theta) = 0. \tag{2.2″}$$

But $G(\bar{\theta}, \theta) = 0$ implies that θ is in the same rectangle as $\bar{\theta}$, and, by the F-cc property of RM, (2.2″) holds. Conversely, Equations (1′), (2.1′), and 2.2′), which constitute the system $G(\theta, \bar{\theta}) = 0$, imply $G(\bar{\theta}, \theta) = 0$. This completes the proof of symmetry. It follows that the covering is a partition.

Next, we choose the set called a flagpole. It is defined by the equations $a_2 = 0$ and $b_1 = 1$. Hence $H(\theta) = (H^1, H^2) = (a_2, b_1) - (0, 1)$; $H^1 = a_2 - 0$, $H^2 = b_1 - 1$; in our earlier notation we have $\alpha^{**} = 0$, $\beta^{**} = 1$.[4] The parameter vectors are split as follows: $a = (a^*, a^{**})$, where $a^* = a_1$ and $a^{**} = a_2$. $b = (b^*, b^{**})$ where $b^* = (b_2, b_3)$ and $b^{**} = b_1$. Hence the Jacobian J can be written (using the A-equation in form (1)) as

$$J = \begin{array}{c} \\ \partial G^1/ \\ \partial G^{21}/ \\ \partial G^{22}/ \\ \partial H^1/ \\ \partial H^2/ \end{array} \begin{pmatrix} /\partial a^* & /\partial b^* & /\partial a^{**} & /\partial b^{**} \\ 1 & (0,0) & \bar{b}_2/\bar{b}_1 & 0 \\ 0 & (1,0) & 0 & -(\bar{b}_2/\bar{b}_1) \\ 0 & (0,1) & 0 & \bar{a}_1 + (\bar{b}_2/\bar{b}_1)\bar{a}_2 \\ 0 & 0 & 1 & 0 \\ 0 & 0 & 0 & -1 \end{pmatrix}, \tag{2*}$$

Solving the system $G(\bar{\theta}, \theta) = 0$, $H(\theta) = 0$ for the components of θ (i.e., for the five parameters without the overbars), we write the solution as

$$\hat{\theta} = \tau(\bar{\theta}) = (\hat{a}_1, \hat{a}_2, \hat{b}_1, \hat{b}_2, \hat{b}_3)$$

where

$$\hat{a}_1 = -\left(\frac{\bar{b}_2}{\bar{b}_1}\right) \cdot 0 + \bar{a}_1 + \left(\frac{\bar{b}_2}{\bar{b}_1}\right)\bar{a}_2 = \bar{a}_1 + \left(\frac{\bar{b}_2}{\bar{b}_1}\right)\bar{a}_2$$

$$\hat{a}_2 = 0$$

$$\hat{b}_1 = 1$$

$$\hat{b}_2 = \left(\frac{\bar{b}_2}{\bar{b}_1}\right) \cdot 1 = \left(\frac{\bar{b}_2}{\bar{b}_1}\right)$$

$$\hat{b}_3 = F(\bar{\theta}) - \left[\bar{a}_1 + \left(\frac{\bar{b}_2}{\bar{b}_1}\right)\bar{a}_2\right] \cdot b_1. \tag{3}$$

Define $g(m, \theta)$ as indicated by the formula, with $\hat{\theta} = (\hat{\theta}^*, \hat{\theta}^{**})$, $\hat{\theta} = \tau(\hat{\theta})$

$$g(m, \theta) = G(\hat{\theta}, \theta)\big|_{\hat{\theta}^{**}=(\alpha^{**}, \beta^{**})=(0,1)}^{\hat{\theta}^* = m}.$$

For instance, to find $g^1(m, a)$, we start with the formula

$$G^1(\hat{\theta}, \theta) = a_1 + (\hat{b}_2/\hat{b}_1)a_2 - (\hat{a}_1 + (\hat{b}_2/\hat{b}_1)\hat{a}_2), \qquad (\nabla)$$

which is obtained from the formula for $G^1(\bar{\theta}, \theta)$ in Equation (1), p. 6, by replacing in the RHS of $(\nabla)\bar{a}_j$ by $\hat{a}_j$ and $\bar{b}_k$ by $\hat{b}_k$. In turn, we replace $\hat{a}_2$ and $\hat{b}_1$ by their flagpole values, 0 and 1 respectively. Also, in the RHS of (∇), we replace $\hat{b}_2, \hat{a}_1, \hat{b}_3$ by m_1, m_2, and m_3 respectively.

As a result of these substitutions, with $m = (m_1, m_2, m_3)$, the LHS of (∇) becomes $g^1(m, \theta)$ and Equation (∇) becomes

$$\begin{aligned} g^1(m, \theta) &= a_1 + (m_1/1)a_2 - \left(m_2 + \frac{m_1}{1} \cdot 0\right) \\ &= a_1 + m_1 a_2 - m_2. \end{aligned} \qquad (\nabla\nabla)$$

Hence, the first equilibrium message equation is

$$g^1(m, a) \equiv a_1 + m_1 a_2 - m_2 = 0. \qquad (4.1)$$

Analogous substitutions yield the two other equilibrium message equations:

$$g^{21}(m, b) \equiv -m_1 b_1 + b_2 = 0. \qquad (4.21)$$

and

$$g^{22}(m, b) \equiv m_2 b_1 - m_2 + b_3 - m_3 = 0. \qquad (4.22)$$

Similarly, the outcome function h, defined by

$$h(m) =: F(\hat{\theta}) \Big|_{\substack{\hat{\theta}^* = m \\ \hat{\theta}^{**} = (0, 1)}} \qquad (5)$$

is found to be

$$h(m) = \hat{a}_1 \hat{b}_1 + a_2 \hat{b}_2 + \hat{b}_3 = m_2 \cdot 1 + 0 \cdot m_1 + m_3 = m_2 + m_3.$$

We can now directly verify that, for an equilibrium message m, it is the case that $h(m) = F(\theta)$ – that the mechanism is F-optimal.

Let m be an equilibrium message for θ. Then

$$\begin{aligned} h(m) &= m_2 + m_3 \\ &= m_2 + (m_2 b_1 - m_2 + b_3) \quad \text{by (4.2.2)} \\ &= m_2 b_1 + b_3 \\ &= (a_1 + m_1 a_2)b_1 + b_3 \quad \text{by (4.1)} \end{aligned}$$

$$= \left(a_1 + \frac{b_2}{b_1} a_2 \right) b_1 + b_3 \quad \text{by (4.2)}$$
$$= a_1 b_1 + a_2 b_2 + b_3$$
$$= F(\theta). \qquad \qquad \text{Q.E.D.}$$

The existence requirement is also satisfied, since – given (a, b) – the three linear equation system (4) is solvable (uniquely) for m_1, m_2, and m_3. Hence our mechanism does realize the goal function F.

It remains to observe that System (4) is privacy preserving: Equation (4.1) involves a's but no b's, while Equations (4.2) involve b's but no a's. This completes the example.

REMARK 1. Let us assume that, for a given $\bar{\theta}$, all Jacobian matrices of $G(\bar{\theta}, \theta)$ have a constant rank over the parameter space as θ varies. If, as above, we also assume that the Jacobian J in [2] is nonsingular at a point, or on a subset, of the parameter space, it follows that there exists a partitioning of the vectors a and b into $a = (a^*, a^{**})$ and $b = (b^*, b^{**})$ such that the Jacobians J^1 and J^2 are (square and) nonsingular at the same points of the parameter space.

Hence, if we assume the nonsingularity of J (together with the smoothness of G and that $G(\theta, \theta) = 0$), we can conclude that the covering generated by G is a partition and that a (smooth) flagpole exists, at least locally. In this sense, the nonsingularity of the smaller matrices is not an additional assumption.

Conversely, if we assume the nonsingularity of the two smaller matrices (at the same subset of the parameter space) then a nonsingular J can be constructed as above. So the two assumptions are equivalent.

REMARK 2. We have seen that when the Jacobian $\partial G / \partial \theta$ has maximal rank (equal to the dimension d of its range), then G represents a partition and has a smooth transversal obtained by fixing certain components of θ – choosing a flagpole parallel to coordinate planes.

It is natural to ask whether these conclusions are necessarily false when the Jacobian is of rank lower than maximal. The following example shows that this is not the case. In this example, G represents a partition and there is a transversal with properties mentioned above, even though the rank of the Jacobian is less than maximal.

Our example is the two-dimensional augmented inner product where the goal function is $F \equiv a_1 b_1 + a_2 b_2 + b_3$ and every one of the five parameters ranges over all real values except that $b_1 \neq 0$.

As shown in the above example, an rRM covering is represented by the following three equation system, where the first equation, which defines the (maximal) A-side of the rectangle is

$$G^1(\bar{\theta}, a) \equiv \bar{b}_1 a_1 + \bar{b}_2^* a_2 + \bar{b}_3^* - F(\bar{\theta}) = 0. \tag{1}$$

The B-equations are

$$G^{21}(\bar{\theta}, b) \equiv (\bar{b}_2/\bar{b}_1)b_1 + b_2 = 0, \tag{2.1}$$

and

$$G^{22}(\bar{\theta}, b) \equiv [\bar{a}_1 + (\bar{b}_2/\bar{b}_1)\bar{a}_2]b_1 + b_3 - F(\bar{\theta}) = 0. \tag{2.2}$$

Next, consider a modification of our equation system in which equations (2.1)–(2.2) are left unchanged, but Equation (1) is replaced by

$$G^{1\sim}(\bar{\theta}, a) \equiv (G^1(\bar{\theta}, a))^3 = 0. \tag{1'}$$

It is seen that, because of the sign-preserving properties of the cubic, the modified system defines the same covering (hence a partition) and the same transversal as the original system. However, at a point $\theta = (a, b)$ belonging to $V(\bar{\theta})$, we have $G^1(\bar{\theta}, a) = 0$, and hence the first row of the Jacobian of the modified system consists of zeros, so the rank of the Jacobian $\partial G/\partial \theta$ equals $2 < 3 = d$. This illustrates the point made at the beginning of this remark.

2.3.3 Flagpoles: A Walrasian Example

2.3.3.1 Preliminaries (Model, Assumptions, Notation)

The Walrasian example is interesting for two reasons: as an illustration of the flagpole technique of construction, and for its importance in economic theory. It is interesting that systematic application of the method of rectangles followed by the method of flagpoles "discovers" the Walrasian mechanism.

The example, whose phase one was studied in Chapter 1, Section 1.6, is extremely simple: pure exchange, two goods (X, Y), and two traders (1, 2). Their preferences are represented by quasi-linear utility functions, linear in Y and quadratic in X.

In the notation used in Section 2.1.3.3, the equilibrium conditions are

$$x = \frac{(b_2 - a_2)}{b_1 + a_1}$$

$$p = \frac{(a_1 b_2) + a_2 b_1}{b_1 + a_1}.$$

The price p is always positive, because we assumed that the four parameters (a's and b's) are J positive.

We take the goal function $F_w(\theta)$ at θ to be the quantity of the second trader's net trade $x_2 = x$; i.e.,

$$F_w(\theta) = (b_2 - a_2)/(b_1 + a_1), \tag{2}$$

where

$$\theta = (a, b), \qquad a = (a_1, a_2), \qquad b = (b_1, b_2).$$

2.3.3.2 Constructing the Walrasian Mechanism

The first step is to derive an rRM correspondence in equation form. This is done in Section 2.1.3.3.

We use the abbreviations

$$\bar{F} = (\bar{b}_2 - \bar{a}_2)/(\bar{b}_1 + \bar{a}_1)$$

$$\bar{p} = (\bar{a}_1 \bar{b}_2 + \bar{a}_2 \bar{b}_1)/(\bar{b}_1 + \bar{a}_1).$$

As shown in 2.1.3.3, the equations that define the generic $A \times B$ rectangle, in the G-equation form, are

$$G^1(\bar{\theta}, a) \equiv a_1 \bar{F} + a_2 - \bar{p} = 0 \tag{3.1}$$

$$G^2(\bar{\theta}, b) \equiv -b_1 \bar{F} + b_2 - \bar{p} = 0. \tag{3.2}$$

The preceding derivation is valid both for the case $\bar{F} = 0$ and $\bar{F} \neq 0$.[63] The first case is interesting, because it corresponds to situations in which the initial endowment allocation is Pareto optimal.

It is shown in Section 2.1.3.3 that the covering C_V is a partition. The next step is to select – construct – a flag pole.

According to the general recipe, we select one of the a's and one of the b's and define a flagpole by assigning admissible fixed values to those two

---

[63] However, the rectangles generated by points with $\bar{F} = 0$ are somewhat special because then the a_1, b_1 coordinates are unlimited.

parameters. We must do it in such a way that the resulting Jacobian is non-singular for all values of $\bar{\theta}$. Hence we cannot fix either a_2 or b_2, because then the resulting Jacobian would become singular whenever $F = 0$. Therefore, the flagpole must be defined by fixing the values of a_1 and b_1.

By hypothesis, the fixed values must be positive. Any positive numbers are admissible; we choose $a_1 = b_1 = 1/2$. The set of points in the (four-dimensional) parameter space (a_1, b_1, a_2, b_2) satisfying these two conditions is the flagpole, denoted by P.

We thus obtain a system of four equations that determine (uniquely) the point on the flagpole P that represents the point $\bar{\theta}$. These are

$$G^1 = 0, \qquad G^2 = 0, \qquad H^1 = 0, \qquad H^2 = 0. \qquad (*)$$

The first two equations of $(*)$ are (3.1) and (3.2), and the second two have $H^1 \equiv a_1 - 1/2$, and $H^2 \equiv b_1 - 1/2$.

The 4×4 Jacobian of this system is the matrix J given by

$$
J = \begin{array}{c} \\ \partial G^1/ \\ \partial G^2/ \\ \partial H^1/ \\ \partial H^2/ \end{array}
\begin{array}{c} /\partial a_2 \;\; /\partial b_2 \;\; /\partial a_1 \;\; /\partial b_1 \\ \begin{pmatrix} 1 & 0 & \bar{F} & 0 \\ 0 & 1 & 0 & -\bar{F} \\ 0 & 0 & 1 & 0 \\ 0 & 0 & 0 & 1 \end{pmatrix} \end{array},
$$

where the rows correspond to the four equations in the order that they appear in $(*)$, and the order of the columns is a_2, b_2, a_1, b_1.

Because the solution is unique, we write it as $\theta^* = \tau(\bar{\theta})$ where θ^* is a representative of the "source" $\bar{\theta}$, and τ is the "*index*" function. To solve the four-equation system $(*)$ for (a_1, b_1, a_2, b_2), we substitute the values $a_1^* = b_1^* = 1/2$ into Equations (3), and so obtain

$$a_2^* = \bar{p} - \bar{F}/2 \qquad (7.1)$$
$$b_2^* = \bar{p} + \bar{F}/2. \qquad (7.2)$$

Conversely,

$$\bar{F} = b_2^* - a_2^* \qquad (8.1)$$
$$\bar{p} = (b_2^* + a_2^*)/2. \qquad (8.2)$$

The next step is to construct the mechanism, and verify that it realizes the goal function.

Following the mechanism construction procedure outlined in Section 2.3.1, we define the message space M as a set that contains a set M' that is in one-to-one correspondence with $\tau(\Theta)$; this is the set of points on the flagpole P that represent points $\bar{\theta}$ in Θ

In the Walrasian example it is natural to use the Euclidean 2-space as M. The generic element of M is $m = (m_1, m_2)$ where

$$m_1 = b_2^* = \bar{p} + \bar{F}/2 \tag{9.1}$$
$$m_2 = a_2^* = \bar{p} - \bar{F}/2. \tag{9.2}$$

And, conversely,

$$\bar{F} = m_1 - m_2 \tag{10.1}$$
$$\bar{p} = (m_1 + m_2)/2. \tag{10.2}$$

We obtain the equilibrium equations $g^1 = 0$, $g^2 = 0$ by substituting into Equations (3) the values of $\bar{F}$ and $\bar{p}$ in terms of the messages m_i, as given in Equations (10). We then get

$$g^1(m, a) \equiv a_1(m_1 - m_2) + a_2 - (m_1 + m_2)/2 = 0 \tag{11.1}$$
$$g^2(m, b) = -b_1(m_1 - m_2) + b_2 - (m_1 + m_2)/2 = 0. \tag{11.2}$$

Equations (11) show that the mechanism is informationally decentralized (privacy preserving) because (11.1) contains no b's and (11.2) contains no a's.

It remains to construct the outcome function $h(m)$. The recipe for this step is

$$h(m) = F(a_1^*, a_2^*, b_1^*, b_2^*),$$

where the values of the asterisked parameters are as defined in equation system (*) – equations (7) and (10) – with $a_1^* = b_1^* = 1/2$, and the other two parameters are expressed as functions of m.

$$\begin{aligned} h(m) &= (b_2^* - a_2^*)/(b_1^* + a_1^*) \\ &= [(\bar{p} + \bar{F}/2) - (\bar{p} - \bar{F}/2)]/(1/2 + 1/2) \\ &= \bar{F} \\ &= m_1 - m_2. \end{aligned} \tag{12}$$

We next show that the mechanism (M, g^1, g^2, h) we have constructed is F-optimal; this means that if $g^1(m, a) = 0$ and $g^2(m, b) = 0$, then $h(m) = F(a, b)$.

Now, clearly if $g^1(m, a) = 0$ and $g^2(m, b) = 0$, then

$$g^2(m, b) - g^1(m, a) = 0.$$

But, by Equations (3) and (12),

$$0 = g^2(m, b) - g^1(m, a) = -(b_1 + a_1)h(m) + (b_2 - a_2),$$

which yields

$$h(m) = (b_2 - a_2)/(b_1 + a_1) = F(a, b).$$

Existence of equilibrium message for each $\theta \in \Theta$ is obvious.

It follows that the mechanism realizes F. It is, in fact, equivalent to, but not identical with the customary Walrasian mechanism. (The latter uses x and p as messages, and in that mechanism $h(p) = x$.)

2.3.4 Unique Solvability Implies Partition

Notation:

$$G : \bar{\Theta} \times \Theta \to \mathbb{R}^d$$
$$g : P \times \Theta \to \mathbb{R}^d$$
$$\psi : \bar{\Theta} \to P$$

($\dim P \le d \le \dim \Theta = \dim \bar{\Theta}$).

DEFINITION 2.3.4.1. (g, ψ) is a *condensation* of G if, for all θ and $\bar{\theta}$ in Θ,

$$g(\psi(\bar{\theta}), \theta) = G(\bar{\theta} \cdot \theta). \tag{1}$$

G *represents* V if, for all $\bar{\theta}$ in Θ,

$$V(\bar{\theta}) = \{\theta \text{ in } \Theta : G(\bar{\theta}, \theta) = 0\}. \tag{2}$$

The equation $g(p, \theta) = 0$ is said to be *uniquely solvable for* p if, for every θ in Θ,

$$\text{there exists a } p' \text{ in } P \text{ such that } g(p', \theta) = 0, \tag{3.1}$$

and, for every θ in Θ and for all p', p'' in P,

$$\text{if } g(p', \theta) = 0 \text{ and } g(p'', \theta) = 0, \text{ then } p' = p''. \tag{3.2}$$

THEOREM 2.3.4.1. If (g, ψ) is a condensation of G, and the equation $g(p, \theta) = 0$ is uniquely solvable for p, for every θ in Θ, then the covering C_V of Θ generated by V is a partition.

Proof: Suppose the point $\hat{\theta} D$ belongs to $V(\theta')$ and to $V(\theta'')$. We show that [4] is satisfied.

Because $V(\theta')$ and $V(\theta'')$ have the point $\hat{\theta}$ in common, and because G represents V, we may conclude that

$$G(\theta', \hat{\theta}) = 0 \qquad \text{and} \qquad G(\theta'', \hat{\theta}) = 0. \tag{5}$$

Because (g, ψ) is a condensation of G, it follows that if $p' = \psi(\theta')$, and $p'' = \psi(\theta'')$, then we may conclude that

$$g(p', \hat{\theta}) = 0 \qquad \text{and} \qquad g(p'', \hat{\theta}) = 0.$$

But then, by unique solvability,

$$p' = p''$$

$$\psi(\theta') = \psi(\theta''). \tag{6}$$

The assumption, that (g, ψ) is a condensation of G, directly yields (7.1) and (7.2) for all θ;

$$g(\psi(\theta'), \theta)) = G(\theta', \theta), \tag{7.1}$$
$$g(\psi(\theta''), \theta)) = G(\theta'', \theta). \tag{7.2}$$

But (6) makes the left-hand sides of (7.1) and (7.2) identical. Hence

$$G(\theta', \theta) = G(\theta'', \theta) \qquad \text{for all } \theta.$$

It follows from Equation (2), because G represents V, that

$$V(\theta') = V(\theta''). \tag{4}$$

This completes the proof.

2.4 Analytic Aspects

When the correspondence V is self-belonging, $G(\theta', \theta') = 0$ for all θ' – the Equation $G(\theta', \theta) = 0$ has a solution for $\theta = \theta'$ – therefore so has $g(p', \theta') = 0$, where $p' = \psi(\theta')$.

Therefore, when g and ψ are smooth (at least of class C^1), and the Jacobian $\partial g / \partial p$ is square and nonsingular, the implicit function theorem applies and it follows that $g(p, \theta) = 0$ for (p, θ) in a neighborhood of θ' follows is locally uniquely solvable.

For *global* unique solvability – "univalence" – we need additional conditions, for example, those on the minors of the Jacobian, as well as on the domain of g, as specified in the various theorems by Gale and Nikaido

(1965) A simple additional condition is that the function G be linear in its second argument, θ. The condition is the case in several of our examples.

2.4.1 Phase Two via Condensation. General Principles

Since we are in phase two, we take as given the covering correspondence $V : \Theta \Rightarrow \Theta$ and its equation equivalent, written[64] in equation form most succinctly as

$$G(\bar{\theta}, \theta) = 0, \qquad (*)$$

where $G : \Theta \times \Theta \to \mathbb{R}^d$, the equation form is equivalent to the set-theoretic form

$$G(\bar{\theta}, \theta) = 0 \qquad \text{if and only if } \theta \in V(\bar{\theta}).$$

We assume that $2 \leq d \leq k$ where $k = \dim \Theta$. Since V is assumed to be rectangular, "decentralized", the equilibrium equation system for two agents $(*)$ can be written as[65]

$$G^i(\bar{\theta}, \theta^i) = 0, \qquad i = 1, 2, \qquad (**)$$

where

$$G^i : \Theta \times \Theta^i \to \mathbb{R}^{d_i}, \quad 1 \leq d_i \leq k_i, \quad d_1 + d_2 = d.[66]$$

It is often convenient to write $(*)$ in the equivalent form

$$G_s(\bar{\theta}, \theta) = 0, \qquad s = 1, \ldots, d, \qquad (***)$$

where 0 is the real number zero and $G_s : \Theta \times \Theta \to \mathbb{R}$ is a real-valued function.

In the decentralized form we sometimes write $(**)$ as

$$G_{1,s'}(\bar{\theta}, \theta^1) = 0, \qquad G_{2,s''}(\bar{\theta}, \theta^2) = 0,$$
$$s' = 1, \ldots, d_1, \qquad s'' = 1, \ldots, d_2, \qquad \theta^i \in \Theta^i, \qquad i = 1, 2, \qquad (****)$$

with $G_{1,s'}$ and $G_{2,s''}$ each real-valued.

In this section we go from an equation system (such as $(*)$ or its equivalents) indexed by the *parameter* vector $\bar{\theta}$ to an equilibrium equation system, $g(m, \theta) = 0$ or $g^i(m, \theta^i) = 0$, $i = 1, 2$, indexed by the *message* vector

---

[64] In Equation $(*)$, $\underline{0}$ is the null element of $\mathbb{R}^d$.

[65] In $(**)$, the symbol $\underline{0}$ denotes the null element of $\mathbb{R}^{d_i}$.

[66] $\Theta = \Theta^1 \times \Theta^2$, $k_i = \dim \Theta^i$, $i = 1, 2$; $k_1 + k_2 = k$.

m, where m is an element of a message space M. Except for trivial cases, $\dim M < \dim \Theta$. The two equation systems are equivalent in the sense that $g(m, \theta) = 0$ if an only if $G(\bar{\theta}, \theta) = 0$.

As shown in Chapter 3 (Section 3.5.1) and also in Chapter 2 (Section 2.2.3.1) above, there is a general procedure for making such a transition; it involves the construction of a *transversal T* to the covering C_V of the parameter space Θ generated by the correspondence V when that correspondence is self-belonging – when $\bar{\theta} \in V(\bar{\theta})$ for all $\bar{\theta}$ in Θ.

One technique of constructing a transversal, that of "flagpoles," is described in Section 2.3.1 of this chapter.

In this section, we present another technique for making the transition to a message-indexed system, called *the method of condensation*, abbreviated CM. It is based on the 1996 result due to Mount and Reiter (abbreviated in references as M/R) and reproduced as Theorem 4.4.6 in Chapter 4. The next few pages provide a brief outline of the notation and procedures of condensation.

Let $x = (x_1, \ldots, x_m) \in X$ and $y = (y_1, \ldots, y_n) \in Y$ be points in Euclidean spaces of dimensions m and n, respectively. The components of the vector x are called *primary* variables, those of y *secondary*. Also, let $w \in W$ be a point in the Euclidean space W of dimension $r \leq m$.[67] We say that the "smooth"[68] function $\Gamma^\sigma(w, y)$, $\sigma \in \{1, \ldots, N\}$ is an *r-condensation* of the function $\Phi^\sigma(x, y)$ if there exist r "smooth" functions $A_i : X \to \mathbb{R}^r$, $i = 1, \ldots, r$, such that

$$\Phi^\sigma(x, y) = \Gamma^\sigma(A_1(x), \ldots, A_r(x), y) \qquad (+)$$

for all $(x, y) \in U \times V \subset X \times Y$, where U and V are respectively neighborhoods of the points $p \in X$ and $q \in Y$.[69,70]

We refer to the functions Φ^σ as *candidates for condensation*, and to $A(\cdot) = (A_1(\cdot), \ldots, A_r(\cdot))$ as the *condensing mapping*. Γ^σ is the *condensed* form of Φ^σ. It is assumed that each candidate function Φ^σ, $\sigma = 1, \ldots, N$, belongs to the continuous differentiability class $C^{\alpha+1}$ with $\alpha \geq 2$ – a "smoothness" assumption).

---

[67] We speak of *trivial condensation* when $\dim W = \dim X$, i.e., when $r = m$.

[68] See condition in Theorem 4.4.6 of Chapter 4.

[69] $\Gamma^\sigma : W' \times U \to \mathbb{R}$, $W' \subseteq W$, W' a neighborhood of a point $p' \in W$, $p' = A(p)$ where $A(p) = (A, (p), \ldots, A_\tau(p))$, $\Phi^\sigma : U \times V \to \mathbb{R}$. The symbols U and V are unrelated to the U and V symbols for the covering correspondence in earlier sections.

[70] Our local concept of condensation can be made global under stronger assumptions such as those used by Gale and Nikaido (1965, 1968, 1999).

In applications of condensation techniques in mechanism theory, to make the transition from a given parameter-indexed system $G_s(\bar{\theta}, \theta) = 0$, $s = 1, \ldots, d$ to a message-indexed system $g_s(m, \theta) = 0$, $s = 1, \ldots, d$, we naturally make the equilibrium functions G_s into candidates for condensation. But to design a mechanism that realizes the given goal function[71] $F : \Theta \to Z$, we must also construct an outcome function $h : M \to Z$. This is accomplished by also making F into a candidate. Thus, in the case of mechanisms, the complete list of candidates is $(G_1, \ldots, G_d, F)$. (In the general condensation theory notation the list of candidates is $(\Phi^1, \ldots, \Phi^N)$. Hence G_s, $s = 1, \ldots, d$, correspond to $\Phi^1, \ldots, \Phi^{N-1}$, and F corresponds to Φ^N.) As for the arguments of G, the vector $\bar{\theta}$ will play the role of $\bar{x}$ the "primary" variable, while θ will constitute a component of the "secondary" vector variable y.[72]

Theorem 4.4.6 states conditions for the existence of an r-condensing mapping $A(\cdot) = (A^1(\cdot), \ldots, A_r(\cdot))$. These involve "smoothness" of the candidate functions (see above), and the ranks of their Hessians (defined below). A *necessary* condition for r-condensibility is that the rank of the bordered Hessian, denoted BH, not exceed r – that is

$$\text{rank}\,(BH) \leqq r. \tag{I}$$

A set of *sufficient* conditions for r-condensibility consists of the above Condition (I) on the rank of the bordered Hessian BH, together with the requirement that the (nonbordered) Hessian H^* be of rank exactly r – that is

$$\text{rank}\,(H^*) = r. \tag{II}$$

Suppose that our list of candidates $(G_1, \ldots, G_d, F)$ satisfies the smoothness conditions as well as the two sufficient conditions for some (non-trivial) $r < d + 1$. How do we then construct the r-condensing functions $A_1, \ldots, A_r$ and the r-condensed functions $\Gamma^1, \ldots, \Gamma^{d+1}$?

The constructive proof of Theorem 4.4.6 answers these questions. In what follows we provide a simplified and less than rigorous exposition of these procedures.

The condensing functions, $A_i(\cdot)$, are defined by the relations

$$A_i(x) = \left.\frac{\partial \Phi_{\alpha_i}(x)}{\partial y_{\beta_i}}\right|_{y=q}, \qquad i = 1, \ldots, r,$$

---

[71] Z is the outcome space.

[72] In the next section, we introduce certain auxiliary variables $\hat{y}$, so that the role of y will be played by $(\theta, \hat{y})$, rather than just by θ. Hence θ becomes a component of y.

where the indices α_i and β_i are so chosen, and the x_j's so numbered that the Jacobian matrix

$$\tilde{H} = \left(\frac{\partial A_i(x)}{\partial x_i} \right)_{\substack{t=1,\ldots,r \\ i=1,\ldots,r}}$$

is nonsingular. The existence of such indexation is guaranteed by Condition (II) of the theorem.

Write $x^* = (x_1, \ldots, x_r)$, $x^{**} = (x_{r+1}, \ldots, x_m)$ and $x = (x^*, x^{**})$, so that $\tilde{H} = \frac{\partial H}{\partial x^*}|_{x=p}$. Consider now the equation system

$$w_i = A_i(x^*, x^{**}), \, i = 1, \ldots, r. \tag{++}$$

Its local[73] solvability for x^* in a neighborhood of the point (p, q) is guaranteed by the smoothness of the candidate functions and rank condition (II). Write the solution of the preceding equation system $(++)$ as

$$x_i^* = \phi_i(w, x^{**}) \qquad i = 1, \ldots, r,$$

so that, for all x,

$$\phi_i(A(x), x^{**}) = x_i, \qquad i = 1, \ldots, r. \tag{$\circ$}$$

It remains to define the r-condensed functions $\Gamma^\sigma, \sigma = 1, \ldots, N$. This is accomplished in two steps. We first define a *"precursor" function* Γ'^σ of Γ^σ for each σ. Its definition is

$$\Gamma'^\sigma(w, x^{**}, y) = \Phi^\sigma(\phi^1(w, x^{**}), \ldots, \phi_r(w, x^{**}), x^{**}, y),$$

$$\sigma = 1, \ldots, N, \tag{+++}$$

where $w = (w_1, \ldots, w_r)$, $w \in \mathbb{R}^r$.

Next, in equation system $(+++)$, we set

$$w = A(x^*, x^{**}), \qquad \text{i.e., } w_i = A_i(x), \qquad i = 1, \ldots, r.$$

We then obtain from $(+++)$ the following sequence of equalities for each $\sigma \in \{1, \ldots, N\}$:

$$\begin{aligned}
\Gamma'^\sigma(w, x^{**}, y) &= \Phi^\sigma(\phi_1(A(x), x^{**}), \ldots, \phi_r(A(x), x^{**}), x^{**}, y) \\
&= \Phi^\sigma(x_1, \ldots, x_r, x^{**}, y) \qquad \text{by Equation } (\circ) \\
&= \Phi^\sigma(x^*, x^{**}, y) \qquad \text{by definition of } x^* \\
&= \Phi^\sigma(x, y) \qquad \text{by definition of } x, x^*, x^{**}.
\end{aligned}$$

---

[73] Global solvability would follow from linearity, or by imposing Gale–Nikaido type conditions. (In some of our examples we luckily have linearity.)

Thus

$$\Gamma^\sigma(A(x), x^{**}, y) = \Phi^\sigma(x, y) \qquad \text{for all } \sigma = 1, \ldots, N, \qquad (\Delta)$$

and all (x, y) in appropriate neighborhoods. But this is not yet the desired condensation formula. To satisfy the definition of condensation we must have

$$\Gamma^\sigma(A(x), y) = \Phi(x, y) \text{ free of } x^{**} \qquad \text{for all } \sigma \text{ and all } (x, y), \quad (\Delta\Delta)$$

rather than the precursor formula (Δ). Can we get rid of the argument x^{**} appearing in (Δ)? Miraculously, the answer is in the affirmative.

Since, as shown in Theorem 4.4.6,

$$\frac{\partial \Gamma'^\sigma}{\partial x^{**}} \equiv 0, {}^{74}$$

the precursor Γ'^σ is independent of x^{**}, so that we can define the condensed function Γ^σ by

$$\Gamma^\sigma(w, y) = \Gamma'^\sigma(w, \xi^{**}, y),$$

where ξ^{**} is any admissible value of x^{**}. With this substitution in (Δ), we obtain $(\Delta\Delta)$, so that $A(\cdot)$ and the Γ^σ functions satisfy the definition of condensation.

The preceding exposition provides a constructive method of finding a condensation for the equation system $G(\bar\theta, \theta) = 0$ and the goal function[75] $F(\bar\theta)$, when the smoothness conditions are satisfied by the functions G and F, and rank Conditions (I) and (II) by their Hessians. (In this context we view the use of the implicit function theorem (IFT) as a constructive step. In our main examples constructivity is due to their linearity.)

In the following subsections we illustrate the construction procedures by two familiar examples: the Walrasian, and the augmented two-dimensional inner product. In both cases it turns out that the equation systems to be solved are linear (more precisely, affine), so the results hold globally, and there is no need to involve the IFT, or the more complex Gale–Nikaido conditions.

It turns out, however, that we require a slight extension of Theorem 4.4.6 to obtain R-minimizing[76] condensation. The extension is dealt with in Section 2.4.2.1 on "amplification."

---

[74] Note that, in (Δ), x^{**} is also "hiding" in the argument $x = (x^*, x^{**})$ of the mapping function $A(x) = A(x^*, x^{**})$.

[75] The argument of $F(\cdot)$ is taken as $\bar\theta$, rather than θ, since condensation applies to the primary variables, hence here the components of $\bar\theta$.

[76] Hence minimizing the dimension of the message space for a given covering correspondence $V(\cdot)$. This follows from the collary in Section 4.4.7 of Chapter 4.

Preceding that discussion is a subsection that provide the definitions of the Hessian matrices used in Section 4.4.6 and in sections below.

2.4.2 The Mount–Reiter Condensation Theorem (Sufficiency)

Smoothness assumptions. We are given N functions[+]. $\Phi^\sigma : U \times V \to \mathbb{R}$, $i = 1, \ldots, N$, U a neighborhood of p, and V a neighborhood of q. (The Φ^σ's are called the *candidates* for condensation.) Each Φ^σ belongs to continuous differentiability class $C^{\alpha+1}$ with $\alpha \geq 2$.[+] $N \geq 1$.

To state sufficient conditions of condensibility M/R introduces certain matrices of derivatives of the functions Φ^σ.

To start with, define the matrices (Hessians)

$$H^\sigma(x, y) = H^\sigma = \left(\frac{\partial^2 \Phi^\sigma}{\partial x_i \partial y_j} \right)_{i=1,\ldots,m;\ J=1,\ldots,n} , \qquad \sigma = 1, \ldots, N.$$

Each H^σ is an $m \times n$ matrix (m rows, n columns); written out fully, it is

$$H^\sigma = \begin{pmatrix} \partial^2 \Phi^\sigma/\partial x_1 \partial y_1 \ldots \partial^2 \Phi^\sigma/\partial x_1 \partial y_n \\ \cdots\cdots\cdots\cdots\cdots\cdots\cdots\cdots\cdots \\ \partial^2 \Phi^\sigma/\partial x_m \partial y_1 \ldots \partial^2 \Phi^\sigma/\partial x_m \partial y_n \end{pmatrix}.$$

Now define $H(x, y) = H = (H^1 \vdots H^2 \vdots \cdots \vdots H^n)$, an m by $N \cdot n$ matrix (m rows, $N \cdot n$ columns).

Next, define the column vectors

$$\Phi_x^\sigma(x, y) = \begin{pmatrix} \partial \Phi^\sigma/\partial x_1 \\ \vdots \\ \partial \Phi^\sigma/\partial x_m \end{pmatrix}, \qquad \sigma = 1, \ldots, N.$$

In turn define the "bordered" Hessian $BH = BH(x, y)$ by

$$BH(x, y) = BH = \left(\Phi_x^1 \vdots \Phi_x^2 \vdots \cdots \vdots \Phi_x^N \vdots H^1 \vdots H^2 \vdots \cdots \vdots H^N \right)$$

$$= \left(\Phi_x^1 \vdots \Phi_x^2 \vdots \cdots \vdots \Phi_x^N \vdots H \right)$$

an m by $N + N \cdot n$ matrix (m rows, $N + N \cdot n$ columns).

When the matrices or H^σ or H are evaluated at the point $y = q$, so that they become functions of x alone, this is indicated by an asterisk. Thus, in particular,

$$H^*(x) = H^* = H(x, q) \quad \text{and} \quad H^{\sigma *}(x) = H^\sigma(x, q), \quad \sigma = 1, \ldots, N.$$

[+] In M/R, the Φ^σ functions are written as F_i, and α is written as k. Some of the notation is changed to avoid confusion with our mechanism design notation.

The Condensation Theorem. Theorem 4.4.6 (ii) states sufficient conditions for condensing the functions $\Phi^1(x, y), \ldots, \Phi^N(x, y)$ respectively into functions

$$\Gamma^1(A_1(x), \ldots, A_r(x), y), \qquad \Gamma^2(A_1(x), \ldots, A_r(x), y), \ldots,$$

$\Gamma^N(A_1(x), \ldots, A_r(x), y)$ so that there is a neighborhood $W' \times V$ of a point (p', q), $p' \in \mathbb{R}^r$, $W' \subset \mathbb{R}^r$, $1 \leq r < N$, and $\Gamma^\sigma : W' \times V \to \mathbb{R}$ such that for every $(x, y) \in U \times V$, and every $\sigma \in \{1, \ldots, N\}$,

$$\Phi^\sigma(x, y) = \Gamma^\sigma(A_1, (x), \ldots, A_r(x), y). \tag{+}$$

Note that only the primary variables x are being condensed.

The sufficient conditions are

(I) For all $(x, y) \in U \times V$

$$\text{rank}\,(BH(x, y)) \leqq r$$

and

(II) rank $(H^*)) = r$ for every $x \in U$.

When (I) and (II) are satisfied, there exist r functions $A_1(x), \ldots, A_r(x)$, where the functions $A_\mu(\cdot)$, $\mu = 1, \ldots, r$ are of class C^α, a neighborhood W' of $p' \in ((A_1(p), \ldots, A_r(p))$ in $\mathbb{R}^r$, and N functions Γ^σ of class C^α such that (+) holds for all $(x, y) \in U' \times V' \subset X \times Y$.

2.4.2.1 Amplification

This subsection is devoted to an extension of the M/R Theorem A.3.(ii), essential for applications to mechanism design problems. The extension will be referred to as *amplification*.

First, we present a simple example that shows the need for an extension. In this example $N = 1$, $m > 2$, $n = 1$, and the real-valued function to be condensed is

$$\Phi(x, y) = y_1 \varphi_1(x) + \varphi_2(x);$$

e.g., more specifically, with $n = 3$,

$$\Phi(x, y) = y_1(x_1 + x_2 + x_3) + x_1 x_2 x_3,$$

where $x_i > 0$, $i = 1, 2, 3$ and $x_1 \neq x_2 \neq x_3 \neq x_1$. ($y_1$ is a real number and so is every x_i, $i = 1, 2, 3$). Here

$$H(x, y) = \binom{1}{1} = H(x, q) = H^*,$$

and

$$BH(x, y) = \begin{pmatrix} y_1 + x_2 x_3 \vdots 1 \\ y_1 + x_1 x_3 \vdots 1 \\ y_1 + x_1 x_2 \vdots 1 \end{pmatrix}.$$

Now by direct inspection we observe that $\varphi_1(x) = x_1 + x_2 + x_3$ and $\varphi_2(x) = x_1 x_2 x_3$ can be used as the "condensing" functions $A_1(\cdot)$, $A_2(\cdot)$ of Theorem 4.4.6, with $r = 2$, and[78] $\Gamma : \mathbb{R}^2_{++} \times \mathbb{R}$, with

$$\Phi(x, y) \equiv \Gamma(A_1(x), A_2(x), y),$$

where

$$\Gamma(w_1, w_2, y) = y_1 w_1 + w_2 \qquad \text{and} \qquad y = y_1$$

and

$$A_1(x) = x_1 + x_2 + x_3, \qquad A_2(x) = x_1 x_2 x_3.$$

However, condition (II) of the theorem is not satisfied for $r = 2$ since rank $H^2 = 1$.[79] Hence the need for an extension ("amplification") of Theorem 4.4.6.

The amplification remedy can be illustrated on the preceding example as follows. We introduce an auxiliary[(*)] secondary variable $\hat{y}_2$, with the requirement that the value of $\hat{y}_2$ at the point q be $q_2 = 1$, and define the amplified function – to be condensed – as

$$\hat{\Phi}(x, y) = y_1 \varphi_1(x) + \hat{y}_2 \varphi_2(x), \qquad y = (y_1, \hat{y}_2).^{[80]}$$

The amplified Hessians are as follows:

$$\hat{H}(x, y) = \begin{pmatrix} 1 \vdots x_2 & x_3 \\ 1 \vdots x_1 & x_3 \\ 1 \vdots x_1 & x_2 \end{pmatrix} = \hat{H}^*,$$

with rank $(\hat{H}^*) = 2$

---

[78] More precisely, the domain of Γ is a subset of $\mathbb{R}^2_{++}$ because of the inequalities $x_1 \neq x_2 \neq x_3 \neq x_1$.

[79] For $r = 1$, Condition (I) is violated, since rank $(BH) = 2$ when $x :> 0$ and $x_1 \neq x_2 \neq x_3 \neq x_1$.

[(*)] Here y_1 is called an original secondary variable.

[80] Note the change in the meaning of the symbol y!

For the bordered Hessian, we have

$$B\hat{H}(x, y) = \begin{pmatrix} y_1 + \hat{y}_2 x_2 x_3 & \vdots & 1 & x_2 x_3 \\ y_1 + \hat{y}_2 x_1 x_3 & \vdots & 1 & x_1 x_3 \\ y_1 + \hat{y}_2 x_1 x_2 & \vdots & 1 & x_1 x_2 \end{pmatrix}.$$

Hence rank $(B\hat{H}(x, y)) \leqq 2$, since the first column is a linear combination of the other two columns. In fact, rank $(B\hat{H}(x, y)) = 2$ under the inequalities assumed for the x_i's. So Theorem 4.4.6 works for the amplified function $\hat{\Phi}$.

When $N > 1$, more than one auxiliary-secondary variable may be present. (In what follows, we may sometimes omit the circumflex symbol ($\wedge$) when the situation is clear from the context.)

2.4.2.2 Mechanism Design

Returning to the mechanism design model, the functions $G_s(\bar{\theta}, \theta)$ correspond to the functions $\hat{\Phi}^\sigma$ – they are among the "candidates" – the functions to be condensed. $\bar{\theta}$ corresponds to x, the vector of primary variables to be condensed, while θ (without the overbar) corresponds to the "original" (not auxiliary) secondary variables. Amplification is needed when $G_s(\bar{\theta}, \theta)$ is of the form

$$G_s(\bar{\theta}, \theta) = G_{s1}(\bar{\theta}, \theta) + G_{s2}(\bar{\theta}).$$

Therefore, we introduce an auxiliary variable $\hat{y}_s$, so that after amplification we are dealing with

$$\hat{G}_s(\bar{\theta}, y) = G_{s1}(\bar{\theta}, \theta) + \hat{y}_s G_{s2}(\bar{\theta}), \qquad s = 1, \ldots, d,$$

where

$$y = (\theta, \hat{y}), \qquad \hat{y} = (\hat{y}_1, \ldots, \hat{y}d).$$

(In fact, some $\hat{y}_s$'s may be superfluous when $G_{s_2}(\bar{\theta}) \equiv 0$, i.e., when at this point, there is no additive term depending on $\bar{\theta}$ but free of θ. However, uniform notation seems desirable.)

Hence,

$$
\hat{H}^{\sigma} =
\begin{pmatrix}
\hat{G}^{s}_{\bar{\theta}_1\theta_1} & \ddots & \hat{G}^{s}_{\bar{\theta}_1\theta_n} & \vdots & \hat{G}^{s}_{\bar{\theta}_1\hat{y}_1} & \ddots & \hat{G}^{s}_{\bar{\theta}_1\hat{y}_d} \\
\vdots & & \vdots & \vdots & \vdots & \vdots & \vdots \\
\hat{G}^{s}_{\bar{\theta}_m\theta_1} & \ddots & \hat{G}^{s}_{\bar{\theta}_m\theta_n} & \vdots & \hat{G}^{s}_{\bar{\theta}_m\hat{y}_1} & \ddots & \hat{G}^{s}_{\bar{\theta}_m\hat{y}_d}
\end{pmatrix}
$$

and

$$
B\hat{H} =
\begin{pmatrix}
\hat{G}^{1}_{\bar{\theta}_1} & \ddots & \hat{G}^{d}_{\bar{\theta}_1} & \vdots & & \vdots & & \vdots & & \vdots \\
& & & \vdots & \hat{H}^1 & \vdots & \hat{H}^2 & \vdots & \ddots & \vdots & \hat{H}^d \\
\vdots & & \vdots & & & \vdots & & \vdots & & \vdots \\
\hat{G}^{1}_{\bar{\theta}_m} & & \hat{G}^{d}_{\bar{\theta}_m} & \vdots & & \vdots & & \vdots & & \vdots
\end{pmatrix}
$$

where

$$
\hat{G}^{s}_{\bar{\theta}_i\theta_j} = \frac{\partial^2 \hat{G}_s}{\partial \bar{\theta}_i \partial \theta_j}
\quad \text{and} \quad
\hat{G}^{s}_{\bar{\theta}_i\hat{y}_t} = \frac{\partial^2 \hat{G}_s}{\partial \bar{\theta}_i \partial \hat{y}_t}.
$$

2.4.3 Walrasian Mechanism Construction

As above, the Walrasian Goal function is

$$
F = \frac{b_2 - a_2}{a_1 + b_1},
$$

and we write

$$
\bar{F} =: F(\bar{\theta}) = \frac{\bar{b}_2 - \bar{a}_2}{\bar{a}_1 + \bar{b}_1},
$$

where, by hypothesis,

$$
\bar{a}_1 + \bar{b}_1 > 0 \quad \text{and} \quad \bar{a}_2 + \bar{b}_2 > 0.
$$

The method of rectangles yields a (reflexive) covering with the equilibrium functions $G^1(\bar{\theta}, a)$, $G^2(\bar{\theta}, b)$ given by

$$
G^1(\bar{\theta}, a) = 0 : a_1\bar{F} + \overbrace{(\bar{b}_1\bar{F} - \bar{b}_2)}^{\Phi^1} + a_2 = 0 \tag{0}
$$

$$
G^2(\bar{\theta}, b) = 0 : b_1\bar{F} - b_2 + \overbrace{(\bar{b}_2 - \bar{b}_1\bar{F})}^{\Phi^2} = 0 \tag{00}
$$

We also set

$$
\Phi^3 =: F(\bar{\theta}). \tag{000}
$$

The three expressions, labeled Φ^i, $1 = 1, 2, 3$, are our candidates for condensation.

2.4.3.1 Recapitulating Notation

$$\bar{\theta} = (\bar{a}, \bar{b}); \qquad \theta = (a, b), \qquad \bar{a} = (\bar{a}_1, \bar{a}_2),$$
$$b = (\bar{b}_1, \bar{b}_2) \qquad a = (a_1, a_2), \qquad b = (b_1, b_2)$$

$$\bar{F} =: \frac{\bar{b}_2 - \bar{a}_2}{\bar{b}_1 + \bar{a}_1}.$$

As yet not amplified candidates for condensation $\rightarrow$
$$\begin{cases} \Phi^1 \equiv a_1 \bar{F} + (\bar{b}_1 \bar{F} - \bar{b}_2) + a_2 \\ \Phi^2 = b_1 \bar{F} - b_2 + (\bar{b}_2 - \bar{b}_1 \bar{F}) \\ \Phi^3 = \bar{F}. \end{cases}$$

2.4.3.2 Need for Amplification

Calculate the (nonamplified) matrix H:

Without amplification (i.e., with $y = (a_1, b_1, a_2, b_2)$), we find

$$H^1 = \begin{array}{c|cccc} & /\partial a_1 & /\partial a_2 & /\partial b_1 & /\partial b_2 \\ \hline /\partial \bar{a}_1 & \bar{F}_{\bar{a}_1} & 0 & 0 & 0 \\ /\partial \bar{a}_2 & \bar{F}_{\bar{a}_2} & 0 & 0 & 0 \\ /\partial \bar{b}_1 & \bar{F}_{\bar{b}_1} & 0 & 0 & 0 \\ /\partial \bar{b}_2 & \bar{F}_{\bar{b}_2} & 0 & 0 & 0 \end{array},$$

where

$$\bar{F} = \frac{\bar{b}_2 - \bar{a}_2}{\bar{b}_1 + \bar{a}_1}.$$

Then

$$H^1 = (\bar{F}_{\bar{\theta}} \underset{\sim}{0} \underset{\sim}{0} \underset{\sim}{0}),$$

where $\underset{\sim}{0}$ is a 4×1 column vector of zeros.

Similarly,

$$H^2 = (\underset{\sim}{0} \underset{\sim}{0} \tilde{F}_{\bar{\theta}} \underset{\sim}{0}).$$

Since

$$\Phi^3 = \bar{F},$$

we get

$$H^3 = (0000).$$

Hence, $H = (H^1 \, H^2 \, H^3) = (\bar{F}_{\bar\theta}000 \vdots 00 \, \bar{F}_{\bar\theta}0 \vdots 0000).$

So (with or without Φ^3), rank H = rank H^* = 1.

However, it is clear that in fact the four primary variables in $\bar\theta = (\bar{a}_1, \bar{a}_2, \bar{b}_1, \bar{b}_2)$ appearing in Φ^1, Φ^2, Φ^3 can be condensed into two functions. In fact, setting

$$z_1 = \bar{F}, \qquad z_2 = b_1 \bar{F} - \bar{b}_2,$$

we obtain

$$\Phi^1 = a_1 z_1 + a_2 + z_2$$
$$\Phi^2 = b_1 z_1 - b_2 - z_2$$
$$\Phi^3 = z_1.$$

Without amplification, Theorem 4.4.6 (ii) with $r = 2$ is not satisfied, since rank $H^* \neq 2$, so Condition II is violated.

This illustrates the need for the amplification procedure.

2.4.3.3

We introduce the auxiliary secondary variables $\hat{y}_1$, $\hat{y}_2$, $\hat{y}_3$, (one for each Φ^i function), so that the amplified functions $\hat{\Phi}^i$ are

$$\hat{\Phi}^1 = a_1 \bar{F} + a_2 + (\bar{b}_1 \bar{F} - \bar{b}_2) \cdot \hat{y}_1$$
$$\hat{\Phi}^2 = b_1 \bar{F} - b_2 + (\bar{b}_2 - \bar{b}_1 \bar{F}) \cdot \hat{y}_2$$
$$\hat{\Phi}^3 = \bar{F} \cdot \hat{y}_3.$$

(Note that $\bar{b}_2 - \bar{b}_1 \bar{F} = \frac{\bar{b}_1 \bar{a}_2 + \bar{b}_2 \bar{a}_1}{\bar{b}_1 + \bar{a}_1}$.)

Then

		a_1	a_2	b_1	b_2	$\hat{y}_1$	$\hat{y}_2$	$\hat{y}_3$	
	$\bar{a}_1$	$\bar{F}_{\bar{a}_1}$	0	0	0	$\bar{b}_1 \bar{F}_{\bar{a}_1}$	0	0	
$\hat{H}^1 =$	$\bar{a}_2$	$\bar{F}_{\bar{a}_2}$	0	0	0	$\bar{b}_1 \bar{F}_{\bar{a}_2}$	0	0	$= \hat{H}^{*1}.$
	$\bar{b}_1$	$\bar{F}_{\bar{b}_1}$	0	0	0	$\bar{F} + \bar{b}_1 \bar{F}_{\bar{b}_1}$	0	0	
	$\bar{b}_2$	$\bar{F}_{\bar{b}_2}$	0	0	0	$-1 + \bar{b}_1 \bar{F}_{\bar{b}_2}$	0	0	

Next,

$$
\hat{H}^2 = \begin{array}{c|cccc|c|c|c}
 & a_1 & a_2 & b_1 & b_2 & \hat{y}_1 & \hat{y}_2 & \hat{y}_3 \\
\hline
\bar{a}_1 & 0 & 0 & \bar{F}_{\bar{a}_1} & 0 & 0 & -\bar{b}_1 \bar{F}_{\bar{a}_1} & 0 \\
\bar{a}_2 & 0 & 0 & \bar{F}_{\bar{a}_2} & 0 & 0 & -\bar{b}_1 \bar{F}_{\bar{a}_2} & 0 \\
\bar{b}_1 & 0 & 0 & \bar{F}_{\bar{b}_1} & 0 & 0 & -\bar{b}_1 \bar{F}_{\bar{b}_1} - \bar{F} & 0 \\
\bar{b}_2 & 0 & 0 & \bar{F}_{\bar{b}_2} & 0 & 0 & -\bar{b}_1 \bar{F}_{\bar{b}_2} + 1 & 0
\end{array} = \hat{H}^{*2}.
$$

Finally,

$$
\hat{H}^3 = \frac{a_1 \quad a_2 \quad b_1 \quad b_2 \quad \hat{y}_1 \quad \hat{y}_2 \quad \hat{y}_3}{(0 \quad 0 \quad 0 \quad 0 \quad 0 \quad 0 \quad \bar{F}_{\bar{\theta}})} = \hat{H}^{*3} \approx (\bar{F}_{\bar{\theta}}).
$$

Hence, omitting 0-columns and repetitious columns, we have

$$
\hat{H}^* \approx \left(\bar{F}_{\bar{\theta}} : \bar{b}_1 \bar{F}_{\bar{\theta}} + \begin{bmatrix} 0 \\ 0 \\ \bar{F} \\ -1 \end{bmatrix} \right).
$$

Hence, performing elementary operations, we have

$$
\hat{H}^* \approx \begin{bmatrix} \bar{F}_{\bar{a}_1} & \vdots & 0 \\ \bar{F}_{\bar{a}_2} & \vdots & 0 \\ \bar{F}_{\bar{b}_1} & \vdots & \bar{F} \\ \bar{F}_{\bar{b}_2} & \vdots & -1 \end{bmatrix} = \begin{bmatrix} -\dfrac{\bar{b}_2 - \bar{a}_2}{(\bar{b}_1 + \bar{a}_1)^2} & 0 \\[2ex] -\dfrac{1}{\bar{b}_1 + \bar{a}_1} & 0 \\[2ex] \dfrac{1}{\bar{b}_1 + \bar{a}_1} & \bar{F} \\[2ex] -\dfrac{\bar{b}_2 - \bar{a}_2}{(\bar{b}_1 + \bar{a}_1)^2} & -1 \end{bmatrix}.
$$

Consider the submatrix that consists of the second and last rows of $\hat{H}^*$,

$$
\begin{bmatrix} \bar{F}_{\bar{a}_2} & 0 \\ \bar{F}_{\bar{b}_2} & -1 \end{bmatrix},
$$

whose determinant $\bar{F}_{\bar{a}_2} = \frac{1}{\bar{b}_1 + \bar{a}_1} \neq 0$ by hypothesis.
   Hence rank $H^* = 2$.

Now look at BH to check Condition (I).

	$\hat{\Phi}^1$	$\hat{\Phi}^2$	$\hat{\Phi}^3$	$(\hat{\Phi}^1, \hat{y}_1)$	$(\hat{\Phi}^3, \hat{y}_3)$
$\bar{a}_1$	$(a_1 + \hat{y}_1\bar{b}_1)\bar{F}_{\bar{a}_1}$	$(b_1 - \bar{b}_1\hat{y}_2)\bar{F}_{\bar{a}_1}$	$\hat{y}_3\bar{F}_{\bar{a}_1}$	$\bar{b}_1\bar{F}_{\bar{a}_1}$	$\bar{F}_{\bar{a}_1}$
$\bar{a}_2$	$(a_1 + \hat{y}_1\bar{b}_1)\bar{F}_{\bar{a}_2}$	$(b_1 - \bar{b}_1\hat{y}_2)\bar{F}_{\bar{a}_2}$	$\hat{y}_3\bar{F}_{\bar{a}_2}$	$\bar{b}_1\bar{F}_{\bar{a}_2}$	$\bar{F}_{\bar{a}_2}$
$\bar{b}_1$	$(a_1 - \hat{y}_1\bar{b}_1)\bar{F}_{\bar{a}_1} + \bar{F}_{\hat{y}_1}$	$(b_1 - \bar{b}_1\hat{y}_2)\bar{F}_{\bar{b}_1} - \hat{y}_2\bar{F}_2$	$\hat{y}_3\bar{F}_{\bar{b}_1}$	$\bar{F} + \bar{b}_1\bar{F}_{\bar{b}_1}$	$\bar{F}_{\bar{b}_2}$
$\bar{b}_2$	$(a_1 + \hat{y}_1\bar{b}_1)\bar{F}_{\bar{a}_1} - \hat{y}_1$	$(b_1 - \bar{b}_1\hat{y}_2)\bar{F}_{\bar{b}_2} + \hat{y}_2$	$\hat{y}_3\bar{F}_{\bar{b}_2}$	$-1\bar{b}_1\bar{F}_{\bar{b}_2}$	$\bar{F}_{\bar{b}_2}$

where $BH \approx$ is shown at left of the table.

The above is a matrix BH rank-equivalent.

Next, by subtraction of multiples of columns, we obtain

$$BH \approx \begin{array}{cccc} \hat{\Phi}^1 & \hat{\Phi}^2 & (\hat{\Phi}^1, \hat{y}_1) & (\hat{\Phi}^3, \hat{y}_3) \\ \begin{pmatrix} 0 & 0 & \vdots & -1 & \vdots & \bar{F}_{\bar{a}_1} \\ 0 & 0 & \vdots & 0 & \vdots & \bar{F}_{\bar{a}_2} \\ \bar{F} & -\bar{F} & \vdots & \bar{F} & \vdots & \bar{F}_{\bar{b}_1} \\ -1 & +1 & \vdots & -1 & \vdots & \bar{F}_{\bar{b}_2} \end{pmatrix} \end{array}.$$

Clearly, the first two columns are eliminated (by the 3rd column). Hence, only the last two columns remain, and we conclude that

$$\text{rank } (BH) \leqq 2,$$

and so condition (I) of Theorem 4.4.6 (i) is satisfied.[81]

We are thus entitled to apply the theorem *in amplified form*. We shall show in the next section that $\bar{\theta}$ can indeed be condensed to two functions of its four components $(\bar{a}_1, \bar{a}_2, \bar{b}_1, \bar{b}_2)$. Not surprisingly, the two functions are

$$\bar{F} = F(\bar{\theta}) = \frac{\bar{b}_2 - \bar{a}_2}{\bar{b}_1 + \bar{a}_1} \qquad \text{and} \qquad \bar{b}_2 - \bar{b}_1\bar{F}.$$

THE "ALGORITHM" FOR CONDENSATION (M/R NOTATION). Although Theorem 4.4.6 (ii) is an existence theorem, it is important to note that the proof provides a "constructive"[82] procedure for condensation when the sufficient conditions are satisfied. We recapitulate the notation and procedure.

The condensing functions $A_1(x), \ldots, A_r(x)$ are obtained as follows. Since, by condition (II), the matrix H^* has rank r, there exists a subvector

---

[81] In fact, rank $(BH) = 2$, as seen if we take rows 2 and 4, so $(BH) = \bar{F}_{\bar{a}_2} = -\frac{1}{\bar{b}_1 + \bar{a}_1} \neq 0$ by hypothesis.

[82] A step in the construction involves solving a system of equations that can be nonlinear. In such a case "solving" might be difficult, or require resort to computational procedures that are approximate.

$\xi = (\xi_1, \ldots, \xi_r)$ of $x = (x_1, \ldots, x_m)$ and a subset of r columns such that the submatrix $\tilde{H}$ formed from the r ξ-rows and the r columns is nonsingular. Without loss of generality, let $\xi = (x_1, \ldots, x_r)$. Each column of H^* is of the form

$$\begin{pmatrix} \partial^2 \Phi^\sigma / \partial x_1 \partial y_j \\ \vdots \\ \partial^2 \Phi^\sigma / \partial x_r \partial y_j \end{pmatrix}$$

for some $i \in \{1, \ldots, N\}$, $j \in \{1, \ldots, n\}$. Let the columns of the nonsingular matrix $\tilde{H}$ correspond to $i = \alpha_1, \ldots, \alpha_r$ and $j = \beta_1, \ldots, \beta_r$. Then the condensing functions $A_1(x), \ldots, A_r(x)$ are defined as follows:

$$A_1(x) = \left. \frac{\partial \Phi^\sigma{}_{\alpha_1}}{\partial y_{\beta_1}} \right|_{y = q}, \ldots, \quad A_r = \left. \frac{\partial \Phi^\sigma{}_{\alpha_r}}{\partial y_{\beta_r}} \right|_{y = q}$$

In turn the functions Γ^σ (the condensed counterparts of the Φ^σ) are given by

$$\Gamma^\sigma(w_1, \ldots, w_r, x_{r+1}, \ldots, x_m, y)$$
$$= \Phi^\sigma(h_1(w_1, \ldots, w_r, x_{r+1}, \ldots, x_m), \ldots, \phi_r(w_1, \ldots, w_r, x_{r+1}, \ldots, x_m),$$
$$x_{r+1}, \ldots, x_m, y),$$

where the functions $h_1(\cdot), \ldots, h_r(\cdot)$ are the respective solutions for $(x_1, \ldots, x_r)$ of the equation system

$$w_i = A_i(x_1, \ldots, x_m), i = 1, \ldots, r. \tag{$\wedge$}$$

(The local solvability is guaranteed by the implicit function theorem, since the Jacobian $\tilde{H}$ is nonsingular by hypothesis, the $A_\mu(x)$ functions are of class at least C^2 in view of the smoothness assumptions on the Φ^σ's, and – by construction – there exist values of x and w satisfying ($\wedge$). To obtain *global* solvability, additional assumptions would have to be made, e.g., those in Gale and Nikaido. We are treating the solution of ($\wedge$) as a step in the "algorithm." In practice, this may turn out to be a stumbling block.)

2.4.3.4 Constructing the Condensing Functions for the Amplified Walrasian

We show first how to obtain the *condensing functions* $A_1(x)$, $A_2(x)$. Here $\bar{\theta}$ corresponds to x and $(\theta, \hat{y})$ to y in the M/R notation. Take the columns corresponding to the pair

(Φ^1, a_1) and $(\Phi^1, \hat{y})$; then, by the "algorithm,"

$$A^1(\bar{\theta}) = \frac{\partial \Phi^1}{\partial a_1} \qquad A^2(\bar{\theta}) = \frac{\partial \Phi^1}{\partial \hat{y}_1}.$$

But

$$\frac{\partial \Phi^1}{\partial a_1} = \bar{F}^1, \qquad \frac{\partial \Phi^1}{\partial \hat{y}_1} = (\bar{b}^1 \bar{F} - \bar{b}_2).$$

These are, of course, the obvious condensations.

Having found the condensing mapping $A(x)$, the next step is to construct the condensed counterparts, denoted by Γ^σ, of the originally given functions Φ^σ, so that

$$\Phi^\sigma(x, y) = \Gamma^\sigma(A_r, (x), \ldots, A_r(x), y) \qquad \sigma = 1, \ldots, N. \qquad (+)$$

In the Walrasian example (with a slight change in notation) we seek the functions $\Gamma^1, \Gamma^2, \Gamma^i (w_1, w_2, \theta)$, $i = 1, 2, 3$ such that for all $\bar{\theta}, \theta$ in Θ, $\Phi^i = \Gamma^i(\bar{\theta}, (\theta, \hat{y}))\big|_{\hat{y}=(1,1,1)} = \Gamma^i(A_1(\bar{\theta}), A_2(\bar{\theta})\theta)$ $i = 1, 2, 3$.

Consider a 2×2 submatrix $\tilde{H}$ of H^* of rank 2 guaranteeing that rank $H^* = 2$. Specifically, let $\tilde{H}$ consist of elements in rows of H^* corresponding to differentiation with respect to $\bar{a}_2$ and $\bar{b}_2$, and columns corresponding to the differentiation of Φ^1 with respect to a_1 and $\hat{y}_1$.

That is,

$$\tilde{H} = \begin{array}{c} \\ /\partial \bar{a}_2 \\ /\partial \bar{b}_2 \end{array} \overset{\displaystyle (\Phi^1, /\partial a_1) \quad (\Phi^1, /\partial \hat{y}_1)}{\left[\begin{array}{cc} \bar{F}_{\bar{a}_2} & \bar{b}_1 \bar{F}_{\bar{a}_2} \\ \bar{F}_{\bar{b}_2} & -1 + \bar{b}_1 \bar{F}_{\bar{b}_2} \end{array} \right]}.$$

Writing $L = \bar{b}_1 + \bar{a}_1$, we have

$$\det \tilde{H} \begin{vmatrix} -\dfrac{1}{L} & -\dfrac{\bar{b}_1}{L} \\ \dfrac{1}{L} & -1 + \dfrac{\bar{b}_1}{L} \end{vmatrix} = \frac{1}{L} \neq 0.$$

As an intermediate step, introduce the equation in general notation:

$$w_1 = A_1(x), \quad w_2 = A_2(x), \ldots, \quad w_r = A_r(x);$$

hence in the Walrasian example $(++)$ $w_1 = \bar{F}$, $w_2 = \bar{b}_1 \bar{F} - \bar{b}_2$.

Next, partition the vector $\bar{\theta}$ of the primary variables into $\bar{\theta} = (\bar{\theta}^*, \bar{\theta}^{**})$ where the elements of $\bar{\theta}^*$ correspond to the variables that index the rows of $\tilde{H}$. Then $\bar{\theta}^* = (\bar{a}_2, \bar{b}_2)$, $\bar{\theta}^{**} = (\bar{a}_1, \bar{b}_1)$. Note that $\tilde{H}$ is the Jacobian of the system $(++)$ with respect to the elements of $\bar{\theta}^*$, and that the conditions for the applicability of the implicit function theorem are satisfied.[83]

Therefore, at least *locally*,[84] system $(++)$ can be solved for $\bar{\theta}^*$ in terms of w_1, w_2, and $\bar{\theta}^{**}$. The solution is written as $\bar{\theta}^* = \phi(w, \bar{\theta}^{**})$ or, more explicitly, as

$$\begin{cases} \bar{a}_2 = \phi_1(w_1, w_2, \bar{a}_1, \bar{b}_1), \\ \bar{b}_2 = \phi_2(w_1, w_2, \bar{a}_1, \bar{b}_1). \end{cases}$$

In the Walrasian example, system $(++)$ is

$$w_1 = \frac{\bar{b}_2 - \bar{a}_2}{\bar{b}_1 + \bar{a}_1}, \qquad w_2 = \bar{b}_1 \cdot \frac{\bar{b}_2 - \bar{a}_2}{\bar{b}_1 + \bar{a}_1} - \bar{b}_2.$$

Solving for $\bar{a}_2$ and $\bar{b}_2$, we obtain

$$\bar{a}_2 = \phi_1(w_1, w_2, \bar{a}_1, \bar{b}_1) = -(\bar{a}_1 w_1 - w_2)$$
$$\bar{b}_2 = \phi_2(w_1, w_2, \bar{a}_1, \bar{b}_1) = \bar{b}_1 w_1 - w_2.$$

We are now ready to construct the functions Γ^1, Γ^2, and Γ^3. The general recipe is

$$\Gamma^\sigma(w, y) = \Phi^\sigma\left(\overbrace{\phi(w, x^{**})}^{= x^*}, x^{**}, y \right), \qquad \sigma = 1, \ldots, N.$$

(Contrary to appearances, the RHS does *not* depend on $x^{**!}$) Hence, in the Walrasian example,

$$\Gamma^i(w, \theta) = \Phi^i(\phi(w, \bar{\theta}^{**}), \bar{\theta}^{**}, (\theta, \hat{y}))\big|_{\hat{y}=(1,1,1)}, \qquad i = 1, 2, 3.$$

In particular,

$$\Gamma^1(w_1, \theta) = a_1 \frac{\phi_2 - \phi_1}{\bar{b}_1 + \bar{a}_1} + a_2 + \left(\bar{b}_1 \cdot \frac{\phi_2 - \phi_1}{\bar{b}_1 + \bar{a}_1} - \phi_2 \right) \hat{y}_1 \bigg|_{\hat{y}_1 = 1},$$

where ϕ_j stands for $\phi_j(w, \bar{a}_1, \bar{b}_1)$, $j = 1, 2$; $w = (w_1, w_2)$, and $\theta = (a_1, a_2, b_1, b_2)$.

Noting that

$$\frac{\phi_2 - \phi_1}{\bar{b}_1 + \bar{a}_1} = \frac{(\bar{b}_1 w_1 - w_2) + (\bar{a}_1 w_1 + w_2)}{\bar{b}_1 + \bar{a}_1} = \frac{(\bar{b}_1 + \bar{a}_1) w_1}{\bar{b}_1 + \bar{a}_1} = w_1,$$

[83] By hypothesis, the functions $A_\mu(\cdot)$, $\mu = 1, 2$, are of at least class C^1, the Jacobian is non-singular, and the equations $(++)$ are satisfied at $\bar{\theta} = \bar{p}$ since the A_μ are partial derivatives at that point.

[84] Also globally if additional assumptions on $\bar{H}$ along the lines of Gale–Nikaido are made.

we find that

$$\Gamma^1(w, \theta) = a_1 w_1 + a_2 + (\bar{b}_1 w_1 - (\bar{b}_1 w_1 + w_2))$$
$$= a_1 w_1 + a_2 + w_2.$$

In turn

$$\Gamma^2(w, y) \equiv b_1 \bar{F} - b_2 + (\bar{b}_2 - \bar{b}_1 \bar{F}) \hat{y}_2 \big|_{\hat{y}_2 = 1}$$
$$= b_1 \frac{\phi_2 - \phi_1}{\bar{b}_1 + \bar{a}_1} - b_2 + \left(\phi_2 - \frac{\phi_2 - \phi_1}{\bar{b}_1 + \bar{a}_1} \right)$$
$$= b_1 w_1 - b_2 + [(\bar{b}_1 w_1 - w_2) - \bar{b}_1 w_1]$$
$$= b_1 w_1 - b_2 - w_2,$$

and

$$\Gamma^3(w, y) = \bar{F} \cdot \hat{y}_3 \big|_{\hat{y}_2 = 1} = \frac{\phi_2 - \phi_1}{\bar{b}_1 + \bar{a}_1} = w_1.$$

2.4.3.5 Verifying the Privacy-Preserving Property of the Mechanism

We observe that each $\Gamma^i(w, \theta)$, $i = 1, 2$, inherits the property of being independent of θ_j, $j \neq i$, which means that we have a privacy-preserving mechanism. In the usual mechanism notation, $\Gamma^i(w, y)$ is written as $g^i(m, \theta^i)$ and $\Gamma^3(w, y) = h(w) \equiv m_1$. The message space M is a subset of $\mathbb{R}^2$, and the equilibrium equations are

$$g^1(m, \theta^1) \equiv g^1(m, a) \equiv a_1 m_1 + a_2 + m_2 = 0,$$
$$g^2(m, \theta^2) \equiv g^2(m, b) \equiv b_1 m_1 - b_2 - m_2 = 0.$$

2.4.3.6 Verification of F-Optimality and Existence

It remains to show that this mechanism realizes the goal function

$$F(a, b) \equiv \frac{b_2 - a_2}{b_1 + a_1}.$$

F-optimality. Let $g_i(m, a) = 0$ and $g_2(m, b) = 0$, that is,

$$a_1 m_1 + a_2 + m_2 = 0$$
$$b_1 m_1 - b_2 - m_2 = 0,$$

hence

$$(a_1 + b_1)m_1 + (a_2 - b_2) = 0.$$

Therefore,

$$h(m) \equiv m_1 = \frac{b_2 - a_2}{b_1 + a_1} = F(\theta),$$

as was to be shown.

Existence. By hypothesis, the covering $V(\cdot)$ is self-belonging – for every $\theta \in \Theta, \theta \in V(\theta)$ – hence $G(\theta, \theta) = 0$.

Now, by construction in Theorem 4.4.6,

$$\phi^{\sigma\prime}(x, y) = \Gamma^\sigma(A(x), y) \qquad \text{for all } (x, y).$$

In the Walrasian example, $\sigma = 1, 2, \phi^\sigma(x, y) = 0 \Leftrightarrow G^\sigma(\bar{\theta}, \theta) = 0$.
Also,

$$A^1(x) = A^1(\bar{\theta}) = \left.\frac{\partial \hat{\Phi}^1}{\partial a_1}\right|_{\hat{y}_1=1} = \bar{F}^1 \left(= \frac{\partial G^1}{\partial a_1}\right)$$

$$A^2(x) = A^2(\bar{\theta}) = \left.\frac{\partial \hat{\Phi}^1}{\partial \hat{y}_1}\right|_{\hat{y}_1=1} = \bar{b}_1 \bar{F} - \bar{b}_2.$$

We have

$$G^1(\theta, \theta) = 0 \text{ (by self-belonging)}.$$

Hence,

$$g^i(w, \bar{\theta}^i) = 0 \text{ when } w = A(\bar{\theta}). \text{ That is, } g^i(w, \theta^i) = 0 \text{ if } w_i = A^i(\theta).$$

This proves existence. Hence, the mechanism constructed by the condensation method is decentralized, and does realize the Walrasian goal function.

2.4.4 Phase Two of Mechanism Design via Condensation for the Augmented Two-Dimensional Inner Product

2.4.4.1 Example 2. Mechanism Construction By Condensation

In this section we design a (maximal A-set) mechanism that realizes the goal function $F(\theta) = a_1 b_1 + a_2 b_2 + b_3$, defined on $\Theta = \mathbb{R}^5 \backslash \{b_1 \neq 0\}$. We use the equilibrium equation system $G(\bar{\theta}, \theta) = 0$ obtained by rRM in phase one, with the first equation ($G^1 = 0$) divided by $\bar{b}_1 \neq 0$.[85] In the notation used previously, the system is as follows:

$$G^1(\bar{\theta}, a) \equiv a_1 + a_2 \left(\frac{\bar{b}_2}{\bar{b}_1}\right) - \left(\bar{a}_1 + \bar{a}_2 \left(\frac{\bar{b}_2}{\bar{b}_1}\right)\right) = 0$$

$$G^{21}(\bar{\theta}, b) \equiv b_1 \cdot \left(\frac{\bar{b}_2}{\bar{b}_1}\right) - b_2 = 0$$

$$G^{22}(\bar{\theta}, b) \equiv b_1 \cdot \left(\bar{a}_1 + \bar{a}_2 \left(\frac{\bar{b}_2}{\bar{b}_1}\right)\right) + b_3 - F(\bar{\theta}) = 0.$$

In order to facilitate the calculation of the Hessians used in the condensation procedure, we use the following abbreviations:

$$\bar{F} = \bar{a}_1 \bar{b}_1 + \bar{a}_2 \bar{b}_2 + \bar{b}_3 = F(\bar{\theta})$$

$$\bar{B} = \frac{\bar{b}_2}{\bar{b}_1}$$

$$\bar{K} = \bar{a}_1 + \bar{a}_2 \left(\frac{\bar{b}_2}{\bar{b}_1}\right).$$

In amplified form the candidates for condensation are denoted by Φ's (with circumflexes where appropriate); $\hat{\Phi}^1 = \hat{G}^1$, $\Phi^2 = G^{21}$, $\hat{\Phi}^3 = \hat{G}^{22}$, and $\Phi^4 = \hat{y}_3 \bar{F} K$. Explicitly, using the new abbreviations,

$$\hat{\Phi}^1 \equiv a_1 + a_2 \bar{B} - \hat{y}_1 \bar{K}$$
$$\Phi^2 \equiv b_1 \bar{B} - b_2$$
$$\hat{\Phi}^3 \equiv b_1 \bar{K} + b_3 - \hat{y}_2 \bar{F}$$
$$\hat{\Phi}^4 \equiv \hat{y}_3 \bar{F},$$

where $\hat{y}_1$, $\hat{y}_2$, $\hat{y}_3$ are the auxiliary variables used in amplification. After differentiation, we set $\hat{y}_1 = 1$, $i = 1, 2, 3$. The fourth candidate is introduced as a convenience in constructing the outcome function $h(m)$ needed to complete the mechanism.

Next, we construct the bordered Hessian *BH*, in this case a 5 by 11 matrix (see the *BH* table below), and choose a (maximal rank) nonsingular "test" submatrix *T*. This submatrix is formed from rows of *BH* corresponding to the elements $(\bar{a}_1, \bar{b}_1, \bar{b}_3) = \bar{\theta}^*$ of $\bar{\theta}$ and the columns of *BH* for $(\partial \hat{\Phi}^1 / \partial a_2, \partial \hat{\Phi}^3 / \partial b_1, \partial \hat{\Phi}^3 / \partial \hat{y}_2)$. The condensing mapping $A(\cdot) = (A^1(\cdot), A^2(\cdot), A^3(\cdot))$

---

[85] This division does not affect the equilibrium values and does not affect decentralization properties. It does help the condensation process.

is then defined by the relations

$$A_1 = \frac{\partial \Phi^1}{\partial a_2} = \bar{B}, \qquad A_2 = \frac{\partial \Phi^3}{\partial b_1} = \bar{K}, \qquad A_3 = \frac{\partial \Phi^3}{\partial \hat{y}_2} = -\bar{F},$$

where $\bar{B}$, $\bar{K}$, $\bar{F}$ are defined as above. We note from the BH-table that both BH and H^* have rank 3.

Following the prescribed procedure we consider the equation system

$$w_i = a^i(\bar{\theta}), \; i = 1, 2, 3,$$

that is,

$$w_1 = \frac{\bar{b}_2}{\bar{b}_1} \qquad w_2 = \bar{a}_1 + \bar{a}_2 \, \bar{B}, \qquad w_3 = -(\bar{a}_1 \bar{b}_1 + \bar{a}_2 \bar{b}_2 + \bar{b}_3).$$

We solve this system for the components of $\bar{\theta}^* = (\bar{a}_1, \bar{b}_2, \bar{b}_3)$ as functions of $w = (w_1, w_2, w_3)$ and of $\theta^{**} = (\bar{a}_1, \bar{b}_1)$. We find $\bar{a}_1 = w_2 - \bar{a}_2 w_1$, $\bar{b}_2 = w_1 \bar{b}_1$, $\bar{b}_3 = -w_3 - w_2 \bar{b}_1$, abbreviated as $\bar{\theta}^* = \phi(w, \bar{\theta}^{**})$. Using these solutions, we note that $\bar{B} = w_1$, $\bar{K} = w_2$, and $\bar{F} = -w_3$.

Finally, these results enable us to obtain the condensed functions Γ^i, $i = 1, 2, 3, 4$, according to the general recipe

$$\Gamma^i(w, \theta) = \hat{\Phi}^i(\phi(w, \bar{\theta}^{**}), \bar{\theta}^{**}, \theta, \hat{y})\big|_{\hat{y}=(1,1,1)}.$$

Thus,

$$\Gamma^1(w, \theta) = \hat{\Phi}^1(\phi(w, \bar{\theta}^{**}), \bar{\theta}^{**}, \theta, \hat{y}_1)\big|_{\hat{y}_1=1}.$$
$$= a_1 + a_2 \bar{B} - 1 \cdot \bar{K} = a_1 + a_2 w_1 - w_2,$$
$$\Gamma^2(w, \theta) = \Phi^2(\phi(w, \bar{\theta}^{**}), \bar{\theta}^{**}, \theta)$$
$$= b_1 \bar{B} - b_2 = b_1 w_1 - b_2,$$
$$\Gamma^3(w, \theta) = \hat{\Phi}^3(\phi(w, \bar{\theta}^{**}), \bar{\theta}^{**}, \theta, \hat{y}_2)\big|_{\hat{y}_2=1}$$
$$= b_1 \bar{K} + b_3 - \bar{F}$$
$$= b_1 w_2 + b_3 + w_3,$$
$$\Gamma^4(w, \theta) = \hat{\Phi}^4(\phi(w, \bar{\theta}^{**}), \bar{\theta}^{**}, \theta, \hat{y}_3)\big|_{\hat{y}_3=1}$$
$$= \hat{y}_3 \bar{F} = 1 \cdot (-w_3) = -w_3.$$

Since, to get realization, we want to have the outcome function to have the F-optimality property, we define the outcome function by

$$h(w) = \Gamma^4 = \bar{F},$$

that is,

$$h(w) = -w_3.$$

2.4.4.2 Verification of F-Optimality, Existence and Decentralization

To verify F-optimality of the mechanism, suppose that the three equilibrium conditions hold – that is, $\Gamma^1 = \Gamma^2 = \Gamma^3 = 0$. Then

$$
\begin{aligned}
h(w) = -w_3 &= b_1 w_2 + b_3 && \leftarrow \text{by } \Gamma^3 = 0 \\
&= b_1 (a_1 + a_2 w_1) + b_3 && \leftarrow \text{by } \Gamma^1 = 0 \\
&= b_1 \left(a_1 + a_2 \frac{b_2}{b_1} \right) + b_3 && \leftarrow \text{by } \Gamma^2 = 0 \\
&= a_1 b_1 + a_2 b_2 + b_3 && \leftarrow \text{by elementary algebra} \\
&= F(\theta). && \leftarrow \text{by definition of } F
\end{aligned}
$$

Hence, at equilibrium, $h(w) = F(\theta)$, and so the F-optimality condition holds. Existence property is also easily verified (see below). Finally, Γ^1 is independent of b while Γ^2 and Γ^3 are independent of a. Hence the privacy-preserving mechanism defined by

$$
M \subseteq \mathbb{R}^3, \quad g^1(m, a) = \Gamma^1(w, \theta)\big|_{w=m}, \quad g^{21}(m, b) = \Gamma^2(w, \theta)\big|_{w=m},
$$
$$
g^{22}(m, b) = \Gamma^3(w, \theta)\big|_{w=m}, \quad \text{and} \quad h(m) = \Gamma^4(w)\big|_{w=m} = -w_3
$$

realizes F and is informationally decentralized. More explicitly, we have

$$
\begin{aligned}
g^1(m, a) &\equiv a_1 + a_2 m_1 - m_2 \\
g^{21}(m, b) &\equiv b_1 m_1 - b_2 \\
g^{22}(m, b) &\equiv b_1 m_2 + b_3 + m_3 \\
h(m) &\equiv -m_3.
\end{aligned}
$$

The message equation system is, of course,

$$
g^1(m, a) = 0, \qquad g^{21}(m, b) = 0, \qquad g^{22}(m, b) = 0.
$$

It is uniquely solvable for $m = (m_1, m_2, m_3)$ as a function of (a, b):

$$
m_1 = \frac{b_2}{b_1}; \qquad m_2 = a_1 + a_2 m_1 = a_1 + a_2 \left(\frac{b_2}{b_1} \right)
$$
$$
m_3 = -(b_1 a_2 + b_3) = - \left(b_1 \left(a_1 + a_2 \left(\frac{b_2}{b_1} \right) \right) \right) + b_3.
$$

This proves the existence property of realization.

Since agent 1 only verifies $g^1(m, a) = 0$, while agent 2 checks the equations $g^{21}(m, b) = 0$, $g^{22}(m, b) = 0$, the mechanism is informationally decentralized (privacy preserving).

(Condensation) BH Matrix for Augmented Inner Product (Showing: rank $(BH)=3$)

$\partial(\cdot)/\partial\theta$	$\partial\Phi^1$	$\partial\Phi^2$	$\partial\Phi^3$	$\partial\Phi^4$	$\partial\Phi^1_{a_2}$ $=\partial\bar B$	$\partial\Phi^1_{\dot y_1}$ $=\partial(-\bar K)$	$\partial\Phi^1_{b_1}$ $=\partial\bar B$	$\partial\Phi^1_{b_2}$ $=\partial(-1)$	$\partial\Phi^3_{b_1}$ $=\partial\bar K$	$\partial\Phi^3_{\dot y_3}$ $=-\partial\bar F$	$\partial\Phi^4_{\dot y_3}$ $=\partial\bar F$
	1^*	2^*	3^*	4^*	1^{**}	2^{**}	3^{**}	4^{**}	5^{**}	6^{**}	7^{**}
$/\partial\bar a_1$	$-\hat y_1$	0	$b_1\cdot1-\hat y_2\bar b_1$	$\hat y_3\cdot\bar b_1$	0				1	$-b_1$	
$/\partial\bar a_2$	$-\hat y_1 B$	0	$b_1 B-\hat y_2\cdot\bar b_1$		b_2				B	$-b_2$	
$/\partial\bar b_1$	$-(a_2-\hat y_1\bar a_2)\cdot\left(\frac{1}{\bar b_1}\right)$	$-b_1\frac{\bar a_2 b_2}{\bar b_1^2}$	$-b_1\frac{\bar a_2 b_2}{\bar b_1^2}-\hat y_2\cdot\bar a_1$	$\hat y_3\cdot\bar a_2$	$-\frac{b_2}{\bar b_1^2}$				$-\frac{\bar a_2 b_2}{\bar b_1}$	$-\bar a_1$	
$/\partial\bar b_2$	$(a_2-\hat y_1\bar a_2)\cdot\left(\frac{1}{\bar b_1}\right)$	$\frac{b_1}{\bar b_1}$	$b_1\frac{\bar a_2}{\bar b_1}-\hat y_2\bar a_2$		$\frac{1}{\bar b_1}$				$\frac{\bar a_2}{\bar b_1}$	$-\bar a_2$	
$/\partial\bar b_3$	0	0	$-\hat y_2\cdot1$	1	0			Null		-1	
Relations of columns	$1^*=-5^{**}$ $+a_2\cdot1^{**}$ $(\hat y_1=1)$	$2^*=b_1\cdot1^{**}$	$3^*=b_1\cdot5^{**}$ $+6^{**}$ $(\hat y_3=1)$	$4^*=-6^{**}$ $(\hat y_3=1)$		$2^{**}=-5^{**}$	$3^{**}=1^{**}$				$7^{**}=-6$

$F(\theta)=a_1 b_1+a_2 b_2+b_3$
$\bar F=F(\theta)$
$\bar B=b_2/b_1$
$\bar K=\bar a_1+\bar a_2\bar B$

$\hat\Phi^1=a_1+a_2\bar B-\hat y_1\bar K$
$\Phi^2=b_1\bar B-b_2$
$\hat\Phi^3=b_1\bar K+b_3-\hat y_2\bar F$
$\hat\Phi^4=\hat y_3\bar F$

Test Matrix (T)

	1^{**}	5^{**}	6^{**}
$/\partial\bar a_1$	0	1	$-\bar b_1$
$/\partial\bar b_2$	$\frac{1}{\bar b_1}$	$\frac{\bar a_2}{\bar b_1}$	$-\bar a_2$
$/\partial\bar b_3$	0	0	-1

rearranged (triangular):

$$\approx\begin{pmatrix}1/\bar b_1 & \bar a_2 b_1 & -\bar a_2\\ 0 & 1 & -\bar b_1\\ 0 & 0 & -1\end{pmatrix}$$

$$\det T=(-1)\left(-\frac{1}{\bar b_1}\cdot1\right)$$
$$=\frac{1}{\bar b_1}\neq0\text{ by hyp.}$$

Columns other than $1^{**},5^{**},6^{**}$ are linearly dependent on $1^{**},5^{**},6^{**}$. Hence rank $BH=3$.

2.5 Overlaps

2.5.0 Constructing a Mechanism When the Parameter-Indexed Product Structure Is Not a Partition: An Example

The example is extremely simple, but not trivial. The goal function is what may be called "augmented hyperbolic" or "augmented one-dimensional inner product." For the sake of continuity, although at the cost of some repetition, we present both phases, one and two, consecutively.

The algebraic formula for the goal function is

$$F(a, b) = a_1 b_1 + b_2$$

so that $\Theta^1 = \{\theta^1 : \theta^1 = a_1, a_1 \in \mathbb{R}\}$;

$$\Theta^2 = \{\theta^2 : \theta^2 = (b_1, b_2), (b_1, b_2) \in \mathbb{R}^2\}, \Theta = \Theta^1 \times \Theta^2 = \mathbb{R}^3.$$

The construction of a covering (phase one) would be very simple if we restricted the parameter space by ruling out points with $b_1 = 0$. In that case, using left-RM, and choosing the maximal A-set in order to guarantee reflexivity, we define the A-set by the relation $F(a, \bar{b}) = F(\bar{a}, \bar{b})$, i.e.,

$$a_1 \bar{b}_1 + \bar{b}_2 = \bar{a}_1 \bar{b}_1 + \bar{b}_2.$$

Since $\bar{b}_1 \neq 0$,

$$A(\bar{\theta}) = \{a_1 \in \mathbb{R} : a_1 = \bar{a}_1\} = \{\bar{a}_1\}. \tag{1}$$

In turn, the corresponding B-set is defined by the requirement that

$$F(a, b) = F(\bar{a}, \bar{b}) \qquad \text{for all } a \in A(\bar{\theta}).$$

That is,

$$\bar{a}_1 b_1 + b_2 = \bar{a}_1 \bar{b}_1 + \bar{b}_2. \tag{2}$$

Thus the covering correspondence is

$$\begin{aligned} V(\bar{\theta}) &= V^1(\bar{\theta}) \times V^2(\bar{\theta}) \\ &= \{\bar{a}_1\} \times \{(b_1, b_2) \in \mathbb{R}^2 : \bar{a}_1 b_1 + b_2 = \bar{a}_1 \bar{b}_1 + \bar{b}_2\}. \end{aligned} \tag{3}$$

In equation form, we have

$$G^1(\bar{\theta}, a) \equiv a_1 - \bar{a}_1 = 0 \tag{4.1}$$

$$G^2(\bar{\theta}, b) \equiv \bar{a}_1 b_1 + b_2 - (\bar{a}_1 \bar{b}_1 + \bar{b}_2) = 0. \tag{4.2}$$

We skip the formalities of making the transition to message form. It is obvious that this can be accomplished by setting $m_1 = \bar{a}_1$ and $m_2 = \bar{a}_1 \bar{b}_1 + \bar{b}_2$. Then the message-form equations become

$$g^1(m, a) \equiv a_1 - m_1 = 0 \tag{5.1}$$

$$g^2(m, b) \equiv m_1 b_1 + b_2 - m_2 = 0, \tag{5.2}$$

and a natural outcome function is $h(m_1, m_2) \equiv m_2$. It turns out that the mechanism in this case is the parameter transfer, PT_{ab}, from agent 1 to agent 2.

But if we do not exclude the zero value for b_1, things get more interesting, although more complicated. We then divide our analysis into two cases: Case (i) when $\bar{b}_1 \neq 0$ and Case (ii) when $\bar{b}_1 = 0$. In what follows, we use the left-RM (L-RM) method throughout, and start with the maximal A-set to assure reflexivity. This guarantees that we construct a maximally coarse covering, and therefore the mechanism has the informational efficiency property of maximal coarseness.[86]

CASE (i): CONSTRUCTING $V(\bar{\theta})$ WHEN $\bar{b}_1 \neq 0$. In this case the derivation of the covering correspondence yields the same formulae as those obtained above in Equations (3) and (4). There is a difference, however: even though $\bar{b}_1 \neq 0$ in Case (i), the value $b_1 = 0$ is not ruled out.

CASE (ii): CONSTRUCTING $V(\bar{\theta})$ WHEN $\bar{b}_1 = 0$. Here the maximal A-set is defined, as always in L-RM, by $F(a, \bar{b}) = F(\bar{a}, \bar{b})$, but when $\bar{b}_1 = 0$, this becomes

$$a_1 \cdot 0 + \bar{b}_2 = \bar{a}_1 \cdot 0 + \bar{b}_2,$$

which is the identity $0 = 0$. The parameter a_1 ranges over all real values. Thus,

$$A(\bar{\theta}) = \mathbb{R}. \tag{6.1}$$

The B-set is again defined by the condition $F(a, b) = F(\bar{a}, \bar{b})$ for all $a \in A(\bar{\theta})$, i.e., by

$$a_1 b_1 + b_2 = \bar{a}_1 \cdot 0 + \bar{b}_2 = \bar{b}_2 \quad \text{for all } a_1 \in \mathbb{R}. \tag{6.2}$$

---

[86] The complications arising in using L-RM, maximal A, do not arise with R-RM, maximal B, even when all of $\mathbb{R}^3$ is the parameter space. In the latter approach we use at PT_{ab} and the covering is a partition. But our purpose in this section is to gain insight into mechanism construction when the covering is not a partition. For that purpose, L-RM, maximal A, with $F = a_1 b_1 + b_2$ is particularly instructive. (For more detail on the R-RM approach, see the Appendix.)

Setting $a_1 = 0$ we obtain $b_2 = \bar{b}_2$, hence $a_1 b_1 = 0$. Then setting $a_1 = 1$ yields $b_1 = 0$. So, when $\bar{b}_1 = 0$, we find

$$B(\bar{\theta}) = \{(b_1, b_2) \in \mathbb{R}^2 : b_1 = 0, \ b_2 = \bar{b}_2\}, \tag{7.1}$$

and

$$V(\bar{\theta}) = \mathbb{R} \times \{(b_1, b_2) \in \mathbb{R}^2 : b_1 = 0, b_2 = \bar{b}_2\}. \tag{7.2}$$

Equivalently, when[87] $\bar{\theta} = (\bar{a}_1; \bar{b}_1, \bar{b}_2)$ and $\bar{b}_1 = 0$, the relation $\theta \in V(\bar{\theta})$, $\theta = (a_1; b_1, b_2)$, $a = a_1$, $b = (b_1, b_2)$, can be expressed by the following system of equations:

$$
\begin{aligned}
G^1(\bar{\theta}, a) &\equiv 0 = 0 \quad (\text{or } G^1(\bar{\theta}, a) \equiv a_1 \cdot 0 = 0) \\
G^{21}(\bar{\theta}, b) &\equiv b_1 = 0 \\
G^{22}(\bar{\theta}, b) &\equiv b_2 - \bar{b}_2 = 0.
\end{aligned}
\tag{7.3}
$$

The next stage of the mechanism construction process is the choice of an SDR. But to accomplish this, we first describe the covering C_V of Θ generated by the correspondence V. It is most helpful at this stage to look at the geometry of the covering.

The Covering C_V when $\bar{b}_1 = 0$.

First, we study the "rectangles"[88] generated by V in Case (ii), when $\bar{b}_1 = 0$. Consider a three-dimensional diagram, with a_1 on the vertical axis, while the axes for b_1 and b_2 are in the horizontal plane.

Then $K = V(\bar{\theta})$ for $\bar{\theta} = (\bar{a}_1; \bar{b}_1, \bar{b}_2) = (\bar{a}_1; 0, \bar{b}_2)$ is a vertical line (parallel to the a_1-axis) lying in the (b_2, a_1)-plane, (defined by the condition $b_1 = 0$), and intersecting the b_2-axis at the point $\bar{b}_2$, or, more precisely, at the point $(\bar{a}_1; b_1, b_2) = (0; 0, \bar{b}_2)$.

Since b_2 is free to range over all reals, the family of all these rectangles (lines) for Case (ii) fills the whole plane $b_1 = 0$.

The description of rectangles generated in Case (i) is somewhat more complicated. As seen in Equation (3), when $\bar{b}_1 \neq 0$, the rectangle for a given $\bar{\theta} = (\bar{a}_1; \bar{b}_1, \bar{b}_2)$, $\bar{b}_1 \neq 0$ is the set

$$V(\bar{\theta}) = \{\bar{a}_1\} \times \{(b_2, b_3) \in \mathbb{R} : \bar{a}_1 b_1 + b_2 = \bar{a}_1 \bar{b}_1 + \bar{b}_2\}.$$

---

[87] We often find it helpful to separate the a-components from the b-components by a semicolon rather than a comma.

[88] Subsequently, we dispense with the inverted commas when referring to a set $K = K_1 \times K_2$ where $K_1 \subseteq \Theta^1$ and $K_2 \subseteq \Theta^2$ as a rectangle.

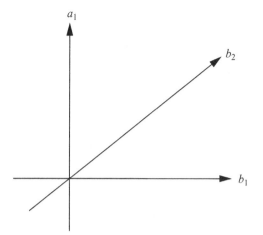

Figure 2.5.1 AugHyperbolic.

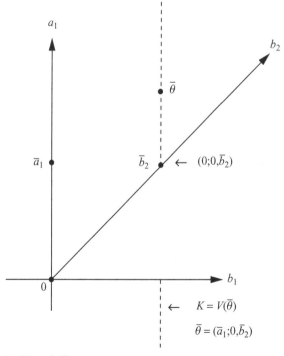

Figure 2.5.2 AugHyperbolic.
(*Note*: The value of a_1 does not affect $K = V(\bar{\theta})$ when $\bar{\theta}$ belongs to category (ii)).

That is, $V(\bar{\theta})$ is a straight line in the (horizontal) $a_1 = \bar{a}_1$ plane, defined by the equation

$$b_2 = -\bar{a}_1 b_1 + \bar{F}, \qquad (8)$$

where $\bar{F} = F(\bar{a}, \bar{b}) = \bar{a}_1 b_1 + \bar{b}_2$. Thus, the value of $\bar{a}_2$ determines both the level at which the line lies and its slope.

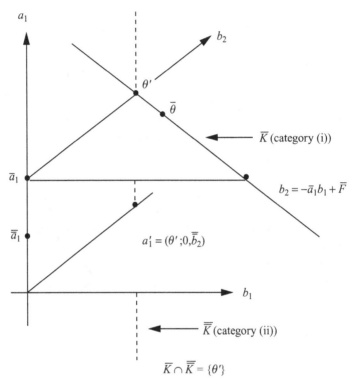

Figure 2.5.3 AugHyperbolic. Showing the intersection θ' of $\bar{K}$; of category (i) with $\bar{\bar{K}}$ of category (ii).

Note that if two parameter points $\bar{\theta} = (\bar{a}_1; \bar{b}_1, \bar{b}_2)$ and $\bar{\bar{\theta}} = (\bar{\bar{a}}_1; \bar{\bar{b}}_1, \bar{\bar{b}}_2)$ have the same a-component, that is, if $\bar{a}_1 = \bar{\bar{a}}$, then the two rectangles $\bar{K} = V(\bar{\theta})$, $\bar{\bar{K}} = V(\bar{\bar{\theta}})$ lie in the same horizontal plane, but also have the same slope; hence they are either distinct and parallel (when $F(\bar{\theta}) \neq F(\bar{\bar{\theta}})$) or coincide (when $F(\bar{\theta}) = F(\bar{\bar{\theta}})$ even though $\bar{\theta} \neq \bar{\bar{\theta}}$). Hence when $\bar{a}_1 = \bar{\bar{a}}_1$, there are no nontrivial overlaps. But, in fact, there are no overlaps altogether, since then the two rectangles $\bar{K}$ and $\bar{\bar{K}}$ lie in two different horizontal planes.

We thus see that there can be no nontrivial overlaps between two rectangles of the same category – both generated by $\bar{\theta}$ of the same case: either both

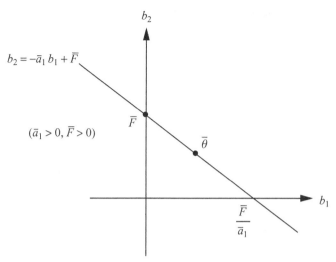

Figure 2.5.4 AugHyperbolic. A horizontal cross-section at level $a_1 = \bar{a}_1$; note that $\partial b_2/\partial b_1 = -\bar{a}_1$.

of Case (i) or both of Case (ii). But there are common points that involve rectangles of different categories.

Consider a rectangle $\bar{K}$ such that (i) holds, i.e., $\bar{K} = V(\bar{\theta})$, $\bar{b}_1 \neq 0$. Call this a category (i) rectangle and also consider a rectangle such that $\bar{\bar{K}} = V(\bar{\bar{\theta}})$, $\bar{\bar{b}}_1 = 0$, which is called category (ii) (see Figures 2.5.3 and 2.5.4).

Since all rectangles of category (ii) are in the plane $b_1 = 0$, a point of overlap must also have $b_1 = 0$. But then, at such a point we have $b_2 = \bar{b}_2 = \bar{\bar{b}}_2$ and $a_1 = \bar{a}_1$. So points $(a_1; b_2, b_3) = (\bar{a}_1; 0, \bar{b}_2)$ with $\bar{b}_2 = \bar{\bar{b}}_2$, are points of (nontrivial) overlaps, and these are the only such points. Clearly, the covering is not a partition.

It is helpful to know the location of overlaps because any point of a rectangle K that is not a point of overlap with any (distinct) other rectangle can serve as an SDR point.

A rectangle K of category (i) in the covering C_V can be characterized by

$$K = \{(a_1; b_1, b_2) \in \mathbb{R}^3 : \text{there exist numbers } p \text{ and } q \text{ such that}$$
$$a_1 = p \text{ and } b_2 = -p\,b_1 + q\}. \tag{9.1}$$

Such a rectangle will sometimes be denoted K_{pq}. For such a rectangle, in defining an SDR we avoid points of overlap by setting $b_1 = 1$. That is, for $K = K_{pq}$ of category (i) as defined by Equation (9.1), we define the value of the SDR function $\Lambda : C_V \rightarrow \Theta$ by

$$\Lambda(K) = (p; 1, s) \text{ where } s = -p + q. \tag{10.1}$$

As for a rectangle K in C_V of category (ii), it can be characterized by

$$K = \{(a_1; b_1, b_2) \in \mathbb{R}^3 : h_1 = 0, h_2 - r \text{ for some } r\}. \tag{9.2}$$

For such K, we choose the SDR value

$$\Lambda(K) = (0; 0, r). \tag{10.2}$$

Next, we proceed to check that our choice of the function Λ satisfies the two parts of the definition of SDR:

$$\Lambda(K) \in K \tag{1}$$

$$K' \neq K'' \Rightarrow \Lambda(K') \neq \Lambda(K''). \tag{2}$$

For category (i), and hence $b_1 = 1$, $b_2 = -p + q$. Substituting these values into the equation $b_2 = -pb_1 + q$ we obtain $-p + q = -p \cdot 1 + q$, which is an identity. So SDR (1) is satisfied.

To check SDR (2) for category (i), suppose $\Lambda(K') = \Lambda(K'')$. Now $\Lambda(K') = (p'; 1, -p' + q')$ and $\Lambda(K'') = (p''; 1, -p'' + q'')$, so $p' = p''$ and $-p' + q' = p'' + q''$. But then $p' = p''$ and $q' = q''$, hence $K' = K''$. Therefore SDR (ii) is also satisfied in category (ii).

Now consider a rectangle K of category (ii). We have $K = \{(a_1; b_1, b_2) \in \mathbb{R}^3 : b_1 = 0, b_2 = r\}$, so a_1 can take any numerical value, in particular $a_1 = 0$. But $(0; 0, r) = \Lambda(K)$. So SDR (1) is satisfied.

To check SDR (2) for category (ii), suppose $\Lambda(K') = \Lambda(K'')$. Now $K' = \{(a_1; b_1, b_2) \in \mathbb{R}^3 : b_1 = 0, b_2 = r'\}$ and $K'' = \{(a_1; b_1, b_2) \in \mathbb{R}^3 : b_1 = 0, b_2 = r''\}$. Therefore, $\Lambda(K') = (0; 0, r')$ and $\Lambda(K'') = (0; 0, r'')$. But $\Lambda(K') = \Lambda(K'')$ implies $r' = r''$, and $r' = r''$ implies $K' = K''$. Hence our function Λ satisfies SDR (1) and SDR (2) in both categories.   Q.E.D.

Having constructed an SDR function, it remains to make a transition to message form. To simplify matters we choose the transversal $T = \Lambda(C_V)$ as our message space M.

We start by constructing the individual equilibrium correspondences $\mu^1 : \Theta^1 \Rightarrow M$, and $\mu^2 : \Theta^2 \Rightarrow M$, using the set-theoretic formulation.

The individual correspondence μ^1 is defined as follows:

$$\text{for } m \text{ in } M \quad \text{and} \quad \theta^1 \text{ in } \Theta^1,$$

$m \in \mu^1(\theta^1)$ if and only if $\exists K$ in C_V such that $\theta^1 \in K_1$.

Here it is understood that $K = K_1 \times K_2 \subseteq \Theta^1 \times \Theta^2$, so that K_1 is the projection of K onto the parameter space Θ^1 of the first agent.

The definition of μ^2 is analogous (just replace 1's by 2's). Then the group (social) correspondence $\mu : \Theta \Rightarrow M$ is defined as the intersection of the two individual correspondences:

$$\mu(\theta^1, \theta^2) = \mu^1(\theta^1) \cap \mu^2(\theta^2),$$

more directly, by the following: for $\theta \in \Theta$ and $m \in M$,

$$m \in \mu(\theta) \quad \text{if and only if } \exists \, K \text{ in } C_V \quad \text{such that } \theta \in K.$$

Next, we describe the *verification scenario*, both in set-theoretic and analytic form.

There are two types of message vectors:

$$m' = (p; 1, s) \quad \text{for some } (p, s) \in \mathbb{R}^2$$

and

$$m'' = (0; 0, r) \quad \text{for some } r \in \mathbb{R}.$$

Suppose the coordinator or central computer proposes a message of type $m' = (p; 1, s)$. According to the definition of the message correspondence μ^1, agent 1 will say "yes" if and only if there exists a rectangle K^* in the covering[89] C such that his/her parameter value is "covered" by the Θ^1-projection of K^*; formally, if $K^* = K_1^* \times K_2^*$, $K^* \in C$, $K_1^* \subseteq \Theta^1$, $K_2^* \subseteq \Theta^2$, and $\theta^1 \equiv a_1 \in K_1^*$, and $m' = \Lambda(K^*)$. (This requires that agent 1 know that such a K^* exists in the covering C, but agent 1 need not know whether $\theta^2 \equiv (b_1, b_2)$ is a point in K_2^*. Thus the informational decentralization requirements are not violated.)

Agent 2 will say "yes" if and only if there exists a rectangle $K^{**} = K_1^{**} \times K_2^{**}$ in C such that $m' = \Lambda(K^{**})$ and her parameter value is "covered" by K_2^{**}, i.e., $\theta^2 = (b_1, b_2) \in K_2^{**}$.

Could it happen that both agents say "yes," but $K^* \neq K^{**}$? If that were the case, since $\Lambda(K^*) = m'$ and $\Lambda(K^{**}) = m'$, we would have a situation where $\Lambda(K^*) = \Lambda(K^{**})$ but $K^* \neq K^{**}$, thus violating rule (2) of SDR's. It follows that both agents will say "yes," i.e., $m' \in \mu(\theta)$ for $\theta = (\theta^1, \theta^2)$, if and only if there exists K in C such that $m' = \Lambda(K)$, $K = K_1 \times K_2 \subseteq \Theta^1 \times \Theta^2$ and $\theta^1 \in K_1$, $\theta^2 \in K_2$.

Note that such a rectangle K would "automatically" be of Category (i), since only such rectangles have representatives $\Lambda(K)$ with $b_1 = 1$.

---

[89] We write C for C_V.

Also note that $\theta^1 \in K_1$ when $\Lambda(K) = (p; 1, s)$ means that $p = a_1$, while $(b_1, b_2) \in K_2$ means that $pb_1 + b_2 = p + s$.

In the case where the coordinator proposes a message of type $m'' = (0; 0, r)$, agent 1 says "yes" if and only if there is a rectangle $K \in C$, $m'' = \Lambda(K)$, and $\theta^1 = a_1 \in K_1$. But, by construction of Λ, it must be the case that $K_1 = \mathbb{R}$, hence condition $a_1 \in K_1$ is necessarily satisfied with K^* of Category (ii).

Agent 2 says "yes" if and only if $\theta^2 = (b_1, b_2) \in K_2$, i.e., $b_1 = 0$ and $b_2 = r$.

In Summary, the *equilibrium conditions* are as follows.

If $m = m' = (p; 1, s)$, then $m' = \Lambda(K)$ where $K = K_{pq}$ of Category (i), and

$$g^1(m', a) \equiv a_1 - p = 0$$
$$g^2(m', b) \equiv pb_1 + b_2 - (p + s) = 0.$$

If $m = m'' = (0; 0, r)$, then $m'' = \Lambda(K)$, where $K = K_r$ of category (ii), and the *equilibrium conditions* are

$$g^1(m'', a) \equiv 0 = 0 \text{ (or } g^1(m'', a) \equiv 0 \cdot a_1 = 0)$$
$$g^{21}(m'', b) \equiv b_1 = 0$$
$$g^{22}(m'', b) \equiv b_2 - r = 0.$$

To complete the construction of the mechanism we define the *outcome function*, $h : M \to Z$; in this case $h : M \to \mathbb{R}$, since we have specialized to $Z = \mathbb{R}$.

If $m = m'$, we set $h(m') \equiv p + s$; if $m = m''$, we set $h(m'') = r$.

To verify F-optimality, consider first the case $m = m'$. Here $h(m') \equiv p + s = pb_1 + b_2 = a_1 b_1 + b_2 = F(\theta)$. When $m = m''$, $h(m'') = r = b_2 = F(\theta)$ since $b_1 \neq 0$. So the mechanism is F-optimal.

Next we check *existence*. First, let $\theta = (a_1; b_1, b_2)$, with $b_1 \neq 0$. Then $0 = (p; 1, s)$ will satisfy the equilibrium conditions $g^1(m, a) = 0$, $g^{21}(m, b) = 0$ provided $p = a_1$ and $s = -p + q$ with $q = a_1 b_1 + b_2$.

On the other hand, if $\theta = (a_1; b_1, b_2)$ with $b_1 = 0$, then $m'' = (0; 0, r)$ satisfies the equilibrium conditions provided $r = b_2$. Thus in all cases an equilibrium message for any given $\theta \in \Theta = \mathbb{R}^3$ exists.

Thus, we have constructed a decentralized and minimally coarse message mechanism that realizes the given goal function $F(\theta) = a_1 b_1 + b_2$ over the full $\mathbb{R}^3$ parameter space. The design procedure used was "algorithmic"; that no guessing was involved.

APPENDIX

Following up on comments made in footnote 1, page 3, we show that the right-RM approach with maximal B-set for $F(\theta) = a_1 b_1 + b_2$ generates a partition when the parameter space Θ is all of $\mathbb{R}^3$.

When R-RM is used, the maximal B-set is defined by $F(\bar{a}, b) = F(\bar{a}, \bar{b})$ – here by

$$\bar{a}_1 b_1 + b_2 = \bar{a}_1 \bar{b}_1 + \bar{b}_2. \tag{+}$$

Thus, for every $\bar{\theta}$ in $\mathbb{R}^3$, whether $\bar{b}_1 \neq 0$ or $\bar{b}_1 = 0$, we have[90]

$$B_R(\bar{\theta}) = \{b \in \mathbb{R}^2 : \bar{a}_1 b_1 + b_2 = \bar{a}_1 \bar{b}_1 + \bar{b}_2\}.$$

The corresponding A-set is the Θ^1 space, denoted by $A^*(B_R(\bar{\theta}), \bar{\theta})$; it is defined by the relation

$$a_1 b_1 + b_2 = \bar{a}_1 \bar{b}_1 + b_2 \qquad \text{for all } b \in B_R(\bar{\theta}). \tag{++}$$

Substituting into $(++)$ the value of b_2 obtained from $(+)$, we get

$$a_1 b_1 + (\bar{a}_1 \bar{b}_1 + \bar{b}_2 - \bar{a}_1 b_1) = \bar{a}_1 \bar{b}_1 + \bar{b}_2,$$

and then,

$$(a_1 - \bar{a}_1) b_1 = 0 \qquad \text{for all } b_1 \in \mathbb{R}.$$

For $b_1 = 1$, this yields

$$a_1 = \bar{a}_1.$$

Thus, for all $\bar{\theta}$ in $\mathbb{R}^3$,

$$A^*(B_R(\bar{\theta}), \bar{\theta}) = \{\bar{a}_1\}.$$

Therefore,

$$V_R(\bar{\theta}) = V_R^1(\bar{\theta}) \times V_R^2(\bar{\theta})$$
$$= \{\bar{a}_1\} \times \{b \in \mathbb{R}^2 : \bar{a}_1 b_1 + b_2 = \bar{a}_1 \bar{b}_1 + \bar{b}_2\},$$

where $V_R^1(\bar{\theta}) \subseteq \Theta^1$ and $V_R^2(\bar{\theta}) \subseteq \Theta^2$.

Consequently, every set K of the covering C_R generated by V_R is of the form

$$K = K_1 \times K_2$$
$$= \{p\} \times \{b \in \mathbb{R}^2 : p b_1 + b_2 = q \text{ for some two numbers } p, q\},$$

where $K_i \subseteq \Theta^i$, $i = 1, 2$.

---

[90] In this appendix we use the subscripts R and L to distinguish sets obtained through R-RM from those derived through L-RM.

By contrast, category (ii) sets in C_L (the covering generated by L-RM with maximal A) are of the form

$$K = K_1 \times K_2 \subseteq \Theta^1 \times \Theta^2$$

with $K = \mathbb{R}$, not a singleton $\{p\}$ as in $K_1 \in C_R$.

Clearly, the two coverings are not the same: $C_R \neq C_L$. In particular, the set $A^*(B_R(\bar{\theta}), \bar{\theta}) = \{\bar{a}_1\}$ is not maximal for $\bar{\theta}$ with $\bar{b}_1 = 0$, since $A_L(\bar{\theta}) = \mathbb{R}$ is a proper superset of $\{\bar{a}\}$ and remains in the same F-contour set when $\bar{b}_1 = 0$. Nevertheless, both coverings, C_R and C_L are reflexive RM's.

We now proceed to show that C_R is a partition. Suppose $\bar{K}$ and $\bar{\bar{K}}$ are two sets in C_R. Then $\bar{K} = \{\bar{p}\} \times \{b_1 \in \mathbb{R}^2 : \bar{p}\, b_1 + b_2 = \bar{q}\}$ and $\bar{\bar{K}} = \{\bar{\bar{p}}\} \times \{b_1 \in \mathbb{R}^2 : \bar{\bar{p}}\, b_1 + b_2 = \bar{\bar{q}}\}$. We shall show that if $\bar{K}$ and $\bar{\bar{K}}$ have a point $\hat{\theta}$ in common, then any point θ belonging to $\bar{K}$ must also belong to $\bar{\bar{K}}$, and vice versa.

Suppose $\hat{\theta} = (\hat{a}_1; \hat{b}_1, \hat{b}_2)$ belongs both to $\bar{K}$ and $\bar{\bar{K}}$. Then $\hat{a}_1 = \bar{p}$ and $\hat{a}_1 = \bar{\bar{p}}$. Also, $\bar{p}\, \hat{b}_1 + \hat{b}_2 = q$ and $\bar{\bar{p}}\, \hat{b}_1 + \hat{b}_2 = \bar{\bar{q}}$. But $\hat{a}_1 = \bar{p}$ and $\hat{a}_1 = \bar{\bar{p}}$ imply $\bar{p} = \bar{\bar{p}}$. Hence the equalities involving b's can be written as

$$a_1^* \hat{b}_1 + \hat{b}_2 = \bar{q},$$

and

$$a_1^* \hat{b}_1 + \hat{b}_2 = \bar{\bar{q}},$$

where $a_1^* = \bar{p} = \bar{\bar{p}}$. It follows that $\bar{q} = \bar{\bar{q}}$. Consider now any $\theta = (a_1; b_1, b_2)$. Suppose $\theta \in \bar{K}$, i.e., $a_1 = \bar{p}$ and $\bar{p}b_1 + b_2 = \bar{q}$. But since $\bar{p} = \bar{\bar{p}}$ and $\bar{q} = \bar{\bar{q}}$, it follows that $a_1 = \bar{\bar{p}}$ and $\bar{\bar{p}}\, ab_1 + b_2 = \bar{\bar{q}}$. Hence $\theta \in \bar{\bar{K}}$ as well. Similarly, for every θ in Θ, $\Theta \in \bar{\bar{K}}$ implies $\Theta \in \bar{K}$. Hence $\bar{K} = \bar{\bar{K}}$. It follows that C_R is a partition.

The equation form of the covering correspondence V_R is

$$\begin{cases} G^1(\bar{\theta}, a) \equiv a_1 - \bar{a}_1 = 0 \\ G^2(\bar{\theta}, b) \equiv \bar{a}_1 b_1 + b_2 - (\bar{a}_1 \bar{b}_1 + \bar{b}_2) = 0. \end{cases} \tag{+++}$$

A natural transition to message form is to set

$$m_1 = \bar{a}_1$$
$$m_2 = \bar{a}_1 \bar{b}_1 + \bar{b}_2.$$

The message equilibrium equations are

$$g^1(m, a) \equiv a_1 - m_1 = 0$$
$$g^2(m, b) \equiv m_1 b_1 + b_2 - m_2 = 0,$$

where $m = (m_1, m_2) \in \mathbb{R}^2$.

With the outcome function $h(m) \equiv m_2$, we have a mechanism (M, g^1, g^2, h), $M = \mathbb{R}^2$, that realizes the goal function $F(\theta) = a_1 b_2 + b_2$. We recognize this mechanism as PT_{ab}, the parameter transfer from agent 1 to agent 2.

It is striking that the functions G^1, G^2 in Equations $(+++)$ define V_R in equation form over all of $\Theta = \mathbb{R}^3$ have the same form as Equations (4.1), (4.2) V_L for $\bar{\theta}$ with $\bar{b}_1 \neq 0$. This observation leads us to take another look at C_L, the covering generated by V_L. We first note that the equation system $G(\bar{\theta}, \theta) = 0$ there derived for $\bar{\theta}$ with $\bar{b}_1 \neq 0$ is solvable (not uniquely) for $\bar{\theta}$ given any $\theta \in \mathbb{R}^3$, namely by setting $\bar{\theta}$ equal to any given θ. This gives us $G(\bar{\theta}, \theta) = 0$ for every θ in $\mathbb{R}^3$. But this means that the vertical rectangles obtained in Case (ii) $\bar{b}_1 = 0$ for L-RM, are superfluous: the rectangles generated by $G(\bar{\theta}, \theta) = 0$ cover the whole parameter space $\Theta = \mathbb{R}^3$. We have not just overlaps, but also redundancy. In fact, if we remove from C_L the superfluous vertical rectangles we are left with the covering that is precisely equal to C_R, this reduced C_L covering, say $C'_L = C_R$, is still rRM, but no longer redundant. And, as we have seen above, it leads to a decentralized mechanism that realizes the goal function $F(\theta) = a_1 b_1 + b_2$, is free of redundancy or even overlaps, and is informationally efficient (in the sense of maximal coarseness).

2.6 Informational Efficiency

2.6.1 Main Results

We use three concepts included in the concept of informational efficiency. The two principal ones are *maximal coarseness* and *informational size* (mainly, cardinality for finite spaces, and vectorial dimension for Euclidean spaces). The third concept is *equation efficiency*, measured by taking into account the number of equations each agent must verify.

We study each concept in the setting of the *reflexive rectangles method*. First, we find that among decentralized mechanisms that realize a goal function, rRM constructs a maximally coarse covering. It is also true that a maximally coarse covering yields an rRM mechanism. The relationship of rRM to information size of the message space is more complicated. It can happen that an rRM covering (or mechanism) fails to have a message space of minimal size. This is shown by examples in this section. However, it is shown in 2.6.5 that if $m^*(F)$ is the minimal informational size attainable by an informationally decentralized mechanism that realizes the goal function F, then there exists an rRM covering of the domain of F, and a decentralized rRM mechanism that realizes F whose message space also has size $m^*(F)$.

In Section 2.6.7 we provide more detailed results for Euclidean cases with parameter spaces of low dimension.

2.6.2 The Maximality of Reflexive RM-Coverings

DEFINITION 2.6.2.1. (a) A covering C' of Θ is a *coarsening* of a covering C of Θ if for every $k \in C$, $\exists k' \in C'$ such that

$$k \subseteq k'.$$

(b) C' is a *proper* coarsening of C if it is a coarsening of C and if there exists k^* in C and k'^* in C' such that

$$k'^* \supseteq k^*, \qquad \text{but } k'^* \neq k^*.^{91}$$

(c) A covering of Θ is called *self-belonging* if it is generated by a self-belonging correspondence.

(d) A covering C of Θ is *eligible* if it is rectangular, F-cc (for some given function F), and self-belonging.

(e) An eligible covering C of Θ is called *maximal*[92] if it has no proper eligible coarsening.

THEOREM 2.6.2.1 (Sufficiency). If C is a reflexive[93] RM for F on Θ, then it has no proper eligible coarsening – C is maximal.

Proof: Suppose C is reflexive RM, but not maximal. Then there exists a proper, eligible coarsening C' of C. That is, C' is rectangular, F-cc, and self-belonging. Because C' is a coarsening of C' it follows that, for every $k \in C$, there is a k' in C' such that $k' \supseteq k$, $k' = A' \times B' \subseteq \Theta^1 \times \Theta^2$, and k' is contained in the contour set of F that contains k. Also, there are sets $A \subseteq \Theta^1$, $B \subseteq \Theta^2$, with $k = A \times B$.

Because $k \subseteq k'$, it follows from rectangularity of C and C' that

$$A' \supseteq A, \qquad B' \supseteq B. \tag{*}$$

---

[91] C is a refinement of C'.

[92] This term seems natural in that a "maximal" coarsening maximizes informational efficiency of a mechanism as measured by the degree of coarseness of its covering.

[93] I.e., both left-RM and right-RM.

Let $a \in A$ and $b' \in B'$. Because C and C' are self-belonging and F-cc, there exists $\bar{\theta} \in k$ such that k is the image of $\bar{\theta}$ by the generating correspondence, and the contour set of F that contains $\bar{\theta}$ also contains k. But k is a subset of k'. Hence the contour set that contains k' is the same as the one that contains k'. It follows from the inclusions labeled (*) that

$$(a, b') \in F^{-1}(F(\bar{\theta})),$$

and also $k' \subseteq F^{-1}(F(\bar{\theta}))$.

Hence, by the definition of $B^*(A, \bar{\theta})$ we have[94]

$$(a, b') \in A \times B^*(A, \bar{\theta}) = A \times B.$$

The equality follows from the fact that C is assumed to be reflexive, and hence left-RM.

Thus, $b' \in B'$ implies $b' \in B$. But b' is an arbitrary element of B'. Hence $B' \subseteq B$. Therefore, by (*),

$$B' = B.$$

Recall that C is reflexive RM, and therefore it is right-RM. Hence, we can show that

$$A = A'$$

by reasoning similar to that used to show that $B' = B$. It then follows that

$$K' = K.$$

This shows that C' is not a proper coarsening of C. Thus, the supposition that C is not maximal leads to a contradiction. This contradiction completes the proof.

THEOREM 2.6.2.2 (Necessity). If C is a rectangular F-cc covering of Θ that is maximal (that is, there is no eligible proper coarsening of C), then C is a reflexive-RM covering of Θ.

Proof: Suppose, to the contrary, that C is maximal and is not a reflexive RM covering. Without loss of generality, suppose C is not left-RM. Then there exists $\bar{\theta}$ and $k = A \times B \in C$ such that

$$B \neq B^*(A, \bar{\theta}).$$

---

[94] The set $B^*(A, \bar{\theta})$ is defined as the union of all sets $B \subseteq \Theta^2$ such that $\bar{\theta} \in A \times B$ and $A \times B \subseteq F^{-1}(F(\bar{\theta}))$.

It follows from the definition of $B^*(A, \bar{\theta})$ that

$$B \subsetneq B^*(A, \bar{\theta})$$

Hence,

$$k \subsetneq A \times B^*(A, \bar{\theta}). \tag{**}$$

Write $k' = A \times B^*(A, \bar{\theta})$,
so that (**) becomes

$$k' \supsetneq k. \tag{+}$$

Consider the collection

$$C' = (C \setminus \{k\}) \cup \{k'\}.$$

C is a covering. The inclusion (+) implies that C' is an eligible covering, because C is an eligible covering, and, from its definition, k' is rectangular, F-cc and self-belonging. Clearly C' coarsens C because, for every set r of C, there is a set r' of C' such that $r \subseteq r'$. This is so because all sets r in C other than k have their identical twins $r' = r$ in C'; and for k in C there is k' in C' with $k \subseteq k'$. Moreover, the coarsening C' is proper because $k' \neq k$. This contradicts the hypothesis that C is maximal, and thus proves the theorem.

2.6.3 Informational Efficiency: General Considerations

A theory of design of economic mechanisms must consider the "cost" in terms of resources, of operating a given mechanism – otherwise every design problem can be solved by using a complete revelation mechanism, or a parameter transfer. In a given design problem these mechanisms, along with many others, might be infeasible in that the resources required to operate any of them might not be available. The resources required are determined by activities that fall under one of three headings:

- Observing the environment;
- Communicating;
- Computing.

A decentralized mechanism that realizes a given goal function, F, determines how finely each agent must observe her component of the environment. This accuracy is formalized by the rectangular covering of the parameter space – a characteristic of the given mechanism.

The amount of communication required by the mechanism is measured by the informational size of its message space. Coarseness of a covering is a set-theoretic concept; size of the message space can be set-theoretic or analytic.

These two indicators or measures of information processing requirements are related, but not equivalent. They are related, because the messages used by the mechanism index the sets in the covering from which the mechanism is constructed. But, to put it informally, the "size" of the index set depends on the "number" of rectangles in the covering, not the "size" of the rectangles. The size of the sets is a property of the covering, and is, loosely speaking, related to the coarseness of the covering. We show in Chapter 3, Section 3.7.4 that coarseness of the covering and informational size of the message space are different concepts. Examples in this section illustrate that point.

The resource costs associated with the computing required to operate a mechanism are determined by their computational complexity. We do not study computational complexity of goal functions, or of the computations performed by agents in this book.[95] However, when the mechanism is given in equation form, rather than set theoretically, an intuitively appealing rough indicator of the burden of calculation imposed by the mechanism is the number of equations that have to be evaluated by agents – referred to as *equation efficiency*, briefly, *eq-efficiency*. The concept of equation-efficiency is formalized by the eq-vector $(q_1, \ldots, q_N)$, where q_i is the nonnegative integer that specifies the number of equations to be checked by agent i in the verification scenario. Given two alternative mechanisms π' and π'' that each realize a goal function F, we say that π' is strictly more equation-efficient than π'' if $q_i' \leq q_i''$ for all $i = 1, \ldots, N$, and at least one of the inequalities is strict.

A mechanism π is *eq-efficient* if it realizes the given F and there is no mechanisms strictly more eq-efficient than π. We show by example that a mechanism can be eq-efficient without being m-efficient. The example appears toward the end of Section 2.6.6. That eq-efficiency is formalized by a vector shows that the concept of eq-efficiency is useful where different agents have different resources or different skills with which to carry out the required verifications.

The number of equations that characterizes a message verification scenario is meaningful only if the equilibrium functions are "smooth," in the sense that justifies the application of the implicit function theorem;

---

[95] Mount and Reiter (2002) presents a formal model of computation that applies to computations performed in a setting in which functions of real variables are computed, and in which computations are carried out by human beings with the aid of machines. A formal analysis of complexity of computations is presented in that book, and examples of its application to models in economics and game theory are given.

in particular, such that the Jacobian of the equation system that defines the message correspondence, as well as the equilibrium of the mechanism, satisfies a rank condition.[96]

The informational size of the message space[97] is defined in the more general setting of topological spaces, but in the case of Euclidean parameter spaces and equation systems that satisfy the smoothness conditions imposed about, we can take the size of a message space to be its dimension. In fact, continuity of the functions is sufficient to justify this. We denote the size of the Euclidean message space M by dim M.

In this book we confine attention to three components of informational efficiency – coarseness of the covering, informational size of the message space, and, in cases where regularity conditions are satisfied, to eq-efficiency. (The concept of redundancy also plays a role.) The concept of informational efficiency is similar to that of production or technological efficiency where the question is whether any input quantity could be reduced without increasing the requirements for other inputs or decreasing output, "other things being equal."

Ideally, we would like to have an algorithm for designing decentralized mechanisms that realize a given goal function, and that are informationally efficient – specifically, that have maximally coarse coverings, and message spaces of minimal informational size – and that is generally applicable. We present such an algorithm for the case of finite environments in Chapter 3, Section 3.4. But the case of Euclidean environments is less satisfactory. We do not have an algorithm that is generally applicable and constructs a mechanism that realizes a given goal function, and whose message space has minimal dimension. Further, we cannot assure that the covering generated has no redundant sets, although in examples where the Jacobian has maximal rank, the covering is a partition, and therefore has no redundant sets. This suggests a possible generalization; if the equilibrium system is linear, as is the case in many examples, there is an algorithm that produces a mechanism that realizes the goal function and has an rRM – maximally coarse – covering. We use this algorithm for the inner product goal function, and also for the Walrasian goal function, with a suitably chosen domain. But in nonlinear cases the usual difficulties presented by nonlinearity prevent development of an algorithmic approach to minimizing the dimension of the message

---

[96] The standard textbook condition is that the relevant functions be continuously differentiable (C^1) and have Jacobians of the highest rank permitted by the dimension of the matrix. See somewhat less demanding conditions in Hurwicz (1969), and Mount and Reiter (1974). Also Gale and Nikaido (1965) and Nikaido (1968) for global conditions.

[97] See Mount and Reiter (1974).

space. However, the rectangles method – rRM – construction applied to a given goal function, followed by the *N*-step construction, does in all cases construct coverings that cannot be properly coarsened.

Coarsening a covering associated with a mechanism does not raise, and can lower, the informational costs associated with the mechanism. Informally, an agent who, for instance, must "observe" his endowment with high precision would generally have to do some – in some cases, a considerable amount – of work to make that observation. We also show that in Euclidean environments coarsening does not raise, and may – but does not necessarily – lower, the dimension of the message space. This is particularly clear when the covering is a partition. However, it is not the case that coarseness-minimal mechanisms – a class that is the same as reflexive RM mechanisms – always minimize the dimension of the message space. We have examples, presented in subsequent sections, in which a coarseness-minimal mechanism uses a message space whose dimension is higher than the minimum dimension for mechanisms that realize that particular goal function.

We show in the next section that, for a given goal function, there always exists an rRM covering, hence maximally coarse, that generates a mechanism whose message space has minimal dimension among *all* decentralized mechanisms – not restricted to those rRM constructed by rRM – that realize the given goal function.

2.6.4 A Comment on Informational Efficiency Concepts

In the preceding discussion there are three concepts of informational efficiency, based respectively on the coarseness of coverings, the number of equations to be verified by each agent, and the dimension of the message space.

The coarseness concept is set-theoretic and so applicable regardless of the analytic properties of the correspondences and mechanisms (e.g., smoothness, ranks of Jacobians, etc.). But the other two concepts relate to a narrower class of structures, those in which correspondences, transversals, and equilibrium functions are "smooth" – satisfy conditions in which it is meaningful to speak of the number of equations.

The dimension of the message space is a positive integer. Therefore message spaces are ordered by their dimension. In contrast, the other two concepts lead to only partial orderings. Hence two mechanisms may be noncomparable either in terms of coarseness, or, where regularity conditions make counting equations meaningful, by their equation-number vectors. This results in a multiplicity of noncomparable mechanisms that are either minimally coarse or equation-efficient.

We can recognize a fourth candidate for an informational efficiency property, that of *redundancy*. A rectangle in a covering C is redundant if the set of rectangles K that remain after deleting K is a covering. This set-theoretic concept induces a partial ordering of mechanisms. Coarseness-maximality does not imply nonredundancy, nor does nonredundancy imply coarseness-maximality.

When the parameter space is a finite set, each redundant rectangle in a covering increases the size of the message space by one additional message – the label of that redundant rectangle. Since we have an algorithm for constructing minimal F-cc rectangular coverings, we can be assured that redundant rectangles do not arise.

When the parameter space is Euclidean there might be redundant rectangles that do not increase the dimension of the message space. In such a case the property of redundancy in the covering would itself be redundant.

Example 3.7.4 shows two different coverings of the parameter space. If the two coverings are superimposed so that the resulting covering has redundant rectangles, the dimension of the message space remains the same.

2.6.5 Minimal Informational Size Is Achievable by an rRM Mechanism

In this section we analyze the relationship between two concepts of informational efficiency: maximal coarseness of the covering and minimum size of the message space – a central issue in mechanism design. When the parameter space is finite the cardinality of the message space is its informational size. When the parameter space is a Euclidean space, or a subset of it with a nonempty interior, its (finite) dimension is its informational size. We know from examples (in Sections 2.6.6, 2.5, and this section) that maximal coarseness of the covering does not by itself imply minimal dimension of the message space constructed from it. There are examples in which two maximally coarse coverings lead to message spaces of different informational size.

When the parameter space is finite there is an algorithm for constructing a mechanism whose message space has minimum size.[98] (See Chapter 3,

---

[98] This algorithm also applies to cases in which the parameter space is Euclidean, but the goal function does not satisfy regularity conditions. See the example shown in Figure 3.4.1.l 7, and the hyperbolic example 2.5.0, 2.5.1.

Section 3.4.1.) For the Euclidean smooth case, we only have the existence result shown in Section, 2.6.5.2, but not an algorithm for locating a mechanism whose message space is of minimal informational size in the class of mechanisms with maximally coarse coverings, nor an algorithm for constructing a mechanism with a message space whose message space has minimal dimension. However, there is a constructive procedure for constructing an rRM mechanism that realizes F when we know a nonrRM mechanism that realizes F. This procedure is used in the proof of 2.6.5.2.

2.6.5.2 Minimal Size Message Spaces versus rRM Mechanisms: Lemma A and the Theorem

Consider a privacy-preserving mechanism $\pi = (M, g^1, g^2, h)$ or $\pi = (M, \mu^1, \mu^2, h)$ realizing a given goal function $F : \Theta \to Z, \Theta = \Theta^1 \times \Theta^2$. Such a mechanism generates a covering of Θ by F-cc "rectangles," i.e., sets of the form $K = K_1 \times K_2$, where $K_1 \subseteq \Theta^1$ and $K_2 \subseteq \Theta^2$, and $K \subseteq F^{-1}(z)$ for some z in Z. We write[99] $K = \{\theta \in \Theta : g(m, \theta) = 0\}$, or [100] $K = \{\theta \in \Theta : m \in \mu(\theta)\}$ where $m \in M$. We call m the "label" of K when the preceding equalities hold. Each rectangle has one and only one label.

It may happen that there are two rectangles, say $K^{(1)}$ and $K^{(2)}$ in C^π, with $K^{(1)} \neq K^{(2)}$, but $K_1^{(1)} = K_1^{(2)}$ or $K_2^{(1)} = K_2^{(2)}$, both rectangles in the same contour set, but with different labels. That is, there is $z \in Z$ such that $K^{(i)} \subset F^{-1}(z), i = 1, 2$, but $K^{(i)} = \{\theta \in \Theta : g(m^{(i)}, \theta) = 0\}, i = 1, 2$, and $m^{(1)} \neq m^{(2)}$.

LEMMA A. Given a privacy-preserving mechanism π realizing the given goal function F, there exists a privacy-preserving rRM mechanism with the same or lower size (dimension or cardinality) of the message space.

Proof: Let C_1^π be the projection of the covering C^π into the subspace Θ^1. Formally,

$$C_1^\pi = \{K_1 \subseteq \Theta^1 : K_1 = \text{proj}_{\Theta^1}(K), K \in C^\pi\}.$$

Next, define the set

$$A_1^\pi = \{K_1 \subseteq \Theta^1 : K_1 \in C_1^\pi\}.$$

---

[99] $g(m, \theta) = 0 \Leftrightarrow g^1(m, \theta^1) = 0$ and $g^2(m, \theta^2) = 0$ where $\theta = (\theta^1, \theta^2)$
[100] $\mu(\theta) = \mu^1(\theta^1) \cap \mu^2(\theta^2)$ where $\theta = (\theta^1, \theta^2)$.

Note that, for every point $\bar{\theta}^1 \in A_1^\pi$, there is $\bar{\theta}^2 \in \Theta^2$ such that $A_1^\pi \times \{\bar{\theta}^2\} \subseteq F^{-1}(F(\bar{\theta}^1, \bar{\theta}^2))$.

We now proceed to carry out the "two-step convergence" procedure. That is, for each $K_1 \in C_1^\pi$, we construct a maximal Θ^2-set compatible with K_1. Formally, we construct the set

$$B^*(K_1, \bar{\theta}) = \bigcap_{\theta^1 \in K_1} \hat{B}(\theta^1, \bar{\theta}),$$

where

$$\hat{B}(\theta^1, \bar{\theta}) = \{\theta^2 \in \Theta^2 : (\theta^1, \theta^2) \in F^{-1}(F(\bar{\theta}))\}.$$

Note that we have now obtained a left-RM covering of Θ, to be denoted say by C', and that C' is a coarsening of C^π. In turn we carry out the second step of "two step convergence," starting with the projection of C' in Θ^2 and carrying out the procedure formally defined by constructing $\bar{A}(\bar{\theta}) = A^*(B(\bar{\theta}), \bar{\theta})$ where $B(\bar{\theta}) = B^*(K_1, \bar{\theta})$.

Thus we obtain a right-RM covering of Θ, say C''. Now C'' is a coarsening of C', hence also of C^π. But C'' is a maximally coarse rRM.

Now we proceed to allocate messages to the rectangles of C''. Since C^π covers Θ, given any rectangle K'' of C'', there exists at least one rectangle K of C^π such that $K \cap K'' \neq \varnothing$. From among rectangles K of C^π satisfying the preceding set inequality choose an arbitrary $\bar{K} \in C^\pi$. Suppose the "label" of $\bar{K}$ is $\bar{m}$; i.e., $\bar{K} = \{\theta \in \Theta : g(\bar{m}, \theta) = 0\}$ or $\bar{K} = \{\theta \in \Theta : \bar{m} \in \mu(\theta)\}$. Then in the newly constructed rRM covering C'', give to the rectangle K'' the label $\bar{m}$. That is, we set $K'' = \{\theta \in \Theta : g(\bar{m}, \theta) = \{\theta \in \Theta : \bar{m} \in \mu(\theta)\}$.

It may happen that there is a rectangle[101] $\hat{K}$ in C^π with label $\hat{m}$ other than $\bar{m}$, but also intersecting K''. That is, $\hat{m} \neq \bar{m}$, $\hat{K} = \{\theta \in \Theta : g(\hat{m}, \theta) = 0\} = \{\theta \in \Theta : \hat{m} \in \mu(\theta)\}$, and $\hat{K} \cap K'' \neq \varnothing$.

But allocating to K'' the label $\bar{m}$ will not violate the F-cc requirement for C'', since the "two-step convergence" results in an F-cc covering so that there is an outcome $z \in Z$ such that $K'' \subseteq F^{-1}(z)$. Also, since π realizes F, and both $\bar{K}$ and $\hat{K}$ intersect K'', $\hat{K} \subseteq F^{-1}(z)$.[102]

The label allocation process produces a message space M^* for a decentralized rRM mechanism $\Pi^* = (M^*, \mu^{1*}, \mu^{2*}, h^*)$, with M^* constituting a subset of M. In fact, M^* may be a proper subset if some elements such as $\hat{m} \in M$ above fail to be used as labels for any rectangles in C''.

---

[101] Or even that there are more than two such rectangles.

[102] The two inclusions for $\bar{K}$ and $\hat{K}$ use the same z as the inclusion for K''.

A generic rectangle $K'' = K_1'' \times K_2''$ in π^* was already defined in the "two-step" procedure as

$$K'' = \tilde{A}(\bar{\theta}) \times B(\bar{\theta})$$

for a properly selected point $\bar{\theta}$.

Since $M^* \subseteq M$, we may define the outcome function h^* of π^* as follows: for $m \in M^*$,

$$h^*(m) = h(m),$$

where h is the outcome function of the originally given mechanism π.

We have thus obtained a decentralized rRM mechanism, say $\pi^* = (M^*, \mu^1, \mu^2, h) = (M^*, g^1, g^2, h)$, $M^* \subseteq M$. Hence, by the monotonicity of size (dimension or cardinality) with regard to inclusion,[103]

$$\begin{cases} \dim M^* \leqq \dim M \text{ if } \Theta \text{ is Euclidean, finite-dimensional:} \\ \quad \text{and } \#M \leqq \#M \text{ if } \Theta \text{ is finite} \end{cases} \quad (+)$$

Among privacy-preserving mechanisms realizing a given goal function $F : \Theta \to Z$, $\Theta = \Theta^1 \times \Theta^2$, there is at least one such mechanism with a message space M of minimal size (dimension or cardinality). This is so because we are assuming either $\Theta \subseteq E^n$, a finite-dimensional Euclidean space, and the message space M is also assumed a subset of a finite-dimensional Euclidean space, say E^m, $m < \infty$, and for nonempty M, $\dim M$ is a nonnegative integer, or because we are assuming Θ to be a finite set.

THEOREM. For every goal function F defined on a subset Θ of a finite-dimensional Euclidean parameter space E^N, or on a finite set Θ, (in either case $\Theta = \Theta^1 \times \Theta^2$), there exists a decentralized (privacy-preserving) rRM, hence maximally coarse, mechanism realizing F whose message space is of minimal size in the class of such mechanisms.

Proof: The conclusion follows from Lemma A and the two inequalities in $(+)$. For finite Θ it also follows from Theorem 3.4.1.1 in Chapter 3.

2.6.6 Two rRM Coverings of Different Informational Size for the Same Goal Function: An Example

Consider the goal function

$$F(a, b) = a_1 b_1 + a_2 b_2 + b_3 + a_1^2,$$

where $b_2 \neq 0$ and $a_2 > 0$.

[103] In separable metric (hence Euclidean) spaces. See Hurewicz and Wallman (1948).

We construct two different left-RM coverings, and show that they are reflexive, nonredundant, and symmetric, so that the resulting covering is a partition. It turns out that the corresponding mechanisms are parameter transfers, one from agent 1 to agent 2; the other vice versa. It follows that rRM does not necessarily minimize the dimension of the message space, even if the covering it constructs is nonredundant, or even a partition. (This is in contrast to the situation with the augmented inner product example where $F(a, b) = a_1 b_1 + a_2 b_2 + b_3$, and where reflexive RM does yield mechanisms whose message spaces have minimum dimension.)

The first mechanism, denoted π', uses as a point of departure the A-set defined by the equation

$$F(a, \bar{b}) = F(\bar{a}, \bar{b}),$$

or explicitly,

$$a_1 \bar{b}_1 + a_2 \bar{b}_2 + \bar{b}_3 + a_1^2 = F(\bar{a}, \bar{b}). \tag{1}$$

To find the corresponding B-set, we solve Equation (1) for a_2 and substitute the solution into the equation $F(a, b) = F(\bar{a}, \bar{b})$. The solution of Equation (1) for a_2 is (since $\bar{b}_2 \neq 0$),

$$a_2 = \frac{1}{\bar{b}_2} \left(\bar{F} - a_1 \bar{b}_1 - \bar{b}_3 - a_1^2 \right) \tag{2}$$

where $\bar{F}$ is an abbreviation for $F(\bar{a}, \bar{b})$.

Substituting the expression for a_2 from Equation (2) into $F(a, b) = \bar{F}$, we obtain

$$a_1 b_1 + \frac{b_2}{\bar{b}_2} \left(\bar{F} - \bar{b}_3 - a_1 \bar{b}_1 - a_1^2 \right) + b_3 + a_1^2 - \bar{F} = 0. \tag{3}$$

This relation must be an identity in a_1, so the coefficients of the powers of a_1 must vanish. This yields three equations:

$$b_1 - \frac{b_2}{\bar{b}_2} \bar{b}_1 = 0 \text{ (from terms linear in } a_1) \tag{4.1}$$

$$-\frac{b_2}{\bar{b}_2} + 1 = 0 \text{ (from terms quadratic in } a_1) \tag{4.2}$$

$$\frac{b_2}{\bar{b}_2} (\bar{F} - \bar{b}_3) + b_3 - \bar{F} = 0 \text{ (from other terms).} \tag{4.3}$$

Using equations (4.2), (4.1), and (4.3) in turn, we find that this system of equations is equivalent to

$$b_1 = \bar{b}_1, \qquad b_2 = \bar{b}_2, \qquad b_3 = \bar{b}_3.$$

Hence the B-set is defined by

$$B = \{(b_1, b_2, b_3) : b_j = \bar{b}_j; \; j = 1, 2, 3\},$$

and it becomes clear that we are dealing with parameter transfer from agent 2 to agent 1. Thus, the message space M' of π' has dim $M' = 4$.

Next, we check reflexivity, that is, whether $A^*(B, \bar{\theta})$ is the original A-set. To do this we substitute the values of the b_j's in the set B into the equation $F(a, b) = \bar{F}$. This gives the equation

$$a_1 \bar{b}_1 + a_2 \bar{b}_2 + \bar{b}_3 + a_1^2 = F(\bar{a}, \bar{b}),$$

which is precisely Equation (1) defining the original set A. Hence we do have a reflexive RM covering.

Next, we show that this rRM covering is nonredundant; we do this by showing that it is a partition. The proof relies on Theorem 3.6.1, which states that if a covering is rRM and symmetric then it is a partition. It remains to prove symmetry.

For this purpose we write the equations of the covering correspondence in equation form as $G(\bar{\theta}, \theta) = 0$, or more explicitly as

$$G^1(\bar{\theta}, a) = 0$$
$$G^2(\bar{\theta}, b) = 0,$$

where

$$G^1(\bar{\theta}, a) \equiv a_1 \bar{b}_1 + a_2 \bar{b}_2 + \bar{b}_3 + a_1^2 - F(\bar{a}, \bar{b})$$

and

$$G^2(\bar{\theta}, b) \equiv (G^{21}(\bar{\theta}, b), \; G^{22}(\bar{\theta}, b), \; G^{23}(\bar{\theta}, b)),$$

with

$$G^{2j}(\bar{\theta}, b) \equiv b_j - \bar{b}_j, \quad j = 1, 2, 3.$$

$G(\bar{\theta}, \theta)$ is said to be symmetric if

$$G(\bar{\theta}, \theta) = 0 \implies G(\theta, \bar{\theta}) = 0.$$

To prove symmetry of our $G(\bar{\theta}, \theta) = 0$ system we first note that $G^2(\bar{\theta}, b) = 0$ implies $G^2(\theta, \bar{b}) = 0$, since $b = \bar{b}$ is the same as $\bar{b} = b$. As for $G^1(\bar{\theta}, a) = 0$, or $F(a, \bar{b}) - F(\bar{a}, \bar{b}) = 0$, the interchange of $\bar{\theta}$ and θ yields $F(\bar{a}, b) - F(a, b) = 0$. However, since the interchange left $b = \bar{b}$, we are entitled to rewrite $F(\bar{a}, \bar{b}) - F(a, \bar{b}) = 0$ by replacing b by $\bar{b}$ in both expressions in the equation, thus obtaining $F(\bar{a}, \bar{b}) - F(a, \bar{b}) = 0$, which is the original equation $G^1(\bar{\theta}, a) = 0$. This completes the proof of symmetry, and hence shows that the covering is a partition. This completes the analysis of the first covering and its generating correspondence.

Now the second covering generates a mechanism π''. For the second covering, using the L-RM correspondence, we choose to define the set A by

$$A(\bar{\theta}) = \{(a_1, a_2) : a_1 = \bar{a}_1, a_2 = \bar{a}_2, a_2 > 0\}. \tag{1}$$

Clearly, this will be the parameter transfer from agent 1 to agent 2. Agent 1 sends two messages $m_1^1 = a_1$; $m_2^1 = a_2$, and agent 2 sends one message:

$$m^2 = F\left(m_1^1, m_2^1, b\right). \tag{*}$$

Thus, dim $M'' = 3$, which shows that π'' is not m-efficient.

Again we substitute the values from the A-equations into $F(a, b) = F(\bar{a}, \bar{b})$, obtaining the B-equation:

$$\bar{a}_1 b_1 + \bar{a}_2 b_2 + b_3 + \bar{a}_1^2 = \bar{a}_1 \bar{b}_1 + \bar{a}_2 \bar{b}_2 + \bar{b}_3 + \bar{a}_1^2. \tag{2}$$

To verify reflexivity, we consider the set $A^*(B, \bar{\theta})$ and ask whether it is the original set A. For this purpose we solve equation (2) for b_3 and substitute the solution into $F(a, b) = \bar{F}$.

The solution of (2) for b_3 is

$$b_3 = -\bar{a}_1(b_1 - \bar{b}_1) - \bar{a}_2(b_2 - \bar{b}_2) + \bar{b}_3.$$

Its substitution into $F(a, b) = F(\bar{a}, \bar{b})$ yields

$$(a_1 - \bar{a}_1)\, b_1 + (a_2 - \bar{a}_2)\, b_2 + \left(a_1^2 - \bar{a}_1^2\right) = 0, \tag{3}$$

which must be an identity in b_1 and b_2. Let b_1 be any nonzero number and b_2 so chosen that $(a_1 - \bar{a}_1)\, b_1 + (a_2 - \bar{a}_2)\, b_2 = 0$. (By hypothesis, $b_1 \neq 0$!) Then (3) becomes

$$a_1^2 - \bar{a}_1^2 = 0,$$

and since (by hypothesis) $a_1 > 0$, $\bar{a}_1 > 0$, it follows that

$$a_1 = \bar{a}_1. \tag{4.1}$$

Hence, by equation (3) together with $a_1 = \bar{a}_1$,

$$(a_2 - \bar{a}_2)\, b_2 = 0.$$

Hence,

$$a_2 = \bar{a}_2, \tag{4.2}$$

and Equations (4.1), (4.2) bring us back to the original A-set. Hence, we have reflexivity.

It remains to verify symmetry. Here the $G(\bar{\theta}, \theta) = 0$ system consists of

$$G^1(\bar{\theta}, a) \equiv (G^{11}(\bar{\theta}, a), G^{12}(\bar{\theta}, a)) = 0,$$

with

$$G^{1i}(\bar{\theta}, a) \equiv (a_1 - \bar{a}_1) = 0, \quad i = 1, 2,$$

and

$$G^2(\bar{\theta}, b) \equiv (a_1 - \bar{a}_1)\, b_1 + (a_2 - \bar{a}_2)\, b_2 + \left(a_1^2 - \bar{a}_1^2\right) = 0.$$

When θ and $\bar{\theta}$ are interchanged, it still remains the case that $a = \bar{a}$. As for $G^2(\bar{\theta}, b) = 0$, it becomes

$$(\bar{a}_1 - a_1)\, \bar{b}_1 + (\bar{a}_2 - a_2)\, \bar{b}_2 + \left(\bar{a}_1^2 - a_1^2\right) = 0,$$

but, since $b_j = \bar{b}_j$, the preceding relation can be rewritten as

$$(\bar{a}_1 - a_1)\, b_1 + (\bar{a}_2 - a_2)\, b_2 + \left(\bar{a}_1^2 - a_1^2\right) = 0,$$

which is equivalent to the original B-equation (3). Thus we have symmetry, hence partition and therefore nonredundancy.

One important conclusion is that a nonredundant rRM covering can yield a mechanism with higher than minimum dimension of the message space.

Furthermore, although π' is not m-efficient, it does have the property of being eq-efficient, assuming nondegeneracy[104]

$$\pi' \text{ is eq-efficient.} \qquad (**)$$

Proof: Suppose π' is not eq-efficient. Then there exists $\pi^{\#}$ whose equation numbers are $q_1^{\#} \leqq 1$, $q_2^{\#} \leqq 3$, with one of the two inequalities strict. It seems obvious that $q_1^{\#} < 1$, i.e., $q_1^{\#} = 0$, is impossible – since this would mean that agent 1 supplies no information. So it must be that $q_2^{\#} < 3$,, i.e., $q_2^{\#} \leqq 2$. But that is also impossible for the following reasons.

Since the set A in π' is maximal, either $A^{\#} = A$ or $A^{\#}$ is a refinement of A in π'. But if $A^{\#} = A$ while $B^{\#} \neq (B$ in π', it follows that $B^{\#}$ coarsens B

---

[104] To make equation counting meaningful, we assume nondegeneracy, as defined in Hurwicz and Weinberger (1990). To define nondegeneracy, consider a mapping $G : W \twoheadrightarrow \mathbb{R}^k$. G is said to be *nondegenerate* at $W_0 \in W$ if the range (image) of its derivative (differentiable) $G_w(W_0; \omega)$ as ω varies is the whole space $\mathbb{R}^k \dot{G}_w$ is linear in ω.

in π'.[105] But this cannot be true since π' is maximally coarse. So $A^\#$ is a nontrivial refinement of A.

Since coverings are represented by nondegenerate equation systems, the $A^\#$ covering is representted by more equations than A, i.e., $q^\# > 1$. Thus, contrary to our hypothesis, $\pi^\#$ is not more efficient than π' (it is eq-noncomparable). This completes the proof of (**), i.e., of the eq-efficiency of π'.

APPENDIX

Recall that given $\bar{\theta} = (\bar{a}, \bar{b}) \in \Theta^1 \times \Theta^2$, and $\tilde{A} \subseteq \Theta^1$ such that $\bar{a} \in \tilde{A}$ and $\tilde{A} \times \{\bar{b}\} \subseteq F^{-1}(F(\bar{\theta}))$, we define the operator B^* by the relation

$$B^*\left(\tilde{A}, \theta = \bigcup_B \{B \subseteq \Theta^2 : \tilde{A} \times B \subseteq F^{-1}(F\bar{\theta})\}\right)$$

REMARK. The operator B^* is monotone decreasing with regard to the inclusion in the first argument; i.e.,

$$A' \supseteq A'' :\Rightarrow: B^*(A', \bar{\theta}) \subseteq B^*(A'', \bar{\theta}).$$

Similarly, given $\bar{\theta} = (\bar{a}, \bar{b}) \in \Theta^1 \times \Theta^2$ and $\tilde{B} \subseteq \Theta^2$ such that $b \in \tilde{B}$ and $\{\bar{a}\} \times B \subseteq F^{-1}(F(\bar{\theta}))\}$, we define the operator A^* by the relation

$$A^*(\tilde{B}, \bar{\theta}) = \bigcup_A \{A \subseteq \Theta^1 : A \times \tilde{B} \subseteq F^{-1}(F(\bar{\theta}))\}$$

A^* is also monotone decreasing with regard to inclusion in the first argument.

THEOREM. "Two-step convergence"

Given $\bar{\theta}$ and A, such that $\bar{a} \in A, \subseteq \Theta^1$, and $A_1 \times \{\bar{b}\} \subseteq F^{-1}(F(\bar{\theta}))$, let $B_1 = B^*(A_1, \bar{\theta})$. Also let $A_2 = A^*(B_1, \bar{\theta})$.

Then $B_2 = \mathrm{def}\, B^*(A_2, \bar{\theta}) = B_1$.

Proof of the Theorem

(i) Claim: $A_2 = \mathrm{def}\, A^*(B_1, \bar{\theta}) \supseteq A_1$

To show this, it is sufficient to prove that

(i') $A_2 \times B_1 \supseteq A_1 \times B_1$.

---

[105] B in π' is maximally fine.

Note that every set B (hence B_1 in particular) in the definition of $B^*(A_1, \bar{\theta})$ satisfies $A_1 \times B \subseteq F^{-1}(F(\bar{\theta}))$; hence A_1 is among the sets A in the definition of $A^*(B_1, \bar{\theta})$. This implies (i') above, hence also claim (i).

(ii) Claim: $B_2 = \mathrm{def}\, B'(A_2, \bar{\theta}) \subseteq B_1 = \mathrm{def}\, B^*(A_1, \bar{\theta})$.

This follows by monotonicity and Claim (i).

(iii) Claim: $B_2 \supseteq B_1$.

Since $A_2 \times B_1$ is in the level set of $\bar{\theta}$ (i.e., $A_2 \times B_1 \subseteq F^{-1}(F(\bar{\theta}))$), it follows that B_1 is among the sets whose union constitutes $B^*(A_2, \bar{\theta})$. Hence the union $B^*(A_2, \bar{\theta})$ includes B_1, i.e., the Claim (iii).

(iv) Since $B_2 \supseteq B_1$ by (ii), and $B_2 \supseteq B_1$ by (iii), it follows that $B_2 \subseteq B_1$.

Q.E.D.

THREE

Designing Informationally Efficient Mechanisms
Using the Language of Sets

3.1 Introduction

This chapter presents a formal and concise account of the process of designing a decentralized mechanism that realizes a given goal function. The presentation here differs from the one in Chapter 2 in that this process is set-theoretic, whereas in Chapter 2 (and Chapter 4), sets and relations are represented by equations. The set-theoretic formulation is more general, and covers cases in which the set of environments is a finite or discrete set. A merit of the set-theoretic formulation is that it helps make clear the essential logic and properties of our procedures for designing decentralized mechanisms. On the other hand, the formulation in which sets and relations are represented by equations permits the components of a mechanism to be expressed in terms of algebraic expressions that hold across the set of environments, rather than pointwise, as is the case with the set-theoretic formulation. The process of mechanism design is "algorithmic" in both formulations, in the sense that the design process consists of a sequence of prescribed steps that starts with a specified goal function, and results in an informationally efficient decentralized mechanism that realizes the given goal function. Both approaches use the axiom of choice to prove the existence of a transversal. However, the equations approach may in specific instances derive a transversal by algebraic means, or through the use of calculus. In the approach that uses smooth equations to characterize sets and functions, an analysis may require solution of systems of nonlinear equations of high degree. Section 1.8 – the regulation of logging in a National Forest – serves to motivate and illustrate mechanism design, but the formal structure presented in this chapter does not require working through the example. Section 1.9 is revisited in Section 3.8, where it is used to illustrate the formal structures presented in this chapter.

3.2 Mechanism Design

In an existing economy, mechanisms are typically designed in the midst of ongoing economic activity, and it is also often the case that the set of designers includes economic agents who are also engaged in economic activity. Nevertheless, in the interest of clarity, it is helpful to separate the process of mechanism design from the conduct of ordinary economic activity. Therefore, we consider two phases of mechanism theory. The first phase is the *design* phase; the second is the *operating* phase. The design phase takes place before the operating phase. It must be completed before the operating phase can start. (In some cases the design was completed even before the current generation of economic agents was born.) We assume that there is a *designer*, who, possibly together with *assistants,* designs and constructs an informationally decentralized mechanism to be used to organize the activities of present and future economic agents.

More specifically, in the basic set up there is a set of economic agents, $\{1, \ldots, N\}$, a set of (factored) economic environments, $\Theta = \Theta^1 \times \cdots \times \Theta^N$, and a goal function $F : \Theta \rightarrow Z$. We assume that the designer knows the set of agents, the factored parameter space, Θ, and the goal function, F. The designer can share her information with her assistants. The designer does not know which of the possible environments will prevail after the design phase is over. The product of that phase is a decentralized mechanism, $\pi = (M, \mu, h)$. Each agent learns his part of the mechanism; that is, agent i learns $\mu^i : \Theta^i \Rightarrow M$, and possibly the outcome function h. The outcome function translates equilibrium messages into outcomes.

After the design phase is finished, a particular environment θ in Θ materializes, and each economic agent learns his component θ^i of θ. Thus, in the operating phase, each economic agent knows the part of the mechanism that governs her behavior, and her component θ^i of θ. It is possible that the designer, or one of her assistants, is one of the economic agents. In that case, she must function in the design phase knowing only the information that the designer is assumed to have, that is, without knowledge of the value of θ, or of her component θ^i of θ.[1]

Designing a mechanism can be a process that consists of *steps*, and these steps can be *distributed* among assistants to the designer. Although it is tempting to think of the design of the mechanism as itself being decentralized, we use the term "distributed," because the process is not necessarily

---

[1] Otherwise incentives would create an additional problem. Here we can think of designing mechanisms that will operate in the future.

informationally decentralized in the sense in which that term applies to a mechanism.

The basic framework and notation used here is the same as that used in Chapter 2. It consists of

- a parameter space Θ;
- an outcome space Z;
- a single-valued goal function $F : \Theta \to Z$;
- a mechanism $\pi = (M, \mu, h)$,
- where M is the message space of the mechanism;
- $\mu : \Theta \Rightarrow M$ is the (group) equilibrium message correspondence, and
- $h : M \to Z$ is the outcome function.

It is convenient to distinguish between the message space M and the space $M' \subseteq M$, where $M' = \mu(\Theta)$ is the image of Θ under μ, and consists of the subset of messages in M that are actually used by the mechanism.

A mechanism $\pi' = (M', \mu, h')$, where $M' = \mu(\Theta)$, and $h' : M' \to Z$, can be extended to $\pi = (M, \mu, h)$ by defining $h : M \to Z$ by

$$h(m) = \begin{cases} h'(m) & \text{if } m \in M' \\ z^\circ \in Z & \text{if } m \in M \backslash M' \end{cases}.$$

DEFINITION 3.2.1. *The mechanism* $\pi = (M, \mu, h)$ *realizes F if and only if for all* $\theta \in \Theta$

$$h \circ \mu(\theta) = F(\theta).$$

It is implicit in the definition of "realizing" that $\mu(\theta)$ is nonempty for every $\theta \in \Theta$, and that h is defined on $\mu(\Theta)$.

3.2.1 Decentralization

We assume that knowledge of the environment is distributed among a finite set of agents $I = \{1, \ldots, N\}$. Specifically, we assume that

$$\Theta = \Theta^1 \times \cdots \times \Theta^N. \tag{3.2.1}$$

When Θ is the domain of the goal function, F, and (3.2.1) holds, we say that F is *factored*.

We assume that when $\theta \in \Theta$ is the prevailing parameter point, $\theta = (\theta^1, \ldots, \theta^N)$, agent i knows θ^i and does not know θ^j, for any $j \neq i$.[2] In that case no communication from agent i can depend directly on θ^j, for $j \neq i$.[3] Insofar as realization is concerned, this requirement is expressed formally by defining individual equilibrium message correspondences

$$\mu^i : \Theta^i \Rightarrow M, \quad \text{for } i \in I.$$

The set $\mu^i(\theta^i)$ consists of messages $m \in M$ such that when $i's$ parameter value is θ^i, agent i accepts message $m \in M$ as an equilibrium if and only if $m \in \mu^i(\theta^i)$. Thus, agent i's behavior in equilibrium depends only on the component of the environment that she knows.

DEFINITION 3.2.2. A mechanism $\pi = (M, \mu, h)$ is called *informationally decentralized*, briefly *decentralized*, if and only if there exist correspondences $\mu^i : \Theta^i \to M$ such that for all $\theta \in \Theta$, $\mu(\theta) = \bigcap_{i=1}^N \mu^i(\theta^i)$.

That is, $\mu(\theta)$ consists of messages that each agent individually agrees to when the environment is θ.

Our objective here is to design informationally decentralized mechanisms (with desirable informational properties) that realize a given goal function. Consider the situation of a designer of mechanisms. The designer would know the set of agents, I, and the goal function, $F : \Theta \to Z$; that is, she knows the set of environments, the distribution of information about each environment among the agents – the designer knows what information each individual agent would have in each possible environment, but would not herself know that information – and the goal function. The designer's task is to choose a message space, a decentralized message correspondence, and an outcome function that together realize the given goal function. She is to do this using only what she knows, namely, the set of agents, the set of possible environments (including the distribution of information about environments among the agents), and the goal function. The design process generally cannot be decentralized. It is inherent in the design problem that the designer knows the goal function, and the

---

[2] This is a simplification of a more general assumption. Suppose that what agent i knows when the environment is θ is the value $\eta^i(\theta)$ of a function $\eta^i : \Theta \to Y^i$, where Y^i is the set of signals available to agent i. In that case $\eta^i(\theta)$ is what agent i knows about the environment θ. Hence his message can depend only on $\eta^i(\theta)$.

[3] In Section 3.9.2, where mechanisms that implement a goal function in Nash equilibrium are considered, the implementation literature, requires the strategy of an individual agent to depend on the vector $\theta = (\theta^1, \ldots, \theta^N)$, but, according to the requirements of a verification scenario, verification by agent i uses only knowledge by agent i of θ^i.

distribution of information among the agents. On the other hand, decentralization is a property of a mechanism. It concerns the information that each economic agent has about the prevailing environment. Though the designer does not know the prevailing environment she can, in the first phase of mechanism design, distribute her task among her assistants, sharing with them the relevant parts of her information about the goal function, and the structure of the space of environments. In light of the magnitude of the task of designing a decentralized mechanism that realizes a given goal function, it is often desirable to distribute that task among many assistant designers, when that is possible, that is, to *distribute* the process of design. We show how this can be done in the N-step process presented in Section 3.3.

As a guide for the designer, we consider next how a decentralized mechanism that realizes a goal function F structures the parameter space in relation to F.

3.3 Mechanisms and Coverings

The message correspondence $\mu : \Theta \Rightarrow M$ of a mechanism π induces a covering $C = C_\mu$ of the parameter space Θ, as follows. For $m \in M'$, $K \in C_\mu(m)$ if and only if

$$K = \{\theta \in \Theta \mid \theta \in \mu^{-1}(m)\}.$$

Here $\mu^{-1} : M' \Rightarrow \Theta$ is the correspondence defined by

$$\theta \in \mu^{-1}(m) \Leftrightarrow m \in \mu(\theta).$$

Thus, a set K in this covering is the set of all parameter points that give rise to the same message in the mechanism under consideration.

If π realizes F on Θ, then for every point $m \in M'$ and every point in $\theta \in \mu^{-1}(m)$, we have $h(m) = F(\theta)$. It follows that for every set $K \in C_\mu$, $K \subseteq F^{-1}(F(\theta))$. Thus, each set of the covering C_μ is contained in a contour set of the goal function F.

DEFINITION 3.3.2. A set K that is contained in a contour set of F is said to be *F-contour contained*, briefly, *F-cc*; a collection of sets that are each *F-cc* is said to be *F-cc*.

When $\Theta = \Theta^1 \times \cdots \times \Theta^N$ and μ is privacy preserving, $\theta \in \mu^{-1}(m)$ if and only if $\theta^j \in (\mu^j)^{-1}(m)$, for $j = 1, \ldots, N$, where $\theta = (\theta^1, \ldots, \theta^N)$. It follows that

$$\mu^{-1}(m) = (\mu^1)^{-1}(m) \times \cdots \times (\mu^N)^{-1}(m),$$

where $(\mu^i)^{-1}(m) \subseteq \Theta^i$. The proof is immediate.

Thus, the set $\mu^{-1}(m)$ is the product of sets $(\mu^i)^{-1}(m)$ in the individual parameter space Θ^i of agent i. If the message correspondence is privacy preserving, we call the set $\mu^{-1}(m)$ a *rectangle*. It is not a geometric rectangle, except in the case where the set $\mu^{i^{-1}}(m)$ is a geometric rectangle in Θ^i for every $i = 1, \ldots, N$.

If the mechanism π realizes the goal function F, it must be the case, as stated above, that the inverse image of a message is F-contour contained. That is, for all $m \in M' \equiv \mu(\Theta)$, the set $\mu^{-1}(m) \subseteq F^{-1}(z)$, where $h(m) = z$.

Suppose $F(\bar{\theta}) = z$ for some fixed value $\bar{\theta} \in \Theta$. Then for $m \in \mu(\bar{\theta})h(m) = z$. Consequently, $\bar{\theta} \in \mu^{-1}(m)$. Moreover if $\theta' \in \mu^{-1}(m)$, it must be the case that $F(\theta') = z$, because $F(\theta') = h(\mu(\theta')) = h(m) = z$.

Therefore, the set $\mu^{-1}(m) = (\mu^1)^{-1}(m) \times \cdots \times (\mu^N)^{-1}(m)$ is a subset of $F^{-1}(z)$, a contour set of F. That is, $\mu^{-1}(m)$ is F-cc.

To summarize, the covering C_μ induced by the message correspondence μ is

(+)   rectangular

and

(++) F-contour contained, that is, each set $K \in C_\mu$ is a subset of a contour set $F^{-1}(z)$ for some z in the range of F.

The property of rectangularity, namely, that each $K \in C_\mu$ is the product of sets $K^i \in \Theta^i$, $i = 1, \ldots, N$, is a consequence of the privacy-preserving property of the message correspondence, μ, and hence of the fact that a mechanism π that has the message correspondence μ is decentralized.

The relationship between the decentralized mechanism $\pi = (m, \mu, h)$ and the covering C_μ of the parameter space Θ suggests a procedure for constructing decentralized mechanisms that realize a given goal function, when such a mechanism is not known in advance. The idea is to work from the right sort of covering of the parameter space to a mechanism. Without reference to any mechanism, using only knowledge of the goal function F, we construct a covering of the parameter space that satisfies properties (+) and (++). That is, first we construct a rectangular, F-cc covering of Θ, and then we construct a decentralized mechanism from that covering by indexing the sets in the covering by "messages." Furthermore, from the standpoint of informational efficiency it is desirable to make the rectangles in the covering as "large" as possible, in an appropriate sense, because the larger the set in the covering, the less is the information about the environment conveyed by the set, or by the name of the set. Moreover, from the standpoint of informational efficiency, it is also desirable to make the names, or labels, of sets as "small" as possible, in an appropriate sense, because the cost of processing and transmitting small signals is likely to be less than the cost of processing and transmitting large ones. This, along with other considerations related to informational efficiency, is discussed in Section 3.7 and in Chapter 2. Next, we turn to a procedure for constructing a suitable covering.

3.4 A Systematic Process (an Algorithm) for Constructing an rRM Covering

Suppose we are given a factored space of environments $\Theta = \Theta^1 \times \cdots \times \Theta^N$, and a goal function $F : \Theta \to Z$. The first step in the procedure for constructing a decentralized mechanism that realizes F is to construct a correspondence $V : \Theta \Rightarrow \Theta$ with three properties:

$$\text{For every } \theta \in \Theta, V(\theta) \text{ is a rectangle.} \tag{3.4.1}$$

That is, there are sets $K^1, K^2, \ldots, K^N$ $K^i \subseteq \Theta^i$ such that

$$V(\theta) = K^1 \times K^2 \times \cdots \times K^N.$$
$$\text{For every } \theta \in \Theta, V(\theta) \subseteq F^{-1}(F(\theta)). \tag{3.4.2}$$

That is, V is F-cc.

$$\text{For every } \theta \in \Theta, \theta \in V(\theta). \tag{3.4.3}$$

We say that V is *self-belonging* if it satisfies (3.4.3).

We first present the construction for the case of two agents. In that case

$$\Theta = \Theta^1 \times \Theta^2.$$

Define a correspondence $A : \Theta \Rightarrow \Theta^1$ as follows. For an arbitrary point $\bar{\theta} = (\bar{\theta}^1, \bar{\theta}^2) \in \Theta$, define a set $A(\bar{\theta})$ in Θ^1 such that

$$\bar{\theta}^1 \in A(\bar{\theta}), \tag{3.4.4}$$

and

$$A(\bar{\theta}) \times \{\bar{\theta}^2\} \subseteq F^{-1}(F(\bar{\theta})). \tag{3.4.5}$$

Next, define a "rectangle" by choosing a set $B(A(\bar{\theta}), \bar{\theta}) \subseteq \Theta^2$, such that

$$\bar{\theta}^2 \in B(A(\bar{\theta}), \bar{\theta}), \qquad\qquad (3.4.6)$$

and

$$A(\bar{\theta}) \times B(A(\bar{\theta}), \bar{\theta}) \subseteq F^{-1}(F(\bar{\theta})). \qquad\qquad (3.4.7)$$

We define $V(\bar{\theta}) = A(\bar{\theta}) \times B(A(\bar{\theta}), \bar{\theta})$. Then (3.4.4), (3.4.6), and (3.4.7) ensure that $V : \Theta \Rightarrow \Theta$ is self-belonging, rectangular, and F-cc.

Note that this construction can be carried out in steps, each done perhaps by a different assistant designer. This feature also holds when there are more than two agents. We show in Section 3.5 that a mechanism constructed from this covering is decentralized, and does realize the goal function F.

The preceding construction does not take informational efficiency into account in prescribing the sets A and B. For instance, the sets $A(\bar{\theta}) = \{\bar{\theta}^1\}$, $B(A(\bar{\theta}), \bar{\theta}) = \{\bar{\theta}^2\}$ are acceptable. This particular specification results in the covering that leads to the complete revelation mechanism. However, with informational efficiency in mind, we require that the sets A and B be as large as possible without resulting in a rectangle that includes points not in the contour set $F^{-1}(F(\bar{\theta})$. Thus, in a preliminary step we specify $A(\bar{\theta})$ to satisfy 3.4.4 and 3.4.5, as above. In the next step we choose

$$B^*(A(\bar{\theta}), \bar{\theta}) = \cup\{B \subseteq \Theta^2 \mid \bar{\theta}_2 \in B \quad \text{and} \quad A(\bar{\theta}) \times B \subseteq F^{-1}(F(\bar{\theta}))\} \tag{3.4.8}$$

so as to make the B-side of the rectangle as large as possible without going outside the contour set of $\bar{\theta}$, given the set $A(\bar{\theta})$.

This choice of the B-set defines a correspondence $L : \Theta \Rightarrow \Theta$, by

$$L(\theta) := A(\theta) \times B^*(A(\theta), \theta). \qquad\qquad (3.4.9)$$

This is called the *left rectangles method* correspondence, abbreviated *left* RM correspondence. As constructed, it is self-belonging, F-cc and rectangular.

If we had chosen to start with agent 2, we would have started the construction with the preliminary choice of a set $B(\bar{\theta})$ such that for

$$\bar{\theta} = (\bar{\theta}^1, \bar{\theta}^2) \in \Theta,$$
$$\bar{\theta}^2 \in B(\bar{\theta}), \qquad\qquad (3.4.10)$$

and

$$\{\bar{\theta}^1\} \times B(\bar{\theta}) \subseteq F^{-1}(F(\bar{\theta})). \tag{3.4.11}$$

In turn, we would define

$$A^*(B(\bar{\theta}), \bar{\theta})) = \cup\{A \subset \Theta^1 \mid \bar{\theta}^1 \in A \text{ and } A \times B(\bar{\theta}) \subseteq (F^{-1}(\bar{\theta}))\} \tag{3.4.12}$$

and define the right-RM correspondence

$$R : \Theta \Rightarrow \Theta \text{ by } R(\theta) = A^*(B(\theta), \theta) \times B(\theta). \tag{3.4.13}$$

As with L, the right RM correspondence is self-belonging, F-cc, and rectangular.

In general, the left RM and right-RM correspondences are different. However, by using the operators A^* and B^* we can construct a correspondence that is both left-RM and right-RM. We call such a correspondence *reflexive* RM, briefly rRM. To do this we first choose a correspondence $A : \Theta \Rightarrow \Theta^1$ that satisfies conditions (3.4.4) and (3.4.5). Then form the sets $B^*(A(\bar{\theta}), \bar{\theta})$ as described. Second, define $\tilde{B}(\theta) = B^*(A(\bar{\theta}), \bar{\theta})$, and form the right-RM correspondence for $\tilde{B}(\theta)$, using the operator A^* to form the set

$$A^*(\tilde{B}(\bar{\theta}), \bar{\theta}).$$

Let

$$\tilde{A}(\bar{\theta}) = A^*(\tilde{B}(\bar{\theta}), \bar{\theta}).$$

Then the self-belonging, F-cc, and rectangular correspondence,

$$V(\theta) = \tilde{A}(\theta) \times \tilde{B}(\theta),$$

such that

$$\tilde{B}(\theta) = B^*(\tilde{A}(\theta), \theta)$$

and

$$\tilde{A}(\theta) = A^*(\tilde{B}(\theta), \theta),$$

is both left and right RM, that is, *reflexive* RM. If we think of this construction as a dynamic process, then the initial value is the initial step – the choice of the preliminary set either $A(\bar{\theta})$ or $B(\bar{\theta})$, and the stationary value is the result of the final step, $V(\theta) = \tilde{A}(\theta) \times \tilde{B}(\theta)$. This rectangle can also be considered to be a *fixed point* of a mapping defined by the operators A^* and B^*. Examples presented subsequently show that the correspondence V and the covering

C_V that it generates depend on the initial step, that is, on which side of the rectangle is chosen first, and on what set is chosen in that preliminary step.
Formally,

THEOREM 3.4.1 (*Two step rRM construction*). Let $\bar{\theta} \in \Theta = \Theta^1 \times \Theta^2$, let $A_1 \subseteq \Theta^1$, and suppose that $\bar{\theta}^1 \in A_1$. We claim that the set $B_1 := B^*(A_1, \bar{\theta})$ is reflexive. That is, if $A_2 = A^*(B_1, \bar{\theta})$, then $B^*(A_2, \bar{\theta}) = B_1$.

Proof: (*) Note that the operators B^* and A^* are each monotone decreasing with respect to set inclusion.
Thus,

$$A' \supseteq A'' \quad \text{implies} \quad B^*(A', \bar{\theta}) \subseteq B^*(A'', \bar{\theta}).$$

(Similarly for A^*.) To see this, observe that $A_1 \subseteq A_2 = A^*(B_1, \bar{\theta})$. This follows from the definition of A^*, and B^*, and the construction of B_1. Furthermore, by construction we have $A_2 \times B_1 \subseteq F^{-1}(F(\bar{\theta})$. It follows that $B_1 \subseteq B^*(A_2, \bar{\theta})$. But because $A_2 \supseteq A_1$, it follows from (*) that $B_1 \supseteq B^*(A_2, \bar{\theta})$. Thus, we have shown that $B_1 = B^*(A_2, \bar{\theta})$, that is, we have shown that $B^*(A^*(B_1)) = B_1$. This completes the proof.

In the case of two agents the construction can be illustrated graphically. Figures 3.4.1a and 3.4.1b show the two steps of the construction.

A similar construction works for an arbitrary finite number, N, of agents. We begin with notation.

Let $\Theta = \Theta^1 \times \cdots \times \Theta^N$, and for $K^i \in \Theta^i$, $i = 1, \ldots, N$, let $K = K_1 \times \cdots \times K_N$. Thus, K is a rectangle in Θ. We write $K_{-i} = K_1, \ldots, K_{i-1}, K_{i+1}, \ldots, K_N$. The set K_{-i} is an ordered list of sets corresponding to the agents other than agent i in the order $\{1, \ldots, N\}$. Similarly,

$$\Theta^{-i} = \Theta^1 \times \cdots \times \Theta^{i-1} \times \Theta^{i+1} \times \cdots \times \Theta^N.$$

Our construction begins by choosing a sequence of agents $\langle i_1, i_2, \ldots, i_N \rangle$, from the set $\{1, \ldots, N\}$, that is, a permutation of the agents. The construction starts with agent i_1, and continues through the set of agents in the order given by the permutation. For convenience, and without loss of generality, we can consider the agents in the same order as they appear in the set $\{1, \ldots, N\}$. Let $\bar{\theta}$ be an arbitrary point in Θ. The designer constructs a rectangle corresponding to the point $\bar{\theta}$ that has two properties; first, it contains the point $\bar{\theta}$, and second, it is contained in the same contour set of the goal function F as $\bar{\theta}$. We use the following notation.

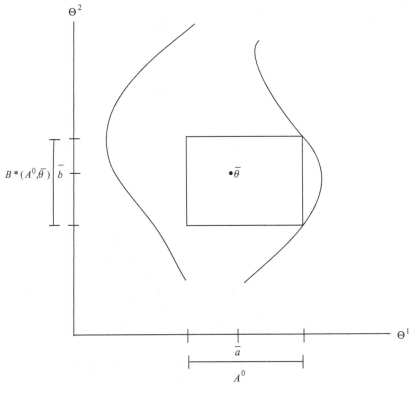

Figure 3.4.1a

The set K_i is the i-side of a rectangle $K = K_1 \times \cdots \times K_N = K_i \times K_{-i}$. We write $K'_{-i} \subseteq K''_{-i}$ to mean that every component of K'_{-i} is a subset of the corresponding component of K''_{-i}.

The designer's construction proceeds in steps. In each step the designer specifies a "side" of the rectangle corresponding to an agent, and does so in steps, agent by agent in order. There is a preliminary step, called the 0th step. In this step the designer specifies a provisional set for agent 1, denoted K_1^0, that satisfies the condition

$$\bar{\theta} \in K_1^0 \times \{\bar{\theta}_{-1}\} = K_1^0 \times \{\bar{\theta}^2\} \times \cdots \times \{\bar{\theta}^N\} \subseteq F^{-1}(F(\bar{\theta})).$$

In the following N steps, the designer constructs the sides of the rectangle corresponding to the point $\bar{\theta}$. This is done by means of operators A_i^*, for $i =$

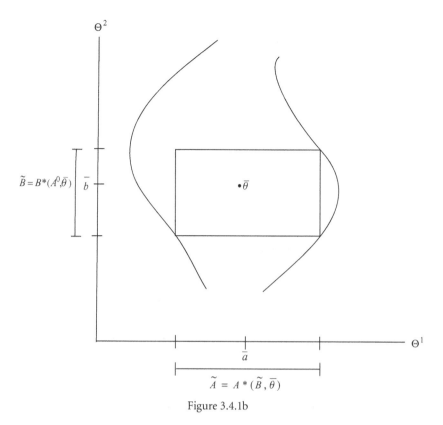

Figure 3.4.1b

$1, \ldots, N$. The operator A_i^* specifies the maximal i-side of an F-cc rectangle that contains the point $\bar{\theta}$, from given sides K_{-i}. We write

$$K_i^* = A_i^*(K_{-i}; \bar{\theta}).$$

Formally, for each $i \in \{1, \ldots, N\}$, we define the operator A_i^* by the relation

$$A_i^*(K_{-i}; \bar{\theta}) = \cup\{K_i' \subseteq \Theta^i : \bar{\theta} \in K_i' \times K_{-i} \subseteq F^{-1}(F(\bar{\theta}))\}. \quad (3.4.14)$$

It is immediately evident that each operator A_i^* is *monotone decreasing with respect to inclusion*, in the sense that
$(+)$ for every $i = 1, \ldots, N$, and every $\bar{\theta}$,

$$\text{if } K'_{-i} \subseteq K''_{-i}, \text{ then } A_i^*(K'_{-i}; \bar{\theta}) \supseteq A_i^*(K''_{-i}; \bar{\theta}).$$

The N steps of the designer's construction are as follows. For agents $2, \ldots, N$, the designer proposes sides

$$K_2 = \left(K_1^0, \{\bar{\theta}^3\}, \ldots, \{\bar{\theta}^N\}, \bar{\theta} \right)$$

$$K_3 = A_3^* \left(K_1^0, K_2, \{\bar{\theta}^4\}, \ldots, \{\bar{\theta}^N\}, \bar{\theta} \right)$$

$$\vdots$$

$$K_i = A_i^* \left(K_1^0, K_2, K_{i-1}, \{\bar{\theta}^{i+1}\}, \ldots, \{\bar{\theta}^N\}, \bar{\theta} \right)$$

$$\vdots$$

$$K_N = A_N^* \left(K_1^0, K_2, \ldots, K_{N-1}, \bar{\theta} \right)$$

and, in the Nth step, the designer constructs the final specification of agent 1's side, namely

$$K_1 = A_1^* (K_2, \ldots, K_N, \bar{\theta}).$$

The N-step construction defines a correspondence $V : \Theta \Rightarrow \Theta$ that is self-belonging, rectangular, and F-cc.

Note that this construction has two "free parameters," the permutation of agents and the choice of the "initial set" in each preliminary step. Thus, even for a given permutation of the agents, and a given point, $\bar{\theta}$, there may be several different rectangles that can be constructed by the N-step procedure.

In Chapter 2, where we define sets and functions by smooth equations, we show how the covering and correspondence described here in set-theoretic terms (without smoothness assumptions) can be constructed by an algebraic procedure. It is not necessary to carry out the construction separately for each parameter point.

Just as the two-step process results in a reflexive rectangle (see Theorem 3.3.1 for two agents) so does the N-step process. To prove this, we first define reflexivity in the setting of $N \geq 2$ agents at an arbitrary hypothetical parameter point $\bar{\theta} \in \Theta$.

DEFINITION 3.4.1. Let C be a rectangular, self-belonging, F-cc covering of Θ. C is called *reflexive*, if and only if for every $\bar{\theta} \in \Theta$, and each rectangle $K = K_1 \times \cdots \times K_N \in C$ such that $\bar{\theta} \in K$, it is the case that for each $i \in \{1, \ldots, N\}$, $K_i = A_i^*(K_{-i}, \bar{\theta})$. If C is generated by a correspondence $V : \Theta \Rightarrow \Theta$ and C is reflexive, we also call V reflexive.

THEOREM 3.4.2. If C_V is a covering of Θ generated by a correspondence V as $\bar{\theta}$ ranges over Θ, that is constructed by an N-step procedure, then C_V is reflexive, F-cc, rectangular, and self-belonging, and so is V.

Proof: Only reflexivity is not obvious. To prove reflexivity we must show that, for an arbitrary $\bar{\theta}$ in Θ, a rectangle $K = K_1 \times \cdots \times K_N$, that is, constructed by the N-step process, $K_i = A_i^*(K_{-i}, \bar{\theta})$, for each $i \in \{1, \ldots, N\}$.

For $i \in \{2, \ldots, N\}$, because K is constructed by the N-step process,

$$K_i = \cup\{K_i' \subseteq \Theta^i : \bar{\theta} \in K_1^0 \times \cdots \times K_{i-1} \times K_i' \times \{\bar{\theta}^{i+1}\} \times \cdots \times \{\bar{\theta}^N\}$$
$$\subseteq F^{-1}(F(\bar{\theta}))\}. \tag{*}$$

It follows that

$$K_{-i} = (K_1, \ldots, K_{i-1}, \{\bar{\theta}^{i+1}\}, \ldots, \{\bar{\theta}^N\}). \tag{\&}$$

From the definition of K, and the assumption that K is constructed by the N-step process, it follows that

$$K_{-i} = (K_1, \ldots, K_{i-1}, K_{i+1}, \ldots, K_N), \tag{**}$$

and that

$$(K_1, \ldots, K_{i-1}, K_{i+1}, \ldots, K_N) \supseteq (K_1, \ldots, K_{i-1}, \{\bar{\theta}^{i+1}\}, \ldots, \{\bar{\theta}^N\}).$$

This implies that $K_{-i} \supseteq A_i^*(K_1, \ldots, K_{i-1}, \{\bar{\theta}^{i+1}\}, \ldots, \{\bar{\theta}^N\})$.

Then, monotonicity of the operators A_i^* yields the relation

$$A_i^*(K_{-i}, \bar{\theta}) \subseteq A_i^*(K_1^0 \times \cdots \times K_{i-1} \times \{\bar{\theta}^{i+1}\} \times \cdots \times \{\bar{\theta}^N\}, \bar{\theta}) = K_i.$$

But

$$\bar{\theta} \in K_i \times K_{-i} \subseteq F^{-1}(F(\bar{\theta})),$$

hence,

$$K_i \subseteq A_i^*(K_{-i}, \bar{\theta}).$$

It follows that $K_i = A_i^*(K_{-i}, \bar{\theta})$, for $i = 2, \ldots, N$.

To see that the conclusion also holds for $i = 1$, note that

$$K_{-1} = (K_2, \ldots, K_N),$$

and hence by the Nth step of the N-step process,

$$K_1 = A_1^*(K_{-1}, \bar{\theta}).$$

We have shown that for all $i = 1, \ldots, N$

$$K_i = A_i^*(K_{-i}, \bar{\theta}).$$

This completes the proof.

Theorem 3.4.2 tells us that the N-step process constructs reflexive RM coverings. It is also the case that *every* reflexive RM covering of the parameter space Θ, for the function F, can be constructed by the N-step process. To see this, suppose that C is a reflexive RM covering of Θ for F, and let $\bar{\theta}$ be an arbitrary point of Θ. Then $\bar{\theta}$ is contained in some rectangle, or possibly several rectangles, in C. Let $K = K_1 \times \cdots \times K_N$ be a rectangle that contains $\bar{\theta}$. Begin the N-step process with $K_1^0 = K_1$ as the preliminary step. The first step constructs $K_2' = \cup\{B \subseteq \Theta^2 : \bar{\theta} \in K_1^0 \times B \times \{\bar{\theta}_3\} \times \cdots \times \{\bar{\theta}_N\} \subseteq F^{-1}(F(\bar{\theta}))\}$. Thus, $K_2' = A_2^*(K_1 \times \{\bar{\theta}_{-2}\}, \bar{\theta})$. Because K is a reflexive RM rectangle, $K_2 = A_2^*(K_{-2}, \bar{\theta})$. Now, $K_1 \times \{\bar{\theta}_{-2}\} \subseteq K_{-2}$. Therefore, $A_2^*(K_{-2}, \bar{\theta}) \subseteq A_2^*(K_1 \times \{\bar{\theta}_{-2}\})$, and hence $K_2 \subseteq K_2'$. But $K_2 \subseteq \{B \subseteq \Theta^2 : \bar{\theta} \in K_1^0 \times B \times \{\bar{\theta}_3\} \times \cdots \times \{\bar{\theta}_N\} \subseteq F^{-1}(F(\bar{\theta}))\}$. Hence, $K_2 \supseteq A_2^*(K_1 \times \{\bar{\theta}_{-2}\}) = K_2'$. Thus, $K_2 = K_2'$.

A similar argument shows that $K_i = K_i'$ for all $i \in \{1, \ldots, N\}$.

We have shown the following.

THEOREM 3.4.3. A covering C of Θ for F is reflexive RM if and only if it can be constructed by the N-step process.

The rRM construction applied to a given goal function can produce several different coverings. All of them are maximally coarse, and therefore are efficient in the sense that they require the agents to observe their environments only as precisely as is necessary to realize the given goal function. We say they are *observationally efficient*. However, the rRM procedure can construct decentralized mechanisms that realize a given goal function, but that have different sized message spaces. Thus, as it stands so far, it is not guaranteed that the rRM algorithm constructs mechanisms that have message spaces that are of minimum informational size, although mechanisms that realize the given goal function and have minimum informational size are among those that are produced by the rRM algorithm. We show next that adding a step to the algorithm can result in mechanisms that have *minimal observational requirements* and also *minimal message spaces*. More specifically, in the case of *finite parameter spaces* the modified rRM construction, called OrRM, results in a covering of the parameter space that leads to a message space that has minimal informational size, and therefore has no redundant rectangles.

3.4.1 OrRM: An Algorithm for Constructing an rRM Covering of a Finite Parameter Space That Is Minimal in the Class of Rectangular, *F*-Contour Contained Coverings

The rRM algorithm for constructing a covering of the level sets of a goal function in its parameter space can construct several different coverings. Each of them is maximally coarse, but they do not necessarily have the same number of sets (see Example 3.6.2). In the case of a finite parameter space, the *number* of sets in a covering is important because, anticipating the construction of a transversal to the covering in the next section, the size of a covering determines the size of the message space of a mechanism based on that covering. In this subsection we modify the rRM construction so that it generates *minimal coverings*, that is, coverings that consist of the smallest possible number of *F*-contour contained rectangles for a given goal function. We show that the covering so constructed, an rRM covering, is minimal in the class of *all F*-contour contained rectangular coverings for the given goal function. It follows that the mechanism constructed from that covering is informationally efficient with respect to two criteria of efficiency: observational efficiency and communication efficiency. The covering constructed by OrRM is maximally coarse, because it is an rRM covering, and, in the case of a finite parameter space, the message space of a mechanism so constructed has minimal informational size in the space of all decentralized mechanisms that realize the given goal function. Furthermore, the covering from which the mechanism is constructed does not contain any superfluous rectangles.

The idea underlying the modification of the rRM algorithm is to choose a special order in which the rectangles are constructed. Specifically, the set constructed first is one in which, for left-RM, the *A*-side is most constrained (in a sense made clear in what follows) (for right-RM, it is the *B*-side), and proceeds in order through those that are successively less constrained, stopping at the first collection of rRM sets that form a covering. This process defines the (self-belonging) covering correspondence V on the full parameter space. It therefore defines the covering C_V, and also ensures that C_V contains no superfluous sets. We call this an *ordered* rRM construction, abbreviated OrRM. The OrRM construction is presented for the case of two agents, first for a goal function that is defined on a finite parameter space, and subsequently for certain special goal functions defined on a continuum, specifically, a Euclidean space, that do not satisfy the regularity assumptions made in Chapters 2 and 4.

Chapters 2 and 4 deal with goal functions defined on Euclidean spaces, and usually assume that they satisfy regularity conditions. In Chapter 2 regular goal functions are usually assumed either to have nonzero Jacobians, or, to satisfy certain rank conditions on bordered Hessian matrices. (Some functions that are not so regular also appear in Chapter 2.) The requirement on the bordered Hessian matrix is imposed when the condensation method is used to construct decentralized mechanisms. These conditions, and the theorems that the condensation method is based on, are presented in Chapter 4. But "between" the finite case and the smooth cases treated in Chapters 2 and 4 there is a class of goal functions defined on continua that do not satisfy smoothness conditions, for instance, step-functions. Goal functions of this kind can arise in applications in which goals are described in ordinary language, or in legal language, perhaps in legislation, or in an administrative context. To represent the intended goal formally in such cases it may be convenient, or necessary, to use step-functions, or functions pieced together from local approximations (splines), as in the Example in Section 1.8. The OrRM method of constructing a covering correspondence can be used in such cases, at least to a certain extent, to construct a minimal covering of the parameter space. It is applied in this subsection to a step-function whose domain is a rectangle in two-dimensional Euclidean space. It is also applied to a function made up of linear pieces. These applications are illustrated graphically. We begin with the case of a finite parameter space.

A Finite Parameter Space

DEFINITION 3.4.1.1. Let

$$\mathbf{B}^{co}(\Theta, F, \hat{\theta}) = \Theta \setminus F^{-1}(F(\hat{\theta})) = \{\theta \in \Theta = \Theta^1 \times \Theta^2 \mid \theta \notin F^{-1}(F(\hat{\theta}))\}.$$

This is the set of all points in the rectangle $\Theta^1 \times \Theta^2$ that are *not* in a given contour set of the goal function F.

The parameter spaces Θ^1 and Θ^2, the goal function F, and the point $\hat{\theta}$ are all fixed in the analysis that follows, so we drop explicit reference to them from the notation and write

$$\mathbf{B}^{co} = \mathbf{B}^{co}(\Theta, F, \hat{\theta}).$$

ASSUMPTION 3.4.1.1. Θ^1 and Θ^2 are finite sets.

Therefore, so is $\Theta = \Theta^1 \times \Theta^2$.

For given $\hat{\theta} \in \Theta^1 \times \Theta^2$, $F^{-1}(F(\hat{\theta})) \subseteq \Theta^1 \times \Theta^2$.

Another piece of notation that is useful is to mark points in the contour set $F^{-1}(F(\hat{\theta}))$ by o and points in $\mathbf{B}^{co}$ by $\times$.

Following the convention used earlier in this chapter for finite sets $\Theta = \Theta^1 \times \Theta^2$, we represent them graphically as a box in which the sides consist of points $a_1, a_2, \ldots, a_n$ of Θ^1, and $b_1, b_2, \ldots, b_m$ of Θ^2. The box is

$$proj_1(F^{-1}(F(\hat{\theta}))) \times proj_2(F^{-1}(F(\hat{\theta}))) \subseteq \Theta^1 \times \Theta^2.^4$$

Let

$$\mathbf{B}(\hat{\theta}) = proj_1(F^{-1}(F(\hat{\theta}))) \times proj_2(F^{-1}(F(\hat{\theta}))).$$

Note that

$$\mathbf{B}(\theta) = \mathbf{B}(\hat{\theta}) \quad \text{for all } \theta \in F^{-1}(F(\hat{\theta})).$$

$\mathbf{B}(\hat{\theta})$ is the smallest box that contains $F^{-1}(F(\hat{\theta}))$.

With the understanding that $\hat{\theta}$ is fixed, we write elements of $\mathbf{B}$ in the coordinates (a, b). Thus, $proj_1(\mathbf{B}) = \{a_1, a_2, \ldots, a_{\bar{p}}\}$, and $proj_2(\mathbf{B}) = \{b_1, b_2, \ldots, b_{\bar{q}}\}$. We use two representations of the contour set. The first uses the set $\mathbf{B}$. Because $\Theta = \Theta^1 \times \Theta^2$ is finite, we can represent $\mathbf{B}$ as a matrix, or table, in which each element (a, b) occupies a "cell" in the matrix. The second is to construct a matrix Q that has the same structure as $\mathbf{B}$, but the entries are either o or $\times$, according to whether the corresponding entry in $\mathbf{B}$ is in the contour set, in which case it is o, or not, in which case it is $\times$. Thus, we can represent the contour set in its *minimal* containing box $\mathbf{B}$ by a $\bar{p} \times \bar{q}$ matrix Q, whose entries are either o or $\times$, where $\bar{p} \le n$, $\bar{q} \le m$. We show a contour set and its containing box in Table 3.4.1.1.

Table 3.4.1.1

1	o	o	$\times$	o
2	–	–	–	–
3	o	o	$\times$	o
4	–	–	–	–
5	–	–	–	–
	1	2	3	4

---

[4] In some cases it is possible to decompose a contour set of F so that there is a collection of pairs of subsets in which each pair forms a rectangular block with the property that the part of the contour set of F in that block can be analyzed separately from the rest of the contour set. That is, there are subset $S_1 \subseteq \Theta^1$ and $S_2 \subseteq \Theta^2$ such that

$$\{proj_1(F^{-1}(F(\hat{\theta})) \cap S_1 \times S_2) \times \Theta^2\} \times \{proj_2(F^{-1}(F(\hat{\theta})) \cap S_1 \times S_2) \times \Theta^1\}$$
$$\subseteq (F^{-1}(F(\hat{\theta})) \cap S_1 \times S_2).$$

Of course, $\Theta^1 \times \Theta^2$ is itself such a block. In specific applications it may be convenient to decompose a contour set in this way. In a general treatment one block, which might as well be $\Theta^1 \times \Theta^2$, suffices.

This matrix, or table, Q is used to construct a rectangular, F-cc, covering of the contour set that is minimal in the set of all F-cc, rectangular coverings of the contour set $F^{-1}(F(\hat{\theta}))$, whether RM coverings or not. There are two versions of the OrRM algorithm. One starts from the A-side and uses the "maximum A-set left-RM" construction. The other starts from the B-side and uses the "maximum B-set right-RM" construction. The two versions do not necessarily yield the same covering, nor do they yield the same marked sets in Q, especially when the numbers of elements in $|proj_1(\mathbf{B})|$ and $|proj_2(\mathbf{B})|$ (respectively equal to the number of columns in Q, and to the number of rows in Q) are not the same. In such a case it is better to use left-RM, when $|proj_1(B)| < |proj_2(B)|$, and right-RM when the inequality is reversed. A similar thing happens in the case of a Euclidean parameter space. In an example, the "augmented inner product" goal function, analyzed in Chapter 2 [2.1.1], the parameter space consists of two real parameters that characterize the first agent, and three that characterize the second. There are only two mechanisms that realize that goal function. One is parameter transfer from agent 1 to agent 2, the other is parameter transfer from agent 2 to agent 1. These mechanisms correspond to F-cc rectangular coverings of the parameter spaces, one to the max A-side RM covering, and the other to the max B-side RM covering. The A-side covering, corresponding to the agent with two parameters, constructs a mechanism with a two-dimensional message space, the other, corresponding to the agent with three parameters, constructs a mechanism with a three-dimensional message space. In the finite case, in the max-A left-RM, (resp. max-B right-RM) the number of choices for A-sets, (resp. B-sets) can depend on the size of $|proj_1(\mathbf{B})|$ (resp. $|proj_2(\mathbf{B})|$). We present the max A-set left-RM version of the algorithm, in a case where the parameter space of agent 1 is not larger than that of agent 2.

The OrRM algorithm also constructs the self-belonging covering correspondence that generates the covering C_V.

The OrRM algorithm.

To begin with, note that the matrix Q might contain several identical rows. For instance, suppose $\bar{q} = 4$, and $\bar{p} = 5$, and suppose that the points (a_1, b_1), (a_2, b_1), (a_4, b_1), and (a_1, b_3), (a_2, b_3), (a_4, b_3) are all in $F^{-1}(F(a_1, b_1))$. Then the matrix Q would have two identical rows, for example, as shown in Table 3.4.1.1.

The rows 1 and 3 are defined to be *equivalent*, because, as is made clear below, they are treated identically by the algorithm.

We begin with an informal discussion of the max A-set left-RM algorithm.

The *first step* is to select a row of Q with the property that the number of entries in that row that are marked $\times$ is a maximum among the rows of Q. Call such a row *maximal (in Q)*. If there are several maximal rows, choose one of them arbitrarily, and name it *Row* 1. We call this a *named row*, and distinguish it from other rows of Q that are not named. Named rows are numbered separately.

The *second step* is to apply the maximal A-set (abbreviated max A-set) version of the left-RM algorithm to *Row* 1. This constructs a rectangle in Q (and the corresponding rectangle in $\mathbf{B}$), which we call K_1. Without confusion we use the same name to refer to a rectangle in Q, and to the rectangle in $\mathbf{B}$ that has entries (a, b) in exactly the matrix positions (cells) that are marked o in Q.

Next, for any point $\theta = (a, b) \in K_1$ let

$$V(\theta) = V(a, b) = K_1.$$

Notice that applying the max A-set left-RM algorithm to rows in Q that are equivalent to *Row* 1 results in the same rectangle K_1.

If K_1 contains all the points in Q marked o, then the covering $C_V = \{K_1\}$ is a covering of the contour set $F^{-1}(F(\hat{\theta}))$.

If there are points of Q marked o that are not in K_1, there must be a point $\theta = (a, b) \notin K_1$. Then there must be at least one row in $Q\backslash\{$rows equivalent to *Row* 1$\}$. Find a row that is maximal in $Q\backslash\{$rows equivalent to *Row* 1$\}$. Name it *Row* 2, and apply the max A-set algorithm to that row, and all rows equivalent to *Row* 2. It follows from the fact that there is at least one point that is marked $\times$ in *Row* 1, but not marked $\times$ in *Row* 2 that the max A-set left-RM algorithm constructs a rectangle $K_2 \not\subset_{\neq} K_1$. Thus, $K_2\backslash K_1 \neq \phi$. For each point $\theta = (a, b) \in K_2\backslash K_1$, let $V(\theta) = K_2$. In other words, for $\theta \in K_2$,

$$V(\theta) = \begin{cases} K_1 & \text{if } \theta \in K_1 \cap K_2, \\ K_2 & \text{if } \theta \in K_2\backslash K_1. \end{cases}$$

If V is defined at every cell in Q that is marked o, then K_1 and K_2 together cover the full contour set.

So, suppose there is a cell in Q marked o at which V is not defined. If such a cell is in *Row* 3 we apply the max A-side left-RM algorithm to *Row* 3. If there is no such cell in *Row* 3, then V is already defined at every cell of that row. We call such a Row *inactive* given the rectangles already constructed. In that case the construction proceeds to the next named Row in which there is an entry o at which V is not defined. Suppose without loss of generality that this is *Row* 4. Then the max A-side left-RM algorithm is applied to *Row* 4. This constructs the set K_3.

This process continues until the first step at which a set K_t, $t \leq \bar{p}$, is reached such that there is no $\theta \in \mathbf{B}$ at which $V(\theta)$ is undefined. The process must stop in at most $\bar{p}$ steps.

Theorem 3.4.1.1 shows that this process guarantees that the covering C_V so constructed consists of the smallest number of F-cc rectangles that can cover the set $F^{-1}(F(\hat{\theta}))$. The covering C_V might contain sets that overlap, but it contains no superfluous sets.

Before presenting a formal treatment, we take up an example that shows the algorithm in action.

EXAMPLE 3.4.1.1. An informal idea of why we might expect the OrRM algorithm to construct a minimal covering is that it starts with an A-side set such that the rectangle that is constructed is the most constrained. That is, it starts with a row with the most entries marked $\times$, and therefore contains elements that will not be covered by other less constrained rectangles. Therefore, the rectangles that are constructed first are ones that would in any case have to be constructed. It might then happen that those rectangles also cover cells that would be covered by other rectangles, ones that could create redundancies if they were constructed too early in the process. The following example illustrates this point, and the process of construction. The example is followed by a formal specification of the algorithm and a statement and proof of Theorem 3.4.1.1.

In this example $\Theta^1 = \{a_1, \ldots, a_6\}$, and $\Theta^2 = \{b_1, \ldots, b_8\}$. The goal function is $F : \Theta^1 \times \Theta^2 \to Z$. The matrix Q can without loss of generality incorporate the effect of the initial step in selecting a row to be considered "next" by first ordering its rows according to the criteria laid out in the informal discussion that precedes this example. If this is done to begin with, the algorithm starts with the top row, and goes through the set of rows from the top row in the order in which they are listed. In this example the reordered matrix Q is shown in Table 3.4.1.2.

Starting with *Row* 1 we apply the *maximal A-set* rRM algorithm. The maximal A-set in *Row* 1 is $A = \{a_1, a_2\}$. Then

$$B^*(A) = \{b_1, b_2, b_6, b_7, b_8\},$$

Table 3.4.1.2

b_1	o	o	×	×	×	×
b_2	o	o	×	×	×	×
b_3	o	×	o	×	×	o
b_4	o	×	×	×	o	o
b_5	×	×	o	o	o	o
b_6	o	o	o	o	o	×
b_7	o	o	o	o	o	o
b_8	o	o	o	o	o	o
	a_1	a_2	a_3	a_4	a_5	a_6

and hence

$$\{a_1, a_2\} \times \{b_1, b_2, b_6, b_7, b_8\} = K_1.$$

(Recall that the max A-side left-RM construction automatically produces reflexive RM rectangles. That is, if A is maximal, then $A^*(B^*(A)) = A$.)

Then for every point $(a, b) \in K_1$ let $V(a, b) = K_1$.

The second row is identical to *Row* 1. The algorithm constructs the same rectangle K_1 for every row that is equivalent to *Row* 1. Therefore, every element in the rows equivalent to *Row* 1 are covered by K_1, and the covering correspondence V is defined for every point in K_1.

Table 3.4.1.3

b_1	1	1	×	×	×	×
b_2	1	1	×	×	×	×
b_3		×		×	×	
b_4		×	×	×		
b_5	×	×				
b_6	1	1				×
b_7	1	1				
b_8	1	1				
	a_1	a_2	a_3	a_4	a_5	a_6

The entries in Q covered by K_1 are indicated in Table 3.4.1.3 by replacing the mark o in a covered cell with the entry 1.

Attention turns to the next row. The third row of Q is the first row that is different from *Row* 1, though it has the same number of × entries (cells marked ×). It is designated *Row* 2. The max A-set for *Row* 2 is $\{a_1, a_3, a_6\}$. Then,

$$B^*(\{a_1, a_3, a_6\}) = \{b_3, b_7, b_8\}.$$

Therefore,

$$\{a_1, a_3, a_6\} \times \{b_3, b_7, b_8\} = K_2.$$

The entries in Q covered by K_1 and K_2, as indicated in Table 3.4.1.4 by the entries 1 and 2, respectively.

Table 3.4.1.4

b_1	1	1	×	×	×	×
b_2	1	1	×	×	×	×
b_3	2	×	2	×	×	2
b_4		×	×	×		
b_5	×	×				
b_6	1	1				×
b_7	1,2	1	2			2
b_8	1,2	1	2			2
	a_1	a_2	a_3	a_4	a_5	a_6

Next, V is defined at the points in K_2 at which V is not already defined. This results in the extension of V as follows:

$$V((a_1, b_3)) = V((a_3, b_3)) = V((a_6, b_3)) = V((a_3, b_7))$$
$$= V((a_3, b_8)) = V((a_6, b_7)) = V((a_6, b_8)) = K_2.$$

The fourth row of Q is different from the third, and is designated *Row 3*. The max A-set is $\{a_1, a_5, a_6\}$. Then $B^*(\{a_1, a_5, a_6\}) = \{b_1, b_7, b_8\}$, and consequently $\{a_1, a_5, a_6\} \times \{b_1, b_7, b_8\} = K_3$.

Table 3.4.1.5

b_1	1	1	×	×	×	×
b_2	1	1	×	×	×	×
b_3	2	×	2	×	×	2
b_4	3	×	×	×	3	3
b_5	×	×				
b_6	1	1				×
b_7	1,2,3	1	2		3	2,3
b_8	1,2,3	1	2		3	2,3
	a_1	a_2	a_3	a_4	a_5	a_6

The entries in Q covered by K_1, K_2, and K_3 are indicated in Table 3.4.1.5 by the entries 1, 2, 3, respectively.

The points that do not already have V values are shown next with their V values. These are

$$V((a_3, b_5)) = V((a_4, b_5)) = V((a_5, b_5)) = V((a_6, b_5))$$
$$= V((a_4, b_7)) = V((a_4, b_8)) = K_3.$$

The fifth row of Q comes next, and is designated *Row* 4. The max A-set is $\{a_3, a_4, a_5, a_6\}$.

$$B^*(\{a_3, a_4, a_5, a_6\}) = \{b_5, b_7, b_8\};$$

therefore,

$$\{a_3, a_4, a_5, a_6\} \times \{b_5, b_7, b_8\} = K_4.$$

The entries in Q covered by $K_1, K_2, K_3,$ and K_4 are indicated in Table 3.4.1.6 by the entries 1, 2, 3, 4, respectively.

Table 3.4.1.6

b_1	1	1	×	×	×	×
b_2	1	1	×	×	×	×
b_3	2	×	2	×	×	2
b_4	3	×	×	×	3	3
b_5	×	×	4	4	4	4
b_6	1	1				×
b_7	1,2,3	1	2,4	4	3,4	2,3,4
b_8	1,2,3	1	2,4	4	3,4	2,3,4
	a_1	a_2	a_3	a_4	a_5	a_6

The elements of K_4 not already assigned receive the assignments

$$V((a_3, b_5)) = V((a_4, b_5)) = V((a_5, b_5)) = V((a_6, b_5))$$
$$= V((a_4, b_7)) = V((a_4, b_8)) = K_4.$$

Unassigned points remain, so the sixth row of Q must be considered. Designate this row as *Row* 5. The max A-set in Row 5 is

$$\{a_1, a_2, a_3, a_4, a_5\}.$$
$$B^*(\{a_1, a_2, a_3, a_4, a_5\}) = \{b_6, b_7.b_8\};$$

therefore,

$$\{a_1, a_2, a_3, a_4, a_5\} \times \{b_6, b_7.b_8\} = K_5.$$

The entries in Q covered by $K_1, K_2, K_3, K_4,$ and K_5 are indicated in Table 3.4.1.7 by the entries 1, 2, 3, 4, and 5, respectively.

Table 3.4.1.7

b_1	1	1	×	×	×	×
b_2	1	1	×	×	×	×
b_3	2	×	2	×	×	2
b_4	3	×	×	×	3	3
b_5	×	×	4	4	4	4
b_6	1	1	5	5	5	×
b_7	1,2,3	1	2,4,5	4,5	3,4,5	2,3,4
b_8	1,2,3	1	2,4,5	4,5	3,4,5	2,3,4
	a_1	a_2	a_3	a_4	a_5	a_6

At this point every element of $\Theta^1 \times \Theta^2$ that is in the contour set under consideration has been assigned a V value. Thus, the construction is completed. The covering is

$$C_V = \{K_1, K_2, K_3, K_4, K_5\}.$$

It is evident that this covering is not redundant, but perhaps not so evident that it is minimal in the class of all F-cc rectangular coverings of Q. Theorem 3.4.1.1 shows this.

Note that the last two rows of Q form an rRM rectangle. If the construction of a covering had started with this rectangle, or had formed it "too soon," then the covering that resulted would have at least one redundant set.

The OrRM construction starting from the B-side generally does not produce the same covering, nor does it necessarily produce a covering that consists of the same number of rectangles. This is illustrated by Example 3.4.1.1.

Next, apply the *maximum B-side right*-OrRM algorithm to Table 3.4.1.2. We do not reorder the columns of Table 3.4.1.2 as we did the rows, but rather number them as shown in Table 3.4.1.8 to display the order in which rectangles are constructed in this example, using the principle that governs the order in which either rows or columns are considered. This is done so as to avoid creating a second matrix, and confusion that might arise from differences in the appearance of the two matrices. It was already noted that the left-OrRM and right-OrRM algorithms do not necessarily construct coverings with the same number of rectangles, and commented that it seems the difference is related to the number of columns compared to the number of rows. But we have not proved this.

Table 3.4.1.8

	Col 6	Col 5	Col 3	Col 1	Col 2	Col 4
b_1	0	0	×	×	×	×
b_2	0	0	×	×	×	×
b_3	0	×	0	×	×	0
b_4	0	×	×	×	0	0
b_5	×	×	0	0	0	0
b_6	0	0	0	0	0	×
b_7	0	0	0	0	0	0
b_8	0	0	0	0	0	0
	a_1	a_2	a_3	a_4	a_5	a_6

The first named column in Table 3.4.1.8 is the fourth column from the left. It has four cells marked ×, the maximum number of cells marked × among the six columns.

This is named *Column* 1, labeled (Col 1), in the table. Applying the max B-side right-RM construction to this column yields the rectangle

$$K_1 = \{a_3, a_4, a_5\} \times \{b_5, b_6, b_7, b_8\},$$

as shown in Table 3.4.1.9. The covering correspondence values are

$$V(a_3, b_5) = \cdots = V(a_5, b_8) = K_1$$

Table 3.4.1.9

	Col 6	Col 5	Col 3	Col 1	Col 2	Col 4
b_1	0	0	×	×	×	×
b_2	0	0	×	×	×	×
b_3	0	×	0	×	×	0
b_4	0	×	×	×	0	0
b_5	×	×	1	1	1	0
b_6	0	0	1	1	1	×
b_7	0	0	1	1	1	0
b_8	0	0	1	1	1	0
	a_1	a_2	a_3	a_4	a_5	a_6

The next named column is column 2, which leads to construction of the set $K_2 = \{a_5\} \times \{b_4, \ldots, b_8\}$, and to defining the covering correspondence at the lone cell in K_2 at which it is not already defined. Thus, $V(a_5, b_4) = K_2$.

Table 3.4.1.10 shows this construction.

Table 3.4.1.10

	Col6	Col5	Col3	Col1	Col2	Col4
b_1	0	0	×	×	×	×
b_2	0	0	×	×	×	×
b_3	0	×	0	×	×	0
b_4	0	×	×	×	2	0
b_5	×	×	1	1	1,2	0
b_6	0	0	1	1	1,2	×
b_7	0	0	1	1	1,2	0
b_8	0	0	1	1	1,2	0
	a_1	a_2	a_3	a_4	a_5	a_6

The rectangle $K_3 = \{a_3\} \times \{b_3, b_5, \ldots, b_8\}$ is the next one constructed, as shown in Table 3.4.1.11.

Table 3.4.1.11

	Col6	Col5	Col3	Col1	Col2	Col4
b_1	0	0	×	×	×	×
b_2	0	0	×	×	×	×
b_3	0	×	3	×	×	0
b_4	0	×	×	×	2	0
b_5	×	×	1,3	1	1,2	0
b_6	0	0	1,3	1	1,2	×
b_7	0	0	1,3	1	1,2	0
b_8	0	0	1,3	1	1,2	0
	a_1	a_2	a_3	a_4	a_5	a_6

The covering correspondence is defined at the one cell not already covered. Thus, $V(a_3, b_3) = K_3$.

Continuing, we get successively

Table 3.4.1.12

	Col6	Col5	Col3	Col1	Col2	Col4
b_1	0	0	×	×	×	×
b_2	0	0	×	×	×	×
b_3	0	×	3	×	×	4
b_4	0	×	×	×	2	4
b_5	×	×	1,3	1	1,2	4
b_6	0	0	1,3	1	1,2	×
b_7	0	0	1,3	1	1,2	4
b_8	0	0	1,3	1	1,2	4
	a_1	a_2	a_3	a_4	a_5	a_6

with $K_4 = \{a_6\} \times \{b_3, b_4, b_5, b_7, b_8\}$, and $V(a_6, b_3) = V(a_6, b_4) = V(a_6, b_5) = V(a_6, b_7) = V(a_6, b_8) = K_4$.

Then,

Table 3.4.1.13

	Col 6	Col 5	Col 3	Col 1	Col 2	Col 4
b_1	5	5	×	×	×	×
b_2	5	5	×	×	×	×
b_3	o	×	3	×	×	4
b_4	o	×	×	×	2	4
b_5	×	×	1,3	1	1,2	4
b_6	5	5	1,3	1	1,2	×
b_7	5	5	1,3	1	1,2	4
b_8	5	5	1,3	1	1,2	4
	a_1	a_2	a_3	a_4	a_5	a_6

and $K_5 = \{a_1, a_2\} \times \{b_1, b_2, b_6, b_7, b_8\}$ and $V(a_i, b_j) = K_5$ for all (i, j) that identify a cell in K_5. Finally, we have Table 3.4.1.14.

Table 3.4.1.14

	Col 6	Col 5	Col 3	Col 1	Col 2	Col 4
b_1	5,6	5	×	×	×	×
b_2	5,6	5	×	×	×	×
b_3	6	×	3	×	×	4
b_4	6	×	×	×	2	4
b_5	×	×	1,3	1	1,2	4
b_6	5,6	5	1,3	1	1,2	×
b_7	5,6	5	1,3	1	1,2	4
b_8	5,6	5	1,3	1	1,2	4
	a_1	a_2	a_3	a_4	a_5	a_6

where $K_6 = \{a_1\} \times \{b_1, \ldots, b_4, b_6, \ldots, b_8\}$, and $V((a_1, b_3)) = V((a_1, b_4)) = K_6$.

This covering consists of six rectangles. It is minimal among right RM coverings, but recalling that max A-side left-OrRM construction resulted in a covering of $\mathbf{B} \backslash \mathbf{B}^{co}$ by five rectangles, we see that it is not minimal in the set of F-cc rectangular coverings of $\mathbf{B} \backslash \mathbf{B}^{co}$.

Formal Treatment

Suppose we are given a finite set $\Theta = \Theta^1 \times \Theta^2$, a goal function $F : \Theta^1 \times \Theta^2 \to Z$, and the sets and notation introduced above. The matrix Q is as defined above for a given contour set. Note that there is an upper bound on the number of rectangles required to cover Q, that is, to cover the cells in Q marked o. Because there is a cell marked o in every column of Q, and there is an F-cc rectangular covering that consists of rectangles that are each confined to its own column of Q, it is not necessary to consider coverings that consist of more than $\bar{q}$ rectangles. (Recall that $\bar{q}$ is the number of columns in Q.) But there might be coverings that consist of fewer than $\bar{q}$ rectangles. Suppose that the number of rows in Q is less than the number of columns in Q.

Let left-OrRM denote the max A-set left-RM algorithm. We show next that the left-OrRM algorithm constructs *minimal coverings*. That is, we show that every F-cc, rectangular covering of the contour set of F contains at least as many rectangles as one constructed by left-OrRM.

ASSUMPTION 3.4.1.1. Suppose that $\Theta = \Theta^1 \times \Theta^2$, and Z are finite sets, $F : \Theta \to Z$, and the matrix Q is defined for each contour set of F such that its named *Rows* are arranged in order with the first, or top, *Row* having the largest number of cells marked $\times$ among the rows of Q, and therefore the smallest number marked o. The second *Row* has the next largest number marked $\times$, but not all in the same columns as *Row* 1. (The possibility that the *number* of cells marked $\times$ in *Row* 2 is the same as in *Row* 1 is not ruled out.) The arrangement and numbering of named *Rows* continues until every named *Row* has a number.

Suppose, without loss of generality, that the number of columns of Q is less than or equal to the number of rows.

Under this assumption it suffices to consider the left-OrRM algorithm.

THEOREM 3.4.1.1. Let C_V be a left-OrRM covering of the contour sets of F, then every rectangular, F-cc (RF) covering of the contour sets of F contains at least as many sets as C_V. C_V is a *minimal covering* of the contour sets of F.

Proof: It suffices to consider one of the contour sets of F, and let $\mathbf{B}\backslash\mathbf{B}^{co}$ and Q be the matrices defined for that contour set.

Suppose the number of cells in *Row* 1 of Q that are marked $\times$ is x_1. Then $y_1 = \bar{q} - x_1 > 0$ is the number of cells in *Row* 1 that are marked o. The smallest number of rectangles that can cover the cells in *Row* 1 that are marked o is 1. There is at least one such rectangle, for instance, the rectangle, R_1, that consists of *all* the cells in Row 1 that are marked o. We seek a covering of Q that has the smallest number of rectangles. Therefore we enlarge R_1 as much as possible. This is accomplished by replacing R_1 by the rectangle

$$K_1 = A_1 \times B^*(A_1),$$

where $A_1 = proj_1 R_1$, and B^* is the operator defined in the left-RM construction in Section 3.3. It is clear that K_1 covers *Row* 1.

The covering correspondence V associated with the covering we are constructing can be defined on K_1, by

$$V(\theta) = K_1, \quad \text{for all } \theta \in K_1.$$

If $V(\theta) = K_1$ for all $\theta \in \mathbf{B} \backslash \mathbf{B}^{co}$, then K_1 covers the entire contour set $\mathbf{B} \backslash \mathbf{B}^{co}$. In that case, $C_V = \{K_1\}$. Therefore, because any rectangular F-cc (RF) covering of the contour set $\mathbf{B} \backslash \mathbf{B}^{co}$ must contain at least one set, the left-OrRM covering C_V is minimal in the class of all RF coverings of $\mathbf{B} \backslash \mathbf{B}^{co}$.

Suppose that not all cells in *Row* 2 are in K_1.

LEMMA 3.4.1.1. A rectangle that covers a cell in a column whose projection on $(\mathbf{B} \backslash \mathbf{B}^{co}) \backslash A_1$ is not empty, cannot cover *Row* 1. That is, a rectangle that

- contains a cell in Q that is marked o, and
- that cell is located in a column whose projection on Θ^1 is not in A_1

cannot cover *Row* 1.

Proof: To verify this, suppose to the contrary that there is a column, say c, such that the only cell that c has in common with *Row* 1 is marked $\times$, and there is an F-cc rectangle, R, that includes a cell in c marked o, and also covers *Row* 1. Let the cell at $(1, c')$ be marked o. Then R includes the cell at $(1, c')$ and a cell at (r, c). If $r = 1$, then $(1, c)$ is marked $\times$, and therefore is not in R.

If $r \neq 1$, then the cells at (r, c') and (r, c) are in R, because R is a rectangle. Therefore, the cell at $(1, c)$ would have to be marked o. But the cell at $(1, c)$ is marked $\times$, which is a contradiction.

It follows that any covering of *Row* 1 must include at least one set that is a subset of K_1, possibly K_1 itself.

Consider named *Row* 2. This set has no more cells marked $\times$ than *Row* 1, and therefore has no fewer cells marked o than *Row* 1. Recall that *Row* 2 is not equivalent to *Row* 1. It follows that *Row* 2 contains a cell marked o in a column, say d, in which the cell at $(1, d)$ is marked $\times$. Lemma 3.4.1.1 assures us that if K is a rectangle that covers *Row* 2, then it cannot also cover any cell in *Row* 1 that is marked o. (A direct proof is as follows: suppose a cell in *Row* 1, say, $(1, d')$, is marked o. Then $d \neq d'$. If K covers both $(1, d')$, and $(2, d)$, then K also covers the cells $(2, d')$ and $(1, d)$. This implies that $(1, d)$ is marked o, which contradicts the statement that $(1, d)$ is marked $\times$.)

We have shown that if K_2 is a rectangle that covers *Row* 2, then $K_2 \not\subset \neq K_1$, though $K_2 \cap K_1$ need not be empty. It follows that any collection of *F*-cc rectangles that covers *Rows* 1 and 2 must contain at least two rectangles.

The collection of left-OrRM rectangles

$$\{K_1 = A_1 \times B^*(A_1), K_2 = A_2 \times B^*(A_2)\}$$

covers both *Row* 1 and *Row* 2 , and consists of exactly two sets. This establishes the proposition that the left-OrRM algorithm constructs a minimal rectangular *F*-cc (RF), covering of *Rows* 1 and 2 that consists of exactly two rectangles.

According to the left-OrRM algorithm, the covering correspondence is V defined as follows:

$$V(\theta) = \begin{cases} K_1 & \text{for all } \theta \in K_1 \\ K_2 & \text{for all } \theta \in K_2 \backslash K_1. \end{cases}$$

Consider *Row* 3. It can be in one of two states:

- every cell in *Row* 3 is covered by either K_1 or K_2,[5] or
- there is a cell in *Row 3* that is not covered by K_1 or K_2.

In the first case *Row 3* is called *inactive given* K_1 and K_2. The covering correspondence V is defined at every cell in *Row* 3. The left-OrRM algorithm goes on to the next named *row* that is *active* (not inactive) *given* K_1 and K_2.

In the second case, there is a cell in *Row 3* marked o, say at *Row 3*, column c, or $(3, c)$ such that the cell at $(1, c)$ is marked $\times$, and another cell at $(3, c')$ marked o such that $(2, c')$ is marked $\times$. (Possibly $c = c'$.)

It is a consequence of Lemma 3.4.1, including the argument in its proof, that when *Row 3* is active there is no *F*-cc rectangle K_3 that also covers either

[5] For example,

	Col 1	Col 2	Col 3
Row 1	x	o	x
Row 2	x	x	o
Row 3	x	o	o

.

Row 1 or *Row* 2. The largest rectangle that covers *Row 3* when *Row 3* is active is

$$A_3 \times B^*(A_3).[6]$$

Define

$$K_3 = A_3 \times B^*(A_3), \text{ and}$$

$$V(\theta) = \begin{cases} K_1 & \text{if } \theta \in K_1 \\ K_2 & \text{if } \theta \in K_2 \setminus K_1 \\ K_3 & \text{if } \theta \in K_3 \setminus K_1 \cup K_2. \end{cases}$$

The left-OrRM construction continues *row* by *row* until the first *row* is reached at which the covering correspondence V is defined at every element in $\mathbf{B} \setminus \mathbf{B}^{co}$. The Proof of Lemma 3.4.1 applies to every *Row j* that is active given the rectangles K_i $i = 1, \ldots, r$, $r \leq j - 1$ that are constructed for preceding active *Rows*. Therefore, at each stage of the construction, any *F*-cc, rectangular covering of the contour set of *F*, $\mathbf{B} \setminus \mathbf{B}^{co}$, must contain at least as many rectangles as the left-OrRm covering C_V. In other words, C_V is a minimal covering in the set of all *F*-cc, rectangular coverings of the contour set $F^{-1}(F(\hat{\theta}))$, and the covering correspondence V is defined on all of $\mathbf{B} \setminus \mathbf{B}^{co}$. Q.E.D.

Next, we consider some simple examples of goal functions defined on a Euclidean parameter space.

The Euclidean Parameter Space
The ideas for constructing minimal coverings presented in the preceding subsection for finite parameters spaces also apply to some cases in which the parameter space is a continuum, for instance, a Euclidean space. Goal functions defined on Euclidean parameter spaces are discussed in Chapters 2 and 4. A goal function can be constructed to model goals that are defined without regard to algebraic representation. For instance, goals that are specified in legislation, or in documents generated for administrative agencies. These can require mathematical formulations that are not so neat and smooth. In such a case the ideas developed to deal with the case of a finite parameter space can sometimes be useful when the parameter space is a continuum, say a Euclidean space, but the goal function is not sufficiently

---

[6] According to the left-OrRM algorithm $A_3 = proj_1(\mathbf{B} \setminus \mathbf{B}^{co} \cap Row\, 3)$, and $B^*(A_3)$ is the largest set β in Θ^2 such that $A_3 \times \beta \subseteq \mathbf{B} \setminus \mathbf{B}^{co}$.

regular for the methods of Chapters 2 or 4 to apply. When the parameter space is Euclidean and the goal function consists of splines pieced together so that some of them have algebraic formulas, and others are defined by means of set generators, a construction that uses algebraic formulas for some parts of the space, and set-theoretic methods for others, may be useful.

In this subsection, we illustrate the use of the ordered rRM procedure for constructing a minimal covering of the level sets of a "nonsmooth" goal function whose domain is a Euclidean parameter space. The illustration is by way of examples in which the parameter space is two dimensional.

We consider the case of two agents. The parameter space is the Cartesian product of two intervals in the real line. The goal function F is a step function. A contour set of F is shown in Figure 3.4.1.1.

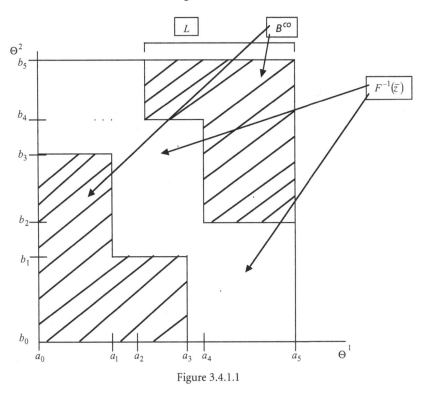

Figure 3.4.1.1

In the Euclidean case the *length* of horizontal lines in $\mathbf{B}^{co}$ plays the role that the number of $\times$s in the rows of the matrix Q play in the finite case.[7] In Figure 3.4.1.1 the longest horizontal line in $\mathbf{B}^{co}$ is one that runs from the right-hand boundary of $\mathbf{B}$ to the contour set as shown in Figure 3.4.1.

---

[7] In a case with more agents, or parameters, "flats" of higher dimension would replace lines.

Starting the max A-set left-RM construction with the A-set taken to be the interval $[a_0, a_2]$, the left-RM algorithm constructs the rectangle K_1 shown in Figure 3.4.1.2.

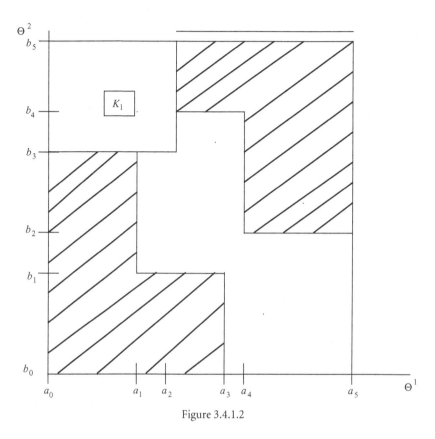

Figure 3.4.1.2

According to the OrRM procedure, every point $(a, b) \in K_1$ takes the value $V(a, b) = K_1$. The next longest horizontal line in $\mathbf{B}^{co}$ to the contour set is shown in Figure 3.4.1.3.

The OrRM procedure constructs the rectangle K_2 shown in Figure 3.4.1.4. Each point in $K_2 \backslash K_1$ is assigned to K_2; that is, $V(a, b) = K_2$ for all $(a, b) \in K_2 \backslash K_1$.

The third longest horizontal line in $\mathbf{B}^{co}$ leads to constructing the rectangle K_3, shown in Figure 3.4.1.5, and to assigning each point in $K_3 \backslash (K_1 \cup K_2)$ to K_3. Thus, $V(a, b) = K_3$ for all $(a, b) \in K_3 \backslash K_1 \cup K_2$.

At this point V has been defined at every point in the contour set. Therefore, the algorithm stops. It constructs a three-set covering with overlapping but not redundant sets.

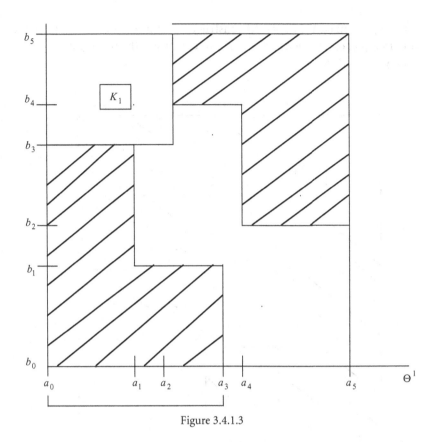

Figure 3.4.1.3

It is also possible to get coverings that consist of four rectangles, one of which is redundant, or five sets, two of which are redundant. These added rectangles are, respectively, the one with corners (a_0, b_3), (a_0, b_4), (a_4, b_3), (a_4, b_4), and the one with corners (a_1, b_1), (a_1, b_2), (a_5, b_1), (a_5, b_2). These are shown in Figure 3.4.1.6.

The next example illustrates a situation in which the goal function consists of linear pieces. It is shown in Figure 3.4.1.7.

According to the OrRM procedure for constructing the covering correspondence V, and the covering C_V that it defines, the A-side construction should start with a point in the contour set $F^{-1}(\bar{z})$ such that the part of the horizontal line through that point that lies in the set $\mathbf{B}$ has a maximal intersection with $\mathbf{B}^{co}$. In this case, it is clear that the vertical segment of the contour set at the point $a = 2$ and all points on the slanted segment between $a = 2$ and $a = 10$ are tied with respect to this criterion. In each case, the length of the relevant line through an arbitrary point of each set is the same,

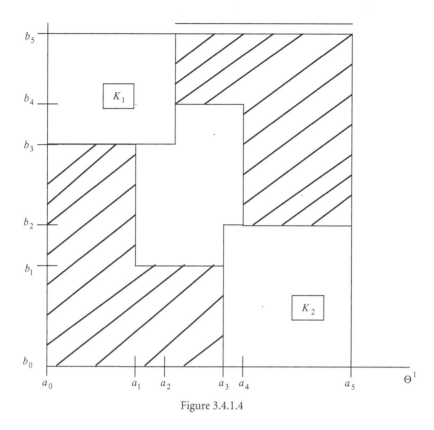

Figure 3.4.1.4

namely the width of **B** minus one point, which is the width of **B**. Thus, the max A-side construction can begin with any point (a, b) such that

$$a = 2 \quad \text{and} \quad 4 \le b \le 14, \tag{+}$$

or,

$$2 < a \le 10 \quad \text{and} \quad 0 < b \le 4. \tag{++}$$

If we begin with a point in $(+)$ then the max A-side algorithm constructs the set K_1, which is the vertical segment defined by the inequalities $(+)$. The covering correspondence is $V(a, b) = K_1$ for all (a, b) that satisfy $(+)$.

If we begin with a point (a, b) that satisfies $(++)$, then the rectangle constructed is the singleton $\{(a, b)\}$, and $V(a, b) = \{(a, b)\}$ for all (a, b) that satisfy $(++)$ and do not satisfy $(+)$. Note that this collection

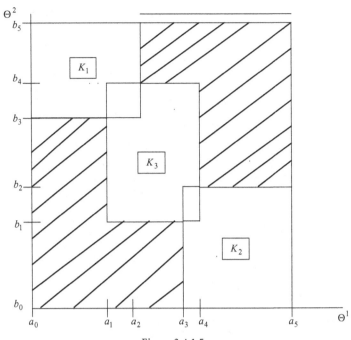

Figure 3.4.1.5

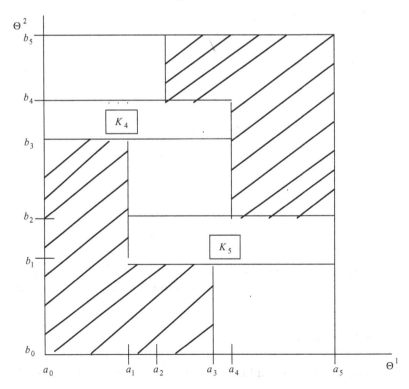

Figure 3.4.1.6

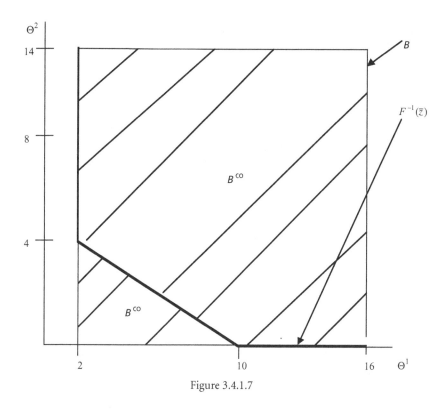

Figure 3.4.1.7

of sets can be described algebraically. The line segment, with end points $(2, 4)$, and $(10, 0)$, has the equation

$$b = -\frac{1}{2}a + 5. \tag{+++}$$

For

$$10 \le a \le 16 \quad \text{and} \quad b = 0. \tag{\#}$$

The max A-side algorithm constructs the set K_2 consisting of all (a, b) that satisfy (#). The correspondence $V(a, b)$ takes the value K_2 at all (a, b) that satisfy (#), but do not satisfy (+) or (++).

Each set K_1, K_2 requires one element to represent it, hence one message. The line segment given by (+++) requires a parameter transfer mechanism.

Thus, the message space consists of the closed line segment given by equation (+++), where the end points are the representatives of the vertical and horizontal segments, respectively.

3.5 Constructing a Mechanism from a Covering
by the Transversals Method (TM)

In Section 3.4 we showed how to construct an rRM correspondence V and its associated covering C_V of Θ. In Section 3.4.1 we show, for a finite environment space, how to construct a covering correspondence, and its associated covering, that consists of a minimum number of rectangles. When the covering C_V consists of a minimum number of sets, a mechanism constructed from that covering has minimum informational size. To construct a mechanism, the next step is to construct a *transversal* for the covering C_V. We use the term *transversal* to the covering C_V despite the fact that it does not have the usual geometric interpretation in finite spaces. Informally, a transversal to a covering C is a subset of Θ that intersects every set $K \in C$ just once, and so is in one-to-one correspondence with C. When the covering is a partition, a transversal consists of one point from each set K in the partition; for every set K, the point can be chosen arbitrarily. But, because the rRM construction can produce a covering that may contain overlapping sets, we need a more general definition of transversal. For this purpose we use the concept of a *system of distinct representatives* (SDR) for a collection of subsets (Hall 1935). A *distinct representative* of a set in a collection of sets is an element that identifies that set uniquely. Thus, when the covering has overlaps, the representative point of a set cannot generally be chosen independently of the representatives of other sets in the covering.

DEFINITION 3.5.1. An SDR for a covering C of Θ is a function $\Lambda : C \to \Theta$ that has two properties:

$$\text{for every } K \in C, \quad \Lambda(K) \in K; \qquad \text{(SDR i)}$$

$$K' \neq K'' \quad \text{implies} \quad \Lambda(K') \neq \Lambda(K''). \qquad \text{(SDR ii)}$$

DEFINITION 3.5.2. Let C be a covering of Θ and let $\Lambda : C \to (\Theta)$ be an SDR for C. The set $T = \Lambda(C)$ is called a *transversal* for C (associated with Λ).

Theorem 3.5.1 shows that if C is a collection of subsets that are generated by a self-belonging correspondence, then C has an SDR, and therefore also has a transversal. (The converse is also true.)

THEOREM 3.5.1. Let C be an arbitrary covering of a set Θ. C has an SDR if and only if C is generated by a self-belonging correspondence $U : \Theta \Rightarrow \Theta$.

Proof: To prove sufficiency, suppose C is generated by a self-belonging correspondence $U : \Theta \Rightarrow \Theta$. Then for each $K \in C$ there exists $\theta_K \in K$ such that $U(\theta_K) = K$. Define $\Lambda : C \to \Theta$ by $\Lambda(K) = \theta_K$. This establishes (i) of Definition 3.5.1. To establish (ii), suppose $\Lambda(K) = \theta_K = \theta_{K'} = \Lambda(K')$. It follows from $\theta_K = \theta_{K'}$ that $U(\theta_K) = U(\theta_{K'})$. Thus $K = K'$.

To prove necessity, suppose C has an SDR $\Lambda : C \to \Theta$. Then by (i) of Definition 3.5.1, for every $K \in C$, $\Lambda(K) \in K$. We define the generating correspondence $U : \Theta \Rightarrow \Theta$ in two steps. First, for $\theta \in \Theta(C)$, let $U_1 : \Lambda(C) \Rightarrow \Theta$ given by $U_1(\theta) = K$ if and only if $\Lambda(K) = \theta$. Second, for $\theta \in \Theta \setminus \Lambda(C)$ define $U_2 : \Theta \setminus \Lambda(C) \Rightarrow \Theta$ as follows. First, for all $\theta \in \Theta$, let $C_\theta = \{K \in C \mid \theta \in K\}$. Note that C_θ is not empty, because C is a covering of Θ. Let $U_2(\theta) = K$ for some arbitrary $K \in C_\theta$. Now, define the correspondence U by

$$
U(\theta) = \begin{cases} U_1(\theta) & \text{if } \theta \in \Lambda(C) \\ U_2(\theta) & \text{if } \theta \in \Theta / C \end{cases}.
$$

Thus, U is a self-belonging correspondence that generates C. The Axiom of Choice is used in both parts of this proof.

The next step is to construct a decentralized mechanism from the rRM correspondence V and a transversal for the covering C_V.

We discuss properties of V and the covering C_V that are relevant to informational efficiency after completing the construction of the mechanism. As we have said, the construction here is set-theoretic.[8]

Returning to the main line of our presentation, we construct a mechanism from a covering of Θ, and a transversal. We do this in steps. Recall that a mechanism consists of a message space, an equilibrium message correspondence, and an outcome function. Our first step is to construct a mechanism *without requiring that the message correspondence preserve-privacy*, that is, we do not require that the mechanism to be decentralized. Subsequently, we construct a decentralized version of the mechanism.[9]

The following notation, definitions, and assumptions are maintained throughout this section.

---

[8] In Chapter 2 sets, correspondences, and functions are given by equations. There we give two systematic methods of construction that are based on a representation of the correspondence V by equations. These are called "flagpole" and "condensation." These general methods presuppose that the covering generated by V is a partition, unlike the methods presented in this chapter. However, in Chapter 2 we also give simple examples that show how transversals can be constructed by algebraic or calculus methods when the underlying coverings have overlaps.

[9] See Chapter 2 for an alternative exposition, and illustrative examples.

We are given

- a goal function $F : \Theta \to Z$;
- a covering C of Θ that is generated by a self-belonging correspondence $V : \Theta \Rightarrow \Theta$;
- Thus, $C_V = C = \{K \subseteq \Theta : K = V(\theta) \text{ for some } \theta \in \Theta\}$.
- C is F-contour contained, (that is, if $K \in C$, then the goal function F is constant on K);
- C has an SDR $\Lambda : C \to \Theta$. Consequently, C has a transversal $T = \Lambda(C)$.

We introduce a set M, the message space, and a function $v : T \to M$. The set M contains, or possibly is the same as, the subset $M' = v(T)$ that consists of the messages actually needed. The function v encodes the elements of the transversal T in the form of messages. (Recall that the elements of T uniquely identify and hence label the sets in the covering.)

Next, we note some properties that are used in the construction of a mechanism. Begin with the goal function F. Because F is a function, it induces a partition of the transversal T such that for each $z \in Z$, $F^{-1}(z)$ has the properties:

$$
\text{(a)} \quad
\left.
\begin{array}{c}
(\theta \in F^{-1}(z) \cap T) \\
\text{and} \\
(\theta' \in F^{-1}(z) \cap T)
\end{array}
\right\}
\Rightarrow F(\theta) = F(\theta'),
$$

and

$$
\text{(b)} \quad z \neq z' \Rightarrow (F^{-1}(z) \cap T) \cap (F^{-1}(z') \cap T) = \varnothing.
$$

Proof: Property (a) follows immediately from the fact that C is an F-cc covering. Property (b) is almost as immediate. Suppose $z \neq z'$, and let $\theta \in (F^{-1}(z) \cap T) \cap (F^{-1}(z') \cap T)$. Then, $\theta \in F^{-1}(z) \cap F^{-1}(z')$. Because F is single-valued, it follows that $z = z'$, which is a contradiction.

This completes the proof.

Because C is a rectangular F-cc covering, it suffices to confine the discussion to a single contour set of F.

Let $F_T : T \to Z$ be the restriction of F to T. The partition induced by F_T on T is the same as the partition induced by F on T.

For a function F defined on a set X we write $P(X, f)$ for the partition induced by F on X. The points of a transversal T have the same description as points of Θ, because T is a subset of Θ. If Θ has a dimension, then the dimension of T would generally be less than the dimension of Θ, but its points, being points of Θ, have the same description as do points of Θ. Hence, in the case in which Θ is a space with coordinates, the points of the transversal have the same number of coordinates as those of Θ that are not in T. We introduce the function $v : T \to M$ in order to encode the points of the transversal in fewer variables than the number of parameters in Θ. More formally, write $v(T) = M' \subseteq M$, and $v^{-1} : v(T) \Rightarrow T$, or equivalently, $v^{-1} : M' \Rightarrow T$. The (single-valued) function v induces the partition $P(T, v) = \{k \subseteq T \mid k \in v^{-1}(m) \text{ for some } m \in M'.\}$.

Recall that for a set $A \subseteq \Theta$ we say that A is F-cc if and only if $(\theta, \theta' \in A) \Rightarrow F(\theta) = F(\theta')$, and a collection E of subsets of Θ is F-cc if and only if every set in E is F-cc.

Lemma 3.5.1 characterizes the collection of inverse images of messages corresponding to the function v.

LEMMA 3.5.1. *The collection $P(T, v)$ is F-cc if and only if $P(T, v)$ is a refinement of $P(T, F) = P(T, F_T)$.*

Proof: $(\Rightarrow)$ Suppose $P(T, v)$ is F-cc. $P(T, v)$ is a refinement of $P(T, F)$ if and only if for every $k \in P(T, v)$ there exists $K \in P(T, F)$ such that $k \subseteq K$. Let $k \in P(T, v)$, and let $\theta \in k$. Write $z = F(\theta)$ and note that there is a set $K \in P(T, F)$ such that $K = F^{-1}(z)$. Because $P(T, v)$ is F-cc, $\theta' \in k \Rightarrow F(\theta') = F(\theta) = z$. Therefore, $k \subseteq K \in P(T, F)$.

$(\Leftarrow)$ Suppose $P(T, v)$ is a refinement of $P(T, F)$. Then it is immediate that $P(T, v)$ is F-cc.

COROLLARY. *If v^{-1} is singleton-valued, then $P(T, v)$ is F-cc.*

DEFINITION 3.5.5. *A function $f : T \to M$ is F-compatible if and only if $P(T, f)$ is F-cc.*

The next step is to construct a mechanism. (Recall that we are temporarily dropping the requirement that it be decentralized.) To do this we must define a message space, a (group) message correspondence, but not the individual message correspondences, and an outcome function. We take the message space to be $M' = v(T)$. Define the outcome function h by

$$h = F \circ v^{-1} : M' \to Z.$$

It follows from Lemma 3.5.1 that h is single-valued.

To define the message correspondence, first, recall that the covering C is F-cc, and define the correspondence

$$\Omega : \Theta \Rightarrow C$$

by

$$\Omega(\theta) = \{K \in C \mid \theta \in K\}.$$

Thus, for each $\theta \in \Theta$, $\Omega(\theta)$ is the collection of sets in C that contain the point θ, or equivalently, cover θ. Note that $\Omega(\theta)$ is never empty, because C is a covering of Θ. Next, assume that v is F-compatible, and define the (group) message correspondence, μ by

$$\mu = v \circ \Lambda \circ \Omega.$$

That is, for all $\theta \in \Theta$,

$$\mu(\theta) = v(\Lambda\,(\Omega(\theta))).$$

Thus, the messages assigned to the point θ are obtained by first looking at the collection of sets in the covering C that cover θ, then considering the subset of the transversal that consists of the distinct representatives of those sets, and finally look at the collection of messages that encode those distinct representatives. It is evident that a mechanism so constructed must realize the goal function. Lemma 3.5.2 establishes this formally.

LEMMA 3.5.2. The mechanism (M', μ, h) realizes F.

Proof: We must show that for every $\theta \in \Theta$,

$$F(\theta) = h(\mu(\theta)).$$

We know that

$$\mu = v \circ \Lambda \circ \Omega$$
$$h = F \circ v^{-1}$$

and that

$$\Omega(\theta) = \{k \in C : \theta \in k\}.$$

Because the covering C is F-cc, if

$$\left(\bar{\theta} \in \bigcup_{k \in \Omega(\theta)} k\right), \text{ then } F(\bar{\theta}) = F(\theta). \tag{#}$$

By the definition of an SDR,

$$\text{for every } k \in C,\ \Lambda\,(k) \in k. \tag{##}$$

It follows from (#) and (##) that for every $k \in \Omega(\theta)$,

$$F(\Lambda(k)) = F(\theta).$$

Therefore, for every $\theta \in \Theta$,

$$F(\Lambda(\Omega(\theta))) = F(\theta). \qquad (\#\#\#)$$

But by (###),

$$F(\theta) = F(\nu^{-1}(\nu(\Lambda(\Omega(\theta))))) = h(\mu(\theta)).$$

That is,

$$
\begin{aligned}
h \circ \mu(\theta) &= F \circ \nu^{-1} \circ \nu \circ \Lambda \circ \Omega(\theta) \\
&= F(\Lambda(\Omega(\theta))) = F(\theta)
\end{aligned}
$$

This completes the proof.

The next step is to modify the mechanism just constructed to make it decentralized.

To do this we must take account of the fact that $\Theta = \Theta^1 \times \cdots \times \Theta^N$. However, to simplify exposition when the notation becomes complex for larger values of N, we take $N = 2$. To construct a decentralized mechanism we must construct individual equilibrium message correspondences $\mu^i : \Theta^i \Rightarrow M'$ and show that the group message correspondence μ can be written as

$$\mu = \bigcap_{i=1,\dots,N} \mu^i.$$

Recall that the message correspondence μ is defined in terms of Ω. We begin the construction by factoring the correspondence Ω. Define

$$\Omega^i : \Theta^i \Rightarrow C$$

as follows.

For $\bar{\theta}^i \in \Theta^i$, $\Omega^i(\bar{\theta}^i) = \{K \in C \mid \text{there exists } \theta^{-i} \in \Theta^{-i}$
such that the point $(\bar{\theta}^i, \theta^{-i}) \in K\}$.

(Recall that $\theta^{-i} = (\theta^1, \dots, \theta^{i-1}, \theta^{i+1}, \dots, \theta^N)$.)

Thus, $\Omega^i(\bar{\theta}^i)$ consists of the sets K in C whose projection on Θ^i covers $\bar{\theta}^i$. Next, consider the set

$$\Lambda \circ \Omega^i(\bar{\theta}^i) \subseteq T.$$

Because Λ is an SDR, every set $K \in \Omega^i(\bar{\theta}^i)$ has a distinct representative in T. Thus, the set $\Lambda \circ \Omega^i(\bar{\theta}^i)$ is in one-to-one correspondence with $\Omega^i(\bar{\theta}^i)$.

Now assume that the function v is injective; that is, v is one-to-one from T onto M'. (Recall that $v(T) = M'$.) Then $v(\Lambda \circ \Omega^i((\bar{\theta}^i))$ is in one-to-one correspondence with $\Lambda \circ \Omega^i(\bar{\theta}^i)$. Because Λ is one-to-one from C to T, it follows that $v(\Lambda \circ \Omega^i(\bar{\theta}^i))$ is in one-to-one correspondence with $\Omega^i(\bar{\theta}^i)$. Now, define

$$\mu^i : \Theta^i \Rightarrow M,$$

by

$$\mu^i(\bar{\theta}^i) = \{m \in M \mid m = (v \circ \Lambda)(K) \text{ for some } K \in \Omega^i(\bar{\theta}^i)\}.$$

Define $\mu : \Theta^1 \times \cdots \times \Theta^N \Rightarrow M$ by $\mu = \bigcap_{i=1,\ldots,N} \mu^i$.
Then, taking $\bar{\theta} = (\bar{\theta}^1, \ldots, \bar{\theta}^N) \in \Theta = \prod_i \Theta^i$,

$$\mu(\bar{\theta}) = \bigcap_i \mu^i(\bar{\theta}^i) = \bigcap_{i=1}^N \{m \in M \mid m = v \circ \Lambda(K^i) \text{ for some } K^i \in \Omega^i(\bar{\theta}^i)\}.$$

Note that for each $\bar{\theta} \in \Theta$, $\mu(\bar{\theta})$ is in one-to-one correspondence with $\bigcap_{i=1}^N \Omega^i(\bar{\theta}^i)$. To see this, suppose $\bar{m} \in \mu(\bar{\theta})$. Then, taking $N = 2$, $\bar{m} \in \mu^1(\bar{\theta}^1) \cap \mu^2(\bar{\theta}^2)$.

But $\bar{m} \in \mu^1(\bar{\theta}^1)$ if and only if $\bar{m} \in v \circ \Lambda(K^1)$ for some $K^1 \in \Omega^1(\bar{\theta}^1)$ and $\bar{m} \in \mu^2(\bar{\theta}^2)$ if and only if $\bar{m} \in v \circ \Lambda(K^2)$ for some $K^2 \in \Omega^2(\bar{\theta}^2)$.

If $K^1 \neq K^2$, then $(v \circ \Lambda)(K^1) \neq (v \circ \Lambda)(K^2)$, because v is injective, and Λ is an SDR. It follows that $\bar{m} \in \mu(\bar{\theta})$ implies $\bar{m} \in v \circ \Lambda(\bar{K})$ for some $\bar{K} \in \Omega^1(\bar{\theta}^l) \cap \Omega^2(\bar{\theta}^2)$.

The converse of the preceding statement is immediate.
To summarize,

$$\bar{m} \in \bigcap_{i=1}^N \mu^i(\bar{\theta}^i) \text{ if and only if}$$

$$\bar{K} \in \bigcap_{i=1}^N \Omega^i(\bar{\theta}^i), \text{ where } \bar{m} = v \circ \Lambda(\bar{K}). \tag{+}$$

It remains to show that the decentralized mechanism (M, μ, h) we have constructed realizes F.

Let $\bar{\theta} \in \Theta$, and suppose $\bar{m} \in \mu(\bar{\theta})$. Then $\bar{m} \in \bigcap_N \mu^i(\bar{\theta}^i)$. It follows from (+) that there is a set $\bar{K} \in \bigcap_i \Omega^i(\bar{\theta}^i)$ in C such that $\bar{m} = v \circ \Lambda(\bar{K})$. Furthermore $\bar{\theta} \in \bar{K}$, because $\bar{K}$ covers $\bar{\theta}^i$ for all i; that is, for all

$$\bar{\theta}^i \in \mathrm{Pr}_{\Theta^i}(\bar{K}).$$

It follows that

$$\bar{\theta} \in \prod_{i=1}^{N} \mathrm{Pr}_{\Theta^i}(\bar{K}) = \bar{K}.$$

Note that $\Lambda(\bar{K}) \in \bar{K}$, because Λ is an SDR.

Because C is an F-cc covering of Θ, and $\bar{K} \in C$, it follows that

$$F(\bar{\theta}) = F(\Lambda(\bar{K})) = F_T(\Lambda(\bar{K})).$$

By construction

$$h = F_T \circ \nu^{-1} : M' \to Z.$$

Therefore,

$$\begin{aligned} h(\bar{m}) &= F_T \circ \nu^{-1}(\bar{m}) = F_T \circ \nu^{-1} \circ \nu \circ \Lambda(\bar{K}) \\ &= F_T(\Lambda(\bar{K})) = F(\Lambda(\bar{K})) = F(\bar{\theta}). \end{aligned}$$

This completes the proof.

In constructing a decentralized mechanism that realizes a goal function $F : \Theta \to Z$ we assumed that the encoding function $\nu : T \to M'$ is injective; that is, in the presence of the other definitions and assumptions, the injectiveness of the encoding function is a sufficient condition for the construction to produce a mechanism that realizes the goal function. Is it possible to complete the construction described in the preceding pages with an encoding function that is not injective? The answer is "no." We show next that injectiveness of ν is a necessary condition for the construction to result in a decentralized mechanism that realizes the goal function $F : \Theta \to Z$. The notation, definitions, and assumptions used in the preceding construction are maintained.

LEMMA 3.5.3. *If the decentralized mechanism (M', μ, h) realizes the goal function $F : \Theta \to Z$, and has the encoding function $\nu : T \to M'$, then ν is injective.*

Proof:[10] We begin with a preliminary proposition. To state the proposition we need some additional notation.

Let $S \subset \{1, \ldots, N\}$ be a subset of agents, and let θ, $\theta' \in \Theta$ be two parameter points. The parameter point $\theta_S \otimes \theta'_{S^c}$ consists of the components

---

[10] This proof is based on a proof given by Antoine Loeper in response to a conjecture that Reiter presented in his course on mechanism design.

of θ corresponding to agents in S, and the components of θ' correspond to agents in the complement of S, denoted S^C. For example, if $N = 5$, and $S = \{1, 3\}$, then $\theta_S \otimes \theta'_{S^C} = (\theta_1, \theta'_2, \theta_3, \theta'_4, \theta'_5)$. Generally, we write $\theta_S \otimes \theta_{S^C} = ((\theta_S \otimes \theta_{S^C})^1, \ldots, (\theta_S \otimes \theta_{S^C})^N)$. We can now state the proposition.

PROPOSITION P. Suppose $K, K' \in C_V$ where $K \neq K'$. Then there exists a subset of agents $S \subset \{1, \ldots, N\}$, and two points $\theta \in K$, and $\theta' \in K'$ such that $\theta_S \otimes \theta'_{S^C} \notin F^{-1}(F(\theta))$.

(Recall that C_V is an rRM covering of the parameter space $\Theta = \Theta^1 \times \cdots \times \Theta^N$ generated by the self-belonging, rectangular, F-cc correspondence $V : \Theta \Rightarrow \Theta$.)

Proof: The sets $K, K' \in C_V$ are written as

$$K = K_1 \times \cdots \times K_N \qquad K' = K'_1 \times \cdots \times K'_N.$$

Define

$$K'' = (K_1 \cup K'_1) \times \cdots \times (K_N \cup K'_N).$$

Suppose P is false. Then,

for every $S \subseteq \{1, \ldots, N\}$ and for every $\theta \in K$,

and $\theta' \in K', \theta_S \otimes \theta'_{S^C} \in F^{-1}(F(\theta))$. $\qquad (*)$

The statement $(*)$ says that K'' is F-cc, because every element in K'' can be written as $\theta_S \otimes \theta'_{S^C}$ for some $\theta \in K$, and $\theta' \in K'$. Note that K'' is rectangular and that $K \subseteq K''$ and $K' \subseteq K''$. Moreover, at least one of these inclusions is strict, because $K \neq K'$. Without loss of generality suppose $K \subset K''$. This contradicts the assumption that K is an rRM rectangle, because $K \subset K'' \subseteq F^{-1}(F(\theta))$.

We return to the proof of Lemma 3.5.3. The proof is by contradiction. So, suppose v is not injective. Then there exist $\bar{\theta}$ and $\bar{\theta}'$ in T such that $\bar{\theta} \neq \bar{\theta}'$, but $v(\bar{\theta}) = v(\bar{\theta}') = m$, for some m in M'. There are two cases:

Case (a) $\quad F(\bar{\theta}) \neq F(\bar{\theta}')$,

Case (b) $\quad F(\bar{\theta}) = F(\bar{\theta}')$.

In Case (a), because the mechanism (M', μ, h) realizes F, we must have

$$h(m) = h(\nu(\bar{\theta})) = F(\bar{\theta}),$$
$$h(m) = h(\nu(\bar{\theta}')) = F(\bar{\theta}')$$
$$F(\bar{\theta}) \neq F(\bar{\theta}'),$$

which is a contradiction.

We turn to Case (b). We continue to suppose that ν is not injective. There are unique sets K, K' such that $\bar{\theta} = \Lambda(K)$ and $\bar{\theta}' = \Lambda(K')$.

Applying Proposition P, there exist

$$\theta \in K, \quad \theta' \in K' \quad \text{and} \quad S \subseteq \{1, \ldots, N\},$$

such that

$$\theta_S \otimes \theta'_{S^C} \notin F^{-1}(F(\theta)). \tag{**}$$

Consider the message correspondence $\mu^i((\theta_S \otimes \theta'_{S^C})^i)$ of agent i. For every $i \in \{1, \ldots, N\}$, either $i \in S$ or $i \in S^C$, but not both.

If $i \in S$, then $K \in \Omega^i((\theta_S \otimes \theta'_{S^C})^i)$. The representative of K in T is $\Lambda(K) = \bar{\theta}$. By hypothesis $\nu(\bar{\theta}) = m$. It follows from the construction of μ^i that $m \in \mu^i((\theta_S \otimes \theta'_{S^C})^i)$.

If $i \in S^C$, then $K' \in \Omega^i((\theta_S \otimes \theta'_{S^C})^i)$. The representative of K' in T is $\Lambda(K) = \bar{\theta}'$. Again, by hypothesis, $\nu(\bar{\theta}') = m$.

Thus, for all $i \in \{1, \ldots, N\} m \in \mu^i((\theta_S \otimes \theta'_{S^C})^i)$. It follows that

$$m \in \bigcap_{i \in \{1, \ldots, N\}} \mu^i((\theta_S \otimes \theta'_{S^C})^i) = \mu((\theta_S \otimes \theta'_{S^C})),$$

and hence that $h(m) \in F(\theta_S \otimes \theta'_{S^C})$. But $h(m) = h(\nu(\bar{\theta})) = h(\nu(\bar{\theta}'))$ implies that $h(m) = F(\bar{\theta}) = F(\bar{\theta}')$, and hence that

$$\theta_S \otimes \theta'_{S^C} \in F^{-1}(F(\theta)) = F^{-1}(F(\theta') = F^{-1}(F(\bar{\theta}) = F^{-1}(F(\bar{\theta}').$$

This contradicts (**), which states that

$$\theta_S \otimes \theta'_{S^C} \notin F^{-1}(F(\theta)) = F^{-1}(F(\theta') = F^{-1}(F(\bar{\theta}) = F^{-1}(F(\bar{\theta}').$$

This completes the proof.

Suppose there are two agents, and that the parameter spaces Θ^1, Θ^2 are finite sets. Then the OrRM construction presented in Section 3.4.1 will produce a minimal covering of the contour map of the goal function, and therefore a mechanism with a minimal size message space.

3.6 Coverings and Partitions

The construction of a mechanism from a covering is considerably simplified when the covering is a partition. If the covering is a partition, then the correspondence Ω is single-valued, that is, for each point $\theta \in \Theta$ there is exactly one set that contains the point θ. In that case the message associated with the parameter value θ (by the encoding function ν) is uniquely determined. That is not the case if θ is covered by more than one rectangle. In that case the task of constructing a mechanism is more difficult. Therefore, it is helpful to know when the rRM procedure generates a partition.[11]

The reflexive rectangles method of constructing a covering of the parameter space Θ is not in general guaranteed to produce a partition of that space. This is true whether or not Θ is finite. Yet in many examples rRM does in fact produce a partition of the parameter space. It is therefore interesting to know what distinguishes the cases in which rRM produces a partition from those in which it produces a covering that is not a partition. An rRM covering, whether or not a partition, is generated by a self-belonging, F-cc correspondence $V : \Theta \Rightarrow \Theta$. Therefore, the question is, "Which additional properties of V determine whether or not the covering it generates is a partition?"[12] Because V depends on F (V must be F-cc) the answer depends both on a property of F, and on a property of V. The property of V is *symmetry*.

DEFINITION 3.6.1. A correspondence $V : \Theta \Rightarrow \Theta$ is said to be *symmetric*, or to *satisfy symmetry*, if $\theta' \in V(\theta) \Leftrightarrow \theta \in V(\theta')$.

REMARK. It is easy to see that if a self-belonging correspondence V generates a partition, then it is symmetric.

Proof: Suppose $\theta' \in V(\theta)$. Certainly $\theta' \in V(\theta')$, because V is self-belonging. Hence, $\theta' \in V(\theta) \subseteq V(\theta')$. Because V generates a partition, it follows that $V(\theta) = V(\theta')$, and hence $\theta \in V(\theta')$.

---

[11] This subject is also discussed in Chapter 2 (unique solvability lemma) in the context of mechanisms in equation form.

[12] Related questions come up when we consider mechanisms that are not constructed from rRM coverings, or coverings that are self-belonging, but not rectangular. What conditions on V ensure that the covering is a partition when V is RM but not necessarily rRM, and more generally yet, when V is self-belonging, but not necessarily rectangular? We take up these questions in a general setting in the Appendix to this chapter, although we are mainly interested in applying the results stated there to rRM coverings.

Before taking up the converse, we consider some necessary conditions.

If the covering generated by an rRM, self-belonging correspondence V is *not* a partition, then there must exist two sets, call them K_1, K_2, generated by V, that have a point, β, in common. Because V is F-cc, both these sets must be subsets of the same contour set of F. Furthermore, neither set can be a subset of the other, because V generates an rRM covering. Therefore, there must be four distinct points in Θ, call them α, β, γ, δ such that

$$F(\alpha) = F(\beta) = F(\gamma) \neq F(\delta) \tag{3.6.1}$$

$$\beta \in K_1 \cap K_2, \qquad \gamma \in K_2 \backslash K_1 \quad \text{and} \quad \alpha \in K_1 \backslash K_2. \tag{3.6.2}$$

Suppose for the sake of simplicity that there are only two agents, 1 and 2. In that case $\Theta = \Theta^1 \times \Theta^2$, and therefore we can write

$$\alpha = (a_1, b_2), \qquad \beta = (a_1, b_1), \qquad \gamma = (a_2, b_1), \qquad \delta = (a_2. b_2).$$

According to 3.6.1, α, β, γ are in the same contour set of F, whereas δ is in a different contour set. Of course, $a_1, a_2 \in \Theta^1$ and $b_1, b_2 \in \Theta^2$. We call a configuration of four points and two sets satisfying 3.6.1 and 3.6.2 an *overlap pattern* (OP), and the four points satisfying 3.6.2 an L-dot *configuration*. The point β is called the *elbow*; the points α and γ are called *fingers*, and the point δ is the *dot*, for reasons that are apparent in Figure 3.6.1, which displays this L-dot configuration. Note that an L-dot configuration is a property of the goal function F, whereas an overlap pattern is a property of the covering generated by V. Furthermore, if V has an overlap pattern, then the points in it that satisfy condition 3.6.1 form an L-dot configuration.

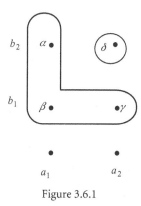

Figure 3.6.1

First, note that for the rRM construction to produce a covering with an overlap it is necessary that F have an L-dot configuration, that is, a set of four points

$$\alpha = (a_1, b_2)$$
$$\beta = (a_1, b_1)$$
$$\gamma = (a_2, b_1)$$
$$\delta = (a_2, b_2)$$

in Θ such that $F(\alpha) = F(\beta) = F(\delta) \neq F(\delta)$. The point β is the elbow of the L-dot configuration.

LEMMA 3.6.1 (Necessity of L-dot). Let C be an F-cc, rRM covering of $\Theta = \Theta^1 \times \Theta^2$. If C is not a partition, then F has an L-dot configuration.

Proof: Suppose C is not a partition. Then there is a point β and two sets, $K_1, K_2 \in C$ such that $\beta \in K_1 \cap K_2$. Let

$$\beta = (a_1, b_1), \qquad a_1 \in \Theta^1, \qquad b_1 \in \Theta^2.$$

Let $U = K_1 \cup K_2$ and let $W = \mathrm{Pr}_{\Theta^1}(K_1) \times \mathrm{Pr}_{\Theta^2}(K_2)$.

Note that $K_1 \backslash K_2 \neq \varnothing$, and $K_2 \backslash K_1 \neq \varnothing$. Otherwise one of the sets K_1, K_2 would be a subset of the other, contradicting either $K_1 \in C$ or $K_2 \in C$.

For any point $y = (y_1, y_2)$ define the sets

$$\Xi(y) = \{x = (x_1, x_2) \mid x_2 = y_2\},$$

and

$$\Psi(y) = \{x = (x_1, x_2) \mid x_1 = y_1\}.$$

$\Xi(y)$ is the longest horizontal line segment through y that lies in W, and $\Psi(y)$ is the longest such vertical line segment.

Note that $\Xi(\beta) \cap K_1 \backslash K_2 \neq \varnothing$ or $\Xi(\beta) \cap K_2 \backslash K_1 \neq \varnothing$, but not both.

To see this, suppose $\Xi(\beta) \cap K_1 \backslash K_2 \neq \varnothing$, and $\Xi(\beta) \cap K_2 \backslash K_1 \neq \varnothing$. Let $x = (x_1, x_2) \in \Xi(\beta) \cap K_1 \backslash K_2$, and let $y = (y_1, y_2) \in \Xi(\beta) \cap K_2 \backslash K_1$. Then $x_2 = b_1$ and $y_2 = b_1$. The sets K_1 and K_2 are each rRM sets. It follows from the rRM construction that $y \in K_1$. But this contradicts the assumption that $y \in K_2 \backslash K_1$.

In summary, we have shown that exactly one of the statements $\Xi(\beta) \cap K_1 \backslash K_2 \neq \varnothing$, $\Xi(\beta) \cap K_2 \backslash K_1 \neq \varnothing$ is true.

A similar argument shows that only one of the sets $\Psi(\beta) \cap K_2 \backslash K_1$ and $\Psi(\beta) \cap K_1 \backslash K_2$ is nonempty.

Furthermore, of the four pairs of statements $(\Xi(\beta) \cap K_i \backslash K_j \neq \varnothing,$ $\Psi(\beta) \cap K_i \backslash K_j \neq \varnothing)$ for $i, j \in \{1, 2\}$ only two of them are possible; if $\Xi(\beta) \cap K_i \backslash K_j \neq \varnothing$, then only $\Psi(\beta) \cap K_j \backslash K_i \neq \varnothing$ is possible. Without loss of generality we suppose that $\Xi(\beta) \cap K_1 \backslash K_2 \neq \varnothing$. Hence $\Psi(\beta) \cap K_2 \backslash K_1 \neq \varnothing$.

Thus, there are a point $x = (x_1, b_1) \in \Xi(\beta) \cap K_1 \backslash K_2$ and a point $y = (a_1, y_2) \in \Psi(\beta) \cap K_2 \backslash K_1$. It follows that $x_1 \in \mathrm{Pr}_{\Theta^1}(U)$, and $y_2 \in \mathrm{Pr}_{\Theta^2}(U)$.

If for every $\beta \in K_1 \backslash K_2$ and every $x \in \Xi(\beta) \cap K_1 \backslash K_2$, and $y \in \Psi(\beta) \cap K_2 \backslash K_1$, it were the case that $F(x_1, y_2) = F(\beta)$, then W would be an F-cc rectangle, thus contradicting K_1 and K_2 in C. Therefore, there must be points, $\alpha, \beta, \gamma, \delta$, where

$$\alpha = x, \text{ or } y,$$
$$\gamma = y \quad \text{if } \alpha = x,$$
$$\gamma = x \quad \text{if } \alpha = y,$$
$$\delta = (x_1, y_2),$$

such that

$$F(\alpha) = F(\beta) = F(\gamma), \text{ and } F(\delta) \neq F(\beta).$$

This concludes the proof.

Lemma 3.6.1 shows that the existence of an L-dot configuration is a necessary condition for the covering C_V to contain overlaps.

On the other hand, the existence of an L-dot configuration, briefly an L-dot, does *not* ensure that the covering generated by V has sets that overlap. This is shown by the following example.

The correspondence $V : \Theta \Rightarrow \Theta$ in this example is constructed by rRM; it is symmetric, and it generates a partition of the parameter space Θ in a case where there is an L-dot configuration in Θ for a given goal function F.

EXAMPLE 3.6.1.

$$\Theta = \Theta^1 \times \Theta^2$$
$$\Theta^1 = \{a_1, a_2\} \qquad \Theta^2 = \{b_1, b_2, b_3\}.$$

For convenience we label the points of $\Theta, \alpha, \beta, \lambda, \delta, \varepsilon$ as shown in Figure 3.6.2.

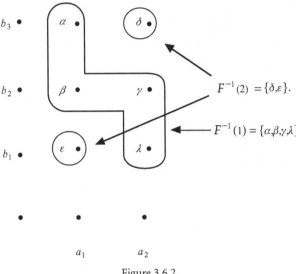

$$F^{-1}(2) = \{\delta, \varepsilon\}.$$

$$F^{-1}(1) = \{\alpha, \beta, \gamma, \lambda\}$$

Figure 3.6.2

The rRM construction can lead to either of the two different correspondences V_1 and V_2, where

$$V_1(\alpha) = V_1(\beta) = \{\alpha, \beta\} = K_1$$
$$V_1(\gamma) = V_1(\lambda) = \{\beta, \gamma\} = K_2$$
$$V_1(\delta) = \{\delta\} = K_3$$
$$V_1(\varepsilon) = \{\varepsilon\} = K_4,$$

which determines the covering $\{K_1, K_2, K_3, K_4\}$ of Θ. Here

$$C_1 = \{K_1, K_2\}$$

is a covering of $F^{-1}(1)$, and

$$C_2 = \{K_3, K_4\}$$

is a covering of $F^{-1}(2)$.

Note that V_1 is symmetric, self-belonging, rectangular and F-cc. Clearly C_1 is a partition of $F^{-1}(1)$, but $F^{-1}(1)$ has an L-dot. Figure 3.6.3 shows this covering.

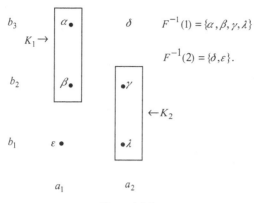

Figure 3.6.3

On the other hand, the rRM construction can also lead to the covering

$$V_2(\alpha) = V_2(\beta) = \{\alpha, \beta\} = K_1$$
$$V_2(\gamma) = \{\beta, \gamma\} = K_2'$$
$$V_2(\lambda) = \{\gamma, \lambda\} = K_2$$
$$V_2(\delta) = \{\delta\} = K_3$$
$$V_2(\varepsilon) = \{\varepsilon\} = K_4.$$

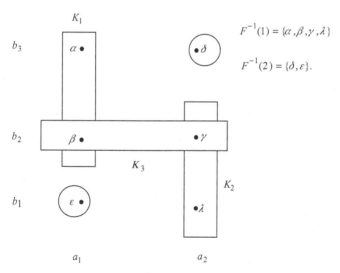

Figure 3.6.4

The correspondence V_2 is *not* symmetric ($\beta \in V_2(\gamma)$, but $\gamma \notin V_2(\beta)$), but it is self-belonging and F-cc. The covering C_{V_2} is not a partition.

Moreover, for later reference we note that the set K_2' is redundant in the sense that if it were removed from the covering C_{V_2} the remaining sets would still be a covering. Figure 3.6.4 shows this covering. Furthermore, as Theorem 3.4.1 assures us, the rRM covering shown in Figure 3.6.4 can be constructed by the two-step process. This is done by taking the initial A-sets to be

$$\{a_1\}, \{a_2\}, \{a_1, a_2\}.$$

The nonredundant covering shown in Figure 3.6.5 results from taking the initial A-sets to be $\{a_1\}, \{a_2\}$.

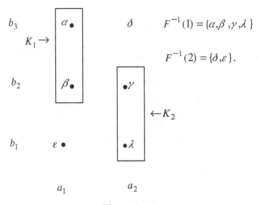

Figure 3.6.5

Of course, the *absence of an L-dot is a sufficient* condition for a covering to be a partition. However, this is not a generally useful condition, because its application requires that the entire domain Θ of F be examined. The following theorem gives a sufficient condition that is more useful, but is more limited in scope, because it applies only to coverings that are generated by an rRM (self-belonging) correspondence. But not every rectangular covering of the parameter space Θ is an rRM covering. Theorem 3.A.4[13] gives conditions that a covering generated by a self-belonging correspondence V, not necessarily rRM, is a partition. As might be expected, these conditions are more complicated.

Again, we suppose that $\Theta = \Theta^1 \times \Theta^2$, where Θ^1 and Θ^2 are arbitrary sets; $F : \Theta \to Z$ is the goal function, and $F^{-1}(F(\theta))$ is the contour set of F containing the point θ.

[13] A numbered statement whose number contains the symbol A appears in the Appendix to this chapter. It is reproduced here for convenient reference. Proofs are given in the Appendix, but are not repeated here.

We write $W(z)$ for the contour set $F^{-1}(F(\theta))$ when $F(\theta) = z$. Fix $z = z^0$, $W = W(z^0)$.

We write C_V for the rRM covering of W generated by V, thus, $C = C_V$.

THEOREM 3.6.1. Let W be an arbitrary contour set of a goal function F. If C_V is an rRM covering of W generated by a self-belonging correspondence $V : W \Rightarrow W$, and if V is symmetric, then C_V is a partition.

Proof: The proof is easier to follow if we lay out its logical structure explicitly.

Let R denote the statement "C_V is an rRM covering of W."
Let S denote the statement "V is symmetric."
Let P denote the statement "C_V is a partition."

In this notation theorem 3.6.1 is

$$\text{"}(R \text{ and } S) \text{ implies } P.\text{"} \qquad (*)$$

We assume R is true. Therefore, $(*)$ is logically equivalent to

$$\text{"}S \text{ implies } P.\text{"} \qquad (**)$$

Notice that $(**)$ is logically equivalent to

$$\text{"not } S\text{" or } P.\text{"} \qquad (++)$$

The statement $(++)$ is true exactly when its negation is false. The negation of $(++)$ is

$$\text{not (not } S \text{ or } P) = \text{"}S \text{ and "not } P.\text{"} \qquad (+++)$$

Our proof assumes "S and not P" and R, and derives a contradiction. This shows that $(+++)$ is false. Therefore, $(++)$ is true, hence $(**)$ is true and $(*)$ is true.

We begin the proof.

Given a covering $C = C_V$ of W and a point $\theta \in W$, define the subcovering $\Omega(\theta)$ by

$$\Omega(\theta) = \{K \in C_V \mid \theta \in K\}.$$

$\Omega(\theta)$ is the collection of rRM rectangles in C_V that cover $\theta \in W$.

For arbitrary $\bar{\theta}, \bar{\bar{\theta}} \in W$, let $\hat{\Omega}(\bar{\theta}, \bar{\bar{\theta}}) = \Omega(\bar{\theta}) \cap \Omega(\bar{\bar{\theta}})$. That is, a set K is in $\hat{\Omega}(\bar{\theta}, \bar{\bar{\theta}})$ if and only if K covers both $\bar{\theta}$ and $\bar{\bar{\theta}}$.

From now on we write $\Omega(\bar{\theta}, \bar{\bar{\theta}})$ for $\hat{\Omega}(\bar{\theta}, \bar{\bar{\theta}})$ where there is no risk of confusion.

If C is not partition of W (that is, "not P''"), then there must be an overlap pattern with points α, β, γ and sets K_1, $K_2 \in C$ such that

(1) $\beta \in K_1 \cap K_2$,
(2) $\alpha \in K_1 \backslash K_2$, $\gamma \in K_2 \backslash K_1$, and
(3) $\Omega(\alpha, \beta) \cap \Omega(\beta, \gamma) = \varnothing$.

(1), (2), and (3) are equivalent to

(i) $\Omega(\alpha, \beta) \neq \varnothing$,
(ii) $\Omega(\beta, \gamma) \neq \varnothing$, and
(iii) if $\Omega(\alpha, \beta) \cap \Omega(\beta, \gamma) \neq \varnothing$, then, for all $K \in \Omega(\alpha, \beta) \cap \Omega(\beta, \gamma)$, $K \subseteq / W$

Next, notice that for any point $\bar\theta \in W$,

(4) $\Omega(\bar\theta) = (\Omega(\bar\theta) \backslash \Omega(\bar\theta, \bar{\bar\theta})) \cup \Omega(\bar\theta, \bar{\bar\theta})$.

That is, the collection of sets that cover a point $\bar\theta$ in W, consists of sets that cover both $\bar\theta$ and $\bar{\bar\theta}$, together with the collection of sets that cover $\bar\theta$ and do not cover $\bar{\bar\theta}$.

It follows that for any $\bar\theta \in W$, and any $\bar{\bar\theta} \in W$, $\bar\theta \neq \bar{\bar\theta}$, either

(a) $V(\bar\theta) \in \Omega(\bar\theta, \bar{\bar\theta})$ or
(b) $V(\bar\theta) \in \Omega(\bar\theta) \backslash \Omega(\bar\theta, \bar{\bar\theta})$,

but not both.

Suppose C is not a partition of W. Then there is an overlap and hence there are points, α, β, γ, and sets K_1, K_2, as in Lemma 3.6.1 satisfying (1), (2), and (3).

Consider $V(\alpha)$. There are two cases labeled (a) and (b) as above for $\bar\theta = \alpha$. Suppose (b) is the case. That is, $V(\alpha) \in \Omega(\alpha) \backslash \Omega(\alpha, \beta)$.

Then,

$$V(\alpha) \notin \Omega(\alpha, \beta).$$

Because V generates the covering C, and $K_1 \in C$, there exists a point v in K_1 such that $V(v) = K_1$. Given the L-dot configuration α, β, γ, where $\alpha = (a_1, b_2)$, $\beta = (a_1, b_1)$, $\gamma = (a_2, b_1)$, and $\delta = (a_2, b_2)$, such that δ is not in the same contour set as the other points, we may assume without loss of generality that $v = (a_1, b_3)$. First, we consider the case in which $v \in V(\alpha)$. If $V(\alpha) = \{\alpha, v\}$, then $V(\alpha) \subseteq K_1$. This would violate rRM. Therefore, there must be a point $\eta \in V(\alpha)$ such that $\eta \notin K_1 = V(v)$. Now, $V(\alpha)$ is an rRM rectangle that includes the points $\alpha = (a_1, b_2)$ $\beta = (a_1, b_1)$,

$\eta = (x, y)$. Without loss of generality we can take $x = a_3$, $y = b_1$. There-fore, $V(\alpha)$ must also include the point $\eta' = (a_3, b_2)$.

Now if $V(\eta') = V(\alpha)$, then $v \in V(\eta')$, but $\eta' \notin V(v) = K_1$. This would violate symmetry of V. So, suppose $\alpha \notin V(\eta')$. Then $\eta' \in V(\alpha)$, but $\alpha \notin V(\eta')$, which violates symmetry.

So suppose $\alpha \in V(\eta')$. Then $V(\eta')$ must also contain v. Consequently $v \in V(\eta')$, but $\eta' \notin V(v)$, which again violates symmetry.

We have shown that $v \notin V(\alpha)$.

But $\alpha \in K_1 = V(v)$, whereas $v \notin V(\alpha)$, which contradicts symmetry of V. Thus, S is false. Hence $(+++)$ is false.

The same analysis applies to $V(\gamma)$ when $V(\gamma) \notin \Omega(\beta, \gamma)$.

Therefore, we may assume the only remaining case, which is

$$V(\alpha) \in \Omega(\alpha, \beta) \text{ and } V(\gamma) \in \Omega(\beta, \gamma).$$

Let $V(\alpha) = K_1 \in \Omega(\alpha, \beta)$, and let $V(\gamma) = K_2 \in \Omega(\beta, \gamma)$.

Then $\beta \in V(\alpha)$. Symmetry of V requires $\alpha \in V(\beta)$.

Similarly, $\beta \in V(\gamma)$, and hence symmetry of V requires $\gamma \in V(\beta)$.

It follows that $\alpha \in V(\beta), \beta \in V(\beta), \gamma \in V(\beta)$ (by symmetry and selfbe-longing of V). Then

$$V(\beta) \in \Omega(\alpha, \beta) \cap \Omega(\beta, \gamma) \cap \Omega(\alpha, \gamma),$$

which, by (iii) shows that

$$V(\beta) \not\subset_{\neq} W.$$

This, contradicts the requirement that $V(\beta)$ is F-cc and hence that it is an rRM rectangle.

Thus in all cases S is false. Therefore $(+++)$ is false, from which it follows that $(++)$ is true. By logical equivalence $(**)$ is true, and because R is true by hypothesis, $(*)$ is true.

This completes the proof.

The following example (Example 3.6.2) shows that the assumption that the covering is rRM is indispensable. The covering in the example is gen-erated by a self-belonging, symmetric correspondence V, but it is not a partition. The covering generated by V is *not* an rRM covering. Note also that the requirement that no set in the covering can be a subset of another in the covering, which is a property of rRM coverings, is alone not sufficient to ensure that the covering generated by V is a partition.

EXAMPLE 3.6.2. Let a contour set of F consist of four points, α, b, γ, δ.
Let

$$V(\alpha) = \{\delta, \alpha, \beta\}$$
$$V(\beta) = \{\alpha, \beta, \gamma\}$$
$$V(\gamma) = \{\beta, \gamma, \delta\}$$
$$V(\delta) = \{\gamma, \delta, \alpha\}.$$

Figure 3.6.6 shows the following level set:

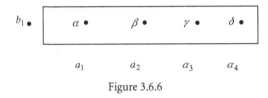

Figure 3.6.6

Observe that no set in C_V is a proper subset of any other.
Furthermore,

$$\beta \in V(\alpha), \text{ and } \alpha \in V(\beta)$$
$$\gamma \in V(\beta), \text{ and } \beta \in V(\gamma)$$
$$\delta \in V(\gamma), \text{ and } \gamma \in V(\delta)$$
$$\alpha \in V(\delta), \text{ and } \delta \in V(\alpha).$$

Therefore, V is symmetric, and also self-belonging. But the covering is not
a partition. It is also not rRM. If it were, we would have

$$V(\alpha) = V(\beta) = V(\gamma) = V(\delta) = \{\alpha, \beta, \gamma, \delta\},$$

and hence that C_V is the partition $\{\{\alpha, \beta, \gamma, \delta\}\}$.

Although we are mainly concerned with rRM coverings, with the correspondences that generate them, and with the mechanisms constructed
from them, there are other mechanisms, including some that are not decentralized, that are constructed from coverings that are not rRM, but are
generated by self-belonging, F-cc correspondences. Such a covering will not
be an rRM covering, and might not even be rectangular. This leads to the
following questions:

- If a covering of the parameter space is a partition, is it generated by a
  self-belonging correspondence, $U : \Theta \Rightarrow \Theta$?

- If a self-belonging correspondence $U : \Theta \Rightarrow \Theta$ generates a covering, what properties of the correspondence assure that the covering it generates is a partition?

We address these questions formally in the Appendix of this chapter. The results in the Appendix are summarized here.

THEOREM 3.A.1. A covering C of Θ is a partition if and only if *every* function $\Lambda : C \Rightarrow \Theta$ that satisfies

(A) $\Lambda(K) \in K$, for every $K \in C$,

is an SDR for C.

Next, we give a characterization of partitions in terms of the generating correspondence, $V : \Theta \Rightarrow \Theta$. First, we define a property that we subsequently show is a property of correspondences that generate partitions.

DEFINITION 3.A.2. Let $\bar{\theta}, \theta', \theta''$ denote points of Θ. A correspondence, $V : \Theta \Rightarrow \Theta$, is *block symmetric* if and only if

(B) $[\theta' \in V(\bar{\theta}) \text{ and } \theta'' \in V(\bar{\theta})] \Rightarrow [\theta' \in V(\theta'') \text{ and } \theta'' \in V(\theta')]$.

Block symmetry is a strengthening of the concept of symmetry. The term "block symmetric" is used because, when (B) is satisfied, there is a permutation of the elements of Θ such that the graph of V consists of blocks ("squares") with the "northeast" and "southwest" vertices on the diagonal of $\Theta \times \Theta$.

It is shown in the Appendix that if a self-belonging correspondence is block symmetric, then it is symmetric.

THEOREM 3.A.2. A covering C of Θ is a partition if and only if there is a block symmetric, self-belonging correspondence that generates C.

The following example shows that symmetry of the generating (self-belonging) correspondence is not sufficient for the covering it generates to be a partition.

EXAMPLE 3.A.1. Let $\Theta = \{a, b, c\}$, and let $V(a) = \{a, b, c\}$, $V(b) = \{a, b\}$, $V(c) = \{a, c\}$. Then V is self-belonging and symmetric, but the covering it generates is not a partition.

However, in this example the covering is reducible in the sense of the following definition.

DEFINITION 3.A.3. An element of a covering C of Θ is *redundant* if eliminating that element from C still leaves a covering of Θ. A covering is *irreducible*[14] if it has no redundant elements; otherwise it is *reducible*.

If C is a finite covering, then it has an irreducible subcovering, which might be C itself. If C is not irreducible, then it has a redundant element. When C is finite, successive elimination of redundant elements must eventually result in an irreducible subcovering. This is not true when C is infinite, as is shown by Dugundji's example (Dugundji, p. 161).

The covering C in Example 3.A.1 can be reduced in two different ways. First, to the covering $C' = \{\{a, b, c\}\}$, which is generated by the (constant) correspondence $U'(\theta) = \{a, b, c\}$, for $\theta \in \{a, b, c\}$, and, second, to the covering $C'' = \{\{a, b\}, \{b, c\}\}$, which is generated by the correspondence $V''(a) = V''(b) = \{a, b\}$, and $V''(c) = \{b, c\}$. Both C' and C'' are irreducible, and V' is symmetric, while V'' is not. Of course, C' is a partition and C'' is not.

Whereas symmetry is not enough to guarantee that the covering generated by a self-belonging correspondence is a partition, but if the covering is irreducible, then symmetry ensures that it is a partition. The converse also holds.

THEOREM 3.A.3. Let C be a covering of Θ. C is a partition if and only if

(i) C is generated by a self-belonging, symmetric correspondence V : $\Theta \Rightarrow \Theta$, and
(ii) C is irreducible.

Theorems 3.A.1, 3.A.2, and 3.A.3 are summarized in Theorem 3.A.4.

THEOREM 3.A.4. The following four propositions are equivalent:

(1) A covering C is a partition;
(2) Every function $\Lambda : C \to \Theta$ that satisfies condition (A) is an SDR for C;
(3) C is generated by a block symmetric, self-belonging correspondence $V : \Theta \Rightarrow \Theta$;
(4) C is an irreducible covering generated by a symmetric, self-belonging correspondence $V : \Theta \Rightarrow \Theta$.

---

[14] The term "irreducible" applied to a covering was introduced by Dugundji (5 p. 160).

What are the relationships between Theorem 3.A.4 and Theorem 3.6.1? The following observations show that the two theorems are not equivalent, and that neither is a generalization of the other.

(1) If a self-belonging correspondence is block symmetric, then it is symmetric. The converse is false, as shown by Example 3.6.2.
(2) If a self-belonging correspondence is rRM is it also irreducible? The answer is "no", as shown by Example 3.6.1b.
(3) If a self-belonging correspondence is irreducible, is it rRM? The answer is "no," as shown by Example 3.6.1b.
(4) If a self-belonging correspondence is rRM, is it block symmetric? The answer is "no," as shown by the example shown in Figure 3.6.7;
(5) If a self-belonging correspondence is block symmetric, is it rRM? The answer is "no." as shown by the example in Figure 3.6.8.

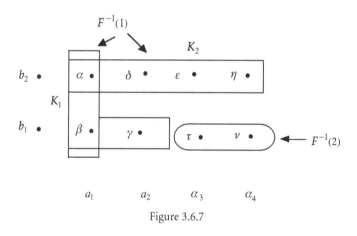

Figure 3.6.7

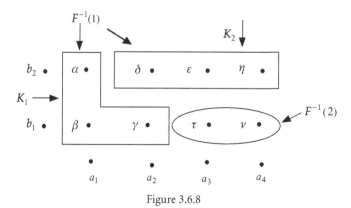

Figure 3.6.8

$$\Theta = \Theta^1 \times \Theta^2 = \{a_1, a_2, a_3, a_4\} \times \{b_1, b_2\}.$$
$$\alpha = (a_1, b_2), \beta = (a_1, b_2), \gamma = (a_1, b_1), \delta = (a_2, b_2),$$
$$\varepsilon = (a_3, b_2), \eta = (a_4, b_2), \nu = (a_3, b_1), \tau = (a_4, b_1)$$
$$F^{-1}(1) = \{\alpha, \beta, \gamma, \delta, \varepsilon, \eta\},$$
$$F^{-1}(2) = \{\nu, \tau\}.$$

Let

$$V(\alpha) = V(\beta) = V(\gamma) = K_1,$$

and

$$V(\delta) = V(\varepsilon) = V(\eta) = K_2.$$

We see that V is block symmetric, but the covering it generates is not rRM.

3.7 Informational Efficiency

3.7.1 Introduction

The informational efficiency of the mechanisms constructed by rRM and the transversals method (TM) is significant for comparing "costs" of alternative mechanisms that realize the same goal. The determinants of informational costs include:

- the precision with which agents are required to perceive their environments in order to operate the mechanism;
- the "amount" of information that the mechanism requires agents to communicate; and
- the complexity of computations required by the mechanism.

The costs related to the first item involve both the means by which agents observe their environments, and the time and effort agents must devote to observing, perhaps introspectively.

The second item involves the infrastructure and institutions by which communication is accomplished. Two kinds of costs are involved here. One is a capital cost, the cost of constructing and maintaining the "pipelines" that messages flow through, in other words, the cost of providing the channel capacity for communication. This includes establishing and maintaining the personal relationships that accompany inter-personal and both intra- and inter-organizational networks through which much communication flows.

The second is a variable cost – the cost of transmitting a particular message among agents. Both items of cost depend on the "size" of the messages to be transmitted.

The third item, the complexity of the computations that agents carry out, includes the time and effort needed to figure out the actions required by the mechanism in the prevailing environment. Those calculations use the observations of the environment, and the messages received by each agent from others, as inputs. Thus, we might expect that the complexity of computation might depend on the messages that are transmitted, as well as on the encoding of observations of the environment. Therefore, we should expect there to be tradeoffs between message size, the precision with which agents are required to report the environment, and computational complexity. Here we assume agents *can* know their own parameters exactly, but might not be required by the mechanism to do so. We do not consider issues of accuracy, nor do we consider costs associated with approximation. Analysis of the costs associated with or resulting from computational complexity depends on the model of computation that is used.[15] Here we do not address computational complexity, except in a limited way. In Chapter 2, where mechanisms in equation form are studied, the number of equations each agent must verify when a mechanism is given in equation form is taken as a rough indicator of the burden of computation. We focus here on the first two components of informational efficiency.

3.7.2 Observational Efficiency

As we saw earlier, a mechanism $\pi = (M, \mu, h)$ that realizes a goal function $F : \Theta \to Z$ induces a covering of the parameter space Θ generated by the correspondence $\mu^{-1} : M \Rightarrow \Theta$. A set $\mu^{-1}(m)$ consists of parameter values that do not have to be distinguished from one another for the agents to agree (or not to agree) to a given message.

---

[15] An analysis of computational complexity in a framework that is applicable to economic mechanisms is presented in Mount and Reiter (2002). The measure of complexity in that model is *delay*. If we assume that an elementary computational step takes a unit of time, then delay is equal to the number of sequential (some steps might be carried out in parallel) elementary computational steps used to complete the required computations. The complexity of the computations required in the Walrasian pure exchange example introduced in Chapter 1 is analyzed. It is shown that there is a tradeoff between communication and computation in that example. The efficient frontier between "size of the message space" and the "delay" is found. Increasing message space size from the minimum possible size, 2 to 3 allows a reduction in complexity (delay) from 3 to 2. Further increases in message space size do not result in further decreases in complexity.

When the mechanism is privacy-preserving, the individual message correspondences μ^i define sets in the individual parameter spaces Θ^i, $i = 1, \ldots, N$ that contain individual parameter values that agent i is not required to distinguish from one another. Thus, the larger these sets are, the lighter is the burden of observation on the agents. The coverings of the parameter space corresponding to the mechanisms under consideration are partially ordered by *coarseness*. That is, the observational requirements associated with different mechanisms are partially ordered by the coarseness of the coverings of the parameter space induced by each mechanism. Thus, the comparison of mechanisms according to the degree of observational precision required to operate the mechanisms is made by comparing the coarseness of their coverings.

We show next that decentralized mechanisms constructed using the reflexive rectangles method, rRM, are *maximal* (maximally coarse) in the set of rectangular coverings generated by mechanisms that realize a given goal function. Thus, a mechanism constructed by rRM can be said to be *maximally efficient* with respect to observational precision. This result also applies to OrRM coverings.

3.7.3 The Maximality of rRM-Coverings

DEFINITION 3.7.3.1. (i) A covering C' of Θ is a *coarsening* of a covering C of Θ if, for every $K \in C$, there is $K' \in C'$ such that $K \subseteq K'$.

(ii) It is a *proper* coarsening if there exists sets $K^* \in C$, and $K'^* \in C'$ such that $K^* \subseteq K'^*$, but $K'^* \neq K^*$.

(iii) A reflexive RM covering C of Θ for F, that has no proper self belonging, rectangular, F-cc (briefly, an RM) coarsening is called *maximal*.

THEOREM 3.7.3.1 (Sufficiency). If C is a reflexive RM (briefly, an rRM) covering of Θ for F, then C is maximal.

Proof: We present the proof first for the case of two agents, and use the notation introduced in Section 3.4.1 for that case.

Suppose C is an rRM covering for F of $\Theta = \Theta^1 \times \Theta^2$, but C is not maximal. Then there exists a proper coarsening C' of C. That is, for every $K \in C$, there is $K' \in C'$ such that $K \subseteq K'$, and at least one set $K \in C$ such that the corresponding set $K' \in C'$ satisfies $K \subsetneq K'$. Because $K' \in C'$, there exist sets $A' \in \Theta^1$, $B' \in \Theta^2$ such that $K' = A' \times B'$. Moreover,

K' is in the contour set of F that contains K. Furthermore, there are sets $A \subseteq \Theta^1$, $B \subseteq \Theta^2$, with $K = A \times B$. Furthermore, because $K \subset_{\neq} K'$, these sets satisfy

$$A' \supseteq A, \quad B' \supseteq B. \tag{*}$$

Let $a \in A$ and $b' \in B'$. By the inclusions (*) above, and because C' is F-cc,

$$(a, b') \in F^{-1}(F(\bar{\theta})),$$

where $\bar{\theta} \in K$, and $K' \subseteq F^{-1}(F(\bar{\theta}))$.

Hence, by the definition of $B^*(A, \bar{\theta})$ in the definition of left-RM, we have

$$(a, \ b') \in A \times B^*(A, \bar{\theta}) = A \times B.$$

Equality follows from the fact that C is reflexive, and hence left-RM.

So, $b' \in B'$ implies $b' \in B$. It follows that $B^* \subseteq B$, because b' is an arbitrary element of B'. Therefore, by (*),

$$B = B'$$

Similarly, because C is reflexive, it is also right-RM. A similar reasoning shows that

$$A = A'.$$

It follows that

$$K = K'.$$

But then C' is not a proper coarsening of C. This contradiction concludes the proof.

THEOREM 3.7.3.2 (Necessity). If C is maximal in the class of RM mechanisms, (that is, if C is a self belonging, rectangular, F-cc covering of Θ that has no proper coarsening), then C is reflexive-RM.

Proof: Suppose C is not reflexive RM. Without loss of generality, suppose it is not left-RM. Then there exists $\bar{\theta}$ and $k = A \times B \in L$ such that

$$B \neq B^*(A, \bar{\theta}).$$

Then it must be the case that

$$B \subset_{\neq} B^*(A, \bar{\theta}).$$

It follows that

$$k \underset{\neq}{\subset} A \times B^*(A, \bar{\theta}).$$ (**)

Write $K' = A \times B^*(A, \bar{\theta})$.
  Then (**) becomes

$$K \underset{\neq}{\subset} K'.$$ (+)

Consider the collection

$$C' = (C \backslash \{K\}) \cup \{K'\}.$$

Because C is a covering, the inclusion (+) implies that C' is a covering. Clearly, C' coarsens C, because every set R in C other than K has its identical twin in C', and for K in C, there is K' in C'such that $K \subseteq K'$. The coarsening is proper because $K' \neq K$. (Moreover, C' is not a superset of C, because it does not contain K.)
  This contradicts the hypothesis that C is maximal.
  This concludes the proof.

Next, we establish the same results for the case where $N > 2$. We use the notation established in Section 3.4 for the discussion of the N-step construction of coverings in the N-agent case, with $N > 2$.

THEOREM 3.7.3.3 (Sufficiency). If C is a reflexive RM covering of $\Theta = \Theta^1 \times \cdots \times \Theta^N$ for F, then C is maximal.

Proof: Suppose C is reflexive RM , but not maximal, and C' is any coarsening of C. Then, for every K in C, $K = K_1 \times \cdots \times K_N \subseteq \Theta^1 \times \cdots \times \Theta^N$, there exists $K' \in C'$ such that $K \subseteq K'$, where $K' = K'_1 \times \cdots \times K'_N \subseteq \Theta^1 \times \cdots \times \Theta^N$, and K' is in the contour set of F that contains K. Suppose $\bar{\theta} \in K$. For any sets $L \in C$, $L' \in C'$ such that $L \subseteq L'$, it follows that

$$L_i \subseteq L'_i \text{ for all } i \in \{1, \ldots, N\}.$$ (*)

For any $i \in \{1, \ldots, N\}$ let $a_i \in L_i$, $b'_i \in L'_i$. If $\bar{\theta} \in L$, then it follows by the inclusion (*), and the assumption that C' is F-cc, that

$$(a_i, b'_i) \in F^{-1}(F(\bar{\theta})).$$

We show next that $L_i \supseteq L_i'$. This inclusion, together with (*), would establish that, for every $i \in \{1, \ldots, N\}$, $L_i \supseteq L_i'$, and thus show that

$$L = L'.$$

By hypothesis, C is reflexive RM. Take $\bar{\theta} \in L$. It follows that

$$(a_i, b_i') \in L_i \times A_i^*(L_{-i}, \bar{\theta}).$$

Thus, $b_i' \in L_i'$ implies $b_i' \in L_i$. Therefore, $L_i \supseteq L_i'$. It follows from (*) that $L_i = L_i'$ for every $i \in \{1, \ldots, N\}$.

It follows that for any sets $K \in C$, $K' \in C'$ such that $K \subseteq K'$, the equality $K = K'$ holds. Thus, if C' is a rectangular, F-cc coarsening of a reflexive RM covering C, then C' is not a proper coarsening of C. It follows that C is maximal. This completes the proof.

THEOREM 3.7.3.4 (Necessity). If C is maximal for F then C is reflexive RM.

Proof: Suppose to the contrary that C is maximal for F, but not a reflexive RM covering. Then there exist $i \in \{1, \ldots, N\}, \bar{\theta} \in \Theta$, and a rectangle $K = K_i \times K_{-i}$ in C such that $K_i \neq A_i^*(K_{-1}, \bar{\theta})$. It follows from the definition of $A_i^*(K_{-i}, \bar{\theta})$ that

$$K_i \underset{\neq}{\subset} A_i^*(K_{-i}, \bar{\theta}).$$

It follows that

$$K \underset{\neq}{\subset} K_i \times A_i^*(K_{i-1}, \bar{\theta}). \tag{**}$$

Write $K' = K_i \times A_i^*(K_{i-1}, \bar{\theta})$. Then (**) becomes

$$K \underset{\neq}{\subset} K'. \tag{+}$$

Now consider the collection of sets,

$$C' = (C \backslash \{K\}) \cup K'.$$

C' is a covering, because C is a covering and the inclusion (+) implies that C' is also a covering. The covering C' coarsens C, because for every set $R \in C$ there is a set $R' \in C'$ such that $R \subseteq R'$. This is so, because every set $R \in C$ except for R' has its identical twin $R = R'$ in C', and for the set $K \in C$, there is $K' \in C'$ such that $K \underset{\neq}{\subset} K'$. Thus, C' coarsens C properly. This contradicts the hypothesis that C is maximal.

This concludes the proof.

We turn next to another aspect of informational efficiency, namely, the *informational size* of the message space of a mechanism. We also consider its relation to coarseness of the covering associated with the mechanism.

3.7.4 Informational Size and Coarseness

Informational Size

Mount and Reiter (1974) introduced a concept of the *informational size of a (topological) space*. To make our discussion of comparisons of informational size self-contained, we discuss briefly the idea that underlies that formal concept. It is the intuitive idea of the *capacity of a space to carry information*.

In ordinary usage information means knowledge about something. In more technical settings information can also mean anything that reduces uncertainty. Shannon's well-known measure of information was developed to analyze the capacity required to transmit signals that go between a sender and a receiver without regard for the meaning of what is transmitted. Jacob Marschak, and others, sought to apply this concept and measure of information in economic settings, and eventually abandoned that enterprise, because it seemed that the "amount" of information as measured by the Shannon formula (entropy) has no necessary relation to the relevance or usefulness or value of the information in economic decision-making.

Information is usually about something. The definition of informational size given in Mount–Reiter (1974) was intended to apply to information about something, and to formalize a notion about the capacity of a mathematical space to "carry" information. However, the concept of informational size is formalized not as a measure of the absolute "size" of a space, but as an ordering of spaces, an ordering that reflects the relative capacities of spaces to carry information. For any two spaces either one of them is informationally larger than the other, or they are not comparable. (Any two finite spaces are comparable. Spaces that have dimension are comparable when certain regularity conditions on mappings are imposed.)

A prototypical instance of a piece of information is:

"Henry's income after taxes in the year 2002 was \$100,000."   (*)

This can be formalized by defining variables whose values identify points in the domain and points in the range of a function. In the sentence (*) the domain $D = N \times Y$ includes values that identify a person, $n = H =$ Henry $\in N$, and the year $y = 2002 \in Y$; the range consists of nonnegative integers interpreted as a number of dollars, and the function $f_1 : D \to I$ specifies the after-tax income in year $y \in Y$ of person $n \in N$. This function formalizes a class of observations, namely, the after-tax income of any specified person in the set N, in any specified year in Y.

We might have also observed:

"Henry lived in a blue house during the year 2002." (**)

This observation is formalized by the function $f_2 : D \to G$, where G is the set of colors of houses under consideration.

It should be clear that the set of functions that can be interpreted as information about entities represented by points in the domain D is very large – perhaps infinite. Even if we were to restrict attention to observations of Henry in the year 2002, there would be a very large – perhaps infinite – number of different possible observations.

These considerations underlie the formal definition of informational size of spaces given in Mount and Reiter (1974). Roughly, if every function defined on a space M' has a corresponding function defined on a space M, and if there are functions defined on M that have no corresponding functions defined on M', then M is said to be informationally larger than M'. The meaning of "corresponding function" uses the idea of lifting functions from M' to M to capture the notion that the two functions involved represent the same observation. 'Lifting functions' is defined as follows.

DEFINITION 3.7.4.1.a Suppose $g : M' \to g(M') = W$ is a function from M' to some set W. If there is a function $\varphi : M \to M'$ that is surjective (here M' might be a subset of M), then the function $f = g \circ \varphi$ is the *lifting of g* to the function $f = g \circ \varphi$ on M.

If there is such a function φ from M to M', then it is evident from Figure 3.7.4.1 that every function on M' can be lifted to a function on M. It is also evident that the function $g \circ \varphi$ represents the same observation as g does. If there is no surjective function from M' to M, then there could be functions on M' with no corresponding functions on M.

The following simple example, in which M and M' are finite sets, illustrates lifting functions.

Suppose $M' = \{x_1, x_2\}$, and $M = \{y_1, y_2, y_3\}$. Then clearly there is a surjective function $\varphi : M \to M'$. For instance,

$$\phi(y_1) = x_1, \qquad \phi(y_2) = \phi(y_3) = x_2.$$

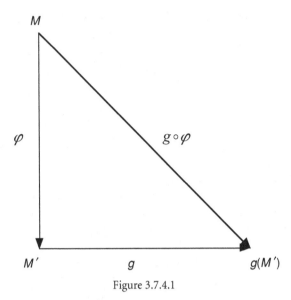

Figure 3.7.4.1

Now if $g : M' \to g(M')$, then the function $f : M \to g(M')$ defined by $f(y) = g(\varphi(y))$ is the function on M associated with g. That is,

$$f(y_1) = g(\varphi(y_1)) = g(x_1),$$
$$f(y_2) = g(\varphi(y_2)) = g(x_2) = g(\varphi(y_3)) = f(y_3).$$

The lifting is not unique. We could have taken

$$\varphi'(y_1) = \varphi'(y_2) = x_1, \qquad \varphi'(y_3) = x_2$$

and as a result gotten

$$f'(y_1) = g(\varphi'(y_1)) = g(x_1) = g(\varphi'(y_2)) = f'(y_2),$$

and

$$f'(y_3) = g(\varphi'(y_3)) = g(x_2).$$

The concept of lifting functions is the idea behind the definition of informational size of a space given in Mount and Reiter (1974), where a (topological) space X is said to be informationally at least as large as a (topological) space Y if and only if there is a (continuous and locally sectioned[16]) function

---

[16] A surjective function $f : X \to Y$ is called *locally sectioned* if its inverse f^{-1} correspondence is locally threaded. A correspondence $\phi : A \Rightarrow B$ is *locally threaded* if for every point $a \in A$ there is an open neighborhood U in A of a, and a continuous function $g : U \to B$ such that $g(a') \in \phi(a)$ for every $a' \in U$.

$\varphi : X \xrightarrow[\text{onto}]{} Y.$[17] These conditions rule out dimension-increasing functions, like the Peano function.

DEFINITION 3.7.4.1.b A set (space) M is informationally at least as large as a set (space) M' if every function on M' can be *lifted* to a function defined on M; it is strictly larger if there is at least one function defined on M' that cannot be lifted to one on M.

In the case in which M and M' are spaces, that is sets with additional structure, for instance Euclidean spaces, the functions that appear in the definition of lifting would naturally be required to satisfy conditions corresponding to the additional structure. In order to accommodate the competitive mechanism, whose message space is Euclidean, as well as more general possibilities, message spaces in the class of topological spaces were considered. This class of course includes Euclidean spaces and, more generally, metric spaces, as well as finite or infinite discrete spaces, the latter with the discrete topology.

Correspondingly, all functions involved are required to be continuous. This is a natural requirement in relation to information, because communication should not amplify small errors too much. But here a technical difficulty complicates matters. A natural measure of size of messages , say, in the case of Euclidean spaces, is *dimension,* that is, the number of variables involved. It seems intuitive that it is more costly to transmit the values of two variables than it is to transmit the value of one variable. In the case of Euclidean spaces, the values of variables are real numbers; the distinction between communicating the values of two real numbers and communicating the value of one real number can disappear unless an additional restriction is imposed. This difficulty would arise if it were possible to encode two real numbers in one real number, communicate that number, and then decode the received value to recover the original two numbers. For concreteness suppose x_1 and x_2 are variables that take values in the unit interval. Then the variable $x = (x_1, x_2)$ has the unit square $I^2 = [0, 1] \times [0, 1]$ as its domain. If it were possible to encode this variable in one real variable, the function representing the encoding would map I^2 into the unit interval $I = [0, 1]$. Of course, there are many such functions. Suppose $\xi : I^2 \to I$ is the encoding function. Then, to communicate the point $x \in I^2$, compute $\xi(x) = y \in I$

---

[17] A number of papers that modify and apply the Mount–Reiter concept of informational size are surveyed in Hurwicz (1986). An alternative condition involving the Lipschitz continuity, due to Hurwicz is also discussed in the cited survey.

and communicate that value to the receiver. To recover the original point x from the value $y = \xi(x)$ we need a function, say ψ, that maps I onto I^2. Furthermore, to be sure we get the original point back, it must be the case that $x = \psi(y) = \psi(\xi(x))$, which is to say that ψ and ξ are inverses of one another. If there were such functions ψ and ξ, and they were both continuous, then there would be no meaningful informational distinction between one real variable and two real variables. (By extending the argument, the number of real variables would not be meaningful as a measure of information content.)

Furthermore, we would require that the image of ψ cover an open set in I^2, because the point to be encoded can be any point in an open set in I^2, (otherwise we are effectively not in I^2). Now, there are continuous functions that map I continuously *onto* I^2. The Peano function, P, whose image of the unit interval is the unit square, is one such continuous, dimension-increasing function. Therefore, when considering lifting functions in order to maintain the distinction between dimensions, the function φ in Definition 3.7.4a is required to be *locally sectioned*. This condition is sufficient to rule out dimension-increasing mappings.

We have shown in Theorem 3.7.4.1 that the rRM method of constructing a covering of the parameter space results in a covering that is maximal. Another desirable informational property of a mechanism is that its message space be as small in informational size as possible. Are these two informational properties equivalent? If not, are they in conflict? That is, is there a tradeoff between communication efficiency, as indicated by the informational size of the message space, and observational precision, as indicated by the coarseness of the covering of the level sets of the goal function?

Suppose that $\pi = (M, \mu, h)$ is a decentralized mechanism that realizes a goal function F, and suppose that the message space of π has minimal informational size. If the covering C_μ of the parameter space induced by the message correspondence is an rRM covering, then Theorem 3.7.4.1 assures us that the covering C_μ is maximally coarse.

Example 3.8.1 shows that the two-step method constructs two rRM coverings, one of them results in a mechanism with a message space of size 2 and the other of size 3. Each mechanism has a maximal covering. (Examination of the two coverings in Figure 3.8.4 and 3.8.5 shows that neither is coarser than the other, but one of them has a redundant set.) More generally, mechanisms that realize a given goal function have at least two properties relevant to informational efficiency: coarseness of the covering and size of the message space. Theorem 3.8.4.3 assures us that a mechanism constructed by the N-step procedure has an rRM covering of the parameter space, and hence is maximally coarse in the set of mechanisms that realize that goal function. Therefore, if a mechanism is constructed by the N-step procedure, or otherwise is known to have an rRM covering (whether or not its message space is of minimal informational size), then its associated covering is maximal.

In the augmented inner product example, with

$$F(a, b) = a_1 b_1 + a_2 b_2 + b_3,$$

the mechanism that has an informationally minimal message space also has the property that the covering of the parameter space that it determines is maximally coarse.[18]

The augmented inner product is a goal function for which rRM constructs two mechanisms, one using left-RM, the other right-RM. One of them is informationally efficient with respect to coarseness and informational size of the message space, whereas the other mechanism does not have a minimum size message space. In that example, parameter transfer from 2 to 1 is never efficient. However, if we took account of computational complexity as a component of informational comparison, parameter transfer from 2 to 1 might sometimes be efficient, perhaps because agent 1 has better computational resources than agent 2.

Suppose, we have a mechanism whose message space has minimal informational size among all RM mechanisms that realize a given goal function. Does it follow that the covering corresponding to that mechanism is maximal? We know from Theorem 3.7.4.1 that if the covering is an rRM covering, then the covering is maximally coarse, whatever the size of the message space.

But suppose that the covering is not rRM. *The following examples show that a mechanism whose message space has minimal informational size need not generate a maximally coarse covering of the parameter space.*

In the first example, Example 3.7.4.2, the parameter space is Euclidean, whereas in Example 3.7.4.3, it is a finite set. The examples indicate that the concepts of informational size of the message space, and of the coarseness of the covering that mechanism generates are quite different. This is perhaps surprising in the case of a finite parameter space, because in that case, the size of the message space is simply the number of distinct messages it contains, and there is a one-to-one correspondence between messages

---

[18] A proof appears in Chapter 2 in the discussion of the condensation method. See also Theorem 4.4.6 in Chapter 4.

and sets in the covering. Therefore, if one message space is informationally smaller than another, it contains fewer messages, and the covering associated with it must contain fewer sets. However, two message spaces can have the same size and yet, as Example 3.8.4.3 shows, the covering associated with one of them can be a coarsening of the covering associated with the other. (In the latter example, the maximally coarse covering has overlaps, while the one that is not maximal is a partition.)

EXAMPLE 3.7.4.2. (Euclidean).

Let the parameter space, $\Theta = \Theta^1 \times \Theta^2$, be two dimensional. For convenience we sometimes write $X = \Theta^1$, $Y = \Theta^2$, and correspondingly x for θ^1, and y for θ^2. Suppose that the goal function F is such that the contour set $F^{-1}(1)$ is the set S shown in Figure 3.7.4.2. It is the trapezoid defined by the two lines labeled L_1, L_2 in Figure 3.7.4.2, together with the line segments in X and Y that complete the trapezoid.[19]

More explicitly, the line L_1 has the equation

$$x + y = 1, \quad \text{where } 0 \le x \le 1, \quad 0 \le y \le 1,$$

and the line L_2 has the equation

$$x + y = 2, \quad \text{where } 0 \le x \le 2, \quad 0 \le y \le 2.$$

The other two line segments are the intervals $[(0, 1), (0, 2)]$ on the Y-axis and $[(1, 0), (2, 0)]$ on the X-axis.

We consider two mechanisms. The first is π, a mechanism that generates the covering C shown in Figure 3.7.4.2. C consists of horizontal line segments that go between L_1 and L_2. The generating correspondence $V(\bar{\theta}) = K_{\bar{\theta}}$ is defined by $V(\bar{\theta}) = \{(x, y) \in F^{-1}(1) \mid y = \bar{y}, \text{ and } 1 \le x + \bar{y} \le 2\}$, where $\bar{\theta} = (\bar{x}, \bar{y})$ and $x \ge 0$, $y \ge 0$.

The unique point $(2 - \bar{y}, \bar{y}) \in L_2$ corresponding to the set $K_{\bar{\theta}}$ is to be the distinct representative of $K_{\bar{\theta}}$. That is, $\Lambda(K_{\bar{\theta}}) = (2 - \bar{y}, \bar{y})$, and the transversal $T = \Lambda(C)$ is the line L_2 itself.

We take the message space of the mechanism to be the line segment $[0, 2] \subset X$. This is defined by choosing the mapping $v : T \to X$ to be $v(2 - \bar{y}, \bar{y}) = 2 - \bar{y}$. This defines the message space of π to be

(i) $M = [0, 2]$.

To define the second mechanism we introduce another line, L_3, into Figure 3.7.4.2, as shown in Figure 3.7.4.3. This line is halfway between L_1

---

[19] For our purposes here, that is all we need to know about the goal function.

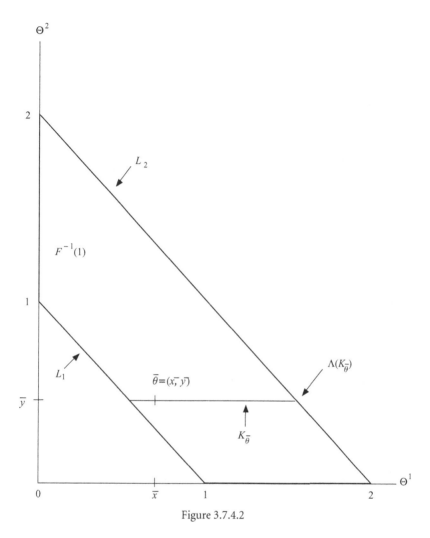

Figure 3.7.4.2

and L_2. Its equation is

$$x + y = 1.5, \quad \text{where } 0 \le x \le 1.5, \quad 0 \le y \le 1.5.$$

This line partitions the contour set $F^{-1}(1) = S$ into two subsets, denoted S_1, S_2, where

$$S_1 = \{(x, y) \in S \mid 1 \le x + y \le 1.5\},$$

and

$$S_2 = \{(x, y) \in S \mid 1.5 < x + y \le 2\}.$$

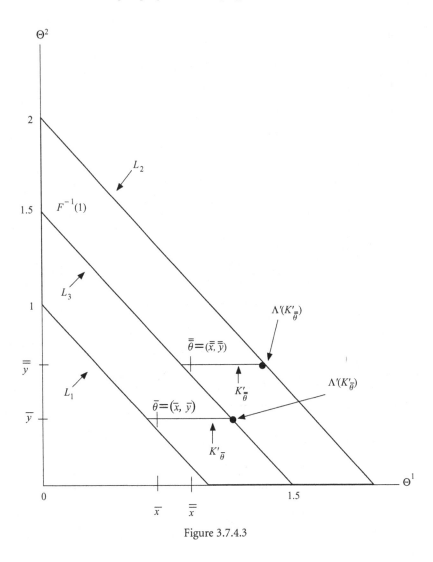

Figure 3.7.4.3

We define the covering C' generated by the correspondence $V' : \Theta \rightrightarrows \Theta$ of the second mechanism. For $\bar{\theta} \in \Theta$, if $\bar{\theta} \in S_1$ then let

$$V'(\bar{\theta}) = K'_{\bar{\theta}} = \{(x, y) \in S \mid 1 \leq x + \bar{y} \leq 1.5, \quad \text{and } y = \bar{y}\},$$

and if $\bar{\theta} \in S_2$ then let

$$V'(\bar{\theta}) = K'_{\bar{\theta}} = \{(x, y) \in S \mid 1.5 < x + \bar{y} \leq 2, \quad \text{and } y = \bar{y}\}.$$

The covering C' generated by V' has the SDR Λ', defined by

$$\Lambda'(K') = K' \cap (L_2 \cup L_3).$$

If $K' \in S_1$ then $K' \cap L_2 \neq \varnothing$, but $K' \cap L_3 = \varnothing$, and, if $K' \in S_2$ then $K' \cap L_2 = \varnothing$, and $K' \cap L_3 \neq \varnothing$.

It follows that if $K' \in S_1$, then $\Lambda'(K'_{\bar\theta}) = (1.5 - \bar{y}, \bar{y}), 0 \leq \bar{y} \leq 1.5$ and if $K' \in S_2$, then $\Lambda'(K'_{\bar\theta}) = (2 - \bar{y}, \bar{y}), 0 \leq \bar{y} \leq 2$.

The transversal is $T' = \Lambda'(C')$.

Next, we define the one-to-one function $v' : T' \to M'$ to obtain the message space M' of the second mechanism π'.

For $K' \subseteq S_1 \Lambda'(K') \in L_3$. Suppose $\Lambda'(K') = (t_1, t_2)$. Then it must be the case that

$$t_1 = 1.5 - t_2, \quad \text{where } 0 \leq t_2 \leq 1.5.$$

Define

$$v'(t_1, t_2) = v'(1.5 - t_2, t_2) = \tfrac{1}{3}t_2.$$

For $K' \subseteq S_2$, $\Lambda'(K') \in L_2$. Then for $\Lambda'(K') = (t_1, t_2)$, it must be the case that

$$t_1 = 2 - t_2, \quad \text{where } 1.5 < t_2 \leq 2.$$

Define

$$v'(t_1, t_2) = v'(2 - t_2, t_2) = 1 + \tfrac{1}{2}t_2.$$

Then the message space is

$$M' = v'(T') = v'(L_2 \cup L_3) = \left[0, \tfrac{1}{2}\right] \cup [1, 2]. \tag{ii}$$

It is clear that C is a proper coarsening of C', but M and M' have the same informational size, that is, $\dim(M) = \dim(M') = 1$. Moreover, M' is a proper subset of M.

EXAMPLE 3.7.6.3 (Finite sets). In this example the parameter space $\Theta = \Theta^1 \times \Theta^2$, where $\Theta^1 = \{a_1, a_2\}$ and $\Theta^2 = \{b_1, b_2\}$. Thus,

$$\Theta = \{(a_1, b_1), (a_1, b_2), (a_2, b_1), (a_2, b_2)\}.$$

Let $\alpha = (a_1, b_2)$, $\beta = (a_1, b_1)$, $\gamma = (a_2, b_1)$, $\delta = (a_2, b_2)$, and suppose $F^{-1}(1) = \{\alpha, \beta, \gamma\}$, and $F^{-1}(0) = \{\delta\}$.

This is shown in Figure 3.7.4.4.

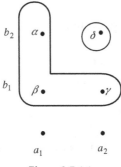

Figure 3.7.4.4

Confine attention to the contour set $F^{-1}(1)$. The smallest message space that is possible for a rectangular covering of $F^{-1}(1)$ consists of two messages, say, m_1 and m_2. A covering of $F^{-1}(1)$ that consists of two rectangles, shown in Figure 3.7.4.5, is $C_1 = \{K_1, K_2\}$, where

$$K_1 = \{\alpha\}, \quad \text{and} \quad K_2 = \{\beta, \gamma\}.$$

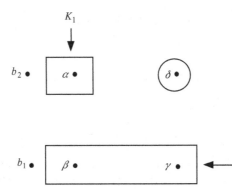

Figure 3.7.4.5

But C_1 has a proper coarsening,

$$C_2 = \{K_1', K_2'\}, \quad \text{where } K_1' = \{\alpha, \beta\} \text{ and } K_2' = \{\beta, \gamma\},$$

as shown in Figure 3.7.4.6.

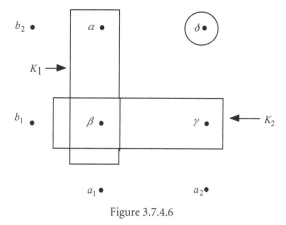

Figure 3.7.4.6

This shows that, although the message space associated with the covering C_1 has minimal informational size, the covering C_1 is not a maximally coarse covering. Note that the covering C_2 is maximally coarse, and the message space it generates has minimal informational size in the set of decentralized (self-belonging, rectangular, and F-cc) coverings of mechanisms that realize the goal function.

Although these examples indicate that informational size of the message space and coarseness of the associated covering are different concepts, in sufficiently regular cases there is a connection between the size of the message space and the "size" of sets in the covering. Suppose the parameter space is $\Theta = R^3$, a Euclidean space, and suppose the goal function is sufficiently smooth. Then level sets of a real-valued goal function will be (locally) two-dimensional smooth manifolds in R^3. A rectangular covering of a level set could consist of two-dimensional rectangles, one-dimensional rectangles, or zero-dimensional rectangles. In the regular case the rectangles will be one dimensional. Correspondingly, the transversal to the covering will be one dimensional. If, as in the case of a revelation mechanism, the sets are zero dimensional, the transversal will be two dimensional. Let the dimension of the level set be d, the dimension of the rectangles in the covering be r, and the dimension of the transversal be t. Then, in the regular case, the relation

$$d = r + t \qquad (\%)$$

will hold.[20] We know from the construction of a mechanism from an rRM covering and a transversal that the dimension of the message space is the

---

[20] The differential approach to mechanisms is explored in Chapter 4, where there is a systematic treatment of the ideas underlying equation (%) , or variants of it.

same as the dimension of the transversal. This follows from the requirement that the mapping $v : T \to M$ be injective. In the regular case this mapping is required to be smooth, and hence dimension preserving. Consequently, if the informational size of the message space (namely its dimension) is smaller, then the dimension of the sets that make up the covering will be larger. Although this relationship is not directly between informational size and coarseness, it suggests that in regular cases the covering corresponding to the smaller message space is either coarser than the original one, or not comparable with it.

The second component of informational efficiency is, as we have indicated, the *informational size* of the mechanism's message space. In the case of a mechanism constructed from an rRM covering, the message correspondence induces the same covering as the one it was constructed from. This suggests that there might be some relationship between the coarseness of the covering and the informational size of the message space.

More specifically, suppose a goal function is given, and consider the class of decentralized mechanisms that realize that goal function. We have shown that an rRM covering C of Θ is generated by a self-belonging correspondence $V : \Theta \Rightarrow \Theta$, and that C is maximal (with respect to the partial ordering of coverings by coarseness, as defined in the preceding subsection) in the class of coverings that are self-belonging, rectangular and F-cc for the given goal function F. A decentralized mechanism, say $\pi = (M, \mu, h)$, constructed from that covering, whether by the method of transversals, or by the condensation procedure (see Chapter 2) also generates a covering of the parameter space, namely, the one induced by the inverse of its message correspondence. We have seen that this covering is the same as the covering C_V generated by V. This connection between the covering and the message space suggests the question: "How is the size of the message space of π related to the coarseness of the covering generated by the message correspondence of π?" More specifically;

(A) "If C is maximally coarse in the class of mechanisms that realize the goal function F, then does the message space M of a decentralized mechanism constructed from that covering have minimal informational size in that same class of mechanisms?

(B) If a decentralized mechanism that realizes F, however constructed, has a message space of minimal informational size, then is the associated covering of Θ maximally coarse in the class of RM mechanisms for F?

If the answer were 'yes' to both questions, then any decentralized mechanism constructed from an rRM covering would be informationally efficient in both senses. However, it is not in general the case that a decentralized mechanism, whose associated covering is maximally coarse, and that realizes the goal function, has a message space that is informationally minimal in the class of decentralized mechanisms that realize that goal function. If the parameter space is finite, the OrRM algorithm constructs a covering that is maximally coarse, and a message space that has minimal informational size among all decentralized mechanisms that realize that goal function.

Example 3.7.4.1 also shows an analogous result in a case in which the parameter space is a Euclidean, and the goal function is smooth. In this example from Chapter 2, the mechanism is represented in equation form. We refer to the goal function in this, and similar examples, as an *augmented inner product* (see Chapter 2).

EXAMPLE 3.7.4.1. There are two agents, with parameter spaces $\Theta^1 = R^2$, and $\Theta^2 = R^3$. We write parameters of agents 1 and 2 as $a = (a_1, a_2)$ and $b = (b_1, b_2, b_3)$, respectively. The goal function is

$$F(a, b) = a_1 b_1 + a_2 b_2 + b_3 + \tfrac{1}{2} a_1^2.$$

There are two mechanisms: one has a message space M_1 whose dimension is 3; the other has a message space M_2 whose dimension is 4. It is shown in Chapter 2 (Section 2.1.3.2) that each of the coverings associated with these mechanisms is constructed by a two-step process, and hence each is a reflexive RM covering. It follows from Theorem 3.7.3.2 that each of these coverings is maximally coarse. The coverings are, of course, not comparable with respect to coarseness. But the two message spaces are comparable with respect to informational size, one being strictly smaller than the other. That is, the message space of the first mechanism is three dimensional, whereas the message space of the second is four dimensional. Thus, *maximal coarseness in the class of rRM mechanisms does not imply minimal message space size of the mechanism.* However, it is an immediate consequence of Theorem 3.7.3.2 that a reflexive RM mechanism that has a message space whose informational size is minimal in the class of mechanisms that realize a given goal function has a maximal covering in that class.

3.8 Section 1.8 Revisited: A Graphical Presentation

We revisit Section 1.8 in order to show how our algorithm constructs a decentralized, informationally efficient mechanism that realizes the goal function in that example. We follow the steps laid out in the Sections 3.2 through 3.5. Here we present the construction graphically, as far as possible.

We use notation and assumptions that are introduced in Section 1.8., but in places we change some assumptions so as to enrich the example, and to show more of the construction. The treatment of Example 1.8 here is somewhat more formal than the exposition in Section 1.8. We begin by defining the sets and functions that appear in Section 1.8. Recall that the function $\varphi = (\varphi_1, \varphi_2)$ maps the interval of possible logging amounts $\lambda \in [0, 1]$ onto the piecewise linear curve $\varphi(\lambda) = (\varphi_1(\lambda), \varphi_2(\lambda)) = (w, n)$, where w denotes the amount of "wood" produced, and n is the amount of "nature" remaining, when the amount of logging is λ. To define the political pressure functions we first define two functions, P_1' and P_2' on the set $\varphi([0, 1]) = \varphi_1([0, 1]) \times \varphi_2([0, 1])$, by the formulas

$$P_1' : \varphi([0, 1]) \to R_+, \qquad P_2' : \varphi([0, 1]) \to R_+.$$

The values

$$p_1 = P_1'(w, n) \quad \text{and} \quad p_2 = P_2'(w, n)$$

are the measures of (maximum) political pressure that agent 1 and agent 2 can bring to bear when the amounts of wood and of nature are (w, n). The political pressure functions are

$$P_i = P_i' \circ \varphi \quad i = 1, 2.$$

Thus, $P_i : [0, 1] \to R_+$ $i = 1, 2$.

We assume that the functions P_i are continuous, and piecewise linear, with linear segments on the intervals $[0, \lambda_1)$, $[\lambda_1, \lambda_2]$, $(\lambda_2, 1]$, and that P_1 is strictly decreasing and P_2 is strictly increasing on $[0, 1]$. Under these assumptions each p-function is uniquely specified by its value at four points, $0, \lambda_1, \lambda_2, 1$. Denote these values a_0, a_1, a_2, a_3 for P_1, and b_0, b_1, b_2, b_3 for P_2. Finally, we suppose that there are numbers, denoted $\tau_{min}^1, \tau_{max}^1, \tau_{min}^2, \tau_{max}^2$, which bound the two functions. Then, the set of environments is $\Theta = \Theta^1 \times \Theta^2$, where

$$\Theta^1 = \left\{ a = (a_0, a_1, a_2, a_3) : \tau_{max}^1 \geq a_0 > a_1 > a_2 > a_3 \geq \tau_{min}^1 \right\},$$

and

$$\Theta^2 = \left\{ b = (b_0, b_1, b_2, b_3) : \tau_{min}^2 \leq b_0 < b_1 < b_2 < b_3 \leq \tau_{max}^2 \right\}.$$

(Recall that in Section 1.8 it was assumed that the set of environments that are possible for the loggers' agent, agent 1, is the set of all pairs, (a_1, a_2), that lie strictly between τ_{max}^1 and τ_{min}^1.)

Note that for any parameter point, $(a, b) \in \Theta$, the graphs of the corresponding functions P_1, P_2 intersect in a unique point $(\lambda^*, \tau^*) \in$

$[0, 1] \times [\tau^1_{min}, \tau^1_{max}] \cap [\tau^2_{min}, \tau^2_{max}]$. Thus, a pair of functions, P_1, P_2 in $\Theta = \Theta^1 \times \Theta^2$, determines a unique point (λ^*, τ^*). We define the goal function $F : \Theta^1 \times \Theta^2 \to R_+$ by the condition that its value at the point $\theta = (a, b) \in \Theta$ be the value λ^* from the unique pair (λ^*, τ^*) so determined.

A typical pair of p-functions is shown in Figure 3.8.1a. It shows one of three possible cases. The other two are shown in Figures 3.8.1b and 3.8.1c.

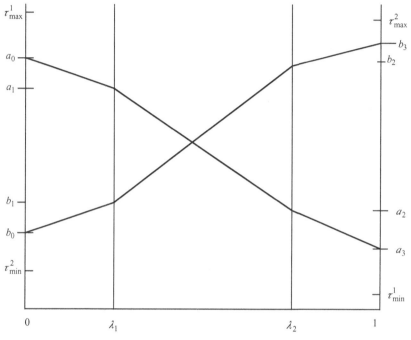

Figure 3.8.1a

Figures 3.8.1b and 3.8.1c show the other two possible cases. In Figure 3.8.1b the point of intersection (λ^*, τ^*) is such that λ^* is between 0 and λ_1, and in Figure 3.8.1c, the intersection of the two p-functions is such that the λ^* is in the rightmost interval.

The individual environment spaces are four dimensional. Hence, the full environment space is eight dimensional – a case that does not lend itself to graphical presentation. However, we can see that in each of the three regions in which the p-functions can intersect, only two parameters per agent determine the point of intersection, and hence the outcome. In the region defined by the condition that λ is in the interval $[0, \lambda_1)$ they are a_0, a_1 for agent 1 and b_0, b_1 for agent 2, and correspondingly in the other two regions. A graphical presentation of the analysis can be given for any

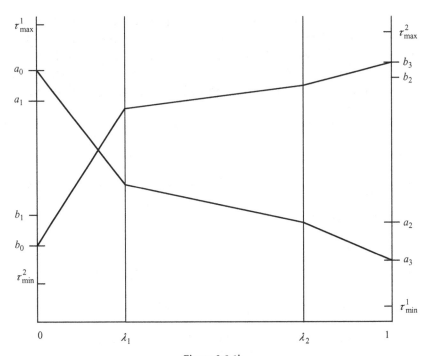

Figure 3.8.1b

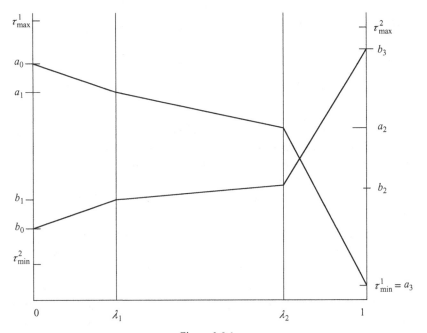

Figure 3.8.1c

one of the regions; the analysis in the other two regions is the same. We take up the case presented in Figure 3.8.1a, in which the p-functions intersect in the middle region, the one in which λ^* is in $[\lambda_1, \lambda_2]$.

The first step in our algorithmic procedure is to construct a covering of the joint parameter space Θ by rectangles. This is accomplished by constructing a correspondence $V : \Theta \Rightarrow \Theta$, that is self-belonging and F-contour contained. First, we choose an arbitrary point $\bar{\theta} = (\bar{\theta}^1, \bar{\theta}^2) = (\bar{a}_0, \bar{a}_1, \bar{a}_2, \bar{a}_3, \bar{b}_0, \bar{b}_1, \bar{b}_2, \bar{b}_3) = (\bar{a}, \bar{b})$.

Next, following the two-step construction, we construct agent 1's side of the rectangle for the given point. This is shown in Figure 3.8.2a.

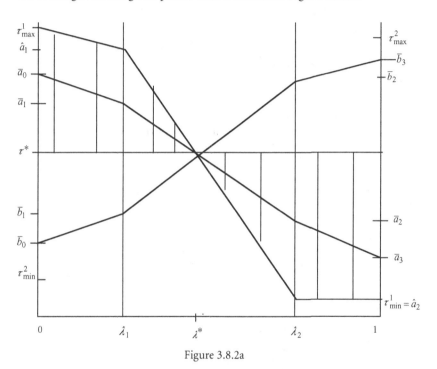

Figure 3.8.2a

Figure 3.8.2a shows that any line segment whose left endpoint is (λ_1, a_1) such that $\tau^* < a_1 \leq \hat{a}_1$, and whose right endpoint is (λ^*, τ^*), is the basis of a parameter point in the set $A(\bar{a}, \bar{b})$. For any point a'_1 that satisfies the condition $(\lambda_1, a'_1); \tau^* < a'_1 < \hat{a}_1$, consider the set of values of a_0 such that $(0, a_0)$ is the left endpoint of a line segment whose right endpoint is in the interval $(\lambda_1, a'_1); \tau^* < a'_1 < a'_0$. We can see in Figure 3.8.2a that this set is not empty. Every such pair of points determines the left endpoint of a line segment that "starts" on the vertical line over the point 0, and whose right endpoint is on the line above λ_1. Furthermore, that point determines the left endpoint of a line segment that passes through the point (λ^*, τ^*), and terminates at the point at which it intersects the vertical line on λ_2. The termination point is the value $\xi_1((\lambda_1, a_1'), (\lambda^*, \tau^*))$ of the function defined in Section 1.9. It is clear that each such line connects at its right endpoint with a line segment that decreases monotonically from the vertical line on λ_2 to the vertical line on 1.

The part of the four-dimensional set of parameter points that is essential here is the set of pairs (a_1, a_2) that characterize the middle line segments that contain the point (λ^*, τ^*); for each such pair we can find the points a_0 and a_3 that complete the specification of the parameter point.

In summary, Figure 3.8.2a shows the set $A(\bar{a}, \bar{b}) \times \{\bar{b}\}$. It should be clear from the graph that the set $A(\bar{a}, \bar{b})$ is the largest set that satisfies the conditions of our construction, and is such that $A(\bar{a}, \bar{b}) \times \{\bar{b}\}$ is in $F^{-1}(F(\bar{a}, \bar{b}))$.

It remains to construct agent 2's side of the rectangle. Figure 3.8.2.b shows the result of this construction.

We have constructed the rectangle $A(\bar{a}, \bar{b}) \times B^*(A(\bar{a}, \bar{b}), \bar{b})$, where $B^*(A(\bar{a}, \bar{b})\bar{b})$ is the set in the parameter space of agent 2 corresponding to the horizontally hatched area in Figure 3.8.2b.

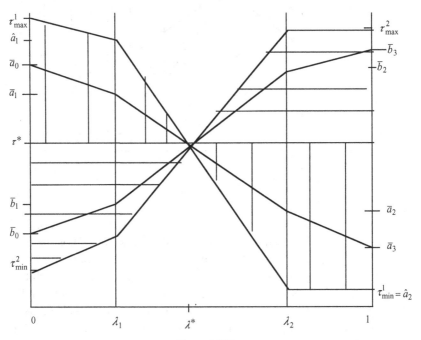

Figure 3.8.2b

Thus, $V(\bar{a}, \bar{b}) = A(\bar{a}, \bar{b}) \times B^*(A(\bar{a}, \bar{b}), \bar{b})$. This is a rectangle in the full parameter space. In order to represent it in a diagram on the page, we note that the defining points are the values of (a_1, a_2) and (b_1, b_2). The rectangle in the parameter space corresponding to these values is shown in Figures 3.8.3a and 3.8.3b.

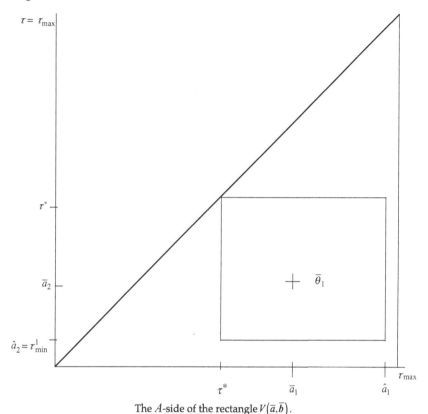

The A-side of the rectangle $V(\bar{a}, \bar{b})$.

Figure 3.8.3a

We have constructed the covering generated by the correspondence $V : \Theta \Rightarrow \Theta$.

The next step is to find a system of distinct representatives (SDR) for that covering. But that is completely obvious from Figure 3.8.2b; we can choose the point $\bar{\theta}$ to be the representative of the set $V(\bar{\theta})$. This choice indeed defines an SDR, because if $\bar{\theta}$ were an element of another set, say, $V(\bar{\bar{\theta}})$, $\bar{\bar{\theta}} = (\bar{\bar{a}}_1, \bar{\bar{a}}_2, \bar{\bar{b}}_1, \bar{\bar{b}}_2); \bar{\bar{\theta}} \neq \bar{\theta}$, then either the two line segments generated by $(\bar{\bar{a}}_1, \bar{\bar{a}}_2)$ and $(\bar{\bar{b}}_1, \bar{\bar{b}}_2)$ intersect at the same point as do the two line segments generated by $\bar{\theta}$, or they intersect at a different point. If they

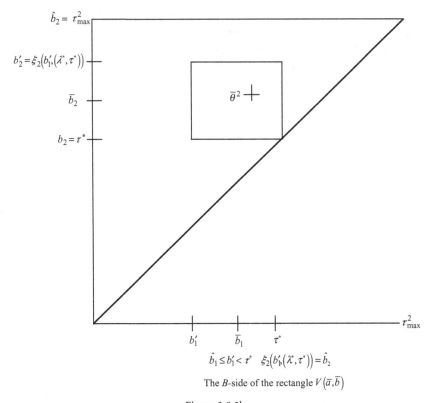

The *B*-side of the rectangle $V(\bar{a},\bar{b})$

Figure 3.8.3b

intersect at the same point, then $V(\bar{\theta}) = V(\bar{\bar{\theta}})$, because by the construction, neither can be a subset of the other.

If they intersect at two different points, then there would be two different points (λ', τ') and (λ'', τ'') such that the line segment corresponding to $\bar{\theta}$ contains both $(\lambda'\tau')$ and (λ'', τ''). But the construction guarantees that the line segments determined by $\bar{\theta}$ have a unique intersection. Thus, given a set in the covering , *any* parameter point in that set can be its representative.

Note that the elements in the SDR are four dimensional. They are the four parameters that determine the two lines that represent the set. But a set $V(\theta)$ is also uniquely associated with the point at which that representative pair of lines intersect. The points of intersection have the form (λ, τ), which is two dimensional.

These two-dimensional points can be chosen as the messages, because the function that associates a point of intersection with the representative of a rectangle in the full parameter space has been shown to be injective, that is, uniquely associated with the representative of the rectangle. We see that the rRM construction produces a mechanism with a two-dimensional message space in this example.

In the original formulation of Section 1.9 the domain of the logging rate, λ, is in the interval $[0, 1]$. This is mapped into the first quadrant of two-dimensional space R_+^2, whose coordinates represent the outputs of "wood" and "nature" that result from logging. The image of the unit interval is assumed to be a continuous curve whose endpoints are $(0, n_{max})$ and $(1, w_{max})$. We assumed that curve to be piecewise linear with kinks at the points $\varphi(\lambda_1) = (\varphi_1(\lambda_1), \varphi_2(\lambda_1))$ and $\varphi(\lambda_2) = (\varphi_1(\lambda_2), \varphi_2(\lambda_2))$. This piecewise linearity is assumed to be inherited by the p-functions, as shown in Figure 1.1.1. This, together with the assumptions that imply that the p-functions have unique intersections over the interval $[0, 1]$, ensures that an environment is characterized by eight parameters, namely, the values of each p-function at the four values $0, \lambda_1, \lambda_2, 1$. Our algorithm for mechanism construction (the rectangles method, followed by the transversals method construction) produces a decentralized mechanism whose message space is two dimensional when applied to that set of environments and goal function. Next, we examine what the algorithmic construction produces when we keep the same goal function, but enlarge the set of environments.

Suppose that instead of approximating the curve $\varphi(\lambda)$ that shows the results of logging at the rate λ at four points $0, \lambda_1, \lambda_2, 1$, we consider n points between 0 and 1. Thus, the points at which there are kinks in the p-functions are $0, \lambda_1, \ldots, \lambda_n, 1$. The assumptions that ensure an intersection of the two p-functions at a point λ^* between 0 and 1 are maintained. In this setting the number of parameters that characterize an environment is $2(n + 2)$. For any environment in the set corresponding to this size subdivision, the intersection appears in one of the intervals $[\lambda_j, \lambda_{j+1})$, for $j = 0, 1, \ldots, n - 1$, and $\lambda_0 = 0$, or in the interval $[\lambda_n, \lambda_{n+1}] = [\lambda_n, 1]]$. As in the case in which $n = 2$, the set of p-functions that intersect in a particular interval, say, $[\lambda_j, \lambda_{j+1})$, the RM construction begins by identifying the class of parameters a_{j-1}, a_j and b_{j-1}, b_j such that the two corresponding p-functions intersect at λ^*, and then extending each of those functions piecewise to the entire interval $[0, 1]$. This process constructs a rectangle in the joint parameter space of the two agents. Construction of a transversal is exactly parallel to what was done in the case $n = 2$. As in that case, there is an injective mapping of the transversal into the two-dimensional space $[0, 1] \times [\tau_{min}^1, \tau_{max}^1] \cap [\tau_{min}^2, \tau_{max}^2]$. The point at which any two p-functions in a particular RM rectangle intersect is the same, and the rectangles are disjoint, and are maximal with respect to inclusion. Hence the point of intersection uniquely identifies that rectangle. Thus, the message consists of two numbers, (λ^*, τ^*), independent of the number of parameters.

Next, we consider a more complex goal function. Suppose the Forester favors the interests of one of the two groups of interested parties over the other. Say he favors more logging, and so is willing to cope with pressure from the preservationists that is not fully offset by countering pressure from the loggers. This can be expressed by a goal function defined as follows. The Forester wants to choose a logging rate such that the pressure from agent 2 – the representative of the preservationists – exceeds the pressure from agent 1 by an amount $\beta > 0$. Thus, the Forester's desired logging rate is $\lambda^{**} \in [0, 1]$ satisfying

$$P_2(\lambda^{**}) - P_1(\lambda^{**}) = \beta. \tag{+}$$

Here we drop the assumption that the p-functions are piecewise linear, but continue to assume that they are strictly monotone. Under these assumptions there is a unique value of λ^{**} that satisfies the condition $(+)$, given $\beta > 0$. This is shown in Figure 3.8.4a for nonlinear p-functions.

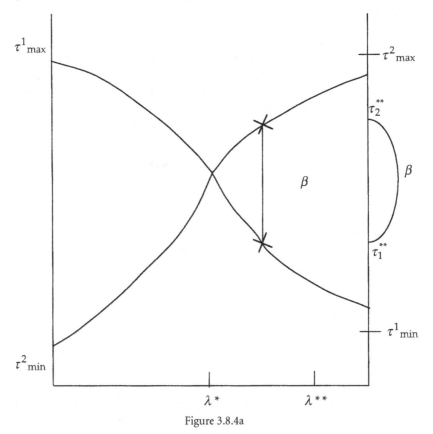

Figure 3.8.4a

Next, we use the rectangles method to construct a covering of the environment spaces. This is shown in Figure 3.8.4b.

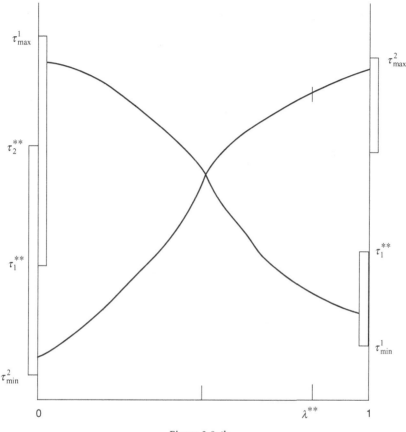

Figure 3.8.4b

The covering is as follows. For agent 1, the relevant rectangle in agent 1's parameter space consists of all p-functions, however represented, whose graph is a curve whose left end point lies in the interval in the line $\lambda = 0$ indicated by the rectangle whose left boundary is in that line. That curve then passes through the point $(\lambda^{**}, \tau_1^{**})$, and terminates in a point that lies in the interval in the line indicated by the thin rectangle inside that line $\lambda = 1$.

For agent 2 the construction is similar. The endpoints of the graph of a p-function that passes through the point $(\lambda^{**}, \tau_2^{**})$ must lie in the intervals indicated by the rectangles outside the lines at $\lambda = 1$, $\lambda = 2$, respectively.

The points of the form $(\lambda, \tau_1, \tau_2)$ constitute an SDR for this covering, and hence can be used as the messages of the mechanism constructed from this covering. It is clear that no smaller message space will work, except in the special case that $\beta = 0$. In that case $\tau_1 = \tau_2$; we are in the case in which the Forester wants to balance the opposing political pressures.

We can see that for each goal function in the family characterized by β, the size of the message space is independent of the number of parameters that characterize the p-functions, that is, of the number of parameters that characterize the environment – in this case, the agents.

The property that the size of the message space is independent of the number of parameters extends to other cases. For instance, in the case where $\beta = 0$, suppose that the linear segments that make up a p-function are replaced by nonlinear segments, so that the graph of a p-function consists of curved segments. The number of parameters might be more or less than the ones needed to characterize linear segments, but as long as the points of intersection of the p-functions are uniquely associated with the RM rectangles, it remains the case that the size of the message space is independent of the number of parameters.

The property that the size of the message space is independent of the number of parameters that characterize agents is a property of the competitive mechanism in exchange environments. There it is well-known that the size of the message space is determined by the number of goods, and the number of agents. It is considered to be an important informational advantage of that mechanism. Section 1.9 suggests that this advantage may also be available in cases that appear at first glance to be quite different.

3.9 Strategic Behavior

3.9.1 Dominant Strategy Implementation

In this section we consider briefly the problem that strategic behavior presents to design of informationally efficient mechanisms. We focus on informational properties of mechanisms in this book, because information processing is costly, and mechanisms that impose information processing tasks that exceed the capacities of human beings, even when equipped with the best information technology available, cannot in fact be operated. But a complete theory of mechanism design should not ignore the effects of distributed information on incentives, and therefore on the operation of decentralized mechanisms when agents have incentives to exploit private information. Indeed, the literature that deals with incentives in mechanism design is extensive, but that literature, with very few exceptions, ignores the burden of information processing. A more complete approach to mechanism design should address both informational and strategic issues.

A few papers in the literature on mechanisms deal with both strategic behavior and informational efficiency. See Reichelstein (1984), Reichelstein and Reiter (1988), Hurwicz (1972), and Williams (1986). These papers show in special contexts that strategic behavior increases informational requirements beyond what would be minimal if the people operating in the mechanism behaved as they were instructed. More specifically, for a given goal function strategic behavior increases the size of the message space that would be required by a decentralized mechanism that realizes that goal function when strategic behavior is ruled out. On the other hand, when informational requirements are ignored, mechanisms can be designed to implement goal functions in a large class. But often these mechanisms impose infeasible informational tasks.[21] The algorithms that we present in this book for constructing informationally efficient decentralized mechanisms that realize a given goal function can, we think, be usefully combined with methods of mechanism design that focus on implementation in the presence of strategic behavior. Although we do not provide a general treatment of this matter in this book, we do suggest ways of including both strategic and informational objectives in a mechanism design process. We show how this might be done in two settings. First, in Section 1.8 we show how an incentive compatible mechanism designed using the revelation principle can be made informationally efficient by applying our algorithm for designing mechanisms. Second, in the case of finite environment spaces we show how a mechanism that implements a goal function in Nash equilibrium can be modified by use of OrRM and the transversals method into a mechanism that is informationally efficient and implements the same goal function in Nash equilbrium.

We begin with the simplest version of Section 1.8. Recall that the decision variable for the Forester is $\lambda \in [0, 1]$, denoting the amount of logging the Forester permits in the given forest. The two functions $P_i : [0, 1] \rightarrow [\tau^i_{max}, \tau^i_{min}]$, $i = 1, 2$, denote respectively a measure of the "amount" of political pressure that agent 1, the representatives of the loggers, can bring to bear on the Forester, and the amount of political pressure that the representative of the preservationists, agent 2, can bring to bear on the Forester, as functions of the amount of logging λ that might prevail[22] Figure 3.9.1.1 is reproduced here for convenient reference.

---

[21] This is not to say that such mechanisms are not valuable. They help establish the limits of feasibility.

[22] We have taken the p-functions $P_i : [0, 1] \rightarrow [\tau^i_{max}, \tau^i_{min}]$, $i = 1, 2$, to be primitives. However, they could be derived from utility functions of each individual logger and for each individual preservationist, and from functions that specify the cost, in effort or money, of creating political pressure. The resulting p-functions would have values determined by the aggregate of those individual contributions given the technology of applying or creating political pressure.

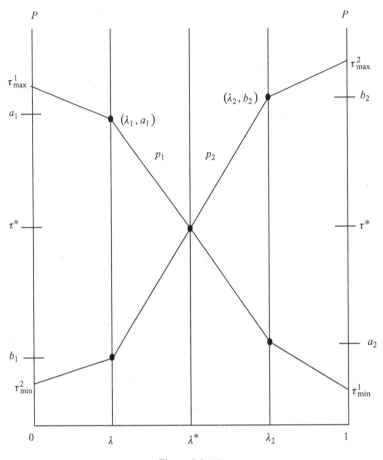

Figure 3.9.1.1

It reflects the simplifying assumption that for all admissible environments $\theta = (\theta^1, \theta^2)$ specified by the parameters $\theta^1 = (a_0, a_1, a_2, a_3)$, $\theta^2 = (b_0, b_1, b_2, b_3)$, we have

(1) $a_0 = \tau^1_{max},$ $a_3 = \tau^1_{min},$ $b_0 = \tau^2_{min},$ $b_3 = \tau^2_{max}$

(2) $a_0 > a_1 > a_2 > a_3,$ $b_0 < b_1 < b_2 < b_3$ (3.9.1)

(3) $a_0 > b_0,$ $a_3 < b_3.$

We assume that in any admissible environment $\theta = (\theta^1, \theta^2)$, θ^i is known by agent i, but not by agent j, $j \neq i$, nor by the Forester.

Suppose that the agents behave strategically. In the verification scenario described in Section 1.9, the Agents replied "yes," or "no" to proposed values of $\lambda \in [0, 1]$. The solution value of λ is the one (unique under our assumptions) to which both Agents say, "yes." It is equivalent in terms of outcome to suppose that each agent i transmits his parameter θ^i to the Forester; the Forester computes the solution (λ^*, τ^*) of the equation $P_1(\lambda, \theta^1) - P_2(\lambda, \theta^2) = 0$, and designates λ^* as the amount of logging he will permit. This process results in the decision called for by the goal function when the agents communicate their parameters truthfully. But, when the agents behave strategically they have incentives not to respond truthfully. Their p-functions are private information. Agent i would like to behave as if the value of her p-function at any value of λ was as large as is consistent with the conditions on the environment that are common knowledge. These are the conditions displayed in Formula (3.9.1). The p-functions that result

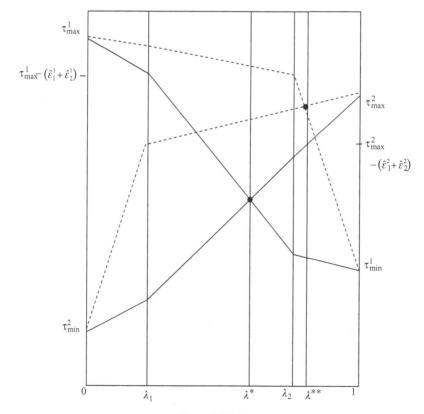

Figure 3.9.1.2

are displayed in Figure 3.9.1.2. That is,

$$\hat{a}_0 = \tau^1_{\max}, \qquad \hat{a}_1 = \tau^1_{\max} - \varepsilon^1, \qquad \hat{a}_2 = \hat{a}_1 - \varepsilon^1, \qquad \hat{a}_3 = \tau^1_{\min}$$
$$\hat{b}_0 = \tau^2_{\max}, \qquad \hat{b}_1 = \tau^2_{\max} - \varepsilon^2, \qquad \hat{b}_2 = \hat{b}_1 - \varepsilon^2, \qquad \hat{b}_3 = \tau^2_{\min}.$$

Strict monotonicity of the p-functions rules out $\varepsilon^i = 0$, $i = 1, 2$ so for simplicity, we assume that there are positive numbers $\hat{\varepsilon}^i = 0$, $i = 1, 2$ that are respectively lower bounds for $\varepsilon^1, \varepsilon^2$.

If $\tau^1_{\max} - 2\hat{\varepsilon}^1 > \tau^2_{\max}$, then agent 1 has an advantage; in that case that the solution λ^{**} of the equation $P_1(\lambda, \hat{a}) - P_2(\lambda, \hat{b}) = 0$ lies in the interval $(\lambda_2, 1]$. Similarly, if $\tau^1_{\max} < \tau^2_{\max} - 2\varepsilon^2$, then $\lambda^{**} \in [0, \lambda_1]$.

Applying the revelation principle here, with the Forester as the mediator, each agent announces his p-function, which is uniquely specified by his parameter θ^i. The Forester then finds the unique value $\hat{\lambda}$ determined by the reported parameter values θ, and announces $\hat{\lambda}$ as the amount of logging permitted. To make this mechanism implement the Forester's goal function, he must create incentives that induce the agents to report their parameter values truthfully. One way the Forester can do this is to introduce another stage in the dialogue between the Forester and the agents. First, the agents report their parameters, $\hat{a}$ for agent 1 and $\hat{b}$ for agent 2. Then in the second stage each agent must *demonstrate* the political pressure that his group can bring to bear at the point λ^{**} that solves the equation $P_1(\lambda, \hat{a}) - P_2(\lambda, \hat{b}) = 0$. But $P_i(\lambda^{**}, \bar{\theta}^i)$ is the maximum political pressure that agent i can actually bring to bear at λ^{**} when her true parameter value is $\bar{\theta}^i$. The disparity is $E^i(\lambda^{**}) = P_i(\lambda^{**}, \hat{\theta}^i) - P_i(\lambda^{**}, \bar{\theta}^i)$. The Forester can observe this disparity. He announces the rule defined in (3.9.2) as his rule of behavior, or decision rule.

$$\text{If} \begin{cases} E^1 > E^2 \\ E^1 < E^2 \\ E^1 = E^2 > 0 \\ E^1 = E^2 = 0 \end{cases} \text{then} \begin{cases} \lambda^* = 0 \\ \lambda^* = 1 \\ \lambda^* = \begin{cases} 0 \text{ with probabilty } 1/2 \\ 1 \text{ with probabilty } 1/2 \end{cases} \\ \lambda^* = \lambda^{**}. \end{cases} \qquad (3.9.2)$$

It is evident that it is best for each agent to announce his true parameter value in the first stage. Thus, agent 1 reports $\hat{a} = \bar{a}$, his true parameter value, and agent 2 announces $\hat{b} = \bar{b}$. This is a revelation mechanism in which truth-telling is a dominant strategy equilibrium.

We turn next to informational considerations. The message space of the revelation mechanism is four dimensional. An environment of each agent is characterized by two parameters, the other two being fixed at commonly known values. Starting with this mechanism we apply the algorithm presented in Sections 3.2 to 3.5. We see that for any admissible environment $(\bar{a}, \bar{b})$ the verification scenario requires the Forester to announce the triple $(\lambda^*, \tau^{1*}, \tau^{2*})$, where agent 1 replies "yes" if and only if $P_1(\lambda^*, \hat{a}) - P_1(\lambda^*, \bar{a}) = 0$, and $\tau^{1*} = P_1(\lambda^*, \bar{a})$, and agent 2 relies "yes" if and only if $P_2(\lambda^*, \hat{b}) - P_2(\lambda^*, \bar{b}) = 0$, and $\tau^{2*} = P_2(\lambda^*, \bar{b})$.

This mechanism is:

- incentive compatible – it is equivalent to the revelation mechanism defined above,
- decentralized, and
- informationally efficient – its message space is three dimensional.

This example suggests a general procedure for making revelation mechanisms into informationally efficient decentralized mechanisms that implement a given goal function. The first step is to start with a revelation mechanism that implements the given goal function, and then apply the rectangles method, to construct a covering correspondence V and the covering C_V that it defines. Then construct an SDR, Λ, an encoding function v, and the message space it maps into, and finally the outcome function, as constructed in Section 3.5.

It is interesting to note that the Forester's introduction of an intermediate step results in a process that roughly resembles the procedure commonly followed when a Federal regulatory agency proposes a new regulation or revises an existing one. It is also the case that Federal agencies operate mechanisms that have several stages. For instance, the process specified by the Internal Revenue Service for determining the amount of income tax to be paid by a taxpayer consists of a sequence of steps, where the number of steps may vary depending on what happens.

3.9.2 Designing Informationally Efficient Nash-Implementing Mechanisms[23]

Earlier sections of this book are devoted to designing informationally efficient decentralized mechanisms that realize a given goal function; strategic behavior of agents is ignored. In this subsection we consider strategic behavior modeled by game forms that Nash implement a given goal function $F : \Theta \to Z$, where $\Theta = \Theta^1 \times \cdots \times \Theta^n$ and Θ^i models the private characteristics of agent i. Given F, we construct informationally efficient game

---

[23] This subsection was written by Stanley Reiter and Adam Galambos.

forms that Nash implement *F*, where *F* satisfies "Maskin monotonicity" and "no veto power."

A game form is a mechanism in the sense defined in preceding sections of this chapter. Here we extend our preceding results to cases where Nash implementation is required. We present a two-stage procedure – an algorithm – for constructing a game form that Nash implements *F*. This algorithm can be used to construct a rectangular *F*-cc covering *C* of Θ that is "monotonically generated." Proposition 3.9.2.2 establishes that this covering is informationally efficient, in a sense made precise in what follows. Following that, Proposition 3.9.2.1 is used to construct a game form that Nash implements *F* and generates the informationally efficient covering *C* by its equilibrium message correspondence. We also show that any covering of Θ generated by the equilibrium message correspondence of a game form must be rectangular, *F*-cc, and monotonically generated.

More precisely, we construct informationally efficient mechanisms (M, μ, h) such that[24] $M = M^1 \times \cdots M^n$ and μ is the Nash equilibrium message correspondence. Such mechanisms are said to have the *Nash property* (Reichelstein and Reiter (1988)). With such a mechanism, a mediator could check the set of possible Nash equilibrium messages (i.e., $\mu(\Theta)$) and ask players to individually verify whether a message would be an equilibrium. Since we are interested in informational efficiency, we would like the set of messages the mediator has to check to be minimal in some sense. Thus, we are looking for Nash implementing game forms that have a minimal set of equilbrium messages. We will construct such game forms by considering the coverings of Θ induced by the Nash equilibrium message correspondences of different game forms that implement *F*.

REMARK. For Nash implementation it is necessary that players condition their strategies on the *entire* profile of types $\theta = (\theta^1, \ldots, \theta^n)$. But the game form (M, h) together with its induced equilibrium correspondence $E : \Theta \Rightarrow M$ is an *informationally decentralized* mechanism. The Nash equilibrium message correspondence can be factored into the correspondences

$$E^i(\bar{\theta}^i) = \{m \in M: mR_i(\bar{\theta}^i)(\bar{m}^i, m^{-i}) \text{ for all } \bar{m}^i \in M^i\}. \quad (3.9.2.1)$$

The correspondence *E* is analogous with the correspondence μ in earlier sections, and the E^i play the role of the μ^i (see Figure 3.9.2.1). Using the language of noncooperative game theory, $E^i(\theta^i)$ is the graph of the *best-response correspondence* of player *i* at θ^i. (M, E, h) is then an informationally

[24] We assume that Θ and *Z* are finite. The set of players is *I*, and $|I| = n$.

decentralized mechanism with the *Nash property* (as in Reichelstein and Reiter (1988, Theorem 2.4)).

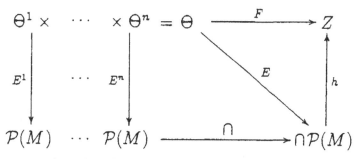

Figure 3.9.2.1 The Nash implementing game form (M, h) together with the Nash equilibrium correspondence E is informationally decentralized. $\mathcal{P}(\cdot)$ denotes the set of all nonempty subsets.

However, incentive compatibility might not be preserved in factoring E and having players announce best-response correspondences rather than individual messages in M. At some state θ some player i might have an incentive to announce the message $\mu^i(\bar{\theta}^i)$ for some $\bar{\theta}^i \in \Theta^i$. In particular, the Nash equilibrium in state $(\bar{\theta}^i, \theta^{-i})$ might be better for player i than the Nash equilibrium in state θ. Although this "false" equilibrium in state $(\bar{\theta}^i, \theta^{-i})$ might not be accessible by i's unilateral deviation from the equilibrium in state θ in the game form (M, h), it could be accessible for i by the false announcement $\mu^i(\bar{\theta}^i)$. The example below illustrates this point.

EXAMPLE: There are two players, and $Z = \{a, b, c, d\}$. Player 1 has two types, $\bar{\theta}^1, \bar{\bar{\theta}}^1$. Player 2 has two types: $\bar{\theta}^2, \bar{\bar{\theta}}^2$. Preferences are

$$R_1(\bar{\theta}^1) = \begin{matrix} a \\ c \\ b \\ d \end{matrix}, \quad R_1(\bar{\bar{\theta}}^1) = \begin{matrix} b \\ a \\ d \\ c \end{matrix}, \quad R_2(\bar{\theta}^2) = \begin{matrix} b \\ c \\ a \\ d \end{matrix}, \quad R^2(\bar{\bar{\theta}}^2) = \begin{matrix} c \\ b \\ d \\ a \end{matrix}. \quad (3.9.2.2)$$

All preferences are strict; the top element is the most preferred. Consider the goal function F shown below:

$$
\begin{array}{c|cc}
 & \bar{\theta}^1 & \bar{\bar{\theta}}^1 \\
\hline
\bar{\theta}^2 & a & b \\
\bar{\bar{\theta}}^2 & c & d
\end{array} \quad (3.9.2.3)
$$

The following game form Nash implements F. Player 1 has strategy space $M^1 = \{m_1', m_1''\}$ and player 2 has strategy space $M^2 = \{m_2', m_2''\}$. (Let $M = M^1 \times M^2$.) The outcome function h is given by

$$
\begin{array}{c|cc}
 & m_1' & m_1'' \\
\hline
m_2' & a & b \\
m_2'' & d & c
\end{array}
\qquad (3.9.2.4)
$$

The Nash equilibrium message correspondence is

$$E((\bar{\theta}^1, \bar{\theta}^2)) = (m_1', m_2'), \qquad (3.9.2.5)$$

$$E((\bar{\theta}^1, \bar{\bar{\theta}}^2)) = (m_1'', m_2''), \qquad (3.9.2.6)$$

$$E((\bar{\bar{\theta}}^1, \bar{\theta}^2)) = (m_1'', m_2'), \qquad (3.9.2.7)$$

$$E((\bar{\bar{\theta}}^1, \bar{\bar{\theta}}^2)) = (m_1', m_2''). \qquad (3.9.2.8)$$

The mechanism (M, E, h) is informationally decentralized, because we can factor E into the best response correspondences E^1 and E^2:

$$E^1(\bar{\theta}^1) = \{(m_1', m_2'), (m_1'', m_2'')\}, \qquad E^1(\bar{\bar{\theta}}^1) = \{(m_1'', m_2'), (m_1', m_2'')\},$$
$$(3.9.2.9)$$

$$E^2(\bar{\theta}^2) = \{(m_1', m_2'), (m_1'', m_2')\}, \qquad E^2(\bar{\bar{\theta}}^2) = \{(m_1', m_2''), (m_1'', m_2'')\}.$$
$$(3.9.2.10)$$

It is easy to see that for all states (θ^1, θ^2), we have $E(\theta^1, \theta^2) = E^1(\theta^1) \cap E^2(\theta^2)$. However, sending the messages prescribed by the maps E^1 and E^2 is not always incentive compatible for the players. In state $(\bar{\theta}^1, \bar{\theta}^2)$, player 2 could pretend to be of type $\bar{\bar{\theta}}^2$ and send the message $E^2(\bar{\bar{\theta}}^2) = \{(m_1', m_2''), (m_1'', m_2'')\}$. With player 1 sending $E^1(\bar{\theta}^1) = \{(m_1', m_2'), (m_1'', m_2'')\}$, the outcome would be

$$\{(m_1', m_2'), (m_1'', m_2'')\} \bigcap \{(m_1', m_2''), (m_1'', m_2'')\} = \{(m_1'', m_2'')\}. \quad (3.9.2.11)$$

But $h(m_1'', m_2'') = c$, which is better for player 2 in state $\bar{\theta}^2$ than a, which would have resulted from following the message prescribed by E^2.

As a first step, we now derive some conditions which must be satisfied by a covering of Θ that is induced by the Nash equilibrium message correspondence of some game form implementing F. Suppose we are given a game form (M, h) that Nash implements F, where $M = M^1 \times \cdots \times M^n$ and $h : M \to Z$. "Nash implements F" means that for every $\theta \in \theta$ the unique Nash equilibrium outcome of the game defined by $[R(\theta), M, h]$ is $F(\theta)$. Note that there may be several Nash equilibrium *strategy profiles*

$\bar{m}^*$, $\bar{\bar{m}}^*$, $\ldots \in M$ at a state θ, but they must lead to the same outcome: $h(\bar{m}^*) = h(\bar{\bar{m}}^*) = \cdots$.

For every $\theta \in \Theta$ let $E(\theta)$ be the set of equilibrium messages of $[R(\theta), M, h]$. If there are several equilibrium messages, they must lead to the same outcome in Z, because (M, h) was assumed to Nash implement F. Let $M^* \subseteq M$ be the image of Θ under E. Then E induces a covering of Θ:

$$C^E := \{\{\theta \in \Theta : \bar{m} \in E(\theta)\} : \bar{m} \in M\}. \tag{3.9.2.12}$$

This covering is rectangular – the equilibrium property of $\bar{m} \in M$ can be verified one player at a time. It is also F-contour contained, because (M, h) was assumed to implement F. In this way, every game form $(\bar{m}, \bar{h})$ that implements F induces a covering $C^{\bar{E}}$ of Θ through its equilibrium message map $\bar{E}$. Our goal is to construct *minimal* coverings that are induced by some game form. As in previous sections, we construct minimal, F-cc, rectangular coverings, but now with the additional requirement that these coverings be induced by some game form that implements F. To construct minimal coverings, we note that the covering $C^{\bar{E}}$ induced by a Nash implementing game form $(\bar{m}, \bar{h})$ is not only rectangular and F-cc, but it is also *monotonically generated*.

DEFINITION 3.9.2.1. For $i \in I$, $\bar{z} \in Z$ and $\bar{\theta}^i \in \Theta^i$ let $L(\bar{z}, \bar{\theta}^i) = \{z \in Z : \bar{z} \, R(\bar{\theta}^i) \, z\}$ denote player i's lower contour set of $\bar{z}$ at $\bar{\theta}^i$, and let $L(\bar{z}, \theta) = (L(\bar{z}, \theta^1), \ldots, L(\bar{z}, \theta^n))$. An F-cc covering C of Θ is *monotonically generated* if for all $K \in C$ and for all $\bar{\theta} \in \Theta$

$$\bigcap_{\theta \in K} L(F(K), \theta) \subseteq L(F(K), \bar{\theta}) \implies \bar{\theta} \in K, \tag{3.9.2.13}$$

where $F(K)$ denotes the common value of F at all points in K, and both "$\cap$" and "$\subseteq$" are componentwise.[25]

This condition is derived from *Maskin monotonicity* (Maskin 1999), which is a necessary condition for Nash implementability.

---

[25] By "componentwise" we mean that for $z \in Z$ and $\theta, \bar{\theta} \in \Theta$, $L(z, \theta) \cap L(z, \bar{\theta})$ means

$$(L(z, \theta^1) \cap L(z, \bar{\theta}^1), \ldots, L(z, \theta^n) \cap L(z, \bar{\theta}^n)),$$

and $L(z, \theta) \subseteq L(z, \bar{\theta})$ means

$$[L(z, \theta^1) \subseteq L(z, \bar{\theta}^1)], \ldots, [L(z, \theta^n) \subseteq L(z, \bar{\theta}^n)].$$

We use the same shorthand notation in several places below.

DEFINITION 3.9.2.2. The goal function *F* is *Maskin monotonic* if for all $\bar{\theta}$, $\bar{\bar{\theta}} \in \Theta$ and $\bar{z} \in Z$

$$[F(\bar{\theta}) = \bar{z}] \text{ and } [L(\bar{z}, \bar{\theta}) \subseteq L(\bar{z}, \bar{\bar{\theta}})] \implies F(\bar{\bar{\theta}}) = \bar{z}. \qquad (3.9.2.14)$$

Note that every monotonically generated covering is rectangular.

Whereas Maskin monotonicity is necessary for Nash implementability, it is not sufficient. To ensure that *F* is Nash implementable, we also impose the *no veto power* condition.[26]

DEFINITION 3.9.2.3. The goal function *F* satisfies the *no veto power* condition if for all $\bar{\theta} \in \Theta$ and all $\bar{z} \in Z$

there exists $j \in I$ such that for all $i \neq j$ and for all $z \neq \bar{z}$,

$$\bar{z}R(\bar{\theta}^i)z \implies F(\bar{\theta}) = \bar{z}. \qquad (3.9.2.15)$$

PROPOSITION 3.9.2.1. Assume that $|I| \geq 3$, and $F : \Theta \to Z$ is onto, Maskin monotonic and satisfies no veto power. Then

  (i) A covering of Θ induced by the equilibrium message map of a game form that implements *F* is *F*-cc and monotonically generated.
  (ii) If a covering *C* of Θ is *F*-cc and monotonically generated, then there exists a game form $(\bar{m}, \bar{h})$ that implements *F* and whose equilibrium message map induces a covering $C^{\bar{E}}$ that contains *C*.

REMARK. We cannot guarantee that the covering $C^{\bar{E}}$ induced by the equilibrium message map in (ii) be identical to *C*. However, the construction in the proof guarantees that the only elements that can be in $C^{\bar{E}} \backslash C$ correspond to equilibrium messages that are "no-veto equilibria": messages that are equilibria only when their outcome is most preferred for all players but one. Also, all elements in $C^{\bar{E}} \backslash C$ are redundant in the sense that each is contained (as a set) in some element of *C*. That is, in any state θ a coordinator may use a message from *C*.

Proof: To prove (i), suppose $(\bar{m}, \bar{h})$ implements *F* and $C^{\bar{E}}$ is the covering induced by its equilibrium message map. As discussed above, it is immediate that $C^{\bar{E}}$ is *F*-cc. To see that it is monotonically generated, fix an element *K*

---

[26] Though it is often used with Maskin monotonicity to guarantee Nash implementability, the no veto power condition is not necessary for implementability.

of the covering, and let $\bar{E}(K) = \bar{m}$ be the equilibrium message at all states in K. Let

$$D^i(\bar{m}) := \{h(m^i, \bar{m}^{-i}): m^i \in M^i\} \qquad (3.9.2.16)$$

be the set of outcomes player i can reach from $\bar{m}$ by unilateral deviation. Let $D(\bar{m}) = (D^1(\bar{m}), D^n(\bar{m}))$. Since $(\bar{m}, \bar{h})$ Nash implements F,

$$\text{for all } \theta \in \Theta, \ D(\bar{m}) \subseteq L(\bar{h}(\bar{m}), \theta) \iff \bar{m} \in \bar{E}(\theta). \qquad (3.9.2.17)$$

In particular, for all $\theta \in K$, $D(\bar{m}) \subseteq L(\bar{h}(\bar{m}), \theta)$. Thus

$$D(\bar{m}) \subseteq \bigcap_{\theta \in K} L(\bar{h}(\bar{m}), \theta). \qquad (3.9.2.18)$$

Then for all $\bar{\theta} \in \Theta$,

$$\bigcap_{\theta \in K} L(\bar{h}(\bar{m}), \theta) \subseteq L(\bar{h}(\bar{m}), \bar{\theta}) \implies D(\bar{m}) \subseteq L(\bar{h}(\bar{m}), \bar{\theta})$$

$$\implies \bar{m} \in \bar{E}(\bar{\theta}) \implies \bar{\theta} \in K, \qquad (3.9.2.19)$$

which proves (i).

To prove (ii), suppose the covering C is F-cc and monotonically generated. We construct a mechanism $(\bar{m}, \bar{h})$ that implements F, and we show that its equilibrium message map $\bar{E}$ induces a covering $C^{\bar{E}}$ containing C. Our construction is similar to that in McKelvey (1989).

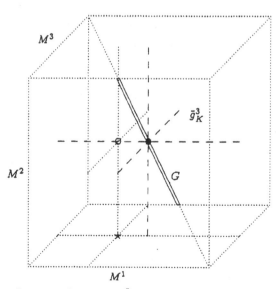

Figure 3.9.2.2 Illustration for denning $\bar{h}$ in the proof of Proposition 3.9.2.1, part (ii)

For each $K \in C$, let

$$g_K := \bigcap_{\theta \in K} L(F(K), \theta) \qquad (3.9.2.20)$$

"monotonically generate" K. Let $G := \{g_K : K \in C\}$, with typical element $g_K = (g_K^1, \ldots, g_K^n)$. For each player, a message will consist of an element of G and either a 0 or a 1, that is, $\bar{m}^i = G \times \{0, 1\}$.

Before we define the outcome function $\bar{h}$ formally, we describe the intuition behind the construction, using Figure 3.9.2.2. Player 1 can move left-right, player 2 can move up-down, player 3 can move in the third dimension. There are three types of points in the message space (the entire cube in Figure 3.9.2.2).

1. At points along the "central diagonal" (the double line), like at •, all players choose the same element of G – say $\bar{g}_K$ – and "1." The outcome is then $F(K)$. Each player can deviate to "off central diagonal points" (the dashed lines). The set of outcomes along the dashed line for player i is $\bar{g}_K^i$. For example, player 3 can reach from • the outcomes $\bar{g}_K^3$ (see Figure 3.9.2.2). Thus, a diagonal point $(\bar{g}_K, \ldots, \bar{g}_K)$ will be an equilibrium at θ if, and only if, for all $i \in I$ we have $\bar{g}_K^i \subseteq L(F(K), \theta^i)$.
2. At "off central diagonal points," like ○, all players $i \in I$ except one (say j) announce the same $\bar{g}_K$ and "1." Then player j can deviate along his dashed line, that is, to any outcome in $\bar{g}_K^j$. The other players can deviate along the dotted lines. Along dotted lines (that is, lines that are not central diagonal and not off central diagonal) all outcomes in Z appear. Thus, the other players $I \backslash \{j\}$ can deviate to any outcome in Z. An off central diagonal point like ○ will be an equilibrium at θ if, and only if, the outcome at this point is preferred by j to all outcomes in $\bar{g}_K^i$ and preferred by all other players to everything in Z.
3. At points like ⋆ that are not central diagonal and not off central diagonal, all players can deviate along dotted lines. That is, all players can deviate to any outcome in Z. Such a point will be an equilibrium at θ if, and only if, all players prefer the outcome at this point to everything in Z.

To define $\bar{h}$ formally, we first number the elements of G: let $c : G \to \{1, 2, \ldots, |G|\}$ be a bijection. For $\bar{m} \in \bar{m}$ let $c^*(\bar{m}) := \sum_{i \in I} c(\bar{m}^i)$ mod $|G|$. Next, we define for each $i \in I$ a function $d_i : G \times G \to Z$ with the property that for all $g_K \in G$, $\{d_i(g_K, g) : g \in G \backslash \{g_K\}\} = \bar{g}_K^i$. This is possible because the assumption that F is onto implies that $|G| \geq |Z|$. Now define $\bar{h}$ as follows:

$$\bar{h}(m^1, m^2, \ldots, m^{|I|})$$
$$= \begin{cases} F(K) & \text{if } m^1 = m^2 = \cdots = m^{|I|} = (g_K, 1) \\ d_j(g_K, g) & \text{if } m^i = (g_K, 1) \text{ for all } i \neq j, m^j \\ & \in \{(g, 0), (g, 1)\}, \ g_K \neq g \\ c^{-1}(c^*(m)) & \text{otherwise.} \end{cases} \quad (3.9.2.21)$$

To show that $(\bar{m}, \bar{h})$ implements F: First, suppose that for arbitrary $\bar{\theta} \in \Theta$, $F(\bar{\theta}) = \bar{z}$. We show next that $\bar{z}$ is a Nash equilibrium outcome. Let $\bar{K}$ denote an element of C containing $\bar{\theta}$. Since C is monotonically generated, $g_K \subseteq L(\bar{z}, \bar{\theta})$. Then each player choosing $(g_K, 1)$ is a Nash equilibrium, because each player i can deviate only to g_K^i given $\bar{h}$, and these outcomes are worse (by the previous sentence). Also, given $\bar{h}$ this strategy profile leads to $\bar{z}$.

Next, suppose that for $\bar{\theta} \in \Theta$, $\bar{m}$ is a Nash equilibrium strategy. Given $\bar{h}$, this means that either $\bar{h}(\bar{m})$ is a most preferred element for at least $n - 1$ players, or all players choose the same $(g_K, 1)$. In the first case, $\bar{h}(\bar{m}) = F(\bar{\theta})$ by no veto power. In the second case, it must be that $g_K \subseteq L(F(K), \bar{\theta})$. But since C is monotonically generated, this means that $\bar{\theta} \in K$, and since C is F-cc, $F(\bar{\theta}) = F(K) = \bar{h}(\bar{m})$.

To show that the covering $C^{\bar{E}}$ contains C: Fix $K \in C$. Each player choosing the message $(g_K, 1)$ is an equilibrium exactly in the states $\theta \in K$, so this message induces K. Each $K \in C$ is thus in $C^{\bar{E}}$.

This completes the proof of Proposition 3.9.2.1.

Now we present the algorithm to construct minimal coverings that are induced by Nash implementing game forms. Our construction relies only on the Maskin monotonicity of F.

We construct the covering for each $\bar{z} \in Z$ separately. The values of a Maskin monotonic F are fully determined by its values at certain important points in Θ. We call these points F-minimal (McKelvey 1989).

DEFINITION 3.9.2.4. Given a goal function F and a state $\bar{\theta} \in \theta$, suppose $F(\bar{\theta}) = \bar{z}$. Then $\bar{\theta}$ is F-minimal for $\bar{z}$ if there does not exist $\bar{\bar{\theta}} \neq \bar{\theta}$ such that

$$F(\bar{\bar{\theta}}) = \bar{z} \quad \text{and} \quad \text{for all } i \in I, \ L(\bar{z}, \bar{\bar{\theta}}^i) \subseteq L(\bar{z}, \bar{\theta}^i). \quad (3.9.2.22)$$

Let $F_{\bar{z}}^{\min} \subseteq \Theta$ denote the set of states that are F-minimal[27] for $\bar{z}$, and $F^{\min} := \cup_{z \in Z} F_z^{\min}$. Let $\mathcal{P}(F_{\bar{z}}^{\min})$ denote the set of nonempty subsets of $F_{\bar{z}}^{\min}$.

DEFINITION 3.9.2.5. Let $S \subseteq F_{\bar{z}}^{\min}$. We say that S has the *generating property* if for all $\bar{\theta} \in \Theta$ the following holds:

$$\bigcap_{\theta \in S} L(\bar{z}, \theta) \subseteq L(\bar{z}, \bar{\theta}) \implies F(\bar{\theta}) = \bar{z}. \tag{3.9.2.23}$$

Algorithm:

---

1. For any subset Q of $F_{\bar{z}}^{\min}$ (i.e., $Q \in \mathcal{P}(F_{\bar{z}}^{\min})$), let $Q_0, Q_1, Q_2, \ldots, Q_{2^Q-1}$ be any ordering of all nonempty subsets of Q such that greater cardinality subsets have lower indices (so that $Q_0 = Q$). Let $r = 0, c = 1$, and $Q = F_{\bar{z}}^{\min}$.

2. *If* Q_r has the generating property, *then* let

$$G^{K_c} = \bigcap_{\theta \in Q_r} L(\bar{z}, \theta), \tag{3.9.2.24}$$

and let $K_c = \{\theta \in \theta : G^{K_c} \subseteq L(\bar{z}, \theta)\}$ be an element of the covering. Increase c by 1. Let $Q = F_{\bar{z}}^{\min} \setminus \cup_{t<c} K_t$. If $Q = \varnothing$, stop. If $Q \neq \varnothing$, let $r = 0$ and go to step 2.

3. *Otherwise* increase r by 1 and go to step 2.

PROPOSITION 3.9.2.2. The covering $\{K_t\}$ constructed above is F-cc, monotonically generated and minimal in the following sense: there does not exist another covering that is coarser and has fewer elements.

Proof: That the covering is F-cc and monotonically generated follows from the generating property, which holds for each element of the cover by step 2. As for minimality, suppose there exists another F-cc, monotonically generated covering C that is coarser and has fewer elements. Then there must exist two elements K_a, K_b of the constructed cover that are contained in the same element C_p of the cover C. Without loss of generality, suppose K_a was constructed before K_b in the algorithm. Since the F-minimal states in K_b were not covered yet when K_a was constructed, and since the algorithm checks the generating property for larger subsets first, the set of F-minimal states in $K_a \cup K_b$ would have been checked first. But this set has the generating property, because $C_p \supseteq K_a \cup K_b$ is part of the monotonically generated cover

---

[27] "Minimal" because these states are minimal in the following partial order $\leq_L$ on the set $\{\theta \in \Theta \colon F(\theta) = \bar{z}\}$: $\bar{\theta} \leq_L \bar{\bar{\theta}} \iff L(\bar{z}, \bar{\theta}) \subseteq L(\bar{z}, \bar{\bar{\theta}})$.

C. Thus, C_p would have been constructed instead of K_a. This completes the proof of Proposition 3.9.2.2.

Once we construct a minimal, F-cc, monotonically generated covering $\bar{C}$ using the algorithm above, we can use Proposition 3.9.2.1 to construct a game form $(\bar{m}, \bar{h})$ that induces a covering $C^{\bar{E}}$ containing C (with all elements in $C^{\bar{E}} \setminus \bar{C}$ contained in some single element of $\bar{C}$ – see the remark after Proposition 3.9.2.1). Then a coordinator running the verification scenario can restrict himself to the messages associated with the covering $\bar{C}$.

Alternatively, we could interpret the covering $\bar{C}$ constructed by the algorithm as the coordination device in a *coordinated ex post equilibrium*.

DEFINITION 3.9.2.6. Given a set of players I with type spaces $\Theta^1, \ldots, \Theta^n$ and preferences $R_i(\theta^i)$, a set of outcomes Z, action spaces $M^1, \ldots, M^n$, an outcome function $h : M \to Z$, and a covering C of Θ, the strategies $s_i^* : C \to M^i$ form a *coordinated ex post equilibrium* if for every $K \in C$, for every $\theta \in K$, and for every player $i \in I$ we have

$$h(s_1^*(K), \ldots, s_n^*(K)) \, R_i(\theta^i) h(\hat{m}^i, s_{-i}^*(K)) \qquad (3.9.2.25)$$

for all $\hat{m}^i \in M^i$.

In the verification scenario, the coordinator does not need to know anything about the state of the world – he just checks all messages in M associated with the covering $\bar{C}$, and asks players to verify individually whether these messages would be an equilibrium. Instead, we can think of the coordinator as having partial knowledge of the state of the world. This partial knowledge is represented by the covering $\bar{C}$ of Θ. Now the coordinator learns which element of the covering $\bar{C}$ contains the state of the world, and recommends actions to the players.[28] Thus the coordinator takes over the coordinating role played – implicitly – by the Nash equilibrium notion. If it is more costly to learn more detailed information about the state of the world, the coordinator would prefer coarser coverings. At the same time, there must be an implementing mechanism that, together with the covering, can implement F in coordinated ex post equilibrium. Thus coverings constructed by the algorithm above are the minimal ones the coordinator could use.

---

[28] In a Bayesian setting, the analogous solution would be the "partial Bayesian approach" to defining correlated equilibrium in Forges (1993, Section 4.4). There an omniscient mediator recommends actions to the players conditional on their types.

APPENDIX: CHARACTERIZATIONS OF PARTITIONS

If a collection of sets C is a covering of Θ, then there is a self-belonging correspondence $V : \Theta \Rightarrow \Theta$ that generates C. What conditions must V satisfy to ensure that C is a partition? Theorems 3.A.1, 3.A.2, and 3.A.3 presented here with proofs, and quoted in Section 3.5 of Chapter 3, provide answers to these questions. To make this appendix self-contained, we repeat some definitions.[29]

DEFINITION 3.A.1. A collection C of sets (equivalently a covering C of Θ) is a *partition*, if and only if, for K, $K' \in C$, either $K \cap K' = \varnothing$ or $K = K'$

The following characterization of partitions in terms of SDRs is straight-forward to prove.

THEOREM 3.A.1. A covering C of Θ is a partition if and only if *every* function $\Lambda : C \to \Theta$ that satisfies

$$\Lambda(K) \in K, \quad \text{for every } K \in C, \tag{A}$$

is an SDR for C .

Proof (*Necessity*):   Suppose C is a partition, and suppose $\Lambda : C \to \Theta$ satisfies (A). We show that K, $K' \in C$, $K \neq K'$ implies $\Lambda(K) \neq \Lambda(K')$. Suppose K, $K' \in C$, and $K \neq K'$. Because C is a partition, $K \cap K' = \varnothing$. Because Λ satisfies (A), $\Lambda(K) \in K$, and $\Lambda(K' \in K')$. Hence, $\Lambda K \neq \Lambda(K')$. Thus, $\Lambda(\bullet)$ is an SDR for C.

Sufficiency: Suppose that every function $\Lambda : C \to \Theta$ that satisfies (A) is an SDR for C. Because the sets $K \in C$ are not empty, there can be many such functions. We choose one such function, $\bar{\Lambda}$, if necessary, using the axiom of choice. Thus, $\bar{\Lambda}$ is an SDR for C.

If C is a partition, there is nothing to prove. So suppose C is not a partition. Then there are two sets K' and K'' in C such that

(a) $K' \cap K'' \neq \varnothing$,
(b) $K' \neq K''$.

---

[29] The material presented here comes from Hurwicz and Reiter (2001).

By (a), there is a point $\theta' \in \Theta$, such that $\theta' \in K'$ and $\theta' \in K''$. Now define the function $\Lambda': C \to \Theta$ by

$$\Lambda'(K) = \bar{\Lambda}(K), \quad \text{for all } K \in C \backslash \{K', K''\}.$$

and

$$\Lambda'(K') = \Lambda'(K'') = \theta'. \qquad (*)$$

Then, for all $K \in C$, $\Lambda'(K) \in K$. But, by (b), $K' \neq K''$, and by $(*)$, $\Lambda'(K') = \Lambda'K''$. Therefore, Λ' is *not* an SDR for C.

This completes the proof.

Next, we give a characterization of partitions in terms of the generating correspondence $V : \Theta \Rightarrow \Theta$. First, we define a property that we show is a property of correspondences that generate partitions.

DEFINITION 3.A.2. Let $\bar{\theta}, \theta', \theta''$ denote points of Θ. A correspondence, $V : \Theta \Rightarrow \Theta$, is *block symmetric* if and only if

$$[\theta' \in V(\theta') \text{ and } \theta'' \in V(\bar{\theta})] \iff [\theta' \in V(\theta'') \text{ and } \theta'' \in V(\theta')]. \quad \text{(B)}$$

We show next that block symmetry is a strengthening of the concept of symmetry. The term "block symmetric" is used because, when (B) is satisfied, there is a permutation of the elements of Θ such that the graph of V consists of blocks ("squares") with the "northeast" and "southwest" vertices on the diagonal of $\Theta \times \Theta$.

REMARK 3.A.1. Symmetry may be defined by the condition

$$\theta' \in V(\bar{\theta}) \iff \bar{\theta} \in V(\theta'). \qquad \text{(S)}$$

To see that (B) implies (S), suppose V is block symmetric. Suppose $\theta' \in V(\bar{\theta})$. We show that $\bar{\theta} \in V(\theta')$. The hypotheses of (B) in the definition of block symmetry are satisfied for $\theta', \theta'', \bar{\theta}$, where $\theta'' = \bar{\theta}$. Therefore, $\theta'' = \bar{\theta} \in V(\theta')$.

THEOREM 3.A.2. A covering C of Θ is a partition if and only if C is generated by a block symmetric, self-belonging correspondence $V : \Theta \Rightarrow \Theta$.

Proof (*Necessity*):   Suppose C is a partition of Θ. Then C has an SDR. To see this, define $\Lambda(K)$ to be any element in K. Because C is a partition, K and K' are disjoint. Thus, $K \neq K'$ implies $\Lambda(K) \neq \Lambda(K')$.

Because C has an SDR, it follows from Theorem 3.A.1 that C is generated by a self-belonging correspondence $V : \Theta \Rightarrow \Theta$. It remains to show that V is block symmetric.

Let $\bar{\theta}, \theta', \theta''$ be elements of Θ that satisfy the hypothesis of (B)–let

$$\theta' \in V(\bar{\theta}) \qquad \text{and} \qquad \theta'' \in V(\bar{\theta}). \tag{i}$$

To prove (B) we show that

$$\theta' \in V(\theta'') \qquad \text{and} \qquad \theta'' \in V(\theta'). \tag{ii}$$

Relation (i) and the self-belonging property of V yield

$$\theta' \in V(\bar{\theta}) \cap V(\theta') \tag{iiia}$$

and

$$\theta'' \in V(\bar{\theta}) \cap V(\theta''). \tag{iiib}$$

Because C is generated by V, there exist C such that

$$\bar{K} = V(\bar{\theta}), \qquad K' = V(\theta'), \qquad K'' = V(\theta''). \tag{iv}$$

C is a partition. Therefore,

$$\bar{K} \cap K' = \varnothing \qquad \text{or} \qquad \bar{K} = K' \tag{v}$$

and

$$\bar{K} \cap K'' = \varnothing \qquad \text{or} \qquad \bar{K} = K''.$$

But Relations (iii.a) and (iii.b) rule out emptiness of the intersections $\bar{K} \cap K'$ and $\bar{K} \cap K''$. Hence $\bar{K} = K'$ and $\bar{K} = K''$. By (iv), this yields

$$V(\bar{\theta}) = V(\theta')$$

and

$$V(\bar{\theta}) = V(\theta'').$$

Using each of these relations in (i) yields the corresponding relation in (ii), and hence V is block symmetric.

This concludes the proof of necessity.

Sufficiency: Suppose that C is generated by a block symmetric, self-belonging correspondence $V : \Theta \Rightarrow \Theta$. We show that C is a partition. That is, we show that for every K, $K' \in C$ either $K \cap K' = \varnothing$ or $K = K'$.

Let K and K' be elements of C. If $K \cap K' = \varnothing$ there is nothing to prove. So, suppose there is $\tilde{\theta} \in K \cap K'$. Then, because C is generated by V, there are elements, $\hat{\theta}$ and $\hat{\hat{\theta}}$ in Θ such that $K = V(\hat{\theta})$ and $K' = V(\hat{\hat{\theta}})$. Thus,

$$\tilde{\theta} \in V(\hat{\theta}) \qquad \text{and} \qquad \tilde{\theta} \in V(\hat{\hat{\theta}}).$$

It follows from (B) and $\tilde{\theta} \in V(\hat{\theta})$ that

for every $\qquad\qquad\qquad \theta \in V(\tilde{\theta}).$

Therefore,

$$V(\hat{\theta}) \subseteq V(\tilde{\theta}).$$

Now, because $\hat{\theta} \in V(\tilde{\theta})$, and $\hat{\theta} \in V(\tilde{\theta})$, by self-belonging, and $V(\hat{\theta}) \subseteq V(\tilde{\theta})$ as just shown, it follows from (B) (with $\hat{\theta}$ here corresponding to θ' in (B), θ to θ'', and $\tilde{\theta}$ to $\bar{\theta}$ in (B)) that

$$\theta \in V(\tilde{\theta}), \theta \in V(\hat{\theta}).$$

Thus,

$$V(\hat{\theta}) \supseteq V(\tilde{\theta}).$$

Therefore,

$$V(\hat{\theta}) = V(\tilde{\theta}).$$

The same argument applied to $V(\hat{\theta})$ and $V(\tilde{\theta})$ shows that

$$V(\hat{\theta}) = V(\tilde{\theta})$$

Therefore,

$$K = V(\hat{\theta}) = V(\tilde{\theta}) = K'.$$

This concludes the proof.

The following example shows that symmetry of the generating (self-belonging) correspondence is not sufficient for the covering it generates to be a partition.

EXAMPLE 3.A.1. Let $\Theta = \{a, b, c\}$, and let $V(a) = \{a, b, c\}$, $V(b) = \{a, b\}$, $V(c) = \{a, c\}$. Then V is self-belonging and symmetric, but the covering it generates is not a partition.

However, in this example the covering is reducible in the sense of the following definition.

DEFINITION 3.A.3. An element of a covering C of Θ is *redundant* if eliminating that element from C still leaves a covering of Θ. A covering is *irreducible* [30] if it has no redundant elements; otherwise it is *reducible*.

If C is a finite covering, then it has an irreducible subcovering, which might be C itself. If C is not irreducible, then it has a redundant element. When C is finite, successive eliminations of redundant elements must eventually result in an irreducible subcovering. This is not true when C is infinite, as shown by Dugundji's example (1966, p. 161).

The covering C in Example 3.A.3 can be reduced in two different ways. First, to the covering $C' = \{\{a, b, c\}\}$, which is generated by the (constant) correspondence $U'(\theta) = \{a, b, c\}$, for $\theta \in \{a, b, c\}$ and, second, to the covering $C'' = \{\{a, b\}, \{b, c\}\}$, which is generated by the correspondence $V''(a) = V''(b) = \{a, b\}$, and $V''(c) = \{b, c\}$. Both C' and C'' are irreducible, and V' is symmetric, while V'' is not. Of course, C' is a partition and C'' is not.

Symmetry is not enough to guarantee that the covering generated by a self-belonging correspondence be a partition, but it is the case that if the covering is irreducible, then symmetry ensures that it is a partition. The converse also holds.

THEOREM 3.A.3. Let C be a covering of Θ. C is a partition if and only if (i) C is generated by a self-belonging, symmetric correspondence $V : \Theta \Rightarrow \Theta$, and (ii) C is irreducible.

Proof: ($\Leftarrow$) Suppose (i) and (ii) hold. We show that V is block symmetric, and hence, by Theorem 3.A.3, that C is a partition. To show that V is block symmetric we must show that V satisfies

$$[\theta' \in V(\bar{\theta}) \text{ and } \theta'' \in V(\bar{\theta})] \Rightarrow [\theta' \in V(\theta'') \text{ and } \theta'' \in V(\theta')]. \quad (B)$$

So, suppose that $\bar{\theta}$ is an arbitrary point of Θ, and consider $V(\bar{\theta})$. Let

$$E(\bar{\theta}) = \{\theta \in V(\bar{\theta}) : V(\theta) = V(\bar{\theta})\}$$

and

$$D(\bar{\theta}) = \{\theta \in V(\bar{\theta}) : V(\theta) \neq V(\bar{\theta})\}.$$

[30] The term "irreducible" applied to a covering was introduced by Dugundji (1966, p. 160).

Note that $V(\bar\theta) = E(\bar\theta) \cup D(\bar\theta)$, and $E(\bar\theta) \cap D(\bar\theta) = \varnothing$. Either $D = \varnothing$ or $D \neq \varnothing$.

Suppose $D \neq \varnothing$. We shall show that $D \neq \varnothing$ leads to the conclusion that the set $K = V(\bar\theta)$ is redundant, thereby contradicting (ii).

Consider $\bar{\bar\theta} \in V(\bar\theta)$. Either $\bar{\bar\theta} \in E(\bar\theta)$ or $\bar{\bar\theta} \in D(\bar\theta)$.

If $\bar{\bar\theta} \in D(\bar\theta)$, then $\bar{\bar\theta} \in \cup_{\theta \in D(\bar\theta)} V(\bar\theta)$.

Now suppose that $\bar{\bar\theta} \in E(\bar\theta)$. Then $V(\bar{\bar\theta}) = V(\bar\theta)$. Let $\hat\theta \in V(\bar{\bar\theta})$. If for all $\bar{\bar\theta} \in E(\bar\theta)$, and all $\hat\theta \in V(\bar{\bar\theta}) \hat\theta \in E(\bar\theta)$, then $D(\bar\theta) = \varnothing$. So we may suppose that $\hat\theta \in (\bar\theta)$. By symmetry, $\bar{\bar\theta} \in V(\bar\theta)$. It follows that $\bar{\bar\theta} \in \cup_{\theta \in D(\bar\theta)} V(\bar\theta)$.

Because $\bar{\bar\theta}$ is an arbitrary point of $V(\bar\theta)$, we have shown that $V(\bar\theta) \subseteq \cup_{\theta \in D(\bar\theta)} V(\bar\theta)$. In order to conclude that $K = U(\bar\theta)$ is redundant, we must show that not every set $V(\theta)$, for $\theta \in D(\bar\theta)$, is equal to $V(\bar\theta)$. But this follows immediately from the definition of $D(\bar\theta)$.

Thus, we have shown that if $D \neq \varnothing$, then $V(\bar\theta)$ is redundant, contradicting (ii). Therefore, we may conclude that $D = \varnothing$.

It then follows from the hypotheses of (B) (which tell us that $\theta' \in V(\bar\theta)$ and $\theta'' \in V(\bar\theta)$) that $\theta' \in V(\theta'')$ and $\theta'' \in V(\theta')$, because it follows from $D = \varnothing$, that for every $\theta \in V(\bar\theta)$, $V(\theta) = V(\bar\theta)$, and hence $V(\theta') = V(\bar\theta) = V(\theta'')$. Thus, (B) is satisfied. Hence, V is block symmetric, and by Theorem 3.A.2, C is a partition.

($\Rightarrow$) Suppose C is a partition. A covering C is a partition if and only if it is generated by a block symmetric, self-belonging correspondence $U : \Theta \Rightarrow \Theta$. Block symmetry implies symmetry. Hence, U is symmetric. Finally, if C is a partition, then it is irreducible. This establishes (i) and (ii).

Theorems 3.A.1, 3.A.2, and 3.A.3 are summarized in Theorem 3.A.4.

THEOREM 3.A.4. The following four propositions are equivalent:

(1) A covering C is a partition;
(2) Every function $\Lambda : C \to \Theta$ that satisfies condition (A) is an SDR for C;
(3) C is generated by a block symmetric, self-belonging correspondence $V : \Theta \Rightarrow \Theta$; and
(4) C is an irreducible covering generated by a symmetric, self-belonging correspondence $V : \Theta \Rightarrow \Theta$.

FOUR

Revelation Mechanisms

4.1 Introduction

This chapter establishes an elementary lower bound on the computational complexity of differentiable functions between Euclidean spaces (actually, differentiable manifolds). The main motivation for this comes from mechanism design theory and as a result, the functions we examine are defined on products of differentiable manifolds and generally have values that are vectors in a Euclidean space. The complexity of computations required by a mechanism determines an element of the costs associated with that mechanism. The lower bound presented in this paper is useful in part because it does not require specification in detail of the computations to be performed by the mechanism, but depends only on the goal function that the mechanism is to realize or implement.

Our lower bound generalizes a bound due to Arbib and Spira (Arbib 1960, Spira 1969, Spira and Arbib 1967) for the complexity of functions between finite sets. The Arbib–Spira bound is based on the concept of *separator sets* for a function. A little later, in Section 4.1.2 of this introduction and in the next paragraph, we discuss briefly the concept and uses of separator sets. A complete description is given in Section 4.2. This concept is used to determine a lower bound to the number of Boolean variables – variables whose values are either 0 or 1 that the function actually depends on. In the finite case the number of variables can be counted easily. But a counting procedure is too crude to be used for functions between infinite sets. Instead, our analysis uses an equivalence relation that corresponds to separator sets in the finite case, and also applies to functions with infinite domains and ranges. The counting procedure is replaced by construction of a *quotient object*.

Consider the case of a function F defined on a product of two sets $S = \{0, 1\} \times \{0, 1\}$ and $T = \{0, 1\}$ with values in the set $Z = \{0, 1\}$. A diagram representing this is $S \times T \to Z$. Arbib and Spira were interested in deciding whether knowledge of all four points in S is required to determine F. In fact such a complete knowledge might not be required. For example, if the function $F(s_1, s_2, t) = s_1 + t$, where $(s_1, s_2) \in S$ and $t \in T$, then we only need information about s_1 and T. That is, to compute F it suffices to know the values of F on the product of T and the subset S_0 of S that consists of points with the second coordinate set to 0. Similarly, one could choose the second coordinate to equal 1 and reach the same conclusion about computing F. On the other hand, for the function $F(s_1, s_2, t) = s_1 + t$, note that since $F(0, 0, t) = t$ while $F(1, 0, t) = 1 + t$, one cannot eliminate any points from the set S_0 and still determine F. Arbib and Spira call S_0 a *separator set* for F. They argue that to evaluate F one needs the values of F on the set $S_0 \times T \subset S \times T$. Therefore, if Boolean coordinates are used on $S \times T$, one needs at least one coordinate on S and one coordinate on T.

To see how quotient objects enter, we examine the same example as above, but we replace Arbib and Spira's argument with a slight variant. Say, two points s and s' in S are *equivalent* if for each $t \in T$, $F(s, t) = F(s', t)$. Denote the collection of equivalence classes for this equivalence relation by Q. In our example it is easy to see that Q consists of only two points. One point is the equivalence class that consists of the points $(0, 0)$ and $(0, 1)$, whereas the other consists of the points $(1, 0)$ and $(1, 1)$. The set Q has three properties that we examine. The first property is as follows. We define a function q that assigns to each point in S its equivalence class, then we can define a function F^* from $Q \times T$ to Z by setting $F^*(y, t) = F(s, t)$ when $q(s) = y$. To compute F we need only F^* and the equivalence relation map q. In other words, we can replace the computation of F with the computation of F^*. Another way of stating this is to say that we can *factor F through the set* $Q \times T$ using the function F^* on the set $Q \times T$. Secondly, there is a less obvious fact. Suppose there is a set X and two functions, one, denoted by p, from S to X, and a function H from $X \times T$ to Z such that F is the composition of the function $p \times Id_T : S \times T \to X \times T$, where Id_T is the identity function on T and H. So we suppose we can replace F by the function H or, equivalently, suppose we can factor F through $X \times T$ using the function H. It then follows that we can factor H through the set $Q \times T$ using the function F^*. In fact, there is a function $\rho : X \to Q$ such that H is the composition of $\rho \times Id_T$ and the function F^*. In Section 4.2 we construct the function ρ. Finally, if S' is a separator set for F in S, then there is a map σ defined on a subset Q' of Q with values in S that is *onto* that separator set S' and is such that the composition $q \circ \sigma$ is the identity on Q'. Furthermore, there is a separator set S' in S that is mapped onto Q by the map q. In summary, separator sets in S are images of Q, so Q can be used to compute F and no set of smaller cardinality than that of Q can be used to compute F.

For those readers who are familiar with category theory, Q, using the maps q and F^*, is a *universal object in a category*. The dimension (when it exists) of the message space of the universal object is the number of variables on which F depends.[1]

The basic construction of the quotient space Q does not use coordinates and is easy to generalize to a discussion of functions from a product $S \times T$ to a set V, where the sets S, T, and Z are differentiable manifolds and the function F is differentiable. Of course, we treat the more general case of a function $F : E^1 \times \cdots \times E^N \to Z$. We place sufficient conditions on the function F to ensure that the quotient Z is a differentiable manifold and that the maps we construct, i.e. F^* and q, are differentiable. Then we work backwards to build coordinates on the quotient that can be pulled back to the original spaces.

Besides an abstract characterization of the number of variables that must be used to compute the function, F, we give an algebraic characterization that uses conditions on the ranks of certain bordered Hessian matrices of F.

The formal presentation of this material is organized as follows. Section 4.2.2 contains the set-theoretic constructions used subsequently. Definitions of F-equivalence (see Definition 4.2.2), of encoded and essential revelation mechanisms are given. It is established (Lemma 4.2.1 and Theorem 4.2.1) that the essential revelation mechanism for a given function, F, is the "smallest" encoded revelation mechanism among encoded revelation mechanisms for F. Section 4.3 deals with the case where the domain of F is a product of differentiable manifolds, and F is differentiable. Simple conditions are given that ensure that the quotient sets (under F-equivalence) are C^0, i.e., topological manifolds (Golubitsky and Guillemin 1973, p. 3) and therefore have dimensions.

The matrices used in the algebraic analysis are defined, and so is the concept of *differentiable separability*. The main results concerning the essential revelation mechanism for a function are established.

---

[1] While we use a concept from category theory, our analysis is self-contained and does not require knowledge of category theory. Category theory is not new to economic theory; Sonnenschein (1974) and Jordan (1982) used concepts from category theory to analyze economic mechanisms.

Section 4.4 contains three propositions, a corollary, and their proofs, namely, Lemma 4.4.1, Theorem 4.4.2, Theorem 4.4.6 and Corollary 4.4.7. These propositions present an altered version of a theorem of Leontief (1947) that is used to obtain the results on encoded revelation mechanisms in Section 4.3. Section 4.4 also contains an example of the constructions required. Corollary 4.4.7 is used in Chapter 2.

The remainder of this introduction contains an informal presentation of background and concepts useful for understanding the formal presentation that follows, and relates the results to the literature on mechanism design. We begin with a brief discussion of computational complexity of functions.

4.1.1 Computational Complexity of Functions

The computational complexity of a function depends on the model of computing used. We use the model of computing presented in Mount and Reiter (1990, 2002). In that model a network consists of a set of elementary processors connected by a directed graph that computes as follows.

Each processor p is a function that receives the values of its inputs, say, $x^1, \ldots, x^s$, from outside the network, or from immediately preceding processors, and computes in one step or unit of time the value of a function $y = f_p(x^1, \ldots, x^s)$. Here $s \leq r$, where r is a given integer parameter, x^i can be a vector of some fixed dimension, say d, and f_p belongs to a specified class $\mathcal{F}$ of vector valued functions. For example, an $(r, 1)$-network of real-valued functions is composed of functions of at most r real variables. Typically, in the finite case, the processors in an (r, d)-network are functions of at most r variables where the variables accept d-tuples of 0's and 1's (i.e., vectors of Boolean values). The class $\mathcal{F}$ is a primitive of the model. Each processor sends the result of its computation to inputs of every successor, i.e., to every processor to which it is connected by a single arc in the graph, or to outside the network if it has no successor.

A network of this kind, called an (r, d)-*network* in Mount and Reiter (1983, 1990, or 2002) is said to compute a function

$$F : E^1 \times E^2 \times \cdots \times E^N \to Z$$

in time t if there is an initial state of the network such that when the values $e^1, \ldots, e^N$ are constantly fed into the network starting from time 0, the value of $F(e^1, \ldots, e^N)$ appears as output of the network at time t. It is important to note that in this model of computing $F(e^1, \ldots, e^N)$, the values of the e^i are passed to an (r, d)-network, and the time required to compute $F(e^1, \ldots, e^N)$ is determined by an analysis of that (r, d)-network.

All computations should be carried out by this (r, d)-network. Therefore, we require that no computations are performed by exchanges of information among the sets E^i prior to passing the knowledge of the e^i to the network. For example, suppose F is a linear function. Then the matrix that represents F algebraically depends on the coordinate system in the spaces E^i. Computations of F can be hidden in coordinate transformations in the space $E^1 \times E^2 \times \cdots \times E^N$.

In the finite case, when $\mathcal{F}$ consists of functions on finite products of finite sets, one can compare (r, d)-networks with *finite state machines* (Arbib 1960, Hopcroft and Ullman 1979, or Mount and Reiter 2002). A finite state machine is a device that processes information using a finite number of inputs, outputs, and internal states. The inputs accepted and the outputs produced are elements of a finite alphabet. The output depends on the internal states of the device and the internal states change and outputs are produced as inputs are accepted. Hopcroft and Ullman (1979, p. 13) give as a simple example of such a machine the control mechanism of an elevator. Inputs are accepted from the call buttons, the outputs are instructions to move (up, down, or stop) and the internal states are directions of motion, current floor and the collection of not yet satisfied requests for service. Every finite (r, d)-network (using d-tuples of Boolean values) is equivalent to a finite state machine (Arbib 1960 or Mount and Reiter 2002) and conversely every finite state machine can be represented as an (r, d)-network.

The *complexity* of F relative to the class of networks characterized by r, d and $\mathcal{F}$ is the minimum over all such networks of the time needed to compute F. If the time is infinite, then F is said to be not computable by networks in that class.

An (r, d)-network $\mathcal{N}$ that computes F in time t may contain loops. It is shown in Mount and Reiter (2002, Theorem 2.1.4) that an (r, d)-network $\mathcal{T}$ can be constructed which is:

(i) free of loops,
(ii) uses the same elementary functions (modules) that $\mathcal{N}$ uses (perhaps with the identity function, projections, and constants added to the functions used by $\mathcal{N}$), and
(iii) computes F in time t.

The network $\mathcal{T}$ is a tree with inputs entering at the leaves and the value of F emerging at the root. The *length of $\mathcal{T}$* is the time needed to compute F. The processors in an (r, d)-network are functions of at most r variables. A node in the tree represents either a function or a leaf and each variable accepts values produced by a predecessor or by a leaf. In a tree that represents an (r, d)-network, each node can have at most r immediate predecessors. It follows that for a fixed r, the number of variables entering the leaves determines a lower bound on the length of a tree that computes F. Thus, the minimum number of variables on which F depends provides a lower bound on the time needed to compute F by (r, d)-networks with elementary functions in the class $\mathcal{F}$.

To arrive at this lower bound it is helpful to view the process of computing F as follows. Each factor E^i in the domain of F is regarded as the parameter space of an agent i, and it is equipped with coordinates. To compute F at the point $e = (e^1, \ldots, e^N)$, each agent sends the coordinates of her parameter point to the (r, d)-network that computes F. Thus, agent i's message, e^i, is the same as that used by a direct revelation mechanism. But it can be the case that some coordinates of E^i are not needed to compute F, then only partial revelation of $e^i \in E^i$ would be required. Therefore, we extend the concept of a revelation mechanism to include partial revelation.

When the domain of F is a differentiable manifold, the number of variables on which F depends is not obvious. Suppose that F is a real-valued function with partial derivatives defined on the Euclidean space $E^1 = \mathcal{R}^2$, ($\mathcal{R}$ denotes the real numbers) where the Euclidean space has specified coordinates, x and y. Then the number of coordinates required to compute F is usually easy to estimate by computing the number of nonzero partial derivatives. For example, the function $F(x, y) = x + y^2$ has partial derivatives in x and y that are both nonzero. One might be tempted to think that $F(x, y)$ is a function more complex than, say, the function x. However, if one treats $\mathcal{R}^2$ as a differentiable manifold, where differentiable coordinate changes are allowed, then the function $F(x, y)$ can be introduced as a coordinate function on $\mathcal{R}^2$, so that $\mathcal{R}^2$ has coordinate functions $F(x, y)$ and y. Having done that, $F(x, y)$ is a function of the one parameter F and is no more complex than x. Thus, the possibility of unrestricted (differentiable) coordinate changes invalidates using the number of nonzero partial derivatives of F, i.e., the number of variables on which F apparently depends, as an indicator of its complexity. Another view of this is as follows. Define an equivalence relation according to which two points a and a' in $\mathcal{R}^2$ are equivalent if F takes the same value at a and a'. The level sets of F are the equivalence classes of this equivalence relation. This set of equivalence classes is a one-dimensional family (indexed by the values of F), and so is no more complex than the level sets of the function x.

We must allow different choices for coordinates. This is especially clear when the space E^i is the parameter space of an agent i. In the individual

E^i there may be nothing intrinsic about the coordinate system used, since agent i's parameters are private to i. Indeed, if E^i is the topological space $\mathcal{R}^2$, agent i may choose to view the space as a vector space and use standard coordinates, or the agent may choose to use polar coordinates. Thus, we should not restrict the choice of coordinates, in the individual E^i.

Beyond that, when F is defined on a product space $E^1 \times \cdots \times E^N$ and the object is to determine the amount of computation required to evaluate $F(e)$, $e \in E^1 \times \cdots \times E^N$, there is a natural restriction on coordinate choices allowed in the product space. The restriction is to allow only coordinate choices that are the product of individual coordinate choices in the separate spaces E^i. A choice of coordinates on $E^1 \times \cdots \times E^N$ in which coordinates on E^i depend on parameters in E^j with $j \neq i$ is ruled out because such a choice can smuggle computation. Suppose, for example, $E^2 = \mathcal{R}^2 - \{\text{the } y_2 \text{ axis}\}$ with coordinates y_1 and y_2, $E^1 = \mathcal{R}^2$ with coordinates x_1 and x_2 and $G(x_1, x_2, y_1, y_2) = x_1 y_1 + x_2 y_2$. To determine the computation required to evaluate G we should certainly consider coordinates $x_1' = x_2$, $x_2' = x_1$, and $y_1' = y_1 + y_2$, $y_2' = y_2$ as a possible choice to be made by the agents. After all, a tax payer's spread-sheet need not have the same line numbers as his tax form. However, a change of coordinates in $E^1 \times E^2$ to the system $x_1'' = G(x_1, x_2, y_1, y_2)$, $x_2'' = x_2$, and $y_1'' = y_1$, $y_2'' = y_2$ hides computation. In the x_i'', y_i'' coordinate system, evaluation of G at a point is no more than reading the first coordinate of the point. The restriction that a coordinate change is allowable only if it is the product of a coordinate change in E^1 and a coordinate change in E^2 leads to the conclusion that all four of the parameters x_1, y_1, x_2, and y_2 are required for the evaluation of G. To see this we again examine the level sets of the function to be computed. Following Arbib–Spira, one must have a sufficient number of parameters from E^1 to be able to distinguish a pair of points $a = (a_1, a_2)$ and $b = (b_1, b_2)$ in E^1 if there is a point z in E^2 such that $G(a, z) \neq G(b, z)$. Define two points a and b in E^1 to be equivalent if and only if $G(a, y) = G(b, y)$ independent of the point y chosen in E^2. If $a_1 \neq b_1$, then $G(a_1, a_2; 1, 0) = a_1 \neq b_1 = G(b_1, b_2, 1, 0)$. A similar argument applies if $a_2 \neq b_2$. Thus, to compute G one needs sufficiently many parameters to distinguish between each two points of E^1. That is, one needs two parameters from E^1. Similarly, one needs two parameters from E^2.

The previous remarks justify the restriction that we choose coordinates that preserve the product structure on $E^1 \times E^2$. It is also clear that if, in the previous example, the function to be evaluated was $G(x_1, x_2, y_1, y_2) = x_1 y_1$, then agent 1 needs only to reveal x_1 while agent 2 needs to reveal only y_1.

With these considerations in mind, we extend the concept of a revelation mechanism to allow for partial revelation of parameters in each allowable coordinate system used in the space E^i. We refer to a mechanism of this type as an *encoded revelation mechanism*. Note that while these mechanisms form a larger class than do revelation mechanisms, the class of encoded revelation mechanism does not include all privacy-preserving mechanisms, or game forms, with the given structure of private information.

In order to make this point clear and to help make this paper self-contained, we include below a brief summary of the formal structure of privacy-preserving mechanisms, and relate encoded revelation mechanisms to them. This is done in Section 4.1.4 of the Introduction.

4.1.2 Separator Sets and Quotients

We formulate the concept of separator sets for the function $F : E^1 \times \cdots \times E^N \to Z$ in terms of an equivalence relation induced on each of the sets E^i by F. The quotients we use to determine the number of variables on which a function F depends is a natural generalization of the argument used in the discussion of the function $G(x_1, x_2, y_1, y_2) = x_1 y_1 + x_2 y_2$. We begin with a set-theoretic presentation that does not assume topological or smoothness conditions of the set E^i or Z. No concept of dimension plays a role in the set-theoretic discussion. When E^i are differentiable manifolds the set-theoretic constructions are used to establish the existence of certain required functions, for which appropriate smoothness conditions can then be verified.

In the case that F is a differentiable function, once the quotient object is constructed the remaining task is to establish conditions that ensure the quotient object has the structure of a differentiable manifold. The conditions we use are rank conditions on certain matrices associated with the function F. The manifold structure on the quotient object allows us to conclude that the dimension of the quotient exists as a topological concept (see Hurewicz and Wallman (1948)) and that the dimension of the quotient is the number of variables required to compute the function. The quotient object is a space with the least number of variables (i.e., least dimension) sufficient to compute the function.

Specifically, for the function $F : E^1 \times \cdots \times E^N \to Z$ we establish that

  (i) for each $1 \leq i \leq N$ there exists a set (E^i/F) and a function $q^i : E^i \to (E^i/F)$,
  (ii) there exists a function $F^* : (E^1/F) \times \cdots \times (E^N/F) \to Z$

such that (E^i/F), q^i, and F^* satisfy the following conditions (See Diagram A). First, $F = F^* \circ (q^1 \times \cdots \times q^N)$. In this case the function F can be *factored* through the space $(E^1/F) \times \cdots \times (E^N/F)$. Second, if for each $1 \leq i \leq N$ there is a function $p^i : E^i \to X^i$, p^i onto X^i, and there is a function $H : X^1 \times \cdots \times X^N \to Z$ for which $F = H \circ (p^1 \times \cdots \times p^N)$, (See Diagram B), then (See Diagram C) for each $1 \leq i \leq N$, there is a unique function $\rho^i : X^i \to (E^i/F)$ such that $\rho^i \circ p^i = q^i$, and such that $H = F^* \circ (\rho^1, \ldots, \rho^N)$.

Arbib and Spira (1960) give a lower bound on the time required for a McCulloch–Pitts neural network to compute F. The bound is expressed as a function of the cardinalities of the separator sets for F in E^i. A subset S^i of E^i is a separator set for the function F in E^i if for each pair of distinct points a, $b \in S^i$ there is a point $z^j \in E^j$, for each $j \neq i$, $1 \leq j \leq N$, where z^j are dependent on a and b, such that $F(z^1, \ldots, z^{i-1}, a, z^{i+1}, \ldots, z^N) \neq F(z^1, \ldots, z^{i-1}, b, z^{i+1}, \ldots, z^N)$. Each separator set in E^i is the image of a subset of (E^i/F) under some *thread* of q^i. By a thread of q^i we mean a function T from (E^i/F) to E^i such that $q^i \circ T$ is the identity function. If the sets E^i are finite, then the cardinality of the set (E^i/F) is an upper bound on the cardinality of each Arbib–Spira separator set for F in E^i. Roughly, the higher the cardinality of a separator set in E^i, the longer it takes to compute F. Thus, the cardinality of the (E^i/F) yields the smallest lower bound on the time required to compute F that can be derived from separator sets. The lower bound on the time required derived from separator sets is a very rough estimate and it is generally not possible to compute F in that time.

Next, we assume that each E^i is a differentiable manifold with appropriate smoothness, and suppose for the sake of discussion that F has values that are real numbers. The lower bound on the time it takes an $(r, 1)$-network to compute a real-valued function of D real variables is, roughly, $\log_r(D)$(See Mount and Reiter 2002). In order to apply that lower bound estimate to the function F we convert the computation of F on $E^1 \times \cdots \times E^N$ to the evaluation of a real-valued function of real variables. Therefore, we are about to consider coordinates explicitly. Since coordinates are usually locally defined functions on differentiable manifolds, the discussion involves neighborhoods of points. A little later we return to the globally defined separator sets and the quotient spaces (E^i/F). By using local coordinates we, unfortunately, enter a thicket of notations. Each of E^i has some coordinate system $(x_{i,1}, \ldots, x_{i,d(i)})$ $(d(i)$ is the dimension of E^i) given in an appropriate neighborhood U^i in E^i, and there is a real-valued function F' of $d(1) + \cdots + d(N)$ real variables such that for each $e = (e^1, \ldots, e^N) \in U^1 \times \cdots \times U^N$, $F(e) = F'((x_{1,1}(e^1), \ldots, x_{1,d(1)}(e^1)), \ldots, (x_{N,1}(e^N), \ldots, x_{N,d(N)}(e^N)))$. The lower bound on computing time for F is then, again roughly, $\log_r(d(1) + \cdots + d(N))$.

However, as one would suspect from the preceding remarks, an incorrect choice of coordinate systems on E^i can lead to a lower bound of $\log_r(d(1) + \cdots + d(N))$ that is too large. Suppose that on U^1, it is possible to ignore the coordinate $x_{1,d(1)}$ and still evaluate F. That is, suppose that for all $(e^2, \ldots, e^N) \in U^2 \times \cdots \times U^N$ and for all e in the neighborhood U^1

$$F(e, e^2, \ldots, e^N) = F'\big(x_{1,1}(e), \ldots, x_{1,d(1)-1}(e), x_{2,1}(e^2), \ldots, x_{N,d(N)}(e^N)\big).$$

When the evaluation of F requires, besides the parameters from E^j, $2 \le j \le N$, only the knowledge of the variables $x_{1,1}, \ldots, x_{1,d(1)-1}$, ignoring the variable $x_{1,d(1)}$ in the evaluation of F'(thus, also the evaluation of F) is the same as replacing the manifold E^i, at least locally, by the space of the variables $x_{1,1}, \ldots, x_{1,d(1)-1}$. The meaning of the phrase, "replacing the manifold E^1", is not entirely clear. A more precise statement is the following. Replace E^1 by the quotient space induced by an equivalence relation, denoted by "$\sim$". The equivalence relation we use is the following one . Two points e and e' in E^1 are equivalent if and only if $(x_{1,1}(e), \ldots, x_{1,d(1)-1}(e)) = (x_{1,1}(e'), \ldots, x_{1,d(1)-1}(e'))$. Note that the equivalence relation used here is not the equivalence relation used to construct E^1/F. If $E^1/(\sim)$ denotes the quotient of E^1 by the equivalence relation "$\sim$" and if $q^1 : E^1 \to E^1/(\sim)$ is the quotient map, then $E^1/(\sim)$ has a natural set of coordinates $(x'_{1,1}, \ldots, x'_{1,d(1)-1})$ induced by the variables $x_{1,1}, \ldots x_{1,d(1)-1}$ of E^1. Furthermore, we can replace F by a map $F^* : E^1/(\sim) \times E^2 \times \cdots \times E^N \to R$ defined by setting $F^*(a', e^2, \ldots, e^N) = F(a, e^2, \ldots, e^N)$ where $q^1(a) = a'$. Now for $e \in U^1$ $F(e, e^2, \ldots, e^N) = F^*(q^1(e), e^2, \ldots, e^N)$. This clears the thicket of notation. Note that we can estimate a lower bound on the computation time to compute F by seeking a lower bound on the time required to compute the function F^*.

Even if, in a given coordinate system, no variable can be eliminated, it is possible that another choice of coordinates might lead to a reduction in the number of variables required to compute F. Furthermore, even if in a particular coordinate system some of the coordinates can be eliminated, we might be able to change coordinates and eliminate a greater number. Therefore, we seek a "good" coordinate system by looking for a "good" quotient. Note that the discussion of "$\sim$" in the previous paragraph shows that if the map q^1 carries two points $(e, e^2, \ldots, e^N)$ and $(e', e^2, \ldots, e^N)$ to the same point, then $F(e, e^2, \ldots, e^N) = F(e', e^2, \ldots, e^N)$. This observation leads us to the following method of choosing quotients. We form the quotient (E^1/F) induced by an equivalence relation "$\approx$," called F-equivalence. Two points $e, e' \in E^1$ are F-equivalent if for all $y \in E^2 \times \cdots \times E^N$, $F(e, y) = F(e', y)$. Next, we add sufficient local conditions on F to guarantee that the quotient of E^1 by the relation "$\approx$" is a differentiable manifold, that the quotient map q^1 is differentiable and that F grows quickly enough to separate points in the appropriate neighborhoods. We then argue that (E^1/F) is the "good" quotient we seek. More generally, conditions are imposed that ensure that the quotient object, $(E^1/F) \times \cdots \times (E^N/F)$, is a topological manifold. Then the dimension of the quotient manifold counts the minimal number of variables required.[2]

Observe that if the quotient map q^1 is one-to-one then no reduction in the number of variables required from E^1 is possible no matter what coordinate system is used.

4.1.3 Algebraic Conditions

An algebraic characterization of the number of variables required to compute a given function F is obtained from a theorem of Leontief (1947).[3]

Suppose that for $1 \le j \le N$, E^i denotes a Euclidean space of dimension $d(i)$, suppose $\mathcal{R}$ denotes the real numbers and suppose that $F : E^1 \times \cdots \times E^N \to \mathcal{R}$ denotes a differentiable function. Assume that for each $2 \le i \le N$, E^i has a coordinate system $\underline{y}_i = (y_{i,1}, \ldots, y_{i,d(i)})$ and denote by $\underline{y}$ the coordinate system $(\underline{y}_2, \ldots, \underline{y}_N)$ on the product $E^2 \times \cdots \times E^N$. We suppose that E^1 has a coordinate system $\underline{x} = (x_1, \ldots, x_{d(1)})$. We seek a "good" quotient for the space E^1, where a good quotient is as described in Section 5.1.2. We use rank conditions on bordered Hessian matrices to construct such a quotient of E^1 (see Mount and Reiter 2002, p. 48). The matrices we call "bordered Hessian" are different from the classical bordered Hessians used in the second derivative test for constrained optima. The matrices we

---

[2] When we assume the existence of certain local threads, this quotient object satisfies universality conditions. We do not know that there is such a universal object that is also as differentiable as the original product $E^1 \times \cdots \times E^N$. Possibly Godement's Theorem (Serre 1965, p. LG 3.27) might resolve this objection.

[3] Abelson used this result to construct a lower bound on the communication complexity of F in a distributed system. In Abelson's paper (1980), communication complexity is the number of real variables that must be transmitted among the processors to compute F. This is essentially the same as the size of the message space in the analysis carried out by Mount Reiter (1974) and in Hurwicz (1986) and Chen (1992).

use are constructed from derivatives of the function F, and reflect the product structure on the product $E^1 \times \cdots \times E^N$. The bordered Hessian we use is denoted $BH_{(x,y)}(F)$. This matrix has rows indexed by coordinates x_i from E^1, and columns indexed by F and the coordinates y from $E^2 \times \cdots \times E^N$. The (x_i, F) entry in $BH_{(x,y)}(F)$ is $\frac{\partial F}{\partial x_i}$, and the (x_i, y_j) entry is $\frac{\partial^2 F}{\partial x_i\, \partial y_j}$. The Hessian (again we abuse the term Hessian), $H_{(x,y)}(F)$, is the submatrix of the bordered Hessian that consists of the columns other than column F. The full bordered Hessian, $FBH_{(x,y)}(F)$ is the bordered Hessian with a row added indexed by F. The entry in position (F, F) is 0. The (F, y_j) entry in the full bordered Hessian is $\frac{\partial F}{\partial y_j}$.

We use conditions on the submatrix $BH_{(x,y)}(F)$ of the full bordered Hessian to guarantee the existence of a manifold structure on the quotient objects (E^i/F). If at each point p of E^1 and each point q of $E^2 \times \cdots \times E^N$ the matrix $BH_{(x,y)}(F)\, |_{(p,q)}$ has rank r and $H(F)_{(x,y)}\, |_{(p,q)}$ also has rank r, then the quotient of E^1 under the equivalence relation "$\approx$" is a manifold of dimension r.

As an example, consider the function

$$K(x, x', y, y') = xy + x'^2 y + 2xy'^2 + 2x'^2 y'^2 = (y + 2y'^2)(x + x'^2)$$

defined on the product $\mathcal{R}^2 \times \mathcal{R}^2 = E^1 \times E^2$, where the variables x, x' are coordinates on E^1 and y, y' are coordinates on E^2. None of the variables can be eliminated from the computation of K. To see this, compute the classical Hessian for K. The classical Hessian for K is the 4×4 matrix with rows and columns indexed by the variables x, x', y, y'. The entry in the (x, x) position of the classical Hessian is $\frac{\partial^2 F}{(\partial x)^2}$, the entry in the (x, y) position is $\frac{\partial^2 F}{(\partial x)\,\partial y)}$, etc. However, the (nonlinear) change of coordinates given by $X(x, x') = (x + x'^2)$, $Y(y, y') = (y + 2y'^2)$ permits K to be written in terms of only two variables, namely,

$$K(x, x', y, y') = X(x, x')Y(y, y').$$

The matrices $BH_{(x,y)}(K)$ and $BH_{(y,x)}(K)$ each has rank equal to 1 as do the matrices $BH_{(X,Y)}(XY)$ and $BH_{(Y,X)}(XY)$.

4.1.4 Privacy-Preserving Mechanisms

The basic setup is as follows. There are N (a positive integer) economic agents, each of whom has a *space of characteristics*. Let E^i denote the space of characteristics of agent i (such as her preference relations). It is assumed that the information about the joint environment $e = (e^1, \ldots, e^N)$ is distributed

among the agents so that agent i knows only her characteristic e^i. A function
$F : E^1 \times \cdots \times E^N \to Z$ is given, which is called the *goal function*. That
function expresses the goal of economic activity. For example, for each
$e = (e^1, \ldots, e^N)$ in $E^1 \times \cdots E^N$, let $F(e)$ denote the Walrasian allocation
(or trade). Agents communicate by exchanging messages drawn from a
message space denoted M. The final or *consensus message*, also called the *group
equilibrium message*, for the environment e is given by a correspondence μ :
$E^1 \times \cdots \times E^N \to M$. Equilibrium messages are translated into outcomes
by an *outcome function* $h : M \to Z$.

A *mechanism* $\pi = (M, \mu, h)$ is said to *realize* the goal function F (on E)
if for all $e \in E$, $F(e) = h(\mu(e))$.[4]

The mechanism (M, μ, h) is called *privacy preserving* if there exist correspondences $\mu^i : E^i \to M$, for $i = 1, \ldots, N$, such that for all $e \in E$,

$$\mu(e) = \mu^1(e^1) \cap \mu^2(e^2) \cap \cdots \cap \mu^N(e^N).$$

This condition states that the set of equilibrium messages acceptable to
agent i can depend on the environment only through the component e^i.
The component e^i is, according to the assumption made above, everything
that i knows about the environment.

From now on we focus on the case in which the characteristics of the agents
are given by real parameters and the mechanisms are privacy preserving. It
has been shown (see Hurwicz (1986) and the references given therein) that in
the case of privacy-preserving mechanisms the inverse image of a point m in
the message space M is a rectangle contained in the level set $F^{-1}(h(m))$. This
fact, in the presence of appropriate smoothness conditions, allows one to
compute a lower bound on the dimension of the message space of a privacy-
preserving mechanism that realizes F. (See Hurwicz 1986 or Hurwicz et al.
1980.)

A revelation mechanism is, of course, one in which each agent transmits his/her parameter value to the message space. (If the mechanism
realizes F then the outcome function h is F itself.) This can be represented as a mechanism in which the message space M is a product
$M = E^1 \times \cdots \times E^N$. If $M^i = E^i$, and if the individual message correspondence of agent i maps the parameter e^i in E^i to $\mu^i(e^i) = E^1 \times \cdots \times E^{i-1} \times$
$\{e^i\} \times E^{i+1} \times \cdots \times E^N$, then the mechanism is a *direct revelation mechanism*. To realize a goal function $F : E^1 \times \cdots \times E^N \to Z$ using the message
space $E^1 \times \cdots \times E^N$ it may be unnecessary for an agent to completely

---

[4] More generally, F can be a correspondence, in which case the definition of realizing F must
be modified, as in Hurwicz (1986).

reveal his/her parameters. For example, suppose there are two agents with environments $E^i = \mathcal{R}^2$, $i = 1$, 2, where the first agent uses coordinates x and y on E^1 while agent 2 uses coordinates z and w on E^2. If the goal function is $F(x, y, z, w) = (x + y)(z + w)$, then the revelation mechanism realizes $F(x, y, z, w)$, but it is also clear that one can construct a mechanism that realizes F in which it is unnecessary for the agents to completely reveal their environmental parameters. One can use the product $\mathcal{R} \times E^2$ as the message space, where the first component $\mathcal{R}$ has coordinate t. Agent 1 uses as message correspondence $v^1(x, y) = (x + y, E^2)$, agent 2 uses $v^2(z, w) = (\mathcal{R}(z, w))$ and the mechanism has as outcome function $h(t, z, w) = t(z + w)$. In this example, agent 2's parameters also enter only through their sum. We do not take advantage of that fact because the point can be made using only agent 1. Agent 1 does completely reveal his/her parameters. The reduction has been achieved by an explicit choice of a coordinate on the space $\mathcal{R}$ and an explicit representation of the function $x + y$. In other words, one can change coordinates in the space E^1, i.e., recode E^i, and use the mechanism $(\mathcal{R} \times E^2, v^1 \cap v^2, t)$ to realize F. This mechanism design recognizes that a simple change of coordinates makes it possible to realize the goal function requiring of agent 1 only a projection of his/her parameters. In the subsequent discussions we will be most interested in the construction of mechanisms that arise from recoding and projection, but it is technically useful to consider mechanisms (M, μ, h) where the message space is a product $M = M^1 \times \cdots \times M^N$ and the message correspondence is the product $g^1 \times \cdots \times g^N$ of functions $g^i : E^i \to M^i$. Such a mechanism $(M^1 \times \cdots \times M^N, (g^1, \ldots, g^N), h)$ is an *encoded revelation mechanism*. We formalize the concept of encoded revelation mechanisms in Section 4.2.1.

Encoded revelation mechanisms that realize a goal function F are a subclass of the class of privacy-preserving mechanisms that realize F. To see that the mechanism $(M^1 \times \cdots \times M^N, (g^1, \ldots, g^N), h)$ is privacy-preserving note that if $\mu^i(e^i) = E^1 \times \cdots \times E^{i-1} \times \{g^i(e^i)\} \times E^{i+1} \times \cdots \times E^N$, then $\mu(e^1) \cap \cdots \cap \mu^N(e^N) = (g^1(e^1), \ldots, g^N(e^N))$. There are simple conditions on the function F that guarantee the existence of a "best" encoded revelation mechanism. Of course, we mean that there is a "best" coordinate system for the realization of the function F by encoded revelation mechanisms constructed using projections of coordinates. What we construct is an encoded revelation mechanism through which each encoded revelation mechanism that realizes F factors. Although the dimension of the message space of this "best" encoded revelation mechanism is a lower bound on the dimensions of message spaces of encoded revelation mechanisms, it is not a lower bound on the dimensions of messages spaces of all privacy-preserving mechanisms that realize a goal function F. Theorems due to Hurwicz, Chen and Abelson, already mentioned, do establish lower bounds on the dimensions of message spaces of privacy-preserving mechanisms that realize F. While those theorems use rank conditions on certain Hessian matrices of F, they do not yield the same bounds as those given by encoded revelation mechanisms.

4.2 Initial Set-Theoretic Constructions

Notation: If X^j, $1 \leq j \leq N$, are sets and X denotes the product set $X^1 \times \cdots \times X^N$, then $X^{\langle -j \rangle}$ denotes the set $X^1 \times \cdots \times X^{j-1} \times X^{j+1} \times \cdots \times X^N$. If $x \in X^1 \times \cdots \times X^N$, and $1 \leq j \leq N$, then $x^{\langle -j \rangle}$ denotes the element $(x^1, \ldots, x^{j-1}, x^{j+1}, \ldots, x^N) \in X^{\langle -j \rangle}$. If $x \in X^j$, if for each $1 \leq i \neq j \leq N$, $z^i \in X^i$ and $z = (z^1, \ldots, z^{j-1}, z^{j+1}, \ldots, z^N) \in X^{\langle -j \rangle}$, then $z^{\langle x @ j \rangle}$ denotes the element $(z^1, \ldots, z^{j-1}, x, z^j, \ldots, z^N)$ of $X^1 \times \cdots \times X^N$.

4.2.1 Encoded and Essential Revelation Mechanisms

DEFINITION 4.2.1. Suppose that E^i, $1 \leq i \leq N$, and Z are sets and suppose that $F : E^1 \times \cdots \times E^N \to Z$ is a function. An *encoded revelation mechanism realizing* F is a triple $(M^1 \times \cdots \times M^N, (q^1, \ldots, q^N), h)$ that consists of:

   (i) a product of sets $M^1 \times \cdots \times M^N$,
   (ii) a collection of functions $q^i : E^i \to M^i, 1 \leq i \leq N$,
   (iii) a function $h : M^1 \times \cdots \times M^N \to Z$, such that for each $(e^1, \ldots, e^N)$ $\in E^1 \times \cdots \times E^N$, $F(e^1, \ldots, e^N) = h(q^1(e^1), \ldots, q^N(e^N))$. The function $(q^1, \ldots, q^N)$ is the message function for the encoded revelation mechanism.

4.2.2 *F*-Equivalence and Encoded Revelation Mechanisms

DEFINITION 4.2.2. Suppose that E^i, $1 \leq i \leq N$, and Z are sets, that $F : \prod_{i=1}^N E^i \to Z$ is a function, and that $1 \leq j \leq N$. Two points x and x' in E^j are F-equivalent in E^j if for each $z \in E^{\langle -j \rangle}$, $F(z^{\langle x @ j \rangle}) = F(z^{\langle x' @ j \rangle})$.

F-equivalence is the relation we introduced in the fourth paragraph of Section 4.1. It is elementary that F-equivalence in E^j is an equivalence relation on points of E^j. Denote by (E^j / F) the collection of F-equivalence classes of E^j : denote by q^j the quotient map from E^j to (E^j/F). That is, q^j carries a point in E^j to the equivalence class of that point under F-equivalence.

The following lemma establishes the sense in which the set $(E^1/F) \times \cdots \times (E^N/F)$ is the smallest product set through which F factors.

LEMMA 4.2.1. Suppose that $E^1, \ldots, E^N$, and Z are sets and suppose that $F : E^1 \times \cdots \times E^N \to Z$ is a function. For each $1 \le j \le N$, denote by q^j : $E^j \to (E^j/F)$ the map that carries each point of E^j to its equivalence class under F-equivalence. Then:

(i) there is a unique function $F^* : (E^1/F) \times \cdots \times (E^N/F) \to Z$ that makes the Diagram A commute;

(ii) if $X^1, \ldots, X^N$ are sets, and if there are functions $p^i : E^i \to X^i$, $1 \le i \le N$, p^i onto X^i, and a function $H : X^1 \times \cdots \times X^N \to Z$ that makes Diagram B commute, then there are uniquely determined maps $\rho^1, \ldots, \rho^N, \rho^i : X^i \to (E^i/F)$, that make Diagram C commute; and

(iii) if $X^1, \ldots, X^N$ are sets, and if there are functions $p^i : E^i \to X^i$, $1 \le i \le N$, and a function $H : X^1 \times \cdots \times X^N \to Z$ that makes Diagram B commute, then for each $1 \le i \le N$, the cardinality of X^i is at least the cardinality of (E^i/F).

We now give a proof of Lemma 4.2.1.

Proof: Define a correspondence $F^* : (E^1/F) \times \cdots \times (E^N/F) \to Z$ by setting $F^*(q^1(e^1), \ldots, q^N(e^N)) = F(e^1, \ldots, e^N)$. It follows immediately from Definition 4.2.2 that this defines a function on $(E^1/F) \times \cdots \times (E^N/F)$. For each $1 \le j \le N$, the map q^j carries E^j onto (E^j/F) because each point in (E^j/F) is the equivalence class of a point in E^j. If $F' : (E^1/F) \times \cdots \times (E^N/F) \to Z$ such that $F' \circ q^1 \times \cdots \times q^N = F$, then for each point $(y^1, \ldots, y^N) \in (E^1/F) \times \cdots \times (E^N/F)$, $(y^1, \ldots, y^N) = (q^1(e^1), \ldots, q^N(e^N))$ for some $(e^1, \ldots, e^N) \in E^1 \times \cdots \times E^N$. Therefore, $F'(y^1, \ldots, y^N) = F'(q^1(e^1), \ldots, q^N(e^N)) = F(e^1, \ldots, e^N) = F^*(q^1(e^1), \ldots, q^N(e^N)) = F(y^1, \ldots, y^N)$. This establishes the uniqueness of the map F^*.

We next show that if $p^i : E^i \to X^i$ and $H : \prod_1^N X^i \to Z$ are functions that make Diagram B commute, then we can factor the map $\prod_1^N p^i$ through the product $\prod_1^N (E^i/F)$. If $x \in X^i$, choose $e, e' \in E^i$ such that $p^i(e') = p^i(e) = x$. For each $w \in E^{\langle -i \rangle}$, set

$$p(w) = (p^1(w^1), \ldots, p^{i-1}(w^{i-1}), p^{i+1}(w^{i+1}), \ldots, p^N(w^N)) \in X^{\langle -i \rangle}.$$

Then $F(w^{\langle e@i \rangle}) = H(p(w)^{\langle p^i(e)@i \rangle}) = H(p(w)^{\langle p^i(e')@i \rangle}) = F(w^{\langle e'@i \rangle})$. It follows that for each i, $q^i(e) = q^i(e')$. Therefore, setting $\rho^i(x) = q^i(e)$ defines a function ρ^i from X^i to (E^i/F). It is clear that Diagram C commutes.

To see the uniqueness of the maps ρ^i, note that if $\rho^{*i} : X^i \to (E^i/F)$, $1 \le i \le N$, are maps that make Diagram C commute when used in place of the maps ρ^i, then for each $x \in X^i$ and each $e \in E^i$ so that $p^i(e) = x$, it follows that $\rho^i(x) = \rho^i(p^i(e)) = q^i(e) = \rho^{*i}(p^i(e)) = \rho^{*i}(x)$. Finally, we turn to assertion *(iii)*. If the maps $p^i : E^i \to X^i$ are onto, then the maps $\rho^i : X^i \to (E^i/F)$ are also onto, therefore the cardinality of X^i is at least that of (E^i/F).[5] If the map $p^i : E^i \to X^i$ is not onto, then replace X^i with the image of p^i. It follows that the image of p^i has cardinality at least that of (E^i/F), while the cardinality of X^i is at least that of the image of p^i.

DEFINITION 4.2.3. Using the notation of Lemma 4.2.1, the triple $((E^1/F) \times \cdots \times (E^N/F), (q^1, \ldots, q^N), F^*)$ is an encoded revelation mechanism realizing F, called an *essential revelation mechanism realizing F*.

The following theorem is a restatement of Lemma 4.2.1 in terms of encoded revelation mechanisms. It states that not only is $(E^1/F)^1 \times \cdots \times (E^N/F^N)$ the product with the smallest cardinality that can be used as the message space for an encoded revelation mechanism, but it is also the case that for every other product space that acts as a message space for an encoded revelation mechanism that realizes F there is a product map onto $(E^1/F) \times \cdots \times (E^N/F)$. This is a characteristic of a universal object in the sense of category theory. Theorem 4.2.1 states that the essential revelation mechanism is a universal object in the category of encoded revelation mechanisms. In order to use the language of category theory, a definition of morphisms between encoded revelation mechanisms must be added. For our purposes it suffices to introduce the concept of *isomorphic encoded revelation mechanisms realizing F*. The mechanism $((E^1/F) \times \cdots \times (E^N/F), (q^1, \ldots, q^N), F^*)$ is then a representative of a class of isomorphic mechanisms. Each member of that class is an essential revelation mechanism realizing F.

DEFINITION 4.2.4. Suppose that $\mathcal{M} = (M^1 \times \cdots \times M^N, (p^1, \ldots, p^N), h)$ and $\mathcal{M}' = (M'^1 \times \cdots \times M'^N, (p'^1, \ldots, p'^N), h')$ are encoded revelation mechanisms realizing a function F. An isomorphism from $\mathcal{M}$ to $\mathcal{M}'$ is

---

[5] It is a standard theorem in set theory that an onto mapping does not increase cardinality, and a set has cardinality at least that of each subset (cf. Lang (1993)).

a collection of one-to-one and onto functions $g^i : M^i \to M'^i$, $1 \le i \le N$ such that Diagram D is a commutative diagram.

THEOREM 4.2.1. Suppose that E^i, $1 \le i \le N$, and Z are nonempty sets and suppose that $F : E^1 \times \cdots \times E^N \to Z$ is a function.

(i) The triple $(E^1/F) \times \cdots \times (E^N/F)$, $(q^1, \ldots, q^N)$, F^*) is an encoded revelation mechanism that realizes F.

(ii) The message function for any other encoded revelation mechanism factors through $(E^1/F) \times \cdots \times (E^N/F)$.

(iii) The set $(E^1/F) \times \cdots \times (E^N/F)$ is the smallest set in cardinality that can be used as an encoded revelation message space for a mechanism that realizes F.

(iv) Finally, the essential revelation mechanism is the unique encoded revelation mechanism $(M^1 \times \cdots \times M^N$, $(p^1, \ldots, p^N)$, $h)$ (to within isomorphism) that realizes F for which the message function is onto, and through which each encoded revelation mechanism that realizes F factors.

4.3 The Topological Case

When E^i are topological manifolds and when F is continuous, it is generally not true that the sets (E^i/F) are manifolds. Even a high degree of smoothness of F is insufficient to guarantee that (E^i/F) is a topological manifold. However, when the (E^i/F) are Hausdorff, a simple condition on the Jacobian of F coupled with a global separation condition does imply that the (E^i/F) are manifolds. When these conditions are satisfied, the essential revelation mechanism has the structure of a manifold, and the dimensions of the (E^i/F) can be used to establish a lower bound on the number of variables, i.e., the number of functions in a coordinate system, that must be passed to a central processor to compute F. This number determines a lower bound for the complexity of the function F.

In this section, we introduce the concept of differentiable separability, which is the Jacobian condition that we use. We then give simple global conditions on the function F to ensure that the sets (E^i/F) are topological manifolds. We begin with some concepts from differential geometry (cf. Golubitsky and Guillemin (1973)).

DEFINITION 4.3.1. Let X and Y be differentiable manifolds. Let $\Phi : X \to Y$ be a differentiable mapping. If at a point $p \in X$ the Jacobian of the mapping Φ has the maximum rank, and if dim $X \ge$ dim Y, then Φ is said to be a *submersion* at p. If Φ is a submersion at each point of X, then Φ is a *submersion*. If a map $g : X \to Y$ is a submersion, then it is known (cf. Golubitsky and Guillemin (1973, p.9)) that the map can be linearized (rectified). That is, if $\dim(X) = n$, $\dim(Y) = m$, and if $p \in X$, we can choose coordinates $(x_1, \ldots, x_n)$ in a neighborhood U of p, and coordinates $(y_1, \ldots, y_m)$, in a neighborhood of g(p) so that for each $q \in U$, $(y_1(g(q)), \ldots, y_m(g(q))) = (x_1(q), \ldots, x_m(q))$.

Notation: Suppose that for $1 \le i \le N$, M^i denotes a topological manifold, for each i, $\underline{p}^i \in M^i$, and $\underline{x}_i$ is a local coordinate system in a neighborhood of $\underline{p}^i$ on M^i. We denote by $\underline{x}$ the coordinate system $(\underline{x}_1, \ldots, \underline{x}_N)$ on the product $M = M^1 \times \cdots \times M^N$. We extend the notation of page 25 and denote by $\underline{x}_{(-i)}$ the coordinate system $(\underline{x}_1, \ldots, \underline{x}_{i-1}, \underline{x}_{i+1}, \ldots, \underline{x}_N)$ on $M^{(-i)}$. If $\underline{z}$ are coordinates on M^i, and $\underline{y}_{(-j)} = (\underline{y}_1, \ldots, \underline{y}_{j-1}, \underline{y}_{j+1}, \ldots, \underline{y}_N)$ are coordinates on $M^{(-j)}$, then $\underline{y}_{(-j)(\underline{z}@j)}$ denotes the coordinates $(\underline{y}_1, \ldots, \underline{y}_{j-1}, \underline{z}, \underline{y}_{j+1}, \ldots, \underline{y}_N)$ on $M^1, \ldots, M^N$.

Next, we introduce a collection of matrices that are generalizations of matrices used by Leontief (1947).

Suppose $E^1, \ldots, E^N$ are Euclidean spaces of dimensions $d_1, \ldots, d_N$, such that the space E^i, $1 \le i \le N$, has coordinates $\underline{x}_i = (x_{i,1}, \ldots, x_{i,d_i})$. Assume that $(\underline{p}^1, \ldots, \underline{p}^N)$ is a point of $E^1 \times \cdots \times E^N$, and assume that U^i is an open neighborhood of the point $\underline{p}^i$, $1 \le i \le N$. We assume that F is a real-valued C^2-function defined on $\overline{U}^1 \times \cdots \times \overline{U}^N$. We require four matrices.

(i) The matrix $BH_{(\underline{x}_i, \underline{x}_{(-i)})}(F) =$
$BH_{((x_{i,1}, \ldots, x_{i,d(i)}), (x_{1,1}, \ldots, x_{i-1,d_{i-1}}, x_{i+1,1}, \ldots, x_{N,d_N}))}(F)$ is a matrix that has rows indexed by $x_{i,1}, \ldots, x_{i,d_i}$ and columns indexed by $F, x_{1,1}, \ldots, x_{(i-1),d_{i-1}}, x_{(i+1),1}, \ldots, x_{N,d_N}$. The entry in the $x_{i,u}$ row and in the F column is $\frac{\partial F}{\partial x_{i,u}}$. The entry in row $x_{i,u}$ and in column $x_{j,w}$ is $\frac{\partial^2 F}{\partial x_{i,u} \partial x_{j,w}}$.

(ii) The matrix $H_{(\underline{x}_i, \underline{x}_{(-i)})}(F)$ is the submatrix of $BH_{(\underline{x}_i, \underline{x}_{(-i)})}(F)$ that consists of the columns indexed by $x_{u,v}$, $u \in \{1, \ldots, i-1, i+1, \ldots, N\}$ and $1 \le v \le d_u$. In other words, we derive H from BH by eliminating the column indexed by the function F. If the number of Euclidean spaces is two, so $F : E^1 \times E^2 \to \mathcal{R}$, we use a slightly less cumbersome notation. Suppose that E^1 has coordinates $(x_1, \ldots, x_p)$ and E^2 has coordinates $(y_1, \ldots, y_q)$. We use as row indices for $BH_{((x_1, \ldots, x_p), (y_1, \ldots, y_q))}(F)$ the variables $x_1, \ldots, x_p$ and as column indices

F, y_1, ..., y_q. The (x_i, F) entry in $BH_{(x_1,...,x_p;y_1,...,y_q)}(F)$ is $\frac{\partial F}{\partial x_i}$ and the (x_i, y_j) entry is $\frac{\partial^2 F}{\partial x_i \partial y_j}$. The matrices $H_{(\underline{x}_i, \underline{x}_{(-i)})}(F)$ and $BH_{(\underline{x}_i, \underline{x}_{(-i)})}(F)$ are matrices of functions in the coordinates $\underline{x}_1$, ..., $\underline{x}_N$ of $E^1 \times \cdots \times E^N$. The conditions we place on the matrices BH and H require that some, but not all, of the variables are to be evaluated at a point. When that partial evaluation takes place we indicate this by adding an asterisk to the H or BH.

(iii) Specifically, the matrix $BH^*_{(\underline{x}_i, \underline{x}_{(-i)})}(F) \mid_{[\underline{x}_i, \underline{p}_{(-i)}]}$ is the matrix that results from evaluating the variables $\underline{x}_1$, ..., $\underline{x}_{i-1}$, $\underline{x}_{i+1}$, ..., $\underline{x}_N$ of the entries of $BH_{(\underline{x}_i, \underline{x}_{(-i)})}(F)$ at the point $p_{(-i)} = (\underline{p}_1, ..., \underline{p}_{i-1}, \underline{p}_{i+1}, ..., \underline{p}_N)$. The matrix $BH^*_{(\underline{x}_i, \underline{x}_{(-i)})}(F) \mid_{[\underline{x}_i, \underline{p}_{(-i)}]}$ is a function of the variables $x_{i,1}$, ..., x_{i,d_i} alone.

(iv) Similarly, the matrix $H^*_{(\underline{x}_i, \underline{x}_{(-i)})}(F) \mid_{[\underline{x}_i, \underline{p}_{(-i)}]}$ is the submatrix of $BH^*_{(\underline{x}_i, \underline{x}_{(-i)})}(F) \mid_{[\underline{x}_i, \underline{p}_{(-i)}]}$ derived by deleting the column indexed by F.

4.3.1 Differential Separability

DEFINITION 4.3.2. Suppose X^1, ..., X^N are differentiable manifolds, where for each $1 \le i \le N$, X^i has dimension d_i. Suppose that $p_i \in X^i$, $1 \le i \le N$, and suppose that for each i, $\phi_i = (\phi_{i,1}, ..., \phi_{i,d_i})$ is a coordinate system in an open neighborhood U^i of p^i. Suppose that $F : \prod_{i=1}^N X^i \to \mathcal{R}$ is a C^2-function. Assume that for $1 \le i \le N$, $\phi_i = \prod_j \phi_{i,j}$ maps U^i onto an open neighborhood V^i of the origin 0^i of a Euclidean space $E^i = \mathcal{R}^{d_i}$ and that ϕ_i carries p^i to 0^i. We assume that E^i has coordinates $(x_{i,1}, ..., x_{i,d_i})$. The function F is said to be *differentiably separable of rank* $(r_1, ..., r_N)$ *at the point* $(p^1, ..., p^N)$ *in the coordinate system* $(\phi_{1,1}, ..., \phi_{N,d_N})$ if for each $1 \le i \le N$, the matrices

$$BH_{((x_{i,1},...,x_{i,d_i}),x_{(-i)})}\left(F \circ \left(\prod \phi_t\right)^{-1}\right)$$

and

$$H^*_{((x_{i,1},...,x_{i,d_i}),x_{(-i)})}\left(F \circ \left(\prod \phi_t\right)^{-1}\right)\Bigg|_{[x_i, 0_{(-i)}]}$$

have rank r_i in a neighborhood of $(0^1, ..., 0^N)$. If F is differentiably separable of rank $(r_1, ..., r_N)$ at $(p^1, ..., p^N)$, and if $r_i = \dim(X^i)$ for each $1 \le i \le N$, then we will say that F is *differentiably separable at* $(p^1, ..., p^N)$ in the coordinate system $(\phi_1 \times \cdots \times \phi_N)$.

The following lemma notes that the ranks of the Hessians used in the previous definition are unchanged by coordinate changes. The proof is a simple computation.

LEMMA 4.3.1. Suppose that for $1 \leq i \leq N$, X^i and Y^i are C^2-manifolds and suppose that $h^i : Y^i \to X^i$ is a C^2-diffeomorphism. Assume that $g : \prod_{i=1}^{N} Y^i \to \mathcal{R}$ and $F : \prod_{i=1}^{N} X^i \to \mathcal{R}$ are C^2-functions such that $g = \prod h^i \circ F$. Suppose that $(q^1, \ldots, q^N) \in \prod_i Y^i$ and let $h^i(q^i) = p^i$. If F is differentiably separable of rank $(r_1, \ldots, r_N)$ at $(p^1, \ldots, p^N)$, then g is differentiably separable of rank $(r_1, \ldots, r_N)$ at $(q^1, \ldots, q^N)$.

We can now define the term differentiably separable for a function defined on a differentiable manifold.

DEFINITION 4.3.3. If $X^i, 1 \leq i \leq N$, are C^2-manifolds, the function $F : X^1 \times \cdots \times X^N \to \mathcal{R}$ is *differentiably separable of rank* $(r_1, \ldots, r_N)$ at the point $(p^1, \ldots, p^N)$ if there is a coordinate system $(\phi_{i,j})$ at the point $(p^1, \ldots, p^N)$ such that F is differentiably separable of rank $(r_1, \ldots, r_N)$ at the point $(p^1, \ldots, p^N)$ in the coordinate system $(\phi_{1,1}, \ldots, \phi_{N,d_N})$.

4.3.2 The Number of Variables on which F Really Depends

If $F : X^1 \times \cdots \times X^N \to \mathcal{R}$ is differentiably separable of rank $(r_1, \ldots, r_N)$ at a point $(p^1, \ldots, p^N)$, then it is possible to write F as a function of variables $\{y_{1,1}, \ldots, y_{1,r_1}, \ldots, y_{N,1}, \ldots, y_{N,r_N}\}$. This assertion, Lemma 4.3.2, is a restatement of Theorem 4.2.1. The proof of Theorem 4.2.1 is to be found in Section 4.4 together with an example of the construction.

LEMMA 4.3.2. Suppose that for $1 \leq i \leq N$, X^i is a C^{k+1}-manifold, $k \geq 2$. Assume,

    (i) $F : X^1 \times \cdots \times X^N \to \mathcal{R}$ is a C^{k+1}- function,
    (ii) $(p^1, \ldots, p^N)$ is a point on $X^1 \times \cdots \times X^N$, and
    (iii) X^i has coordinates $\underline{x}_i$.

A necessary condition that F can be written in the form

$$G(y_{1,1}, \ldots, y_{1,r(1)}, \ldots, y_{N,1}, \ldots, y_{N,r_N}),$$

for $(y_{i,1}, \ldots, y_{i,d_i})$, a coordinate system in a neighborhood of the point $(p^1, \ldots, p^N) \in X^i$, is that the matrix $BH_{(\underline{x}_i, \underline{x}_{(-i)})}(F)$ has rank at most r_i for each i.

Furthermore, a sufficient condition for F to be written in the form $G(y_{1,1}, \ldots, y_{1,r_1}, \ldots, y_{N,1}, \ldots, y_{N,r_N})$, for a C^k-function G in a neighborhood of a point $(p^1, \ldots, p^N)$, is that F is differentiably separable of rank exactly $(r_1, \ldots, r_N)$ at $(p^1, \ldots, p^N)$.

4.3.3 Rank Conditions and Construction of an Essential Revelation Mechanism for F

Lemma 4.3.2 suggests that in the case of a differentiable function F satisfying the rank conditions stated in the lemma, it is possible to construct an essential revelation mechanism whose message space is a topological manifold. We now carry out the construction suggested by the lemma. The main result is given in Theorem 4.3.2 and in Corollary 4.3.3.

DEFINITION 4.3.4. Suppose that X^i, $1 \le i \le N$, and Z are C^k-manifolds and suppose that $F : X^1 \times \cdots \times X^N \to Z$ is a differentiable function. The triple $(M^1 \times \cdots \times M^N, (q^1, \ldots, q^N), h)$ that consists of spaces $M^1 \times \cdots \times M^N$, maps $q^1, \ldots, q^N$, $q^i : X^i \to M^i$, $1 \le i \le N$, and the function $h : M^1 \times \cdots \times M^N \to Z$ is an *encoded C^k-revelation mechanism that realizes F* if

(i) each of the spaces M^i is a C^k-manifold;
(ii) each of the functions q^i, $1 \le i \le N$, and h is a C^k-differentiable function;
(iii) each q^i, $1 \le i \le N$, has a local thread at each point of M^i, and
(iv) $h \circ (\prod_i q^i) = F$.

DEFINITION 4.3.5. Suppose that $F : E^1 \times \cdots \times E^N \to Z$ is a differentiable map from a product of differentiable manifolds $E^1, \ldots, E^N$ to a differentiable manifold Z. The function F *factors through a product of manifolds $X^1 \times \cdots \times X^N$* if there are submersions $p^i : E^i \to X^i$, and a differentiable mapping $H : X^1 \times \cdots \times X^N \to Z$ such that Diagram B commutes.

It has not been established that the essential revelation mechanism is an encoded C^k-revelation mechanism, because the construction given in Theorem 4.2.1 ignores all topological and differentiable structure.

The general outline of the method we use to put a structure on the (E^i/F) is straightforward. We first show that when the rank of $BH_{(\underline{x}_i, \underline{x}_{(-i)})}(F)$ is the same as the dimension of E^i, then for each two points x and x' in E^i, there is an element $y \in E^{(-i)}$ such that $F(x, y) \neq F(x', y)$. Therefore, the set (E^i/F) is E^i. We next appeal to the generalization of a theorem of Leontief and Abelson given in Lemma 4.3.2. This lemma shows that if the rank of $BH_{(\underline{x}_i, \underline{x}_{(-i)})}(F)$ at a point is r_i, then in a neighborhood of the point there is a coordinate system $(x_{i,1}, \ldots, x_{i,d_i})$ and a function G such that $F(x_{1,1}, \ldots, x_{N,d_N}) = G(x_{(-i)}\langle(x_{i,1},\ldots,x_{i,r})@i\rangle)$. We can use the remaining set of coordinates in E^i to determine a subspace S of E^i by setting $x_{i,(r+1)} = 0, \ldots, x_{i,d_i} = 0$. The set S is a submanifold of E^i and the restriction of F to the space $S \times E^{(-i)}$ has the property that the rank of $BH_{((x_{i,1},\ldots,x_{i,r}),\underline{x}_{(-i)})}(\text{restrict } F)$ is the dimension of S. On S, the restriction of F separates points (at least in a neighborhood) and therefore the map from S to (E^i/F) is one-to-one. Some technical fiddling with quotient topologies makes the quotient map, locally, a homeomorphism. Therefore, at least locally, the space (E^i/F) has the same structure as S. The rest of the proof consists of adding enough restrictions to ensure that the local argument can be carried out everywhere on $E^1 \times \cdots \times E^N$.

THEOREM 4.3.1. Suppose that X^i, $1 \leq i \leq N$, is a Euclidean space of dimension $d(i) \geq 1$. Suppose that for each $1 \leq i \leq N$, U^i is an open neighborhood of the origin 0^i of E^i and suppose that F is a C^3-function differentiably separable at each point $(p^1, \ldots, p^N) \in U^1 \times \cdots \times U^N$. Then there is an open neighborhood U of p^i such that for each pair of points x and x' in U, $x \neq x'$, there is a point $w \in U^{(-i)}$ such that $F(x, w) \neq F(x', w)$.

Proof: Denote by $\underline{x}$ the standard coordinate system on E^i and denote by $\underline{y}$ the standard coordinate system on the space $E^{(-i)}$. The matrix $H_{(\underline{x},\underline{y})}(F)|_{[0,0]}$ has rank $d(i)$, by assumption. Set $X = X^i$, set $X^{(-i)} = Y$, denote $\dim(X^{(-i)})$ by $\overline{N}$, and denote d_i by m. We can change coordinates in X and Y separately to coordinates $\underline{z}$ in X and $\underline{w}$ in Y so that the new matrix $H_{(\underline{z},\underline{w})}(F)|_{[0,0]}$ has a 1 in the $z_j \times w_j$ position, $1 \leq j \leq m$, and zero in all the other positions. The Taylor series expansion for $F(z_1, \ldots, z_m, w_1, \ldots, w_{\overline{N}})$ then has the form

$$F(\underline{z}, \underline{w}) = F(0, 0) + \underline{u} \circ \underline{z} + v' \circ \underline{w} + \underline{w} \circ \underline{z} + \underline{z}^T Q\underline{z}$$
$$+ \underline{w}^T Q'\underline{w} + P(z^*, w^*)[z, w],$$

where Q and Q' are square matrices, u and v' are vectors in $\mathcal{R}^m$ and $\mathcal{R}^{\overline{N}}$, respectively, $v' \circ w$ denotes inner product, $\underline{z}^T$ denotes the transpose of the column vector $\underline{z}$, and where $P(z^*, w^*)[z, w]$ is a cubic polynomial in the variables $(z_1, \ldots, z_m, w_1, \ldots, w_{\overline{N}})$ with coefficients that are continuous functions on $U \times V$ evaluated at some point $z^* \in U$ and $w^* \in V$. These coefficients of P are bounded on a ball that is a compact neighborhood of $(0, 0) \in U' \times V'$, $U' \subseteq U$ and $V' \subseteq V$. Then for z, $z' \in U'$ and $w \in V'$, $| F(z, w) - F(z', w) | =$

$$| u \circ (z - z') + w \circ (z - z') + z^T Q z'$$
$$+ P(z'^*, w'^*)[z', w] - P(z^*, w^*)[z, w] |.$$

We suppose that the vector $(z - z') \neq 0$ and denote $(z - z')$ by v. The point w is to be chosen in the set V'. Denote $z'^T Q z' - z^T Q z$ by K and denote $u \circ v$ by L. To complete the proof, it will suffice to show that the function

$$w \circ v + P(z^*, w^*)[z, w] - P(z'^*, w'^*)[z', w] + K + L$$

is not constant on the ball V'. For this it will suffice to show that the function

$$\tilde{Q} = w \circ v + P(z', w^*)[z', w] - P(z'^*, w'^*)[z', w]$$

is not constant on the ball V'. The function $P(z^*, w^*)[z', w] - P(z^*, w^*)[z, w]$ is a cubic $\Sigma_{\alpha, \beta} a_{\alpha, \beta} z^\alpha w^\beta$ in the variables $w_1, \ldots, w_N$ with coefficients $\{a_{\alpha, \beta}(z, z', w, w')\}$ that are functions bounded on $U' \times V'$. Set $w = tv$. The powers of the constants $z_1, \ldots, z_m$ can be combined with the coefficients $a_{\alpha, \beta}$ and therefore $\tilde{Q} = t | v |^2 + a(t)t^3$, where the $a(t)$ is also bounded as a function of t. If $a(t) = 0$ identically in t, then because $v \neq 0$, different values of t produce different values of $\tilde{Q}$. If $a(t) \neq 0$, and $| v |^2 + a(t)t^2 = c$ (a constant), then $a(t) = (c - | v |^2)/t^2$, and therefore $a(t)$ is not bounded as t approaches 0. Therefore, $\tilde{Q}$ is not a constant.

We now give conditions on a function F that is differentiably separable of rank $(r_1, \ldots, r_N)$, so that each of the sets (X^i/F), with the quotient topology, has the structure of a C^0-manifold of dimension r_i. Under these conditions the set-theoretic essential revelation mechanism is a topological essential revelation mechanism.

DEFINITION 4.3.6. If X^i, $1 \leq i \leq N$, are topological spaces, then a real-valued function $F : X^1 \times \cdots \times X^N \to \mathcal{R}$ *induces strong equivalence* on X^i, if the following condition is satisfied. For each $x, x' \in X^i$, such that $x \neq x'$ there is an open neighborhood U of a point $q \in X^{\langle -i \rangle}$, such that $F(u^{\langle x @ i \rangle}) = F(u^{\langle x' @ i \rangle})$ for each $u \in U$, then $F(z^{\langle x @ i \rangle}) = F(z^{\langle x' @ i \rangle})$ for all $z \in X^{\langle -i \rangle}$.

Finding classes of functions that induce strong equivalence is easy. Suppose the X^i are Euclidean spaces with coordinates $\underline{x}_i = (x_{i,1}, \ldots, x_{i,d_i})$, $1 \leq i \leq N$. If for each $1 \leq i \leq N$, $\beta(i) = (\beta(i,1), \ldots, \beta(i,d_i))$ is a sequence of nonnegative integers, denoted by $\underline{x}_i^{\beta(i)}$ the monomial $x_{i,1}^{\beta(i,1)} \cdots x_{i,d_i}^{\beta(i,d_i)}$, and denoted by $\underline{x}_1^{\beta(1)} \cdots \underline{x}_N^{\beta(N)}$ the product of the monomials $\underline{x}_i^{\beta(i)}$. Write

$$F(\underline{x}_1, \ldots, \underline{x}_N) = \Sigma_{\beta(1),\ldots,\beta(N)} A_{\beta(1)\ldots\beta(N)} \underline{x}_2^{\beta(2)} \cdots \underline{x}_N^{\beta(N)},$$

where $A_\beta(\underline{x}_1)$ are polynomials in $\underline{x}_1$. Then for x_1, $x_1' \in X^1$, $F(x_1, x_{(-1)}) = F(x_1', x_{(-1)})$ for $x_{(-1)}$ in an open set in $X^{(-1)}$, if and only if $[A_\beta(x_1) - A_\beta(x_1')]x_2^{\beta(2)} \cdots x_N^{\beta(N)} = 0$ for the $x_2, \ldots, x_N$ chosen arbitrarily in an open set in $X^2 \times \cdots \times X^N$. However, a polynomial vanishes in an open set if and only if each of its coefficients is zero. Therefore, if $F(x_1, x_{(-1)}) = F(x_1', x_{(-1)})$ for the $x_{(-1)}$ chosen in some open set, it follows that for each β, $A_\beta(x_1) - A_\beta(x_1') = 0$. That is, F induces a strong equivalence relation on X^1.

THEOREM 4.3.2. Suppose that E^i, $1 \leq i \leq N$, are C^4-manifolds of dimensions $d_1, \ldots, d_N$, respectively. Suppose $F : E^1 \times \cdots \times E^N \to \mathcal{R}$ is a C^4-function that is differentiably separable on $E^1 \times \cdots \times E^N$ of rank $(r_1, \ldots, r_N)$ where each $r_i \geq 1$. Assume that F induces strong equivalence in E^i for each i. If

  (i) the spaces (E^i/F) are all Hausdorff in the quotient topology,
  (ii) quotient map $q^i : E^i \to (E^i/F)$ is open for each $1 \leq i \leq N$,

then, for each $1 \leq i \leq N$, the space (E^i/F) (with the quotient topology) is a topological manifold (i.e., a C^0-manifold). Furthermore, the quotient map $q^i : E^i \to (E^i/F)$ has a local thread in the neighborhood of each point.

Proof: Suppose that $P^{i*} \in (E^i/F)$, $1 \leq i \leq N$. Choose a point $P^i \in E^i$, $1 \leq i \leq N$, such that $q^i(P^i) = P^{i*}$. Because the function F is differentiably separable of rank $(r_1, \ldots, r_N)$ at the point $(P^1, \ldots, P^N)$, it follows from Theorem 4.4.6 that for $1 \leq i \leq N$, there is an open neighborhood $U^{(-i)}$ of $P^{(-i)}$ in $X^{(-i)}$, an open neighborhood U^i of the point P^i, and a coordinate system $\underline{x}_i = (x_{i,1}, \ldots, x_{i,d_i})$ in E^i such that $x_i(P^i) = (0, \ldots, 0)$ and a C^3-function G defined in a neighborhood of the origin, such that

$$F(z_{1,1}, \ldots, z_{i-1,d_{i-1}}, x_{i,1}, \ldots, x_{i,d_i}, z_{i+1,1}, \ldots, z_{N,d_N})$$
$$= G(z_{1,1}, \ldots, z_{i-1,r_i}, x_{i,1}, \ldots, x_{i,r_i}, z_{i+1,1}, \ldots, z_{N,d_N})$$

for each $z \in U^{\langle -i \rangle}$. Denote by S^{*i} the set of elements $\{x_{i,1}, \ldots, x_{i,r_i}, 0, \ldots, 0\}$ that lie in U^i. Choose in S^{*i} a compact neighborhood S^i of $(0, \ldots, 0)$ (in the induced topology on $S^{*,i}$.) The map q^i carries the set U^i to an open set of (E^i/F) because we have assumed that q^i is an open map. We have assumed that the equivalence relation induced on $X^{\langle -i \rangle}$ by F is strong, therefore the equality

$$F((z_{1,1}, \ldots, z_{i-1,d_{i-1}}), (x_{i,1}, \ldots, x_{i,r_i}), b_1, \ldots, b_{d_i - r_i}, z_{i+1,1}, \ldots, z_{N,d_N})$$
$$= F(z_{\langle -i \rangle \langle (x_{i,1}, \ldots, x_{i,r_i}, 0, \ldots, 0) @ i \rangle})$$

implies that $q_i(x_{i,1}, \ldots, x_{i,d_i}) = q_i(x_{i,1}, \ldots, x_{i,r_i})$ for each $(x_{i,1}, \ldots, x_{i,d_i})$ in U^i. Therefore, $q^i(U^i) = q^i(S^{*i})$. The set S^{*i} was constructed so that q^i is one-to-one on S^{*i}. By assumption, the space (E^i/F) is Hausdorff, therefore the restriction of q^i to S^i is a homeomorphism from S^i to a neighborhood $\mathcal{N}^i$ of p^{*i}. Denote by s^i the inverse of q^i on $\mathcal{N}^i$. It follows that the point $P^{*i} \in X^i$ has a neighborhood N_i that is homeomorphic to a neighborhood of the origin of the space $\mathcal{R}^{r_i}$. Furthermore, the function s^i is a thread of q^i on the set $\mathcal{N}^i$.

The following corollary states that the essential revelation mechanism is a C^0-essential revelation mechanism. In this case, under the assumptions made about F, each C^0-encoded revelation mechanism factors through the C^0-essential revelation mechanism.

COROLLARY 4.3.3. Suppose that E^i, $1 \leq i \leq N$, are C^4-manifolds and that E^i has dimension d_i. Assume that $F : X_1 \times \cdots \times E^n \to \mathcal{R}$ is a real-valued C^4 function that satisfies the following conditions:

(i) there are integers $(r_1, \ldots, r_N)$, $1 \leq r_i \leq d_i$, such that at each point $(P^1, \ldots, P^N) \in E^1 \times \cdots \times E^N$, F is differentiably separable of rank $(r_1, \ldots, r_N)$;
(ii) for each i, the map $q_i : E^i \to (E^i/F)$ is open and (E^i/F) is Hausdorff; and
(iii) for each i, F induces a strong equivalence relation on E^i.

Then the triple

$$((E^1/F) \times \cdots \times (E^N/F), (q^1, \ldots, q^N), F^*),$$

where

(1) each (E^i/F) is given the quotient topology;
(2) the maps $q^i : E^i \to (E^i/F)$ are quotient maps;

(3) $F^* : (E^1/F) \times \cdots \times (E^N/F) \to \mathcal{R}$ is such that

$$F^*(q^1(x^1), \ldots, q^N(x^N)) = F(x^1, \ldots, x^N)$$

for each $(x^1, \ldots, x^N) \in E^1 \times \cdots \times E^N$, is an encoded C^0-revelation mechanism that realizes F. The space (E^i/F) has dimension r_i.

Furthermore, if a triple

$$(X^1 \times \cdots \times X^N, (p^1, \ldots, p^N), H)$$

is such that $p^i : E^i \to X^i$, $H : X^1 \times \cdots \times X^N \to \mathcal{R}$, and the triple is an encoded revelation mechanism that realizes F, then there are continuous maps $\rho^i : X^i \to (E^i/F)$ such that Diagram C commutes, with $Z = \mathcal{R}$.

Proof: We have already shown in Theorem 4.3.2 that the triple

$$((E^1/F) \times \cdots \times (E^N/F), (q^1, \ldots, q^N), F^*),$$

is an encoded revelation mechanism that realizes F. Suppose that $z^{*i} \in X^i$. Denote $(p^1(w), \ldots, p^{i-1}(w), p^{i+1}(w), \ldots, p^N(w))$ by $p^{\langle -i \rangle}(w)$, for each $w \in E^{\langle -i \rangle}$. Choose an element $x^{*i} \in E^i$ such that $p^i(x^{*i}) = z^{*i}$. Suppose that $x'^i \in E^i$, such that $p^i(x^{*i}) = p^i(x'^i) = z^{*i}$. Then for each

$$w \in E^{\langle -i \rangle}, \ F(w^{\langle x^{*i} @ i \rangle}) = H(p^{\langle -i \rangle}(w)^{\langle p^i(x^{*i}) @ i \rangle})$$
$$= H(p^{\langle -i \rangle}(w)^{\langle p^i(x'_i) @ i \rangle}) = F(w^{\langle x'^i @ i \rangle}).$$

Therefore, $q^i(x^{*i}) = q^i(x'^i)$. Set $\rho^{*i}(z^{*i}) = q^i(x^{*i})$. Because the map $p^i : E^i \to X^i$ has a thread in the neighborhood of each point, there is a neighborhood $\mathcal{N}$ of the point z^{*i} and a thread $s_i : \mathcal{N} \to E^i$ such that $p^i(s^i(z^*)) = p^i(z^*)$ for each $z^* \in \mathcal{N}$. Then $\rho^i(z^*) = q^i(s^i(z^*))$. Because both q^i and s^i are continuous, it follows that the map ρ^i is continuous.

4.4 Proofs and Examples

4.4.1 Leontief and Abelson Theorem

The following statement is a classical result sometimes referred to as the "General Theorem on Functional Dependence" (c.f. Widder , 1963).

Notation: If F is a function of one variable and G is a real-valued function of a vector x, then $(F \circ G)(x)$ denotes the composition $F(G(x))$.

THEOREM 4.4.1. Suppose that $\underline{x} = \{x_1, \ldots, x_m\}$ and $\underline{y} = \{y_1, \ldots, y_n\}$ are sets of real variables and suppose $F(\underline{x}, \underline{y})$ and $G(\underline{x})$ are real-valued C^1-functions defined on a neighbourhood U of the point $(p, q) = (p_1, \ldots, p_m, q_1, \ldots q_n) \in \mathcal{R}^m \times \mathcal{R}^n$ that satisfy the following conditions.

(i) $\begin{pmatrix} \frac{\partial F}{\partial x_1} & \cdots & \frac{\partial F}{\partial x_m} \\ \frac{\partial G}{\partial x_1} & \cdots & \frac{\partial G}{\partial x_m} \end{pmatrix}$

is a matrix of rank at most one,

(ii) at p, $\frac{\partial G}{\partial x_1} \neq 0$.

Then there is a function $C(w, y)$, where w is a real variable, such that $F(x, y) = C(G(x), y)$ in some neighborhood of (p, q).

Proof: Because of assumption *(ii)* the equation $w = G(c(w, x_2, \ldots, x_m), x_2, \ldots, x_m) = 0$ has a unique solution in a neighborhood U' of (p, q). Thus, there is a function $c(w, x_2, \ldots, x_m)$ such that $w = G(c(w, x_2, \ldots, x_m), x_2, \ldots, x_m)$ and such that $c(G(x_1, \ldots, x_m), x_2, \ldots, x_m) = x_1$. Set $C(w, x_2, \ldots, x_m, y) = F(c(w, x_2, \ldots, x_m), x_2, \ldots, x_m, y)$. Then

$$\frac{\partial C}{\partial x_j} = \left(\frac{\partial F}{\partial x}\right)\left(\frac{\partial c}{\partial x_j}\right) + \left(\frac{\partial F}{\partial x_j}\right)$$

for $j > 1$. Because

$$w = G(c(w, x_2, \ldots, x_m), x_2, \ldots, x_m),$$

it follows that

$$0 = \frac{\partial G}{\partial x_1} \frac{\partial c}{\partial x_j} + \frac{\partial G}{\partial x_j}$$

for $j > 1$. Further, by condition *(i)*, there is an Ω so that $\frac{\partial F}{\partial x_j} = \Omega \frac{\partial G}{\partial x_j}$ for $1 \leq j \leq m$. Therefore,

$$\frac{\partial C}{\partial x_j} = \Omega \left[\left(\frac{\partial G}{\partial x_1} \frac{\partial c}{\partial x_j} \right) + \frac{\partial G}{\partial x_j} \right] = 0.$$

Hence the function C is independent of the variables $x_2, \ldots, x_m$ and we can write $C(w, x_2, \ldots, x_m, y) = C(w, y)$. Then

$$C(G(x_1, \ldots, x_m), y) = F(c(G(x_1, \ldots, x_m), x_2, \ldots, x_m), x_2, \ldots, x_m, y)$$
$$= F(x_1, \ldots, x_m, y).$$

4.4.2 Leontief's Theorem

Leontief proved the following result (1947).

THEOREM 4.4.2. Suppose F is a function of variables $x_1, \ldots, x_m, y_1, \ldots, y_n$. Set $F_i = \frac{\partial F}{\partial x_i}, 1 \leq i \leq m$. Assume that $(p, q) = (p_1, \ldots, p_m, q_1, \ldots, q_n)$ is a set of values for the variables $(x_1, \ldots, x_m, y_1, \ldots, y_n)$. A necessary and sufficient condition that there exist functions $C(w, y_1, \ldots, y_n)$ and $G(x_1, \ldots, x_m)$ such that $F(x, y) = C(G(x), y)$ in a neighborhood U of the point (p, q) is that

(i) for each $1 \leq i, j \leq m$ and each $1 \leq k \leq n$,

$$\frac{\partial}{\partial y_k}\left[\frac{F_i}{F_j}\right] = 0 \text{ and}$$

(ii) for some j, $F_j(x_1, \ldots, x_m)(p, q) \neq 0$.

Proof: The conditions are clearly necessary. We turn to the proof of the sufficiency. Form the matrix

$$M = \begin{pmatrix} F_1 & \cdots & F_m \\ F_1^* & \cdots & F_m^* \end{pmatrix},$$

where $F_j^* = \frac{\partial F(x,q)}{\partial x_j}$. Condition (i) states that the derivative $\frac{\partial}{\partial y_k}[\frac{F_i}{F_j}] = 0$. Thus the ratio F_i/F_j is independent of y. Also at (p, q), $F_i^*/F_j^* = F_i(x, q)/F_j(x, q)$. It follows that $F_i^*/F_j^* = F_i/F_j$ for all (x, y). Therefore, the matrix M has rank at most one. Further, by assumption, $F_j(p, q) \neq 0$ for some j. The previous theorem shows that we can write $F(x, y) = C(G(x), y)$.

COROLLARY 4.4.3. A necessary and sufficient condition that there exist functions $C(w, y)$ and $G(x)$ such that $F(x, y) = C(G(x), y)$ in a neighborhood of (p, q) is that the matrix $BH_{(x, y)}(F)$ have rank at most one in a neighborhood of (p, q) and $[\frac{\partial F}{\partial x_j}]_{(p, q)} \neq 0$, for some j.

Proof: The necessity of the given rank condition has already been demonstrated. Set $F_j = \frac{\partial F}{\partial x_j}$. Theorem 4.4.2 shows that to prove the sufficiency of the rank condition on $BH_{(x, y)}(F)$, we need only prove that $\frac{\partial}{\partial y_k}[\frac{F_i}{F_j}] = 0$ for each i, j, and k. But

$$\frac{\partial}{\partial y_k}\left[\frac{F_i}{F_j}\right] = \left[\frac{\partial F_i}{\partial y_k}F_j - \frac{\partial F_j}{\partial y_k}F_i\right] \bigg/ F_j^2.$$

By assumption, there is an Ω such that

$$\Omega(F_1, \ldots, F_m)^t = \left(\frac{\partial^2 F}{\partial x_1 \partial y_k}, \ldots, \frac{\partial^2 F}{\partial x_m \partial y_k} \right)^t$$

(M^t denotes the transpose of M). Thus,

$$\Omega \frac{\partial F}{\partial x_i} = \frac{\partial^2 F}{\partial x_i \partial y_k} = \frac{\partial F_i}{\partial y_k}$$

for each i and k. Therefore, $\frac{\partial}{\partial y_k}[\frac{F_i}{F_j}] = 0$ for all k.

COROLLARY 4.4.4. Suppose $F(\underline{x}, \underline{y})$ is a C^2-function of the ordered sets of real variables

$$\underline{x} = (x_1, \ldots, x_m) \qquad \text{and} \qquad \underline{y} = (y_1, \ldots, y_n).$$

A necessary condition that there are functions $C(u, v)$, $A(\underline{x})$, and $B(\underline{y})$ such that $F(\underline{x}; \underline{y}) = C(A(\underline{x}), B(\underline{y}))$ is that the matrices

$$BH_{(\underline{x}, \underline{y})}(F) \qquad \text{and} \qquad BH_{(\underline{y}, \underline{x})}(F)$$

each have rank at most one. Further, if for some $1 \leq j \leq m$ and some $1 \leq k \leq n$, $[\frac{\partial F}{\partial x_j}]_{(p,q)} \neq 0$, and $[\frac{\partial F}{\partial y_k}]_{(p,q)} \neq 0$, then the rank condition is also sufficient for the existence of C, A, and B such that $F = C(A, B)$.

Proof: Because $BH_{(\underline{x}, \underline{y})}(F)$ has rank at most one and $\frac{\partial F}{\partial x_j} \neq= 0$ for some j, it follows from Theorem 4.4.2 that $F(x, y) = C(A(x), y)$ for some A and C. To complete the proof, it will suffice to prove that $C(w, y)$ satisfies the conditions of Corollary 4.4.4 using y_j's as the $x_j's$ and w as x_1. For convenience of notation, assume that $[\frac{\partial F}{\partial x_1}]_{(p,q)} \neq 0$. Then

$$C(w, y) = F(h(w, x_2, \ldots, x_m), x_2, \ldots, x_m, y_1, \ldots y_n).$$

Therefore,

$$\frac{\partial C}{\partial y_j} = \frac{\partial F(h(w, x_2, \ldots, x_m), x_2, \ldots, x_m, y_1, \ldots, y_n)}{\partial y_j}$$

and

$$\frac{\partial^2 C}{\partial w \partial y_j} = \left[\frac{\partial^2 F}{\partial x_1 \partial y_j} \right] \frac{\partial h}{\partial w}.$$

By hypothesis there is a Θ such that $\frac{\partial^2 F}{\partial x_1 \partial y_j} = \Theta \frac{\partial F}{\partial y_j}$ for each j. Therefore,

$$\frac{\partial^2 C}{\partial w \partial y_j} = \Theta \frac{\partial F}{\partial y_j} \frac{\partial h}{\partial w} = \Theta \frac{\partial C}{\partial y_j} \frac{\partial h}{\partial w}.$$

Therefore, by Theorem 4.4.2, $C(w, y) = G(w, B(y))$ if for some y_j, and for

$$w_0 = F(p, q), \qquad \left[\frac{\partial C(w, y)}{\partial y_j} \right]_{(p,q)} \neq 0.$$

However, from the proof of Theorem 4.4.2,

$$C(w, y) = F(h(w, x_2, \ldots, x_m), x_2, \ldots, x_m, y),$$

where $h(F(x_1, \ldots, x_m, q), x_2, \ldots, x_m) = x_1$. If $w_0 = F(p, q)$, because $C(w, y)$ is independent of the variables $x_2, \ldots, x_m$, it follows that

$$C(w_0, y) = F(h(F(p, q), p_2, \ldots, p_m, y) = F(p, y).$$

Therefore, $\frac{\partial C}{\partial y_j} = \frac{\partial F(p,y)}{\partial y_j} \neq 0$ for some j.

COROLLARY 4.4.5. Suppose that for each $1 \leq i \leq r$, $\underline{x}_i$ denotes the ordered set of real variables $(x_{i,1}, \ldots, x_{i,d_i})$. Assume

$$\underline{P} = (\underline{p}_1, \ldots, \underline{p}_p) = (p_{1,1}, \ldots, p_{r,d_r})$$

is a point. A necessary condition that in some neighborhood of the point P there are functions G, A_j, $1 \leq j \leq r$, such that

$$F(\underline{x}_1, \ldots, \underline{x}_r) = G(A_1(\underline{x}_1), \ldots, A_r(\underline{x}_r))$$

is that each matrix $BH_{(\underline{x}_j, \underline{x}_{(-j)})}(F)$ has rank at most one. The condition is also sufficient if for each j, there exists a $k(j)$ such that the derivative

$$\frac{\partial F(\underline{p}_1, \ldots, \underline{p}_{j-1}, \underline{x}_j, \underline{p}_{j+1}, \ldots, \underline{p}_r)}{\partial x_{j,k(j)}} \neq 0.$$

Our results on encoded revelation mechanisms require a slightly altered version of Leontief's theorem. This version is closely related to a result announced by Abelson (1980). We begin with some notation.

Notation: Suppose that X and Y are Euclidean spaces of dimensions m and n, respectively. Assume that X has coordinates $\underline{x} = (x_1, \ldots, x_m)$ and that Y has coordinates $\underline{y} = (y_1, \ldots, y_n)$. Assume that $F_1, \ldots, F_N$ are real valued continuously differentiable functions that are defined on a neighborhood of a point $(a, b) \in X \times Y$. We denote by $BH_{(\underline{x},\underline{y})}(F_1, \ldots, F_N)$ an $(m \times Nn)$ matrix with rows indexed by the variables $x_1, \ldots, x_m$, columns indexed by the functions $F_1, \ldots, F_N$ together with columns indexed by the pairs (F_j, y_ℓ), $1 \le j \le m$, $1 \le \ell \le n$. The entry at position (x_j, F_k) in the matrix is the derivative $\frac{\partial F_k}{\partial x_j}$. The entry at position $(x_j, (F_k, y_\ell))$ is $\frac{\partial^2 F_k}{\partial x_j \partial y_\ell}$. We denote by $\tilde{H}_{(\underline{x},\underline{y})}(F_1, \ldots, F_N)$ the submatrix of $BH_{(\underline{x},\underline{y})}(F_1, \ldots, F_N)$ with rows indexed by x_j, $1 \le j \le m$ and columns indexed by the pairs (F_k, y_ℓ), $1 \le k \le m$, $1 \le \ell \le n$. Thus, $BH_{(\underline{x},\underline{y})}(F_1, \ldots, F_N)$ can be considered to be a matrix consisting of a single row where the jth entry in the row is the matrix $BH_{(\underline{x},\underline{y})}(F_j)$ (cf. Mount and Reiter (2002, p. 211)).

LEMMA 4.4.1. Suppose that X and Y are Euclidean spaces of dimensions m and n, respectively. Assume that X has coordinates $\underline{x} = (x_1, \ldots, x_m)$ and Y has coordinates $\underline{y} = (y_1, \ldots, y_n)$. Assume that $F_1, \ldots, F_N$ are functions from $X \times Y$ to $\mathcal{R}$ that are defined on a neighborhood $U \times V$ of a point (a, b), $a \in X$ and $b \in Y$. A necessary condition that there are functions

$$A_1(x_1, \ldots, x_m), \ldots, A_r(x_1, \ldots, x_m),$$

and functions

$$G_i(W_1, \ldots, W_r, y_1, \ldots, y_n), \ 1 \le i \le N,$$

such that for each $(x_1, \ldots, x_m) \in U$ and $(y_1, \ldots, y_n) \in V$

$$F_i(x_1, \ldots, x_m, y_1, \ldots, y_n) = G_i(A_1, \ldots, A_r, y_1, \ldots, y_n), \ 1 \le i \le N,$$

is that the matrix

$$BH_{(\underline{x},\underline{y})}(F_1, \ldots, F_N)$$

has rank less than or equal to r at each point of $U \times V$.

Proof: Because

$$F_i(x_1, \ldots, x_m, y_1, \ldots, y_n) = G_i(A_1, \ldots, A_r, y_1, \ldots, y_n),$$

it follows that

$$\frac{\partial F_i}{\partial x_j} = \sum_{s=1}^{r} \frac{\partial G_i}{\partial A_s} \frac{\partial A_s}{\partial x_j}$$

and

$$\frac{\partial^2 F_i}{\partial x_j \partial y_k} = \sum_{s=1}^{r} \frac{\partial^2 G_i}{\partial y_k \partial A_s} \frac{\partial A_s}{\partial x_j}.$$

Each of the columns is a linear combination of the r columns

$$\left(\frac{\partial A_i}{\partial x_1}, \ldots, \frac{\partial A_i}{\partial x_m} \right)^t, \quad 1 \le i \le r.$$

Therefore, the matrix $BH_{(x,y)}(F_1, \ldots, F_N)$ has rank at most r.

The next theorem shows that for a product of Euclidean spaces, if F is a differentiably separable function of ranks $(r_1, \ldots, r_n)$, then the rank r_i gives the number of variables required from the space X_i in order to compute the function. We state a more general assertion for sequences of functions that can be used for vector-valued functions (cf. Mount Reiter (2002)).

THEOREM 4.4.6. Suppose that X and Y are Euclidean spaces of dimensions m and n, respectively. Suppose that X has coordinates $\underline{x} = (x_1, \ldots, x_m)$ and that Y has coordinates $\underline{y} = (y_1, \ldots, y_n)$. Assume that $p \in X$, $q \in Y$, that U is a neighborhood of p, V is a neighborhood of q, and that F_i, $1 \le i \le n$, is a C^{k+1}-function, $k \ge 2$, from $U \times V$ to $\mathcal{R}$. Then,

(i) a necessary condition that there is a neighborhood $W \times V$ of a point $(p', q) \in \mathcal{R}^r \times V$, C^k-functions, $k \ge 2$,

$$G_1(W_1, \ldots, W_r, y_1, \ldots, y_n), \ldots, G_N(W_1, \ldots, W_r, y_1, \ldots, y_n)$$

defined on $W \times V$, and C^k-functions $A_1(x_1, \ldots, x_m), \ldots,$ $A_r(x_1, \ldots, x_m)$ defined on $U \times V$ such that for each $1 \le i \le n$,

$$F_i(x_1, \ldots, x_m, y_1, \ldots, y_n) = G_i(A_1(x_1, \ldots, x_m), \ldots,$$
$$A_r(x_1, \ldots, x_m), y_1, \ldots, y_n),$$

is that the matrix $BH_{(\underline{x},\underline{y})}(F_1, \ldots, F_N)$ has rank less than or equal to r at each point of $U \times V$;

(ii) if $BH_{(\underline{x},\underline{y})}(F_1, \ldots F_N)$ has rank at most r in the neighborhood $U \times V$, and if $\tilde{H}_{(\underline{x},\underline{y})}(F_1, \ldots, F_N)\,|_{[\underline{x},q]}$ has rank r at each point of U, then there is a point (p', q) in $\mathcal{R}^r \times Y$, a neighborhood $W \times V$ of (p', q), a neighborhood $U' \times V'$ of (p,q), a C^k-function G defined on $W \times V'$, and C^k-functions $A_1(x_1, \ldots, x_m), \ldots, A_r(x_1, \ldots, x_m)$ defined on a neighborhood of p, such that on $U' \times V'$

$$F_i(x_1, \ldots, x_m, y_1, \ldots, y_n)$$
$$= G_i(A_1(x_1, \ldots, x_m), \ldots, A_r(x_1, \ldots, x_m), y_1, \ldots, y_n),$$

$1 \le i \le n$, for each $(x_1, \ldots, x_m) \in U'$ and $(y_1, \ldots, y_q) \in V'$.

The proof of Theorem 4.4.6 shows how to construct the functions A_i and G_j.

4.4.3 An Example of the Coordinate Construction

As an example, we carry out the constructions for the function

$$F(x_1, x_2, x_3, y_1, y_2, y_3, y_4)$$
$$= F(\underline{x}, \underline{y})x_1(y_1 + y_3 + y_1 y_4) + x_2(y_2 + y_3 - y_1 y_4)$$
$$+ x_2^2(y_1 + y_3 + y_1 y_4) + x_3^2(y_2 + y_3 - y_1 y_4).$$

We first construct the matrix $BH_{(\underline{x},\underline{y})}(F) =$

$$\begin{pmatrix} y_1 + y_3 + y_1 y_4 & 1 + y_4 \\ (y_2 + y_3 - y_1 y_4 + 2x_2(y_1 + y_3 + y_1 y_4) & -y_4 + 2x_2(1 + y_4) \\ 2x_3(y_2 + y_3 - y_1 y_4) & -2x_3 y_4 \end{pmatrix}$$

$$\times \begin{pmatrix} 0 & 1 & y_1 \\ 1 & 1 + 2x_2 & -y_1 + 2x_2 y_1 \\ 2x_3 & 2x_3 & -2x_3 y_1. \end{pmatrix}.$$

The matrix $BH_{(\underline{x},\underline{y})}(F)$ has rank at most 2, and for the point

$(x_1, x_2, x_3, y_1, y_2, y_3, y_4) = (0, 0, 0, 1, 1, 1, 1)$
$= (p, q),\ BH^*_{(\underline{x},\underline{y})}(F)\ |_{[x,q]}$

$$= \begin{pmatrix} 3 & 2 & 0 & 1 & 1 \\ 1 + 6x_2 & -1 + 4x_2 & 1 & 1 + 2x_2 & -1 + 2x_2 \\ 2x_3 & -2x_3 & 2x_3 & 2x_3 & -2x_3 \end{pmatrix}.$$

It is an easy exercise to check that $BH^*(F)$ has rank 2 in $\mathcal{R}^3$. Furthermore, the matrix

$$H^*_{(\underline{x},\underline{y})}(F)\ |_{[p,q]} = \begin{pmatrix} 2 & 0 & 1 & 1 \\ -1 & 1 & 1 & -1 \\ 0 & 0 & 0 & 0 \end{pmatrix}$$

has rank 2. Theorem 4.4.6 states that there are two functions A and B with variables $x_1, \ldots, x_3$, and a function C of two variables such that $F = C(A, B)$. To construct A and B, we first compute the derivatives $\frac{\partial F}{\partial y_i}$, $1 \leq i \leq 4$. The derivatives are

$$\frac{\partial F}{\partial y_1} = x_1 + x_2^2 + x_1 y_4 - x_2 y_4 + x_2^2 y_4 - x_3^2 y_4,$$

$$\frac{\partial F}{\partial y_2} = x_2 + x_3^2, \qquad \frac{\partial F}{\partial y_3} = x_1 + x_2 + x_2^2 + x_3^2,$$

and

$$\frac{\partial F}{\partial y_4} = x_1 y_1 - x_2 y_1 + x_2^2 y_1 - x_3^2 y_1.$$

At the point q these derivatives are

$$\frac{\partial F}{\partial y_1} = 2x_1 - x_2 + 2x_2^2 - x_3^2, \qquad \frac{\partial F}{\partial y_2} = x_2 + x_3^2,$$

$$\frac{\partial F}{\partial y_3} = x_1 + x_2 + x_2^2 + x_3^2,$$

and

$$\frac{\partial F}{\partial y_4} = x_1 - x_2 + x_2^2 - x_3^2.$$

The 2×2 submatrix of H^* whose entries are in the first two rows and columns has rank 2. This is equivalent to the observation that the functions $\frac{\partial F}{\partial y_1} = 2x_1 - x_2 + 2x_2^2 - x_3^2$, and $\frac{\partial F}{\partial y_2} = x_2 + x_3^2$, are independent at the point p. It is the conclusion of the theorem that the functions $\frac{\partial F}{\partial y_1} = 2x_1 - x_2 + 2x_2^2 - x_3^2$, and $\frac{\partial F}{\partial y_2} = x_2 + x_3^2$, can be used as the functions A and B. To check this, set $w_1 = 2x_1 - x_2 + 2x_2^2 - x_3^2$ and $w_2 = x_2 + x_3^2$. We can solve these equations for x_1 and x_2, using the implicit function theorem (Golubitsky and Guillemin 1973, p. 7), because we have already observed that the necessary rank condition is satisfied using the first two rows and first two columns of $H^*_{x,y}(F) |_{[p,q]}$. In this case, of course, the solutions are easily written down. That is, $x_2 = w_2 - x_3^2$, and $x_1 = (1/2)(w_1 + w_2 - 2w_2^2 + 4w_2 x_3^2 - 2x_3^4)$. The final computation in the proof of Theorem 4.4.6 shows that if we substitute these functions in the original function F, we derive a function $G(w_1, w_2, y_1, \ldots, y_4)$ that is independent of the variable x_3. Indeed,

$$G(w_1, w_2, y_1, y_2, y_3, y_4) = (w_1 y_1)/2 + (w_2 y_1)/2 + w_2 y_2 + (w_1 y_3)/2$$
$$+ (3 w_2 y_3)/2 + (w_1 y_1 y_4)/2 - (w_2 y_1 y_4)/2.$$

If we set

$$A_1 = 2x_1 - x_2 + 2x_2^2 - x_3^2,$$

and

$$A_2 = x_2 + x_3^2,$$

then

$$G(A_1, A_2, y_1, y_2, y_3, y_4) = F(x_1, x_2, x_3, y_1, y_2, y_3, y_4).$$

4.4.4 Proof of Theorem 4.4.6

We now turn to the formal proof of Theorem 4.4.6.

Proof: Condition (i) has already been established in Lemma 4.4.1. We turn to the proof of (ii). Because the matrix

$$\tilde{H}_{(\underline{x},\underline{y})}(F_1, \ldots, F_N)|_{[\underline{x},q]}$$

has rank r in the set U, there is a neighborhood U'' of p and an $(r \times r)-$ submatrix of

$$\tilde{H}_{(\underline{x},\underline{y})}(F_1, \ldots, F_N)|_{[\underline{x},q]}$$

that has nonzero determinant everywhere in U''. We can assume, without loss of generality, that the rows of the submatrix are indexed by $x_1, \ldots, x_r$ and that the columns are indexed by $(F_{\alpha(1)}, y_{\beta(1)}), \ldots, (F_{\alpha(r)}, y_{\beta(r)})$. The functions of $\underline{x}$,

$$A_1(\underline{x}) = \frac{\partial F_{\alpha(1)}}{\partial y_{\beta(1)}}(\underline{x}, q), \ldots, \quad A_r(\underline{x}) = \frac{\partial F_{\alpha(r)}}{\partial y_{\beta(r)}}(\underline{x}, q),$$

are C^k-functions of $(x_1, \ldots, x_m)$ in a neighborhood of p. Set

$$z_1 = A_1(x_1, \ldots, x_m), \ldots, \quad z_r = A_r(x_1, \ldots, x_m).$$

Because

$$\frac{\partial A_i}{\partial x_j}(p) = \frac{\partial^2 F_{\alpha(i)}}{\partial x_j \partial y_{\beta(j)}}(p, q),$$

the matrix with (i, j) entry $\frac{\partial A_i}{\partial x_j}(p, q)$ has rank r. Therefore, the implicit function theorem (Golubitsky and Guillemin, 1973) shows that there is a neighborhood U^* of p, and C^k-functions

$$h_1(z_1, \ldots, z_r, x_{r+1}, \ldots, x_m), \ldots, h_r(z_1, \ldots, z_r, x_{r+1}, \ldots, x_m)$$

that are defined on U^* such that

$$z_i = A_i(h_1, \ldots, h_r, x_{r+1}, \ldots, x_m), \tag{4.4.1}$$

$1 \le i \le r$, in the set U^*. Then,

$$h_i(A_1(x_1, \ldots, x_m), \ldots, A_r(x_1, \ldots, x_m), x_{r+1}, \ldots, x_m) = x_i,$$

$1 \le i \le r$, for $(x_1, \ldots, x_p) \in U^*$. Set

$$G_i(w_1, \ldots, w_r, x_{r+1}, \ldots, x_m, y_1, \ldots, y_n)$$
$$= F_i(h_1(w_1, \ldots, w_r, x_{r+1}, \ldots, x_m), \ldots, h_r$$
$$\times (w_1, \ldots, w_r, x_{r+1}, \ldots, x_m), y_1, \ldots, y_q),$$

$1 \le i \le N$. Because

$$G_i(A_1, \ldots, A_r, x_{r+1}, \ldots, x_m, y_1, \ldots, y_n)$$
$$= F_i(h_1(A_1, \ldots, A_r, x_{r+1}, \ldots, x_m), \ldots, h_r(A_1, \ldots, A_r, x_{r+1}, \ldots, x_m),$$
$$(x_{r+1}, \ldots, x_m, y_1, \ldots, y_n) = F_i(x_1, \ldots, x_m, y_1, \ldots, y_n),$$

in order to complete the proof of the assertion it will suffice to show that the function G_i is independent of the variables $x_{r+1}, \ldots, x_m$. Hypothesis (ii) asserts that the column vector

$$\left(\frac{\partial F_i}{\partial x_1}, \ldots, \frac{\partial F_i}{\partial x_m} \right)^t$$

is a linear combination of the columns of the matrix

$$\tilde{H}_{(\underline{x}, y)}(F_1, \ldots, F_N)[x, q]$$

in the neighborhood $U^* \times V$, because BH has rank at most r in $U \times V$, and $\tilde{H}$ has rank r in U^*. Therefore, the column $(\frac{\partial F_i}{\partial x_1}, \ldots, \frac{\partial F_i}{\partial x_m})^t$ is a linear combination of columns indexed by $(F_{\alpha(1)}, y_{\beta(1)}), \ldots, (F_{\alpha(r)}, y_{\beta(r)})$ in the neighborhood $U^* \times V$. It follows, that for each $1 \le i \le N$, and $1 \le t \le m$,

$$\frac{\partial F_i}{\partial x_t} = \sum_{s=1}^{r} C_{i,s} \frac{\partial A_s}{\partial x_t},$$

where the $C_{i,s}$ are functions on $U^* \times V$. Furthermore, if one differentiates Equation 4.4.1 by x_j, for $r + 1 \le j \le m$, it follows that

$$0 = \sum_{t=1}^{r} \frac{\partial A_i}{\partial x_t} \frac{\partial h_t}{\partial x_j} + \frac{\partial A_i}{\partial x_j}.$$

Therefore, if $r + 1 \le j \le m$,

$$\frac{\partial G_i}{\partial x_j} = \sum_{t=1}^{r} \frac{\partial F_i}{\partial x_t} \frac{\partial h_t}{\partial x_j} + \frac{\partial F_i}{\partial x_j}$$

$$= \sum_{t=1}^{r} \left[\sum_{s=1}^{r} C_{i,s} \frac{\partial A_s}{\partial x_t} \right] \frac{\partial h_t}{\partial x_j} + \Sigma_{s=1}^{r} C_{i,s} \frac{\partial A_s}{\partial x_j}$$

$$= \sum_{s=1}^{r} \left[\sum_{t=1}^{r} \frac{\partial A_s}{\partial x_t} \frac{\partial h_t}{\partial x_j} + \frac{\partial A_s}{\partial x_j} \right] C_{i,s} = 0.$$

COROLLARY 4.4.7. (Hurwicz) Write $\underline{x} = (x_1, \ldots, x_m)$, $\underline{y} = (y_1, \ldots, y_n)$ and let $k \geq 2$. Assume that each function $F_i : X \times Y \to \mathcal{R}$, $i = 1, \ldots, N$ is a C^{k+1}-function in a neighborhood $U \times V$ of the point (p, q). Suppose that there is a positive integer $r \in \{1, \ldots, m\}$ such that:

(i) rank$(BH_{(\underline{x}, \underline{y})}) = r$ at each point of $U \times V \subseteq X \times Y$,[6] and
(ii) rank$(\tilde{H}_{(\underline{x}, \underline{y})}|_{(\underline{x}, q)}) = r$ at each point of $U \subseteq X$.

Then there do not exist the following: an integer $r' < r$ and C^k-functions $F^i : \mathcal{R}^{r'} \times V \to \mathcal{R}$, $i = 1, \ldots, N$ in a neighborhood $W \times V$ of (p, q) and C^k-functions $\phi_j : U \to \mathcal{R}$, $j = 1, \ldots r'$ such that for all $i = 1, \ldots N$,

$$F_i(\underline{x}, \underline{y}) = \Gamma_i(\phi_1(\underline{x}), \ldots, \phi_{r'}(\underline{x}), \underline{y}) \qquad (4.4.2)$$

for all $(\underline{x}, \underline{y}) \in U \times V$.

Proof: Suppose, to the contrary, that such an $r' < r$, Γ_i, $i \in \{1, \ldots, N\}$ and ϕ_j, $j \in \{1, \ldots, r'\}$ do exist and satisfy equation 4.4.2.

Then by Theorem 4.4.6 (i), or Lemma 4.4.1, the matrix $BH_{(\underline{x}, \underline{y})}$ is necessarily of rank at most $r' < r$ at each point of $U \times V$. But, $\tilde{H}_{(\underline{x}, \underline{y})}|_{(\underline{x}, q)}$ is a submatrix of $BH_{(\underline{x}, \underline{y})}$ and has rank r on points in $U \times q \subseteq U \times V$. Hence, rank$(BH_{(\underline{x}, \underline{y})}) = r$ at those points of its domain, thus contradicting the requirement that rank$(BH_{(\underline{x}, \underline{y})}) \leq r' < r$ on all of $U \times V$.

REMARK 4.4.1. Assumption (i), rank$(BH_{(\underline{x}, \underline{y})}) = r$, was not used in the proof of the corollary. Also, W is a neighborhood of $p' \in \mathcal{R}^{r'}$, not of p.

REMARK 4.4.2. Under assumptions (i) and (ii) stated in the corollary, Theorem 4.4.6 (ii) states that for $k \geq 2$ there exist C^k-functions, $G_1 : \mathcal{R}^r \times V \to \mathcal{R}, \ldots, G_N : \mathcal{R}^r \times V \to \mathcal{R}$ and for $k \geq 2$, C^k-functions $A_1 : U \to \mathcal{R}, \ldots, A_r : U \to \mathcal{R}$ such that for all $i \in 1, \ldots, N$

$$F_i(\underline{x}, \underline{y}) = G_i(A_1(\underline{x}), \ldots, A_r(\underline{x}), \underline{y}), \qquad (4.4.3)$$

for all $(\underline{x}, \underline{y}) \in U' \times V'$, a neighbourhood of (p, q). More specifically, as seen in the proof of Theorem 4.4.6, Equation 4.4.2 is satisfied, then

$$A_j(\underline{x}) = \frac{\partial F_{\alpha(j)}}{\partial y_{\beta(j)}}(\underline{x}, q), \quad j = 1, \ldots, r, \qquad (4.4.4)$$

---

[6] This assumption is only for later reference. It is not used in the proof of the corollary.

and the functions G_i are defined by

$$G_i(w_1, \ldots, w_r, x_{r+1}, \ldots, x_m, \underline{y})$$
$$= F_i(h_1(\underline{w}, x_{r+1}, \ldots, x_m), \ldots,$$
$$h_r(\underline{w}, x_{r+1}, \ldots, x_m), x_{r+1}, \ldots, x_m, \underline{y}), \quad (4.4.5)$$

after some reordering of the variables. Hence, under assumptions (i) and (ii) stated in the corollary, a condensation of degree r is possible, as stated in Equations (4.4.3), (4.4.4), and (4.4.5) by Theorem 4.4.6 (ii) and this $\underline{r}$ is the minimal feasible degree of condensation, as shown in the corollary.

References

Abelson, H. (1980) Lower bounds on information transfer in distributed systems. *JACM* **27**, 384–92.

Aharoni, R., Nash-Williams, C. St. J.A., and Shelah, S. (1983) A general criterion for the existence of transversals. *Proceedings, London Mathematical Society* **47**, 43–682.

Aizpura, J. and Manresa, A. (1995) A decentralized and informationally efficient mechanism realizing fair outcomes in economies with public goods. *Economic Design* **1**(2), 141–58.

Arbib, M. A. (1960) *Theories of Abstract Automata*. Prentice Hall, Englewood Cliff, New Jersey.

Berge, C. (1963) *Topological Spaces*. Macmillan, New York.

Brualdi, R.A. and Scrimen, E.B. (1968) Exchange systems, matchings and transversals. *Journal of Combinatorial Theory* **5**, 242–57.

Calsamiglia, X. and Kirman, A. (1998) A unique informationally efficient decentralized mechanism with fair outcomes. *Econometrica* **61**(5), 1147–73.

Calsamiglia, X. (1987) Informational requirements of parametric resource allocation processes, in T. Groves, R. Radner and S. Reiter, eds. *Information, Incentives and Economic Mechanisms; Essays in Honor of Leonid Hurwicz*, University of Minnesota Press.

Camacho, A. (1970) Externalities, optimality and informationally decentralized resource allocation processes. *International Economic Review* **11**(2), 318–32.

Chen, P. (1992) A lower bound for the dimension of the message space of the decentralized mechanism realizing a given goal. *Journal of Mathematical Economics* **21**, 249–70.

Damerell, R.M. and Milner, E.C. (1974) Necessary and sufficient conditions for transversals of countable set systems. *Journal of Combinatorial Theory* Series A **17**, 350–79.

Dugundji, J. (1966) *Topology*. Allyn and Bacon, Inc., Boston.

Everett, C.J. and Whaples, G. (1949) Representations of sequences of sets. *American Journal of Mathematics* **71**, 287–93.

Folkman, K.J. (1968) Transversals of Infinite Families With Finitely Many Infinite Members. RAND Corp. memorandum, RM-5676 – PR.

Forges, F. (1993) Five legitimate definitions of correlated equilibrium in games with incomplete information. *Theory and Decision* **35**, 277–310.

Gale, D., Shapley, L. (1962) College admissions and the stability of marriage. *American Mathematical Monthly* **69**, 9–15.

Gale, E. and Nikaido H. (1965) The Jacobian matrix and global univalence of mappings. *Mathematische Annalen* **159**, 81–93.

Golubitsky, M. and Guillemin, V. (1973) *Stable Mappings and Their Singularities*: *Graduate Texts in Mathematics* No 41. SpringerVerlag, New York.

Hall, M., Jr. (1948) Distinct representatives of subsets. *Bulletin American Mathematics Society* **54**, 922–6.

Hall, P. (1935) On representatives of subsets. *Journal of London Mathematic Society* **10**, 26–30.

Hayek, F. (1935) *Collectivist Economic Planning*. George Routledge & Sons, London. (1945) *The Use of Knowledge in Society*. American Economic Review.

Hopcroft, J. E. and Ullman, J. D. (1979) *Introduction to Automata Theory, Languages, and Computation*. Addison Wesley Series in Computer Science, Reading, Massachusetts.

Hurewicz, W. and Wallman, H. (1948) *Dimension Theory*. Princeton University Press, Princeton, New Jersey.

Hurwicz, L. (1960) Optimality and informational efficiency in resource allocation processes, in K. Arrow, S. Karlin, and P. Suppes eds. *Mathematical Methods in the Social Sciences*. Stanford University Press, Stanford, California.

(1972) On informationally decentralized systems, in R. Radner and C.B. McGuire, eds. *Decisions and Organization*, a volume in honor of Jacob Marschak, 297–336.

(1976) On informational requirements for non-wasteful resource allocation systems, Appendix 1 in S. Shulman ed. *Mathematical Models in Economics, Papers and Proceedings of a US-USSR Seminar, Moscow*, 48–50. Publication supported by a grant from NSF-NBER.

(1986) On informational decentralization and efficiency in resource allocation mechanisms, in S. Reiter ed. *Studies in Mathematical Economics, Studies in Mathematics*, Vol. 25. Mathematical Association of America.

and Marschak, T. (2003) Comparing finite mechanisms. *Economic Theory* **21**, 783–841.

(2003) Finite allocation mechanisms: Approximate Walrasian versus approximate direct revelation. *Economic Theory* **21**, 545–72.

Hurwicz, L. and S. Reiter (1990) Constructing decentralized mechanisms by the Method of Rectangles, *Decentralization Conference*, Northwestern University, Evanston, IL.

(1993) *Designing Mechanisms by the Method of Rectangles, Decentralization Conference*, University of California, Berkeley, CA.

(2001) Transversals, systems of distinct representatives, mechanism design and matching. *Review of Economic Design*, 6, no. 2, 289–304.

Hurwicz, L., Radner, R., and Reiter, S. (1975a) A stochastic decentralized resource allocation process: part I, *Econometrica* **43**(2), 187–221.

(1975b) A stochastic decentralized resource allocation process: part II, *Econometrica* **43**(3), 363–93.

Hurwicz, L., Reiter, S., and Saari, D. (1980) *On Constructing an Informationally Efficient Decentralized Process Implementing a Given Performance Function.* Mimeo.

(1980) On constructing an informationally efficient decentralized process implementing a given performance function. Presented at Aix-en-Provence World Congress of the Econometric Society.

Hurwicz. L. and Weinberger, H.F. (1990) A necessary condition for decentralisation and an application to intertemporal allocation. *Journal of Economic Theory* **51**(2) 313–45.

Hurwicz, L. and Reiter, S. (2001) Transversals, systems of distinct representatives, mechanism design and matching, in T. Marschak and T. Ichiishi, eds. *Review of Economic Design*, **6**(2), 289–304. Reprinted in Marschak, T. and T. Ichiishi (2002) *Markets, Games and Organizations*, Springer-Verlag Berlin Heidelberg New York, 163–78.

Hurwicz, L. and H., Weinberg (1990) A necessary condition for decentralization and an application to intertemporal allocation, *Journal of Economic Theory* **51**, 313–45.

Ishikida, T. and Marschak, T. (1996) Mechanisms that efficiently verify the optimality of a proposed action, *Economic Design* 2,1,33–68.

Jordan, J. S. (1982) The competitive allocation process is informationally efficient uniquely. *Journal of Economic Theory* **28**, 1–18.

(1987) The Informational Requirements of Local Stability in Decentralized Allocation Mechanisms, in T. Groves, R. Radner, and S. Reiter, eds. *Information, Incentives and Economic Mechanisms: Essays in Honor of Leonid Hurwicz*, Minneapolis, Minnesota, University of Minnesota Press.

and Xu, D. (1999) On the Communication Complexity of Expected Profit Maximization, *Journal of Economic Theory* **86**, 185–202.

Lang, S. (1993) *Algebra*, 3rd edn, Addison-Wesley Publishing Co., Reading, Massachusetts.

Kelso, A. S., Jr., Crawford, V. P. (1982) Job matching, coalition formation, and gross substitutes. *Econometrica* **50**, 1483–1504.

Lange, O. (1938) On the economic theory of socialism, in *On the economic theory of socialism* ed. B. Lippincott, Minneapolis, University of Minnesota Press, 57–143.

Lerner, A. P. (1927) Statics and dynamics in socialist economics, *Econometrica* **43**, 1–29.

Leontief, W. (1947) A note on the interrelation of subsets of independent variables of a continuous function with continuous first derivatives. *Bulletin of the AMS* 343–50.

Lerner, A. P. (1927) Statics and dynamics in socialist economics, *Econometrica* **43**, 1–29.

(1944) *The Economics of Control*, New York, Macmillan.

MacLane, S. (1971) *Categories for the Working Mathematician*, Springer Verlag, New York.

Manresa, A. (1993) An infinite dimensional extension of the theory of decentralized mechanisms. *Mathematical Social Science* **26**, 157–73.

Marschak, T. A. (1959) Centralization and decentralization in economic organization, *Econometrica*, **27**, 399–430.

(1981) Economic Design, in K. Arrow and M. Intrilligator, eds. *Handbook of Mathematical Economics*, vol. 3, North Holland.

(1987), Price versus direct revelation: informational judgements for finite mechanisms, in T. Groves, R. Radner, and S. Reiter, eds. *Information, Incentives, and Economic Mechanisms: Essays in Honor of Leonid Hurwicz*, University of Minnesota Press, 132–82.

(1996) On economies of scope in communication, *Economic Design*, 2(1), 1–30. Also appears in G.M. Olson, T.W. Malone and J.B. Smith eds., *Coordination Theory and Collaboration Technology*, Lawrence Erlbaum Associates, Mahwah, New Jersey.

and Reichelstein, S. (1998) Network Mechanisms, Informational Efficiency and Hierarchies, *Journal of Economic Theory*, March, 106–41.

(1995) Communication requirements for individual agents in networks and hierarchies, in J. Ledyard, ed. *The Economics of informational Decentralization: Complexity, Efficiency and Stability*; Kluwer Publishing Company, NY: New York 311–46.

Marschak, J. and Radner, R. (1971) *The Economic Theory of Teams*, Yale University Press, New Haven, CN.

Mas Collel, A. (1979) Homeomorphisms of Compact Convex Sets and the Jacobian Matrix, *Siam Journal of Mathematical Analysis*, 10,6, 1105–9.

Maskin, E. (1977) Nash Equilibrium and welfare optimality, mIT.

Maskin, E. (January, 1999) Nash equilibrium and welfare optimality. *Review of Economic Studies* **66**(1), 23–38.

Maskin, E. and Sjostrom, T. (2002) Implementation Theory, in eds. Arrow, K.J., Sen, A.K., and Suyumura, K., Handbook of Social Choice and Welfare, Vol. 1, pp. 237–288, Handbooks in Economics, No. 19, Elsevier, Amsterdam.

McKelvey, R. D. (1989) Game forms for Nash implementation of general social choice correspondences. *Social choice and Welfare* **6**, 139–56.

Mirsky, L. (1971) *Transversal Theory. Science and Engineering* 75, Academic Press, New York and London.

Mount, K. and Reiter, S. (1974) The informational size of message spaces, JET, 8:161–191; *Journal of Mathematical Economics* **8**, 161–92.

Mount, K. and Reiter, S. (1983) *Computation, Communication and Performance in Resource Allocation*; presented at the CEME-NBER Decentralization seminar, University of Minnesota, May 21–23. Northwestern University Mimeo, The Center for Mathematical Studies in Economics and Managerial Science, Northwestern University.

Mount, K. and Reiter, S. (1990) A model of computing with human agents, Discussion Paper No. 890, *The Center for Mathematical Studies in Economics and Managerial Science*, Northwestern University.

(1996) A lower bound on computational complexity given by revelation mechanisms, *Economic Theory* 7(2), 237–66.

(2002) *Computation and Complexity in Economic Behavior and Organization.* Cambridge University Press, Cambridge, UK.

Nash-Williams, C. St. J.A. (1978) Another criterion for marriage in denumerable societies. *Annals Discrete Mathematics* **3**, 165–79.

Nikaido, H. (1968) *Convex Structures and Economic Theory.* Academic Press, New York and London.

(1999) A private communication on univalence.

Osana, H. (August, 2005) Externalities do not necessarily require larger message spaces for realizing pareto-effcient allocations, *Review of Economic Design* **9**(3) 227–69.

Palfrey, T. R. (2002) Implementation Theory, in eds. Aumann, R.J. and S. Hart, Handbook of Game Theory, Elsevier Science BV.

Podewski, K.P. and Steffens, K. (1976) Injective choice functions for countable families. *Journals of Combination Theory Series B* **21**, 40–6.

Radner, R. (1972a) Normative theories of organization: an introduction, in: C.C. McGuire, and R. Radner, eds. *Decision and Organization,* North Holland/ American Elsevier, 177–88.

Radner, R. (1972b) Teams, in: C.C. McGuire, and R. Radner eds. *Decision and Organization,* North Holland/American Elsevier, 189–216.

Radner, R. (1972c) Allocation of a scarce resource under uncertainty: an example of a team, in: C.C. McGuire, and R. Radner eds. *Decision and Organization,* North Holland, American Elsevier, 189–216.

Rado, R. (1967) Note on the transfinite case of Hall's theorem on representatives. *Journal of London Mathematic Society* **42**, 321–4.

Reichelstein, S. (1984) Incentive compatibility and informational requirements, *Journal of Economic Theory* **32**, 384–90.

Reichelstein, S., Reiter, S. (May, 1988) Game forms with minimal message spaces. *Econometrica* **56**(3), 661–92.

and Reiter, S. (1988) Game forms with minimal message spaces, *Econometrica* **53**(3), 661–92.

Roth, A.E. (1984) The evolution of the labor market for medical interns and residents: a case study in game theory. *Journal of Political Economy* **92**, 991–1016.

Saari, D. (1984) A method for constructing message spaces for smooth performance functions, *JET* **33**, 249–74.

Saijo, T. (1988) Strategy reduction in Maskin's Theorem: sufficient conditions for nash implementation, *Econometrica* **56**(3), 693–700.

Serre, J. P. (1965) *Lie Algebras and Lie Groups.* W. A. Benjamin, Inc. New York.

Shelah, S. (1973) Notes on partition calculus, in: A., Hajinal, R., Rado, and V.T. Sos, eds. *Infinite and Finite Sets. (Colloq. Math. Soc. Janos Bolyai)* **10**, 1257–76.

Sonnenschein, H. (1974) An axiomatic characterization of the price mechanism. *Econometrica* **42**, 425–60.

Spira, P. M. (April, 1969) The time required for group multiplication. *Communications of the Association for Computing Machinery* **16**(2), 235–43.

Spira, P. M. and Arbib, M. A. (1967) Computation times for finite groups, semigroups and automata. *Proceedings of IEEE 8th Annals Symptoms Switching and Automata Theory,* 291–5.

Stoenescu, T. and Teneketzis, D. (2004) *Informational Efficiency of Pricing Mechanisms in Unicast Service Provisioning with Routing*, Technical Report, Department of EECS-Systems, University of Michigan (under review at Journal of Economic Theory.)

(2004) *Decentralized Resource Allocation Mechanisms in Networks*, Ph.D. Dissertation, Department of EECS-Systems, University of Michigan.

Tian,G. (1990) Completely Feasible and Continuous Nash Implementation of the Lindahl Correspondence with a Message Space of Minimal Dimension. *Journal of Economic Theory* 51, 443–52.

(2000) *A Uniquely Informationally Efficient Allocation Mechanism in Production Economies*, Mimeo, Texas A and M University.

(2004) A unique informationally efficient allocation mechanism in economies with externalities, *International Economic Review* 45, 79–111.

von Mises, L. (1920) *Economic Calculation in the Socialist Comonwealth*, reprinted in ed. F. Hayek, (1935) *Collectivist Economic Planning*, London, George Routledge & Sons.

Warner, F.W. (1971) *Foundations of Differentiable Manifolds and Lie Groups*. Glenview IL and London, Scott Foresman and Co.

Widder, D. V. (1963) *Advanced Calculus*. Prentice-Hall, New York.

Williams, S. (1984) Implementing a generic smooth function. *Journal of Mathematical Economics* 13, 273–88.

(1986) Realization and nash implementation: to aspects of mechanism design, *Econometrica* 54, 139–51.

Williams, S. (forthcoming) Communication in Mechanism Design. A Differential Approach. CUP.

Index